Critique and Disclosure

Critique and Disclosure

Critical Theory between Past and Future

Nikolas Kompridis

The MIT Press
Cambridge, Massachusetts
London, England

First MIT Press paperback edition, 2011

© 2006 Massachusetts Institute of Technology

MIT Press books may be purchased at special quantity discounts for business or sales
promotional use. For information, please email special_sales@mitpress.mit.edu.

This book was set in Stone Sans and Stone Serif by SNP Best-set Typesetter Ltd., Hong
Kong and was printed and bound in the United States of America.

Library of Congress Cataloging-in-Publication Data

Kompridis, Nikolas.
    Critique and disclosure : critical theory between past and future /
Nikolas Kompridis.
        p. cm.
    Includes index.
    ISBN-13: 978-0-262-11299-4 (hc.: alk. paper)—978-0-262-51653-2 (pb.)
    1. Criticism (Philosophy) 2. Habermas, Jürgen 3. Heidegger, Martin,
1889–1976. I. Title.

B809.3.K67 2007
142—dc22

                                                                2006046711

10 9 8 7 6 5 4 3 2

for Allison

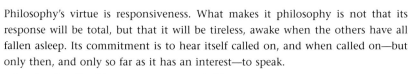

Philosophy's virtue is responsiveness. What makes it philosophy is not that its response will be total, but that it will be tireless, awake when the others have all fallen asleep. Its commitment is to hear itself called on, and when called on—but only then, and only so far as it has an interest—to speak.

—Stanley Cavell, *This New Yet Unapproachable America*

Contents

Preface

At a time when critical theory's future is very much at issue, this book presents a number of arguments about what critical theory should be if it is to have a future worthy of its past. The arguments presented here call for another way to inherit critical theory in light of renewed reflection on the nature of its undertaking, on its relation to time and to its own traditions, and, crucially, on the sources of normativity upon which it should draw. The book is composed of two interanimating and intersecting parts: (1) an elaborate critique of the limitations of Jürgen Habermas's reformulation of critical theory, and the proceduralist interpretation of reason upon which it is based; and (2) an alternative rendering of critical theory, at the center of which is a normatively reformulated interpretation of Martin Heidegger's idea of "disclosure" or "world disclosure." Contrasted are two "visions" of critical theory's role and purpose in the world. On the one side is a vision of critical theory that, in recognition of the value pluralism and social complexity of modernity, restricts itself to the normative clarification of the procedures by which moral and political questions should be settled; on the other, a vision of critical theory that, in recognition of the various ways in which conditions of modernity obscure or foreclose our possibilities, conceives itself as a possibility-disclosing practice. The proposed alternative represents neither a "Heideggerian" critical theory nor a total break with the Frankfurt School tradition of critical theory. Its guiding intention is to return critical theory to itself. To "return to itself," critical theory needs to reclaim the conceptual and normative resources of its own tradition from which it has been cut off and alienated, and to re-attune itself to those sources of normativity in communication with which it receives its calling and undertakes its distinctive philosophical and critical tasks.

The audience for whom this book was written obviously includes Habermasians and Heideggerians, and all those generally interested in the question of how to inherit the German philosophical tradition; however, the circle of intended addressees is much wider and more diverse. I hope that it will have something meaningful to say to social and political theorists, literary and cultural theorists, and feminist and postcolonial theorists wishing to rethink the meaning of reason, the possibilities of human agency, the conditions of modernity, and the practice of critique; in particular, to those who see the need to reformulate our received conceptions of reason, agency, and critique by incorporating (rather than neglecting) the activities through which human beings reflectively and innovatively transform the social practices, cultural traditions, and political institutions that they inherit and pass on.

The form of the book is somewhat unusual in that its arguments are not developed in straightforwardly linear and discrete fashion. Instead, they unfold in a "theme and variation" form. The principal themes of the book—the problem of beginning anew, the normative implications of modernity's relation to time, the cultural role of philosophy and the nature of critical theory's "calling," the meaning and scope of reason, the question of how to inherit and pass on our forms of life, the place of receptivity and self-decentering in our conceptions of reason and agency, and the normative and critical significance of Heidegger's notion of disclosure—are introduced in part I and reappear in subsequent parts of the book, taking on new implications at different points in the argument and in the changing contexts of the argument. As with rondo form in music, the final part, part VI, returns to and "concludes" part I, suggesting answers to the questions first posed there.

Even a superficial reading of this book will reveal its obvious flaws. Despite these flaws it is my hope that the book succeeds in showing the normative and critical potential of a way of thinking and philosophizing that has been greatly misunderstood and sometimes maligned, even though it has been central to the critical practice of Hegel, Marx, Nietzsche, Emerson, Dewey, Mead, Heidegger, Arendt, Gadamer, Adorno, Foucault, Taylor, and Cavell. If the book does succeed in this, then I will have partly discharged my many debts to these thinkers.

Close readers of Habermas will notice that a few elements of the alternative conception of critical theory proposed here can be found in the more "marginal" of Habermas's writings. Thinkers of Habermas's stature leave behind more good undeveloped ideas than less extraordinary thinkers develop in a lifetime. My own intellectual development would have been very different, and I would not have been nearly as clear about my own intellectual agenda, had I not been able to learn a very great deal from Habermas's undeveloped as well as from his fully developed ideas. I am very grateful to Habermas for inviting me to participate in his research colloquium at the University of Frankfurt, where, thanks to a postdoctoral fellowship from the Social Sciences and Humanities Research Council of Canada, I was able to spend three formative years in the company of a very stimulating group of philosophers and social theorists.

I want also to express my gratitude to Peter Dews for an invitation to contribute a paper on Habermas and Heidegger for his collection, *Habermas: A Critical Reader.* The invitation to write that paper gave me the opportunity to articulate in relatively intelligible and cogent form the issues that are at the heart of this book. And because the first draft of that paper was more than 30,000 words long, it became clear that those issues required book-length treatment. What I had in mind back then was a nice short book. It didn't turn out that way, but for the fact that it turned out as a book at all, I am indebted to David Levin for his timely encouragement and support. I am especially grateful to James Bohman for fifteen years of thought-provoking discussion about the topic of disclosure, its critical and normative potential, and its possible role in a renewed critical theory. And I'm also indebted to a great number of other friends and colleagues whose intellectual companionship has been an invaluable source of stimulation and support. I wish, in particular, to thank Martin Bresnick, Mikael Carleheden, Carolin Emcke, Josef Früchtl, Bonnie Honig, Axel Honneth, Jennifer Nedelsky, Claude Piché, and, especially, Jay Bernstein, Joseph Carens, Richard Eldridge, and James Tully. On various occasions and in various ways, whether you realized it or not, you kept my spirits up, and kept me from doubting myself too much, during some very difficult times.

I want also to thank my MIT Press editor, John Covell, for all his help in bringing this book into the marketplace of ideas, and for his choice of three excellent anonymous reviewers. Their valuable criticisms and suggestions helped me improve the book's overall structure and organization, and I wish to thank them as well for their close and attentive reading of the manuscript. And I also want to thank Dana Andrus at The MIT Press for her meticulous editing and valuable suggestions.

I dedicate this long-promised book to Allison Weir for the benefit of her patience and impatience with its progress; for the great good fortune that daily exposes my life to large and restorative doses of her grace, generosity, humor, and beauty; and for reminding me, time and again, that intimacy and criticism are not just compatible with but absolutely essential to the success of any life shared together.

Key to Habermas and Heidegger Citations

BT *Being and Time*, trans. John Macquarrie and Edward Robinson (New York: Harper and Row, 1962)

TCA1 *The Theory of Communicative Action: Reason and the Rationalization of Society*, Vol. 1, trans. Thomas McCarthy (Boston: Beacon Press, 1984)

TCA2 *The Theory of Communicative Action: Lifeworld and System*, Vol. 2, trans. Thomas McCarthy (Boston: Beacon Press, 1987)

PDM *The Philosophical Discourse of Modernity*, trans. Frederick Lawrence (Cambridge: MIT Press, 1987)

NC *The New Conservatism*, trans. Shierry Weber Nicholsen, (Cambridge: MIT Press, 1989)

MC *Moral Consciousness and Communicative Action*, trans. Christian Lenhardt (Cambridge: MIT Press, 1990)

TK *Texte und Kontexte* (Frankfurt: Suhrkamp, 1991)

PT *Postmetaphysical Thinking*, trans. Mark Hohengarten (Cambridge: MIT Press, 1992)

JA *Justification and Application*, trans. Ciaran P. Cronin (Cambridge: MIT Press, 1993)

BFN *Between Facts and Norms: Contributions to a Discourse Theory of Law and Democracy*, trans. William Rehg (Cambridge: MIT Press, 1998)

SS Jürgen Habermas, *Introduction to "Observations on 'The Spiritual Situation of the Age,'"* trans. Andrew Buchwalter (Cambridge: MIT Press, 1985)

WW Jürgen Habermas, "Work and *Weltanschauung*: The Heidegger Controversy from a German Perspective," in Hubert Dreyfus and Harrison Hall, eds., *Heidegger: A Critical Reader* (Oxford: Basil Blackwell, 1992), pp. 186–208

I What Is Critical Theory For . . .

1 Crisis and Critique

How do we renew our cultural traditions, transform our social practices and political institutions, when they break down or are challenged in such a way as to preclude going on as before? For a philosophically and politically diverse group of theorists from Rousseau, Hegel, and Marx to Arendt, Foucault, and Taylor this is *the* philosophical and political question. The urgency of this question arises from a consciousness of crisis, of an awareness of things going, or having gone, terribly wrong. It arises from the need to rethink our commitments to certain ideals and practices, perhaps to break free of them, by imagining previously untried or uncovering previously suppressed possibilities. This very particular need is the need to begin anew—a need marking one's time as a time of need.

To theorists whose thought is self-consciously developed as a response to some deep and abiding experience of crisis, we might wish to give the name "crisis thinkers." Although not always apparent, and certainly too little understood, the experience of crisis may well be the primary inducement to thought in our time, the time of modernity. This is not an accident or some contingent fact about modernity; rather, modernity induces "crisis thinking" because it is inherently crisis generating. A recent observation of Stanley Cavell's identifies precisely what unites these thinkers' response to crisis, identifying as well the source of crisis: "Not whether it is good to have the Enlightenment is our problem, but whether we can survive its solutions."[1]

When Kant proclaimed that "[o]ur age is properly the age of critique, and to critique everything must submit,"[2] he was, of course, trying to show the deep connection between the Enlightenment project—"the project of modernity"—and the practice of critique. But less visible to Kant than to us, is the deep connection between crisis and critique.[3] Once we appreciate the depth of this connection, we will also come to see how complexly enmeshed in the self-understanding of modernity are critique, crisis, and the need to begin anew—how deeply, if I may put it this way, they affect modernity's experience of itself.

The following citations from Hegel's *Phenomenology of Spirit*, Marx's *18th Brumaire of Louis Bonaparte*, and Nietzsche's *Beyond Good and Evil* can help bring the nature of this experience into focus:

It is surely not difficult to see that our time is a birth and transition to a new period. Spirit has broken with what was hitherto the world of its existence and imagination and is about to submerge all this in the past; it is at work giving itself a new form. . . . [F]rivolity as well as the boredom that opens up in the establishment and the indeterminate apprehension of something unknown are harbingers of a forthcoming change. This gradual crumbling is interrupted by the break of day that like lightning all at once reveals the edifice of the new world.[4]

For our part it is our task to drag the old world into the full light of day and to give positive shape to the new one. The more time history allows thinking humanity to reflect and suffering humanity to collect its strength the more perfect will be the fruit which the present now bears within its womb.[5]

More and more it seems to me that the philosopher being *of necessity* a man of tomorrow and the day after tomorrow, has always found himself, and *had* to find himself, in contradiction to his today: his enemy was ever the ideal of today. . . . [P]hilosophers, though they themselves have rarely felt like friends of wisdom but rather like disagreeable fools and dangerous question marks, have found their task, their hard, unwanted, inescapable task, but eventually also the greatness of their task, in being the bad conscience of their time.[6]

In the first citation, Hegel evokes a relation between past and present that involves a dramatic break between a crumbling old world and an imminently emerging new one. The break, when it comes, is sudden; the new world, which emerges as like a lightning flash (*Blitz*), is unprecedented. And the present is construed as that moment in which both the fading of the old world and the imminence of the new world can, and must, be apprehended. Like Hegel, Marx also calls for an apprehension of the present as a "birth and transition" from an old to a new world. Yet both Hegel and Marx are more than a little ambiguous as to whether the emergence of the new is something that is inevitable—something that happens to us or something that we ourselves initiate. For although Marx makes it sound as though *we* are the ones dragging "the old world into the full light of day," he also makes it sound as though the birth of what the "present now bears within" its womb takes place according to a will and logic of its own. This ambiguity may be irremovable, because the new is not something over which we exercise direct control. There is always a contingent aspect to the new, and moreover, once it emerges, the new can possess a self-instituting and self-verifying quality.

Whether the emergence of the new world is regarded as something we ourselves will or something that has a "will" of its own, it is clear that both Hegel and Marx suppose that we are under some normative obligation to help facilitate its birth. Failure to be receptive to the present, attentively attuned to its hidden significance, would mean failure to get into the right normative relation to our own time. That relation arises from a particular normative expectation: that we are *obligated* in some indeterminate sense to bring about the new beginning, obligated to help give "new form" to our form of life by apprehending the present in which we live as a time of "birth and transition." Meeting that obligation requires that we apprehend precisely those possibilities within the present upon whose realization the new form of the world depends. This attentive stance toward the present supposes a complementary stance of anticipatory openness toward the future, to how things might otherwise be. In taking such a stance, however, one is likely to discover that getting into the right relation to one's time may mean living and thinking "in contradiction" to one's time.

In the citation from Nietzsche, being a "philosopher" means being out of step with, in contradiction to, one's time, forced to oppose it, and to act as its "bad conscience."[7] The kind of individual whom Nietzsche calls a "philosopher" is someone who must stretch her thought between today and "tomorrow, and the day after tomorrow." Only a stance of anticipatory openness to the future allows her to endure the state of being in contradiction with her own time. Only the expectation of a future different from the past enables her to persist in her critique of the crisis generating "ideal of today," knowing that the validity of her critique can be established only under the altered social and cultural conditions it normatively prefigures.

Although it may at first seem rather out of place within this tradition of thought, particularly, in its more recent incarnations, it is difficult adequately to understand the nature and aims of Jürgen Habermas's philosophical project unless one sees that it too arises from the consciousness of crisis, from the need to begin anew. This question is at work in Habermas's life-long attempt to bring about "a new beginning" (NC 266)[8] in Germany's political culture by realigning elements of German cultural traditions with the liberal-democratic traditions of the West. It also informs his engagement with the less local problem of sustaining the project of modernity, and his advocacy of a philosophical paradigm change from the "philosophy of the subject" to the model of linguistic intersubjectivity.

Although not Habermas's central philosophical question, the question of how to begin anew, reflectively renewing our traditions and self-critically transforming our social practices and political institutions, is entwined to the central question of Habermas's enterprise: the question of what reason ought to mean. Once we grant that these questions are ultimately inseparable, we are faced with a host of problems that Habermas has been unable to resolve satisfactorily. These problems bear directly not only on the meaning of reason but also on the question of what role philosophy can play in bringing about a new cultural and political beginning that gives new meaning and purpose to our cultural traditions, social practices, and political institutions.

Certainly there are few postwar intellectuals as sensitive as Habermas to the question of how we can self-consciously renew our cultural traditions, particularly, those to which we have a problematic and broken relation. Among German intellectuals there are none more alert to those elements within specifically German cultural and political traditions that must be actively and continuously criticized, and held accountable. However, when Habermas claims that "today we bear a greater responsibility than ever for the proportion of continuity and discontinuity in the forms of life we pass on" (NC 263), the reference of the first-person plural is not restricted to the cultural self-understanding of any nation in particular. This inclusive (necessarily idealized) "we" refers to the shared self-understanding of modernity, and that self-understanding is partly constituted by the responsibility that a culturally and politically heterogeneous *we* is increasingly obliged to assume "for the proportion of continuity and discontinuity in the forms of life we pass on." Whether we think of ourselves as modern, late modern, or postmodern, as political liberals, conservatives, or radicals, as Western or non-Western, this sense of responsibility grows from within the inescapably reflective stance we now must take in consideration of our own cultural and political traditions. Audibly echoing Hegel, Bernard Williams put this state of affairs just right: "There is no route back from reflectiveness."[9] As the twenty-first century unfolds with stupendous inscrutability, and in a state of perpetual insecurity, one of the few things about which we may be certain is that the shelf-life of a naive or taken-for-granted relation to one's traditions will be measured in minutes, if not in time-crunching sound bites. If we can be sure of anything, it is that we are sure to be unsettled.

Since we have become the kind of beings for whom the proportion of continuity and discontinuity of the forms of life we pass on has become an issue for us, we will always be liable to the judgments of a "future present," and thus we will always have something for which to answer. Quite obviously some of our forms of life, some of our traditions and practices, (will) have more for which to answer than others. Still the more we realize that the renewal of cultural traditions is not a process we can simply take for granted, "the more clearly we become conscious of the ambivalence in every tradition" (NC 263). Yet no matter how ambivalently we may relate to any one of our traditions, we cannot self-critically renew our traditions simply by disengaging or extricating ourselves from them. Any like-minded attempt to take a purely objectifying stance toward traditions and forms of life will be self-defeating: because they shape and sustain our identity and self-understanding, our relation to our cultural traditions, even when scrupulously critical, remains one of inescapable dependence.

Though reflectiveness irreversibly defines our relation to our cultural traditions and forms of life, it does not exhaust that relation. It is therefore important to resist the long-standing appeal of one or the other of these two extremes: thinking of ourselves either as standing completely outside of our traditions, in no way affected by or indebted to them, or, as identical with our traditions, fatefully bound to or enclosed within them. I hesitate to designate these two positions as the "liberal" and "communitarian" positions because the meaning of these terms is often as disputable as it is unclear. Whatever name we may wish to give them, it is clear that both of these influential positions are illusory, offering either too much reflective distance or not enough. Traditions, forms of life, call them what you will, are repositories of cultural learning; they bear and transmit an ensemble of holistically structured meanings, ideals, norms, and practices, providing the interpretative and evaluative schemes in terms of which we take up our relations to the world and to one another. The success of any attempt to transcend the limitations of our traditions and forms of life, to surpass their horizons of meaning, will depend on insight, and the acquisition of any such insight will depend crucially (though not exclusively) on the semantic and cultural resources preserved within them. Gadamer's analysis of the *Vorurteile* that structure our practices and languages of interpretation and evaluation has made abundantly clear the extent to which such *Vorurteile* both constrain *and* enable our speech and action. Whether we undertake such an analysis in terms of Gadamerian *Vorurteile*, or Heideggerian *Sinnhorizonte*, or Wittgensteinian *Lebensformen* what we discover is that the success of our attempts to transcend the limitations of our traditions and forms of life depends on abilities and possibilities that traditions and forms of life pass on (or fail to pass on) to their members. They provide resources for, and not just obstacles to, surpassing their limitations. When seen in light of such *interdependence*, the renewal and correction of traditions looks to be co-extensive with self-renewal and self-correction: self-transcendence will necessarily be outward, not upward.[10]

As a reflective process of self-clarification, getting ourselves "right" involves a learning process that demands a complex cognitive and affective engagement with our forms of life and cultural traditions. Whatever it is that stands in need of renewal and reappropriation, is something received in trust by a "we" or "us" to whom it so stands. Thus we could neither correct nor renew our traditions, nor understand ourselves as responsible "for the proportion of continuity and discontinuity in the forms of life we pass on," were we to disengage from or disidentify with them—that is, were we unable or unwilling to regard *as our own* the multiple, conflicting, and troubled traditions we inherit and pass on. A purely objectifying stance (and that includes an ironically skeptical stance) toward the traditions we inherit not only impedes claiming or reclaiming them as our own, it also occludes the ways in which our identities as much as our possibilities are shaped by the traditions we inherit. Moreover an objectifying stance toward traditions poses a threat to their semantic resources in a manner analogous to the threat such a stance poses to the physical (and semantic) resources of nature. The extent to which modernism, or at least, a particular strain of modernism, has been based on this objectifying stance, it has been a vehicle for the destruction of our cultural as well as our natural resources. To become conscious of the ambivalence in every tradition is also, then, to become conscious of the fragility of traditions. It is clearly the case that at any time we may fail to break insightfully from elements in our traditions that are unworthy of our (revised or existing) ethical and political ideals. But we may also fail to retrieve and preserve in renewed form some threatened elements without which further efforts at self-clarification and self-correction would be compromised. And so our sense of responsibility for the renewal of traditions grows with our awareness both of their ambivalence and their fragility.

2   The Problem of Beginning Anew

While there is no route back from reflectiveness, there is no clear, uncontestable route forward. "You must go on," urges the narrator of Beckett's *The Unnameable*.[11] Most surely, we must go on. But if we are to "go on" reflectively rather than blindly, how do we "go on"? To where do we go on? What do we take and what do we leave behind? What of ourselves do we continue, what discontinue? Where or to what do we look for orientation? Do we look to the past? Or do we look to other forms of life? As Hilary Putnam puts it, "Our problem is not that we must choose from among an already fixed and defined number of optimal ways of life; our problem is that we don't know even one *optimal* way of life."[12] In so far as we cannot know the one *optimal* way of life that can serve as a secure normative standard for our own, whatever we determine to be the "right" proportion of the continuity and discontinuity in the forms of life we pass on, will be a determination that is neither final nor indefeasible. The "right" proportion will have to be reviewed and revised *as* we "go on." But even without an "optimal" way of life to which we can appeal, can we not hope for and work toward something better than what we now have? The question then arises as to whether our expectations of, and hopes for, the future can in any way guide our efforts to make sense of the "the proportion of continuity and discontinuity in the forms of life we pass on." But how does our culture open itself up to the future? How does our openness to the future render intelligible (or unintelligible) the ever-shifting constellation of relationships between past, present, and future? Are there better and worse ways to be open to the future—better and worse ways to be open to something new?

Something quite important is missing from Putnam's otherwise perceptive characterization of our situation, and that is the way in which the unavailability of a secure normative standard for determining how we are to go on is intensified by the peculiarly modern experience of time. We must go on—not knowing how or to where—under the vertiginous pressure of modern time. As we are hurled forward into the future at an unprecedented speed, there is less and less time and, therefore, more and more pressure to bring into some intelligible pattern the often obscure and ambiguous relationships between the past, the present, and the future. There is also evidence that as the pressure mounts to render intelligible the discontinuity and change that these relationships undergo, so does the pressure to abandon or regard as useless the effort to make sense of relentless discontinuity and change.

There is perhaps nothing more common today than the insistent, compulsively repeated exhortation to embrace the new, to embrace the future—a future into which we headlong rush as much as into which we are headlong pushed. Perhaps, there is nothing more characteristic of the culture of modernity. Whether it is in the name of "globalization," the "new economy," or the "digital age," no matter how familiar, no matter how transparently ideological or strategic, it is an exhortation with an almost irresistible appeal. Because the source of its power is deeply and inseparably anchored in modernity's self-understanding, the appeal to the "new" retains its power to be a highly persuasive, perhaps the most persuasive, rhetorical device of modern culture. Undeniably, asymmetries of power, various kinds of domination (over human beings, nature, and things), unchecked capitalist growth, and the erosion of the institutions of democratic self-government, individually and in concert, play a very influential role in bringing about massive change in the name of something "new." But by themselves, all these forces do not sufficiently explain the appeal or the seductiveness of the new. Little wonder, then, that Adorno and Benjamin regarded the recurrent appeal to the "new" as an appeal possessing a mythical power tellingly instancing the reversion of "enlightenment to myth."[13] No wonder, too, that such change as we are exhorted to embrace is change we are forced to experience as our unavoidable fate rather than as the outcome of our reflectively exercised agency.

"Keep going, going on, call that going, call that on."[14] We cannot stop the future. We must go on. But why must we go on unreflectively? What presses us to go on toward that which we have had neither the time nor the opportunity to question, reject, or endorse under appropriately reflective conditions? There are different answers that can be adduced. For one, the new is not just seductive; it also arouses fear. So at least one reason why we go on unreflectively is because we are afraid to be left behind, afraid of being rendered out of date, obsolete—the fear of which is not an inessential part of the seduction. But as we have already discussed this is not the only meaning of the new, not the only source of its appeal. The new also contains the promise of something better, a "promise of happiness." It can only be exploited for ideological purposes or for profit *because* it contains this promise: the promise of something better than what we have known. It is this promise that also brings the new into the proximity, if not the domain, of myth.[15]

Is there not a more reflective way for us to be open to the future and to the new—a way that is less inviting of myth? Only as architects of the future who also comprehend the needs of the present can we make sense of the past, suggested the young Nietzsche.[16] He may be right, but it is not self-evident just what his suggestion entails. At the very least, making sense of our past and present seems to demand a way of imagining our future in terms of some utopian project or set of projects that respond to the needs of the present—which supposes, of course, that we have correctly interpreted our present needs. Nonetheless, Nietzsche's suggestion remains a gnomic one, raising as many questions as it is meant to answer. Must we be architects of a fully *determinate* future if we are properly to comprehend the present and make sense of the past? The lately departed twentieth century saw the rise of some truly monstrous architecture created by self-proclaimed "architects of the future." Evidently they suffered from no lack of confidence: either about their own architectural talents or about the legitimacy of the utopia they wanted to build. The architecture of horror that blackened the twentieth century is surely not what Nietzsche had in mind; although, uncannily, he was able to foresee its possibility. But there is no way of getting around the fact that without some explicit normative constraints his call for "architects of the future" appears to be an invitation to disaster. It comes alarmingly close to the most dangerous of modernist fantasies, fantasies in the name of which the architecture of the future becomes a license to annihilate rather than to understand the past.

In Nietzsche's defense, however, it should be said that a determinate future would not, on his view, be a future to which we ought to say *yes*, for it is precisely the demand that the future conform to the determination of our will that leads to nihilism and destructiveness. To imagine the future with complete determinacy would be to deny the indeterminacy essential to the future—essential to the openness of the future. Thus this stance to the future would consist not in its affirmation but in its negation. Yet, despite the inherent dangers of such an undertaking, Nietzsche insists that we must nonetheless engage in imagining the future differently. Why? Is it simply to satisfy the modernist craving for the new, for which the name Nietzsche sometimes serves us a convenient abbreviation? Certainly this is one way to understand Nietzsche's insistence on the new—but it would not be the best way, and not just because it would be untrue to Nietzsche. His insistence on the new has little—if anything—to do with the satisfaction of a desire for the new for its own sake; in fact he regarded this desire as a pathological manifestation of the "ascetic ideal." Rather, the insistence on the new is motivated by the idea that making sense of how we are to "go on" requires that we think from a *new stance*. "Architect of the future" in Nietzsche's sense, then, names an attitude or stance that one is required to assume in order to think anew "the proportion of continuity and discontinuity in the forms of life we pass on." To *think anew* the question of "the proportion of continuity and discontinuity in the forms of life we pass on" is not just one way to make sense of this question, one possible way to be responsive and responsible to it. In Nietzsche's view, it is the *only* way: to make sense of it, to be responsive and responsible to it, *is* to think it anew.

This orientation to the new, to the affirmation of a future different from the past, is the distinctive mark of the "philosopher of the future." Taking Emerson and Nietzsche as exemplars of this type of "philosopher," Stanley Cavell helps us to identify why it is that they arouse our suspicion, and why the new itself arouses another kind of anxiety and fear. "[I]f we are to think anew it must be from a new stance, one essentially *unfamiliar* to us; or, say, from a further perspective that is *uncontrollable* by us."[17] Various and diverse sorts of explanations have been offered to explain why we prefer, or cling to ways of life, patterns of belief, and action orientations with which we are already familiar, and in which we are already feel at "home." While the explanations themselves may be contestable, the tendency they aim to explain is not. The value of Cavell's remark, however, does not consist in serving as one more reminder of this tendency, but in pointing to a link between the unfamiliar and the uncontrollable. It is the latter, so I claim, that best explains why the new makes most moral and political philosophers anxious and suspicious. From a purely cognitive standpoint, the new arouses fear and anxiety because it is not something whose effects we can predict and control. We cannot master what we do not know. From a moral and political standpoint, we are understandably suspicious about any stance or perspective that is uncontrollable. Our suspicion here arises from the assumption that a stance that is uncontrollable is a stance that is morally and politically unaccountable. And so it is quite unclear how thinking anew can be thinking responsibly, how it can be anything more than a dubious source of normativity. Affirming an indeterminate future seems to be no less risky, no less dangerous than affirming a completely determinate one. Whatever the relevant reasons, it would seem that neither the "architects" of a determinate nor an indeterminate future can be held accountable for the future they wish to build.

Even though Nietzsche's recommended stance toward the future may not be altogether "untimely," not quite as existentially remote from and politically incompatible with the pluralistic and fragmented nature of our twenty-first century modernity as first appeared, it nonetheless remains a disturbing prospect. If thinking anew from a new stance means thinking unaccountably, then we would most certainly be evading rather than embracing the responsibility we must bear for "the proportion of continuity and discontinuity in the forms of life we pass on." But perhaps we can save Nietzsche's (and by implication, Emerson's and Cavell's) suggestion from leading to this conclusion, if we recall that to think anew from a new stance arises from an objective not a subjective need. And so it is possible to evaluate the new stance according to the degree to which it illuminates both past and present. Thus, to the degree to which it helps make better sense of the problem of how to go on, the new stance can be assessed by how well it answers the need which gives rise to it.

The challenge, then, is to see how a stance that cannot be controlled can be made accountable.[18] Given the nature of the task, how could we ever reassure ourselves that we have got right, if only provisionally, the proportion of continuity and discontinuity in the forms of life we pass on? How could we confidently—but not blindly—affirm the future we are aiming to build? To what would we owe that confidence? How could we make it accountable? Here is the first draft of an answer to these questions. We would be entitled to our confidence—ethically and epistemically speaking—only if our change of orientation to the future made us insightfully aware of a previously uncritical relation to the past. In other words, a change of orientation to the future in light of the new stance we assume would have to make us more accountable to, more responsible for, the proportion of continuity and discontinuity in the forms of life we pass on. We could not justify an orientation to the future that made us forgetful—or relieved us—of our obligation reflectively and critically to renew our traditions and forms of life. On the other hand, if we were to abandon the continuous, never-ending task of integrating continuity and discontinuity, we would disown our responsibility to those who came before us and to those who will succeed us. Thus we can say that the normativity of the new contains both a problem-solving aspect that answers the ever-present need to make sense of discontinuity against a shifting background of continuity, and a culture-orienting aspect that facilitates a more reflective understanding of and relation to the past.

3   Modernity's Relation to Time

For all that separates him from Nietzsche, Habermas shares with Nietzsche the view that the urgency and inescapability of the problem of self-critically renewing our traditions and forms of life is a function of modernity's relation to time—its "time-consciousness," as Habermas likes to call it. The most extensive discussion of this notion appears in *The Philosophical Discourse of Modernity* where it is positioned as one of the key features of the concept of modernity. I will be exploring the different ramifications of this idea throughout my book, but for the time being I want only to develop the normative connections between modernity's relation to time and the responsibility we must assume for the renewal of our traditions and forms of life.

Habermas introduces the idea of modernity's "time-consciousness" in his explication of Hegel's concept of modernity. "Hegel was the first philosopher to develop a clear concept of modernity" (PDM 4), since Hegel was the first to grasp the implications of modernity's relation to time, a relation constituted by an openness to the "novelty of the future" (PDM 5). More than anything else this openness to the "novelty of the future" is what makes modernity historically distinctive. The expectations that guide modernity's orientation to the future can disclose a horizon of possibility that keeps perpetually open the promise of a future different from the past: it contains the promise of a break with the past, and the promise of a new beginning. There is, unfortunately, a deeply entrenched way to think of this wholly modern idea of beginning anew as involving the complete dismantling of all our previous beliefs and commitments, and starting radically from scratch. This is the way common to Descartes and seventeenth century epistemology, to a popular (but erroneous) reading of Nietzsche, to the avant-garde mentality of modernism, and to the standard modernist understanding of "progress." But there is another way to think of beginning anew—a way that is much less willful, self-undermining, and misguided. It does not require the negation of the past, nor the glorification of a self-creating or self-constituting subject; rather, it requires the recognition of the past as the prehistory of the present, with which it is moreover connected "as by the chain of a continual destiny" (PDM 14). If we are to make sense of a new beginning as something ascribable to our own agency and as something that allows us to "go on" reflectively rather than blindly, we will need accountably to integrate our new beginning with a reflectively appropriated past.

Because of its open, expectant stance to the future, modernity is constantly engaged in reconfiguring its changing relationships to the past, present, and future, rendering the meaning of history subject to an unending conflict of interpretations. Definitive of modernity is the position of the present as the site where new and old, contested pasts and possible futures, constantly collide with one another. That the present will be subject to crisis experiences arising from such disorienting collisions is an unavoidable consequence of this future-oriented stance: the more open to discontinuity we are, the more we have to wrestle with the problem of continuity. Thus, on each occasion in which modernity's time consciousness intensifies, we are pressed into evaluations and decisions concerning the proportion of continuity and discontinuity in the forms of life we pass on.

The experience of the present as a time of crisis is not only due to modernity's openness to the novelty of the future; it is also due to the way in which the future functions as *a source of pressure* brought to bear on currently unsolved problems, on available but unnoticed or unexploited possibilities. In response to this pressure, "there arises an existentially sharpened consciousness of the danger of missed decisions, and neglected interventions. There arises a perspective from which the present state of affairs sees itself called to account as the past of a future present. There arises the suggestion of a responsibility for the connection of one situation to the next, for the continuation of a process that sheds its nature-like spontaneity and refuses to hold out the promise of any taken-for-granted continuity" (PDM 58). The stance toward the future that constitutes modernity's relation to time not only places possibility ontologically higher than actuality, as Heidegger once claimed;[19] it also places an almost unbearable sense of responsibility upon the present. If we are to respond authentically to our consciousness of historical time (in conformity with the obligations to past and present it enjoins), we are compelled to take the ethical perspective of an historically accountable "future present." From this projected ethical perspective we can recognize the past as the "prehistory of the present," to which the present is connected "as by the chain of a continual destiny." Within this ethically reinterpreted historical horizon we bear a special responsibility: we are the ones who must self-consciously renew and correct our forms of life, who must repair what is broken, or break with what seems irreparable. We are the ones who must remake our languages and practices, and make something new out of something old.

By drawing on modernity's relation to time to clarify the responsibility we must bear for the proportion of continuity and discontinuity in the forms of life that we pass on, Habermas has outlined a normatively suggestive picture of what the self-critical renewal of traditions and forms of life demands. This picture suggests that any attempted breaks with the past enjoin a cognitive and an ethical response. From a cognitive standpoint, the activity of making the difference between past and present intelligible demands that it be regarded against a background of continuity which itself cannot be taken for granted, but must be continuously retrieved and re-evaluated. Furthermore such retrieval and re-evaluation is itself answerable to the obligation to get right the proportion of continuity and discontinuity in the forms of life we pass on. Now this cognitive standpoint is intertwined with an ethical-existential standpoint from which we come to see that the problem of getting right the proportion of continuity and discontinuity in the forms of life we pass on, is *our* problem. Coming to see it as our problem means, of course, that our sense of responsibility for self-critically renewing our traditions must have a very strong affective component. Lacking such an affective component, our relation to the past would be marked by inconstancy as much as by denial of responsibility. And this circumstance continues to mark modernity's relationship to the past, the acute insights of Benjamin's critique of the philosophy of history notwithstanding.[20]

4   Renewing the Tradition

I have tried to make explicit the normative implications of Habermas's account of the reflective renewal of traditions because—among other things—I want to draw upon it to evaluate Habermas's stand toward one of his own cultural traditions—the German philosophical tradition that goes back to Kant and Hegel, especially that part of it that goes by the name of "critical theory." The problem of renewing the German philosophical tradition is a problem that Habermas has never taken lightly, and he has treated it as conscientiously and responsibly as could be expected of anyone. No one of his generation or after has done more to renew this tradition, to make it important again. As the principal custodian of Frankfurt School critical theory, Habermas has endeavored to place its considerable insights in the service of reforming the legal and political institutions of liberal democracies. As a rule, Habermas has tried to rescue the Enlightenment elements of the German philosophical tradition, reformulating them in liberal-democratic terms.

Some elements lend themselves to such reformulation with little, if any, resistance—for example, Habermas's reformulation of Kant's categorical imperative and Hegel's concept of recognition in his theory of moral discourse. But there are far too many elements within the German tradition, it would seem, that strongly resist, if not altogether preclude, reformulation in such terms—for example, much of what is considered original in Nietzsche and Heidegger. Therefore Habermas has understandably erred on the side of caution in just what and just how much of the German tradition he regards as reflectively appropriable, re-inheritable. Those ideas, attitudes, and presuppositions within the philosophical and related cultural traditions "that served to make us blind to the Nazi regime" call for a "critical, indeed, a distrustful appropriation" (NC 144). Since Nietzsche and

Heidegger are taken to be the most influential representatives of counter-Enlightenment positions within the German tradition, it seems that there is no other way for critical theorists responsibly to appropriate their thought.

Now as Habermas himself would be the first to point out, the critical, even distrustful, appropriation of traditions must itself be re-evaluated and, when necessary, corrected in light of new, less one-sided or distorted interpretations. In my view, just such a re-evaluation of the German philosophical tradition must now be undertaken in connection with the question of the identity and future of critical theory.[21] I believe that what Adorno said about art in the opening sentences of *Aesthetic Theory* may justifiably be said about critical theory today: it goes without saying that nothing that concerns critical theory goes without saying, let alone without thinking. For all there is to recommend it, Habermas's reformulation has produced a split between new and old critical theory so deep that the identity and future of critical theory are at risk. And that is because the normative gain that issued from the so-called paradigm change to linguistic intersubjectivity is attached to interpretations of critical theory's philosophical sources that have needlessly devalued and misrepresented their critical potential. It is not just that these interpretations go undisputed, even when they have acquired the character of orthodox doctrine; rather, it is that they tend to define the terms of the dispute within critical theory.

As I will endeavor to show, Habermas's reformulation of critical theory not only instituted a change of philosophical paradigm but also a change in critical theory's self-understanding. As a consequence it has come to serve as a "theoretical" barrier to critical theory's own sources in the German philosophical tradition—the sources upon which the continuity of its identity and the possibility of its renewal depends. It is my thesis that the model of critical theory that Habermas's paradigm change has brought about is in need of urgent reassessment if critical theory is to have a future worthy of its past, up to and including Habermas's enormously important contributions. If critical theory is to have such a future, its identity will have to be secured under interpretations of its sources in the German philosophical tradition different from those that have shaped its current self-understanding. To accept the current interpretations as valid and adequate is to risk rendering oneself insensible to just how much has been lost, or given up as theoretically and historically *passé*.

This is not the first (nor the last) time that critical theory must face the problem of how to renew itself, for the problem of renewal, the problem of integrating discontinuity and continuity, is internal to critical theory's self-understanding. Any tradition of inquiry that defines itself by its capacity to reflexively incorporate the sociohistorical conditions and contexts of its own emergence will be one that demands a heightened awareness of its own time. Critical theory's reflective attunement to its own time is not only a source of its theoretical reflexivity; it is also the source of its power to intervene in social life as an agency of positive normative and social change. This interconnection between philosophy and its own time is precisely what the young Hegel had in mind when he wrote of the "need of philosophy" (*Bedürfnis der Philosophie*). According to Hegel, this need arises from the consciousness of "diremption," of division or breakdown (*Entzweiung*)[22]—that is, the consciousness of crisis: "The need of philosophy arises when the power of unification disappears from human life, when oppositions become independent, and lose their living connection and reciprocal relation."[23] Thus philosophy's responsiveness to its own time is a condition of its capacity to be responsible for its own time.

To prevent any misunderstanding, it is essential to point out that the "need" that gives rise to philosophy is not one philosophy already comprehends and to which it is already is in a position to respond. The "need" that gives rise to philosophy also instructs philosophy about its own need—about what philosophy is itself in need of, if it is properly to respond to the need that gives rise to its own activity. Philosophy does not *yet* know what to say, or, for that matter, how to say, whatever needs to be said. Philosophy is called upon to speak without knowing in advance what can answer the need that calls upon it to address, to intervene in, its own time. In this respect, philosophy *receives* its concept of itself from its time, and it is from this stance of receptivity that it is then able to recognize its obligations to its time, able to recognize its own concerns in the concerns that bedevil its own time. Hence philosophy has to be particularly sensitive to the difference that its own time introduces with respect to the past, particularly sensitive to the meaning of significant discontinuities.

The importance attributed to Hegel in the opening pages of *The Philosophical Discourse of Modernity* is due to Hegel's incorporation of modernity's relation to time into his concept of philosophy, as a result of which philosophy's concept of itself is something it "receives" from its own time. Through this incorporation, the concepts of philosophy and modernity mutually elucidate one another: philosophy's tasks and obligations are clarified by its responsiveness to the need from which philosophy arises. Insofar as Habermas holds that this "need" can be answered only through an enlarged and balanced embodiment of the practices of reason, his project is self-consciously continuous with Hegel's and the Young Hegelians. Not only does Habermas understand his own philosophical project to be continuous with Hegel's, he claims that the "need" first thematized by Hegel is the constitutive theme of the philosophical discourse of modernity: the need for self-reassurance.[24]

The reassurance in question concerns modernity's legitimacy, a legitimacy that is supposed to be grounded on reason alone rather than on external authority. Of course, the kind of legitimacy that reason confers upon modernity will depend on what reason is taken to be, on what capabilities are ascribed to it, and what goods it helps to realize. Thus the problem of modernity's self-reassurance is entangled with the problematics of modern reason. If, to use a straightforward example, we think of reason along Cartesian lines, self-reassurance would require certainty in order to reassure convincingly. In Habermas's view, this kind of reassurance is simply unattainable. We should not look for self-reassurance in a form that is incompatible with modernity's relation to time—in a form that "closes off the future as a source of *disruption*" (PDM 12).

While the kind of self-reassurance that Habermas thinks modernity should aim for is much weaker than Cartesian certainty, it should be somewhat stronger than the kind Bernard Williams recommends. Williams uses a much more ordinary term to capture—accurately, I believe—the idea of self-reassurance: *confidence*. For Williams, confidence refers to a mode of conviction very different from certainty.[25] Confidence, in contrast to certainty, is a social good that must be renewed continually by the social practices and cultural traditions to which it lends itself. In this respect Williams's understanding of modernity's need for self-reassurance is closer to Hegel's than it is to Habermas's. Although Habermas derives his understanding of modernity's need for self-reassurance from Hegel, he derives his answer to that need from Kant, in the form of a procedural conception of reason. (I will defer until parts III and IV discussion of how and why this Kantian answer to modernity's need for self-reassurance is normatively incompatible with modernity's relation to time.)

Although the turn to a procedural conception of reason fundamentally alters the character of critical theory, Habermas never wholly abandons his Hegelian construal of critical theory's identity. Thus, when he describes "the self-referentiality of [critical theory's] calling" (TCA2 401), he is reiterating the young Hegel's view of philosophy. Critical theory's calling is self-referential because "it knows that in and through the very act of knowing it *belongs* to the objective context of life that it strives to grasp" (TCA2 401, my emphasis). In this crucial respect, if only in this respect, the self-understanding of critical theory remains the same as it was when Max Horkheimer made use of this self-understanding to distinguish critical theory from traditional theory.[26] It is not just distinctive methodological consequences that follow from this, however, for it is a self-understanding from which *a different kind of knowing* must follow. This normative demand *also* arises from the self-referentiality of critical theory's calling. As a practically oriented inquiry committed to bringing about not only social conditions free from fear and domination but also social conditions conducive to human flourishing, critical theory is theoretically indexed to historically disclosed horizons of possibility. Possibility, however, is no ordinary object of knowledge: it is no object at all. Yet possibility—which here stands for, as much as it requires thinking from, a new stance—is precisely that upon which depends critical theory's capacity to answer the need that gives rise to it. As John Dewey presciently remarked, it is only in light of "possibilities opening up before us that we become aware of constrictions that hem us in and of burdens that oppress."[27] The kind of "knowing" involved here is obviously not the kind of theoretical knowing that leads to abstract knowledge, not a rule-governed cognitive competence which can be tracked along a developmental sequence of discrete stages. By contrast, it involves a *practical* ability to see more in things than they are, which ability cannot be subsumed under rule-like concepts.

Hence the "diagnosis of the times" in which critical theory engages is not strictly descriptive. Critical theory contains an ineliminable normative element that guides its diagnosis. It cannot seek to assume a "view from nowhere"—that is out of the question, since the new view it seeks to assume arises from "within the objective context of life that it strives to grasp." Critical theory's view of things as more than they are, is owed to its ability to articulate what we are already familiar with in the light of possibility. To see things in the light of possibility is the ability to see how they might otherwise be. Such "seeing" requires a reflective responsiveness to historical experience, particularly to experiences of crisis and breakdown—the very experiences that make us reflectively aware of the need to rethink the proportion of continuity and discontinuity in the forms of life we pass on. This kind of "seeing" also involves a genuine re-cognition: seeing differently, as though for the first time, something familiar or taken for granted. So once again, we are presented with the challenge of integrating continuity and discontinuity, the familiar and the unfamiliar, the old and the new.

Because it is normatively and theoretically obligated to attune itself to its own time, critical theory is more vulnerable than other traditions of inquiry to what Alasdair MacIntyre has called "epistemological crises."[28] Although critical theory can count on the continuity of some features of its philosophical self-understanding in order to resolve the inevitable succession of crises that its form of inquiry is heir to, the discontinuity it encounters in the form of various unanticipated normative and historical challenges will require a combination of problem-solving and self-renewal that is sometimes indistinguishable from the practice of reinventing itself. To use a nearly wornout term of art, critical theory will have to undergo a change of paradigm. Of course, a change of paradigm is something a tradition can sustain without the dissolution of its identity, so long as it can successfully integrate the old and the new. Given how critical theory understands its calling, it is not a tradition of inquiry that can settle into, or settle for, a single self-defining paradigm: only in so far as it is prepared to be unsettled is there any hope for it.[29]

It was in response to just such an epistemological crisis that Habermas initiated a change of paradigm from the "philosophy of consciousness" (or "philosophy of the subject") to linguistic intersubjectivity.[30] This involves a change from a paradigm for which the knowledge of objects is primary, to one for which mutual understanding between subjects capable of speech and action becomes primary. Unquestionably the paradigm change to linguistic intersubjectivity made up a rather glaring normative deficit in earlier critical theory. By providing a normative foundation in the potential for reason latent in action oriented to achieving mutual understanding in language, Habermas's quite strenuous theoretical efforts made *plausible* the possibility that such attempts as his to develop the Enlightenment ideals of freedom, reason, and autonomy were not fatally compromised from the start. Hegel, Nietzsche, Heidegger, Adorno, and Foucault had made shockingly clear how much these ideals were ensnared in the net of the objectifying and self-objectifying practices constituting modernity. However, the perspective opened up by Habermas's model of linguistic intersubjectivity makes equally (if not as dramatically) clear that these ideals were not so ensnared in these practices that they could not be retrieved and reconstituted in social practices of a very different character. No small or incidental feature of this achievement is the fact that Habermas has been able to identify sources for resistance to objectification and domination in everyday practice—in the rather "ordinary" acts of achieving mutual understanding in language. In this respect a great part of his remarkable intellectual achievement consists in substantially enlarging the *Spielraum* within which minimally noncoercive and nonrepressive conceptions of modernity's most precious ideals can be reimagined and reformulated.

Of course, all of this was not only a response to the internal problems of old critical theory. The comprehensive conception of reason, truth, language, and society with which this paradigm stands or falls, addresses issues in other domains of inquiry in philosophy and the social sciences, whether they are in close proximity to, or at considerable distance from, critical theory. Above all, the change of paradigm is meant to show that there is more to reason than "instrumental reason," the more of which does not reduce to various practices of objectification and control but points to self-decentering forms of reciprocal recognition and mutual co-operation. By revealing the ways in which "cognitive-instrumental" reason both suppresses and supplants the "moral-practical" and "aesthetic-expressive" dimensions of reason (PDM 314–315)—precisely the dimension of reasons that most clearly enable self-decentering experiences—Habermas argues convincingly for the need to rescue these dimensions of practical reason and re-anchor them in everyday practice. It is an undeniable advantage of his approach that it assimilates—although not half as dialectically and open-mindedly as one would have liked—the deconstructive critiques of reason and subjectivity. Thus he opens up a position from which modernity can affirm as well as criticize, its traditions, practices, and historical self-formation—a position from which it can, if only provisionally, reassure itself. But if it is to retain its identity *as a* critical theory, the paradigm of linguistic intersubjectivity must also remain normatively true to modernity's relation to time. It must preserve, not dismantle, the theoretical constellation Habermas identifies as essential to recovering "the idea of critique nourished on the spirit of modernity" (PDM 53), and that constellation consists of modernity's time-consciousness, its need for self-reassurance, and the problematic meaning as well as unrealized possibilities of modern reason (PDM 43).

Given its component parts, this theoretical constellation is hardly a stable one. The relation between the parts is as subject to changing interpretations as are the parts themselves. Notice how this constellation collapses when modernity's relation to time is subsumed by modernity's claim to autonomy: "Modernity can and will no longer borrow the criteria by which it takes its orientation from the models supplied by another epoch; *it has to create its normativity out of itself*" (PDM 7). That this formulation so closely resembles Kant's claim that "[r]eason is occupied with nothing but itself" is hardly a coincidence.[31] Modernity's claim to autonomy is not just entangled with reason's claim to autonomy; it is, however, unwillingly or unknowingly just as entangled with modern art's claim to autonomy. Like the latter, modernity claims to have created the normative criteria by which it should be judged. Thus the problem of modernity's self-reassurance is squeezed in between two distinct yet interlocking claims: modernity's claim to be self-sufficient, and its claim to be self-creating. Neither of these claims can be successfully redeemed. All they do is induce unending and debilitating sceptical doubts.

This is not the place to go into the various ways these claims can be understood, and the different kinds of skeptical problems they produce.[32] In this context, I wish only to draw attention to the extent to which Habermas's formulation of modernity's claim to autonomy is irreconcilable with his account of modernity's time-consciousness. Indeed, when coupled to the claim to autonomy, modernity's consciousness of time takes the misguided modernist form I criticized earlier. Habermas actually offers two different conceptions of modernity—conceptions that appear to be mutually exclusive in respect of the relation to the past that defines each of them. On the one hand, there is a conception of modernity as a self-creating, self-sufficient *epoch*, without any debts or ties to the past; on the other, a conception of modernity as a fallible, existentially fragile *ethos* whose form of life and whose self-understanding is connected to the past "as by the chain of a continual destiny." In the case of the former, we have a conception of modernity faced with the insurmountable problem of reassuring itself that it is radically unprecedented, that it represents a wholly novel and total break with the past. When it understands itself in this way, modernity becomes the host for the virulent and insatiable skepticisms with which we are now altogether too familiar. In the case of the latter conception, however, the problem of self-reassurance is not posed in a way that is self-defeating from the start. That does not mean it tears itself loose from skeptical doubts about itself once and for all. Rather, it offers much less on which these doubts can feed, and a very different way to live its kind of scepticisms: by acknowledgment rather than by conquest.[33]

5   A Paradigm in Distress

For all of its theoretical ingenuity and practical implications, Habermas's reformulation of critical theory is beset by persistent problems of its own. Although he would not entirely reject my description of these problems, he would most certainly disagree with my estimation of the threat they pose. In my view, the depth of these problems indicate just how wrong was Habermas's expectation that the paradigm change to linguistic intersubjectivity would render "objectless" the dilemmas of the philosophy of the subject (PDM 301). Habermas accused Hegel of creating a conception of reason so "overwhelming" that it solved *too well* the problem of modernity's self-reassurance (PDM 42). It seems, however, that Habermas has repeated rather than avoided Hegel's mistake, creating a theoretical paradigm so comprehensive that in one stroke it *also* solves too well the dilemmas of the philosophy of the subject *and* the problem of modernity's self-reassurance.[34] Although some of the dilemmas of the philosophy of the subject Habermas identifies may indeed be rendered "objectless," there are others, at least as significant, that continue stubbornly to cling to their objects—particularly, those problems that were never really the concern of the paradigm of linguistic intersubjectivity to begin with.[35] No matter how much impressive intellectual energy he expends in addressing these persistent problems, they refuse to let themselves be dissolved: so long as the basic concepts of the theory of communicative action remain unchanged, these problems turn into corrosive agents undermining Habermas's paradigm from within. The problems with which I am concerned in this study are not only of a theoretical nature; they are also of an existential nature, for they are intertwined with the self-understanding of critical theory, and with the question of how to re-inherit the German philosophical tradition.[36]

1. Habermas's very forceful interpretations of the German philosophical tradition from Hegel to Adorno have the advantage of exposing some genuine weaknesses, but the more worrisome disadvantage of blocking the renewal of the tradition's critical resources—this is particularly true of the tradition from Nietzsche to Heidegger and Adorno. Habermas's propensity to reduce this tradition to "negative metaphysics," "aestheticism," and "irrationalism" makes his position even more extreme than Richard Rorty's, for whom this tradition has no public value, only a private value to those with an interest in and a talent for philosophical "self-creation."[37] One can well understand the political anxieties animating these interpretations: for example, the external, and possibly internal, connections between the German tradition and fascist ideology; the provinciality of the German tradition vis à vis developments in postwar Anglo-American philosophy; and its purported "aestheticism" and "romanticism," which valorizes the "extraordinary" (*Außeralltägliche*) and denigrates the everyday. But these anxieties, understandable as they may be, culminate in interpretations that obscure or distort or simply ignore far too much of this tradition's normative and conceptual resources to be accepted without question.

2. The change of paradigm to linguistic intersubjectivity has been accompanied by a dramatic change in critical theory's self-understanding. The priority given to questions of justice and the normative order of society has remodeled critical theory in the image of liberal theories of justice. While this has produced an important contemporary variant of liberal theories of justice, different enough to be a challenge to liberal theory, but not enough to preserve sufficient continuity with critical theory's past, it has severely weakened the identity of critical theory and inadvertently initiated its premature dissolution.[38] One can track the change of identity within Habermas's development in terms of a dramatic shift of emphasis from a Hegelian to a Kantian conception of critical theory—a shift that is initiated after the publication of *Knowledge and Human Interests*, culminating in *Between Facts and Norms*.[39] Although one can provide an adequate explanation of what precipitated this shift in connection with internal problems alone, for example, for a less historicist, more foundationalist theoretical structure, one can enrich this explanation by pointing to an external motivation.

The shift to Kant can be viewed as part of an externally motivated process of purification—namely a purification of the "provincial" elements of critical theory and German philosophy, and not only those parts deserving of critical mistrust. Only Kant's moral universalism and cosmopolitanism survive untainted; they prove normatively and epistemically capable of transcending the provincialism and irrationalism supposedly characteristic of the German tradition from Hegel to early critical theory. The call to *burst every provinciality asunder* (PDM 322), the modus operandi of context-transcending reason, can also serve as the motto of Habermasian critical theory. But as critical theory erases all traces of its own provinciality, it erases its own identity.[40]

To imagine any cultural tradition or form of life that is not in some sense "provincial" is certainly difficult, and it is just as difficult to imagine a total transcendence of what is "provincial." Indeed each and every version of cosmopolitanism will harbor its own provinciality, and not only when it becomes visibly hostile to and intolerant of any trace of provinciality. And it could be very well argued that philosophy as a whole—and not just some particular subtradition—is, or has been, "provincial" in a number of respects. In any case, if "provinciality" is sufficient reason for bursting cultural traditions asunder, it is very hard to see how any of them could survive. Thus it is hard to see what there would be to continue, renew, and correct, and to pass on responsibly to the future. Might it be the case, then, that not everything "provincial" should be burst asunder? If this is indeed the case, then we are compelled to return to the question concerning the proportion of continuity and discontinuity in the forms of life we pass on. But once we take this question far more seriously, we see all the more clearly how much this question is entwined to the question of what reason ought to mean, why it puts into question the idea of reason as a provinciality-bursting power.

3. The gradual erasure of critical theory's identity has been accelerated by Habermas's procedural conception of philosophy, through which the role of philosophy is largely restricted to the problem of designing procedures for determining the validity of generalizable, collectively binding norms. By downsizing his conception of critical theory into an easily categorizable form of normative theory, he has succeeded in bringing it into the philosophical mainstream—into the normal, international "business of science" (PDM 336).[41] But there is a price to be paid for turning critical theory into a "normal science": namely abandoning modernity's time consciousness (for which, *pace* Habermas, the fallibilistic consciousness of the sciences is no substitute). Without a normatively appropriate attunement to its own time, without an openness to historical experience, and without support of the semantic resources of its traditions, critical theory qua normative theory negates itself.

Habermasian critical theory has, I claim, misheard its calling, precisely because it has misinterpreted the problem of self-reassurance one-sidedly in terms of the legitimacy of the normative order of modern societies. The problem of self-reassurance does not reduce to the problem of the legitimacy of our legal and political institutions—to the question of justice. It also has an "existential-ethical" component, concerned with the question of how we can "go on" confidently, trusting that our ideals and norms are not self-undermining, that our ways of life and our form of life do not condemn themselves (to borrow Stanley Cavell's apposite phrase).

In one of his criticism of Habermas's discourse theory of morality, Charles Taylor highlights the false assumption that underlies Habermas's tendency to narrow down the problem of self-reassurance to the problem of normative validity and legitimacy: "[T]he fact that the self is constituted through exchange in language . . . doesn't in any way guarantee us against loss of meaning, fragmentation, the loss of substance in our human environment and our affiliations."[42] It can hardly be claimed that Habermas is not deeply concerned about the loss of meaning, fragmentation, and the general debasement of everyday life. Nonetheless, it remains the case that these issues are not regarded as urgent or as philosophically central as issues of justice and legitimacy. So long as these issues are accorded priority, so long as they are allowed to trump or sideline questions of meaning and meaningfulness, critical theory dismantles the philosophical constellation that has nourished its own idea of critique.

4. By assimilating the liberal position of neutrality toward the good, Habermasian critical theory is supposed to refrain from critically evaluating and normatively ranking "totalities, forms of life and cultures, life-contexts and epochs as a whole" (TCA2 383). Such evaluations can make claims to validity only within the traditions, forms of life, and so forth, from which they arise. It should come as no surprise, however, to find that Habermas does precisely that which his conception of critical theory officially proscribes: critically evaluating and normatively ranking "totalities, forms of life and cultures, life-contexts, and epochs as a whole." Otherwise, he could not engage in his defense of modernity and the Enlightenment project; he could not defend Western rationalism and moral universalism as a standard-bearing cultural learning process; and he could not evaluate and criticize his own cultural traditions.[43] In brief, he could not engage in the activity of critique, for such an activity ineliminably involves just what Habermas asserts must be eschewed. As Habermas elsewhere acknowledges: "If we do not wish to renounce altogether standards of judging a form of life to be more or less misguided, distorted, unfortunate, or alienated, if it is really necessary the model of sickness and health presents itself."[44] But there is no neutral model of "sickness and health" to which critical theory can appeal that does not implicitly or explicitly incorporate some idea/s of the good. Its purported neutrality is as unstable as it is self-defeating. How can it even begin to diagnose the deformation of the lifeworld without presuming some contentful notion of the good? A good that has no significant content has no critical potential.

Rather than assuming a wobbly stance of neutrality, critical theory needs to clarify, to come clean, about the ideas of the good actually motivating and giving the point to its undertaking. Only the false assumption that critique can occupy a normative standpoint analogous to a "view from nowhere" can there be any basis for ruling out appeal to ideas of the good. And only in light of just such ideas can critical theory begin to fulfill its obligations to its own time.[45] Articulating more persuasively, and illuminating more powerfully the goods which motivate and underwrite our critical activity, does much more to generate utopian energies than does an overreaching, and overburdened, universalism.[46] To rest content merely with offering a formal description of the necessary but general conditions of an "undamaged intersubjectivity" (NC 69) is not just to beggar the utopian contents of critical theory, it is to suppress and misrepresent those contents and their sources in the German philosophical tradition. Once modernity's relation to time is forsaken and once appeal to ideas of the good is proscribed, critical theory effectively blocks itself from access to the extraordinary, to utopian energies, and to its own romantic self-understanding. Once it has done all that, it has more or less dissolved itself.

5. Closer inspection shows that the Kuhnian talk of paradigm change is in need of stronger justification than Habermas has provided. For one, he has ignored or denied what his paradigm shares with competing but un-acknowledged paradigms of intersubjectivity. Although they may not be paradigms of intersubjectivity in Habermas's rather narrow sense, they are strikingly misconstrued as straightforward representatives of the philosophy of consciousness or the philosophy of the subject. Quite often the use of these two terms of art appears to be rather arbitrary (or at best a matter of expedience), as though there were no relevant differences between the philosophy of the subject and the philosophy of consciousness, between Hegel and Foucault, on the one hand, and Descartes and Husserl, on the other. Just as apparently arbitrary is the manner by which Habermas subsumes quite heterogeneous philosophical problems and concerns under these categories. There is simply too little conceptual room to make sense of alternative philosophical positions and philosophical problems that can be subsumed neither under the philosophy of consciousness nor under Habermas's model of linguistic intersubjectivity.

By failing to grant sufficient incommensurability between the issues defining his communication paradigm and those of the philosophies of consciousness and the subject, Habermas too quickly concludes that all the problems of the latter have been rendered "objectless" by the paradigm shift to the former. All the relevant problems could have been rendered "objectless" only if they were more or less identical with the problems of the paradigm of mutual understanding. If that were the case, however, Habermas would not really be justified in speaking of a change of paradigm—not if what he means by paradigm change is anything like what Kuhn had in mind when he introduced the term into the philosophy of science. If there is going to be a shift from one paradigm to another, the relevant problems constitutive of the paradigms in question will have to differ a great deal more than Habermas allows. Otherwise, what we are dealing with is not a change of paradigm but a different interpretation of the *same* or *similar* theoretical problems. It should therefore come as no surprise to find that the shift to the paradigm of linguistic intersubjectivity is unable adequately to treat the problems of normative and cultural change central to the German tradition from Hegel to Heidegger and

Adorno. The kind of change to which I refer is the kind of change—be it cultural, normative, semantic, or political—that we can ascribe to our own reflective and practical activity, particularly under conditions of crisis and disorientation. The evolutionary model of social learning and epochal change that Habermas postulates in various texts from *Zur Rekonstruktion des historischen Materialismus* to *The Theory of Communicative Action* does not address these cases of normative and cultural change, since it is social systems, not social actors, who are the principal agencies and repositories of "evolutionary" social learning. The so-called rationalization of the life-world is a process of social learning that takes place behind the backs of social actors: "Its course is neither directed by human intentions nor can it be grasped within the consciousness of a single individual."[47] This is not the only kind of normative and cultural change critical theory needs above all to understand, explain, and facilitate.

6. The most important goal of Habermas's theory of communicative rationality is to provide a comprehensive conception of reason that is not vulnerable to the familiar deconstructive critiques of modern reason. Because it is incarnated in mutual understanding in language, in everyday practices of reciprocal recognition, and because it operates with a wider conception of reason, communicative rationality is not supposed to produce an "other" of reason through what is objectified, excluded, and repressed. Indeed, if it were to do so, it would fail by its own standards. Nonetheless, communicative rationality does produce its own "other" of reason because it denies a *transformative* role for reason, a role it cannot help but deny so long as it is narrowly framed by a procedural conception of rationality that privileges the justificatory role of reason. This is not a problem that is easily rectified, since the basic concepts of communicative rationality are not designed to make sense of—but simply take for granted—the ways in which human beings transform the meanings, ideals, norms, institutions, practices, and traditions they inherit and pass on. Given this state of affairs, one can hardly expect the paradigm of communicative rationality to regard this transformative activity as an activity of reason.

But this transformative activity of reason is just what the idea of communicative reason must presuppose for its successful institution in everyday practice. For example, when Habermas offers his sociological description of the cultural reproduction of the lifeworld, he claims that under modern conditions "the reproduction of the lifeworld is no longer merely routed *through* the medium of communicative action, but is saddled *upon* the interpretative accomplishments of the actors themselves" (TCA2

145). Now, what can this talk of "interpretative accomplishments" mean? A few paragraphs later it turns out that it means no less than the recognition that "the renewal of traditions depends more and more on individuals' readiness to criticize and their ability to innovate" (TCA2 146). If, following Dewey,[48] we regard criticism and innovation as inseparable activities, and, hence, as activities of reason, then it must be the case that a presupposition of the successful employment of public reason requires that the normative space of reasons must be expanded to accommodate and integrate what was previously unseen, unheard, unthought. On such a view, the activities by which we expand the normative space of reason is grasped not as something subject to contingency and luck, or to non-rational acts of "imagination," but as much a part of reason, and as necessary to the success of reason, as testing and justifying norms.

Now this is more or less what Habermas himself implies when he writes that "the yes/no decisions that carry everyday communicative practice no longer go *back* to an ascribed normative consensus, but issue *from* the co-operative interpretation processes of participants themselves" (TCA2 146). If one considers all this from the standpoint of the various breakdowns and crises in the semantic and social dimension that have preoccupied the crisis thinkers of modernity, then the demands with which individuals are said to be saddled are rather enormous indeed. Given that experiences of crisis tend to be the norm rather than the exception, must we not account for the degree to which modern individuals are saddled by the obligation to criticise *and* innovate if they are to ensure the continuity and renewal of their cultural traditions? And must we not identify, as well as foster, the bundled set of reflective, critical, and innovative capacities through which human beings self-critically transform the social practices, cultural traditions, and political institutions which they inherit and pass on? Does a critical theory that has refashioned itself in the image of a liberal theory of justice possess the conceptual and normative resources to take on such a task? Can it remain a *critical* theory, can it remain itself, if it turns its back on this task?

6   Reappropriating the Idea of "World Disclosure"

It is my thesis that Habermas's model of critical theory does not possess the necessary normative and conceptual resources to deal with the problematics of continuity and discontinuity, and of crisis and renewal. This set of problems requires drawing upon an idea that occupies a threatening, if not entirely alien, position vis-à-vis Habermas's philosophical paradigm: Heidegger's idea of "world disclosure." I do not mean to suggest that Habermas's model of critical theory does not possess *any* resources for dealing with this set of problems, for I have already shown how he has contributed to understanding the normative implications of modernity's relation to time, and to explaining why it functions both as an ineliminable and constant challenge to modern forms of life, and as an often neglected normative and conceptual resource. But if there is going to be further progress on this set of problems, and if critically theory is to renew itself, critical theorists will have to draw upon philosophical resources other than those which Habermas's model of critical theory can provide.

In my view, Heidegger's idea of "world disclosure" offers a more promising way of understanding the problematics of continuity and discontinuity, and of crisis and renewal. Properly construed, it is capable of providing the resources for a more persuasive treatment of the six problems identified in chapter 5. Although there are no direct and unmediated connections between those problems and the concept of disclosure as it is typically understood, I will show in parts II through IV, that redescribing this group of problems in terms of the Heideggerian idea of disclosure is something implicitly endorsed by Habermas himself. His response to the challenge that some recent incarnations of this idea pose to his own project takes up most of *The Philosophical Discourse of Modernity*. The great bulk of this book is a response to the skeptical and political dangers that Habermas attributes to this idea, and the ways in which it has evidently seduced a diverse group of highly influential thinkers.

To properly develop the normative and theoretical potential of this idea, however, we need a far less defensive and far more open assessment of its problem-clarifying and problem-solving potential. Much more explicitly than Habermas does, I consider this idea to represent the most important challenge to Habermas's position. I am also of the view that it can render less narrow and more capacious our present conceptions of reason, critique, and philosophy. I am by no means proposing to turn world disclosure into some superconcept under which all of these concepts can be subsumed; rather I am drawing upon the fact that it is *already* implicated in them. My aim is to clarify the normative and conceptual connections that are already there, to make their implications for reformulating the meaning of reason and role of philosophy all the more perspicuous. As will become clear in due course, what I propose to draw from Heidegger does *not* require abandonment of Habermas's best critical insights; rather, it means reassessing them and recombining them with Heidegger's in order to re-envision the future of critical theory.

That world disclosure is a theme which is itself entangled in the political and moral implications of Heidegger's thought poses yet another kind of challenge to those who seek to renew critical theory through a reappropriation of the German philosophical tradition.[49] I am too well aware that what I propose here is practically impossible to do without courting controversy and considerable misunderstanding. The idea of integrating Heidegger's thought into critical theory may be greeted with suspicious resistance if not outright revulsion by some critical theorists. And the idea that Heidegger's thought can contribute to the renewal of critical theory is more likely to be greeted with disbelief (if not derision) than with curiousity. The fact is, both Heidegger's person and his thought have played the role of critical theory's "other": he is the very antithesis of the critical intellectual as critical theorists imagine "him." While it is certainly not my intention to integrate Heidegger's thought into critical theory by sanitizing or normalizing Heidegger's politics and life, as anathema as it may sound to the ears of some, Heidegger's thought is already a part of critical theory, and not just on account of the well-known impact his ideas have had on Habermas and Karl-Otto Apel. Heidegger's thought is simply too much a part of the philosophical tradition from which critical theory ambivalently draws its philosophical energies and orientation. In other words: critical theory has already incorporated its despised "other." Whether it has done so in the right way remains an open question.

Throughout his career Adorno criticized Heidegger with arguments very similar to those relentlessly employed by Habermas throughout his. And although Thomas McCarthy is right to point out that "the basic issues separating critical theory from Heideggerian ontology were not raised post hoc in reaction to Heidegger's political misdeeds but were there from the start' in the early Marcuse's criticisms of Heidegger,"[50] it is nevertheless also the case that many decades later the way in which critical theorists understand these issues has remained virtually unchanged, conceptually frozen by long-unchallenged assumptions. It is an understanding that has become rigid, and in need of extensive reassessment. That it could be sustained so long without need of revision is not unconnected to the fact that Heidegger's life has functioned all too conveniently as a constant indictment of his philosophy, an ever-handy confirmation of the need to treat the philosophy with suspicion and distrust, thereby making unnecessary any serious reassessment of its claims. In the meantime the early Marcuse's genuine interest in the possibilities of combining ontological and materialist forms of critical analysis has been left to languish as a historical footnote, even though its considerable potential has barely been developed either by Heideggerians or Habermasians.[51]

Heidegger's various analyses of the phenomenon of world disclosure—of *In-der-Welt-Sein*, *Lichtung*, *Gestell*, and *Ereignis*—represent his central contribution to twentieth-century philosophy.[52] Through these analyses Heidegger developed an original critique of, as well as an original alternative to, the representationalist epistemologies and the naturalistic ontologies of modern philosophy. He marshaled important new arguments (both transcendental and hermeneutic) against mentalistic accounts of intentionality, against views of agency as disembodied and disengaged, and against "deworlded" conceptions of objectivity and truth. In *Being and Time* and in *The Basic Problems of Phenomenology*, Heidegger argued that prior to confronting the world as though it were first and foremost a super object, or as though it were identical with nature, we operate "always already" with a pre-reflective, holistically structured, and grammatically regulated *understanding* of the world. And so prior to establishing explicit epistemic relations to the world "out there," our theoretical understanding of the world always refers back to, as much as it draws upon, a concerned *practical* involvement with what we encounter in the world—a world we do not "constitute," but into which we are "thrown."

The notion of disclosure refers, in part, to this ontological "pre-understanding" of the world—or understanding of "being." Heidegger's investigation of conditions of intelligibility—of how something can show up as *something* in the first place—took up the radical mode of questioning initiated by Kant's transcendental deduction, but cut much deeper than the epistemologically oriented and monologically posed question of conditions of possible experience. One of the hugely important conclusions of his investigation is that if there is to be any understanding of something "as something" at all, our "understanding must itself *somehow see as disclosed, that upon which it projects*."[53] Whichever Heideggerian term of art one chooses to use, whether it is "world," "being," "clearing," or "background," the basic point is that the "world" or "clearing" *cannot* be "identified with any of the entities that show up in it. It is not to be explained by them as something they cause, or one of their properties, or as grounded in them."[54] Rather, it is that which first makes possible an understanding of those entities as the entities they are. Stephen Mulhall provides a very fine summary of this point:

Knowledge, doubt and faith are relations in which Dasein might stand towards specific phenomena in the world, but the world is not a possible object of knowledge—

because it is not an object at all, not an entity or set of entities. It is that within which entities appear, a field or horizon ontologically grounded in a totality of assignment-relations; it is the conditions for any intra-worldly relation, and so is not analysable in terms of any such relation. What grounds the Cartesian conception of subject and world, and thereby opens the door to scepticism, is an interpretation of the world as a great big object or collection of objects, a totality of possible objects of knowledge, rather than as that wherein all possible objects of knowledge are encountered.[55]

The early Heidegger's "existential analytic" also claims to have discovered a reciprocal relation, an interdependence, between Dasein (human being) and world, between the processes of making sense of the world and making sense of ourselves. Dasein is, only insofar as it is in a world; world (not nature or the cosmos out there!) is, only insofar as Dasein exists.[56] So, in one sense, the world is pre-reflectively disclosed *to* us, yet, in another, the world is disclosed *through* us: it is we who make its disclosure possible. " *'There is' truth only in so far as Dasein is and as long as Dasein is*. Entities are uncovered only *when* Dasein is, and only as long as Dasein *is*, are they disclosed."[57] Thus disclosure involves both receptivity and activity, both openness to and engagement with, what is disclosed. What is disclosed may concern the background structures or conditions of intelligibility necessary to any world- or self-understanding, which I'll refer to as *pre-reflective* disclosure (Heidegger called them *Existenzialen*); or it may concern the ways in which these background structures of intelligibility are reopened and transformed through novel interpretations and cultural practices, which I'll refer to as *reflective disclosure* (or redisclosure). Both pre-reflective and reflective disclosure suppose human receptivity, and although I distinguish between reflective and pre-reflective forms of disclosure, I do not wish to suggest that the difference is to be understood as difference between cognitive and noncognitive processes of disclosure. In both instances what we are speaking of are types of practical cognition occurring at different levels of awareness.

More important is the question of how to understand the interactive relation between pre-reflective and reflective disclosure. I think it must be understood both as a feedback and as an oppositional relation. The circularity is easy enough to grasp. It is only because our understanding of the world is first disclosed to us that we can disclose the world again, and again. The world is not disclosed in one shot. Disclosure is an ongoing process: it is always happening 24/7. Thus it is neither something utterly extraordinary nor something utterly mundane: it is something at once extraordinary and mundane. We must remain mindful of the feedback relation between pre-reflective and reflective disclosure when we to try to grasp their oppositional relation. James Bohman has suggested that the need for new disclosures of the world arises from the tendency of any disclosure of the world to rigidify, and to resist being disclosed anew: because the world has been pre-reflectively disclosed, it must be reflectively and critically disclosed anew. It is most certainly the case that any disclosure of the world will be one that inevitably and unavoidably incorporates hidden relations of power and domination. But what we must be careful not to forget is that our prior understanding of the world resists *and* enables, impedes *and* facilitates, the possibility of disclosing the world anew. Moreover we *can* normatively distinguish "good" from "bad" disclosure by distinguishing between disclosures of the world that more fully and generously create the conditions for reflective disclosure from those that create conditions that obscure their own status *as* disclosures. Put negatively, we can say that a new disclosure of the world cannot eliminate relations of power and domination, but it can bring about a change in the conditions of intelligibility on which those asymmetrical relations depend, giving them much less "ontological" support. Put positively, given our permanent dependence on the conditions of intelligibility supplied by our pre-reflective understanding of the world, the reflective disclosure of world presents itself as unending challenge and task, for what is in need of redisclosure cannot be known in advance of the particular historical contexts in which that need arises.

Now because disclosure renders ambiguously neutral the distinction between "creation" and "discovery," reflective disclosure can be further distinguished according to whether the effect it produces *decenters* or *refocuses* a prior understanding of the world. A reflective disclosure can critically introduce meanings, perspectives, interpretive and evaluative vocabularies, modes of perception, and action possibilities that stand in strikingly dissonant relations to already available meanings and familiar possibilities, to already existing ways of speaking, hearing, seeing, interpreting, and acting. Such a dissonance cannot but disturb the unreflective, taken-for-granted flow of our self-understanding and social practices. This kind of disturbance is not like noise that one can turn off by closing a window or by plugging one's ears, although this is certainly one way to describe metaphorically the resistance to effects of self-decentering. One can characterize these effects as a scrambling of our symbolically structured pre-understanding of the world, putting into defamiliarizing relief our self-understanding and our practices. But the experience of self-decentering is not limited to the scrambling and defamiliarizing of existing patterns of interpretation, action, and belief; it also involves a *push* to enlarge and transform our self-understanding and our practices.

Reflective disclosure can also increase our awareness of previously hidden or unthematized interconnections. Here our shared pre-understanding of the world is not so much challenged and subverted as it is uncovered and rearticulated. Disparate or anomalous facets of our pre-understanding of the world are refocused, breakdowns in languages of interpretation and evaluation are repaired, what was distant or disconnected is drawn together into a *common space* with what is near. From the period following his involvement with National Socialism to the end of his life, Heidegger was more and more preoccupied with this aspect of reflective disclosure. Whether disclosure is of a decentering or a refocusing kind, and sometimes it not easy to distinguish the one from the other, it always arises from a critical impulse, from consciousness of disturbance, breakdown, crisis.

In his later philosophy, Heidegger's account of disclosure takes a "linguistic turn," but this turn is made in an ontological rather than in a semantic-logical direction. Heidegger's "linguistic turn" breaks somewhat with the conception of language in *Being and Time*, where language (*Rede*) opens up or uncovers in a different light something that has already been disclosed independently of language (through concerned involvement with what we encounter in the world). In his later philosophy, Heidegger attributes to language a "primordial" (*ürsprunglich*) world-disclosing function. It is language that first discloses the horizons of meaning in terms of which we make sense of the world and ourselves. As Gadamer later put it, "that human beings have a world at all depends upon, and is presented in, language."[58] It is this more controversial, indeed, notorious, conception of linguistic world disclosure that has become associated with such remarks as "language is the house of being" and it is language that "speaks," not human beings. But Heidegger's view of language must not be taken to refer to language understood in naturalistic terms, not least of all, because it would reduce his view to a version of linguistic relativism. By "language" Heidegger means the ontological context necessary for language in the ordinary sense—that which must obtain if there is to be any understanding *überhaupt*.[59] Although the notion of linguistic world disclosure has been traced back to Herder's and to Humboldt's theories of language, and is certainly present in Nietzsche's various writings, Heidegger first formulates the challenge contained in this notion in its most original and radical terms.[60] Heidegger not only linguistifies disclosure, he historicizes it as well,

making possible accounts of the formation and transformation of historical epochs by tracking changes in ontologies (changes in the "understanding of being").

During the period of *Being and Time* and *The Basic Problems of Phenomenology*, Heidegger claimed philosophy had failed to recognize, let alone, to
grasp in its significance, the phenomenon of world disclosure.[61] Today the
situation is much different. The problem is no longer one of recognizing
and grasping the significance of world disclosure. Its significance has been
recognized and grasped not just by Heidegger, but also by the later
Wittgenstein and by Dewey and, more recently, by Michel Foucault,
Jacques Derrida, Charles Taylor, Hubert Dreyfus, Richard Rorty, and
Cornelius Castoriadis, among others. Now, as we will see, the problem is what
to make of it, how to assess it, how far to take it, and in which direction.

In his own conception of the lifeworld, which plays such an important role both in his social theory and in his philosophy of language,
Habermas has taken it rather far indeed. The "lifeworld" refers to that
grammatically regulated pre-understanding that holistically structures an
intersubjectively shared form of life. Thus it refers to what I called pre-
reflective disclosure, or our pre-understanding of the world. At the same
time Habermas grants that "language is the constitutive organ not only
of thought, but also of both social practice and experience, of the formation of ego and group identities" (CA 221). But what is at issue between
Habermas and Heidegger, and between Habermas and all those who draw
on this notion for various purposes (Foucault, Taylor, Derrida, Castoriadis,
inter alios), concerns the ramifications of Heidegger's later construal of disclosure. Expressing the suspicion and worries discussed above in connection with how we are responsibly to think anew from a new stance,
Habermas claims that Heidegger and those influenced by him *absolutize*
disclosure, robbing human agents of their critical and reflective capacities.
He argues that appeal to this notion in order to describe and explain
processes of semantic, normative, and cultural change involves, among
other things: devaluing reason, devaluing the problem-solving and action-
coordinating functions of language, devaluing everyday practice, and
devaluing the cognitive claims of philosophy. And he argues that the real
appeal of this notion consists in its capacity to provide the skeptical critics
of modern reason with a fatalistic or ecstatic "refuge in something wholly
Other" (PT 8).

These are certainly strong claims; unfortunately, they suppose and reproduce a very questionable interpretation of this, admittedly, controversial

idea. However, it is neither the only nor the best way to take up Heidegger's idea. Charles Taylor has suggested a better alternative. It involves
reconceiving reflective disclosure as "a new department" of reason.[62] This
suggestion does not oppose disclosure to reason; rather, it places world disclosure within reason. This is a suggestion that I have also made, and for
which I will argue in various ways throughout this book. To proceed with
this suggestion requires thinking of disclosure not as the "other" of reason,
but as another voice of reason. But this suggestion is not going to be successfully developed without reconceiving reason itself. If it can be demonstrated that reflective disclosure is indeed "a new department" of reason,
that reason has a place within disclosure as much as disclosure has a place
with reason, then Habermas's strong objections against it are altogether
deprived of the basis upon which they rest. Rather than regarding it as a
threat to reason, as Habermas does, I will argue that disclosure presents us
with the possibility of a new, practice-altering conception of reason, a conception of reason upon which the basis for an alternative model of critical theory can emerge. Habermas's excessive worries about the skeptical
implications of disclosure have obscured the fact that this idea provides
the impetus and the basis for an enlargement of the meaning of reason
in another direction—in the direction of transformation, illuminating
reason's capacity both to transform our practices and our sensibility, and,
in turn, to be transformed by them. In my view, this is the direction to
which the German tradition has been pointing—with varying degrees of
clarity and conviction—since Kant's first critique.

Perhaps more controversial yet is another of Taylor's suggestions. It concerns an implication of the idea of disclosure for our understanding of
agency. In becoming more aware of our role in disclosing the world, we
come to see that "we are responding to something that is not us," and so
we come to see our relation to the world quite differently.[63] We thus
become aware of the possibility of "an articulation of things which would
lay out their meanings for us (and hence where the discourse would not
be that of science) but where the meaning would not be merely human-
centred (and hence the discourse would not be one of self-expression)."[64]
Taylor's remark directs our attention to that side of our agency, and of
reason as well, in which self-decentering *receptivity* plays an indispensable
part, the recognition of which prompts us to reformulate our conception
of them.

But before I can engage directly in analysis and critique of Habermas's
philosophical response to the challenge of disclosure (part III), and before I
can begin to present my alternative (parts IV–VI), I must first examine the

soundness of his claims concerning the internal connections between Heidegger's philosophy and his politics—connections which he, like Adorno before him, considers to be internal, not external. The purpose of this exercise is not to go over what is now rather familiar ground, but to respond to Habermas's *political* critique of disclosure. I argue that this critique fails, and fails for reasons that confirm the depth of the six problems identified in chapter 5.

II Dependent Freedom

1 Disclosure and Intersubjectivity

In two more or less complementary accounts written in the 1980s, Habermas attempted to uncover the links between Heidegger's philosophy and Heidegger's unrepentant engagement with National Socialism. The first of these appeared in the chapter on Heidegger in *The Philosophical Discourse of Modernity*, and the second, in the essay, "Work and *Weltanschauung*," published a few years later. In each of these accounts Habermas postulates an *internal* connection between Heidegger's philosophy and his politics. In *The Philosophical Discourse of Modernity* Habermas argues that the categories of *Being and Time* were rendered fit for duty in the service of National-Socialist revolution simply by displacing the accent from their essentially individualistic orientation to a collectivistic one. "Dasein was no longer this poor Kierkegaardian-Sartrean individual hanging in the air, in *Sorge* . . . now Dasein was the Dasein of the people, of the *Volk*."[1] To further support this connection, Habermas argues that the transition between Heidegger's early and later philosophy cannot be explained properly as a philosophically motivated development, but must be seen as a politically motivated development arising from Heidegger's much belated realization that National Socialism was not the solution to the problem of nihilism, only its most recent and most extreme symptom. It was this disillusionment with fascism, then, that was supposed to have prompted the transition from the activistic impulses of the early philosophy to the fatalistic ones of the late philosophy—from *Being and Time's* assertive "decisionism of empty resoluteness" to the "submissiveness of an equally empty readiness for subjugation" (PDM 141).

[O]nly after this change of attitude did the overcoming of modern subjectivity take on the meaning of an event that is *only* to be undergone. Until then, the decisionism of self-assertive *Dasein*, not only in the existential version of *Being and Time* but also (with certain changes of accent) in the national/revolutionary version of the writings from the thirties, had retained a role in disclosing being. Only in the final phase of working through his disillusionment does the concept of the history of being take on a fatalistic form. (WW, 198)

In "Work and *Weltanschauung*," responding to criticisms of his first account, Habermas argues for a weaker but no less telling connection between Heidegger's philosophy and his politics. Now the decisive connection to be established is between Heidegger's philosophy and the ideologically tainted *Weltanschauung* of the German mandarins. The mandarin *Weltanschauung*, the subject of a well-known study by the historian Fritz Ringer,[2] consisted of a cluster of ideological motifs that defined a pervasive intellectual and academic mentality that flourished in Germany (and in Europe) in the late nineteenth and early twentieth century: antimodern, antidemocratic, and elitist, it typically expressed itself in a shrill critique of "mass civilization." Heidegger evidently incorporated this "scientifically unfiltered diagnosis of crisis" into his philosophical reconstruction of the historical significance of the present (WW 194). For all of the unprecedented originality of *Being and Time*, there is no denying the "connections between the mandarin consciousness of the German professor Martin Heidegger and certain limitations from which the argumentation of *Being and Time* cannot free itself" (WW 191). As a particularly transparent instance of the internal connection between work and *Weltanschauung*, Habermas singles out the analysis of *das Man*—the "one", the "they", the "anyone."[3] Here we can see, claims Habermas, how the mandarin critique of mass civilization and its elitist contempt for the everyday entwines itself around the monological, individualistic (ultimately, solipsistic) premises of *Being and Time*—premises from which it is impossible to arrive at the insight—derived from Hegel and Mead—that we are individualized as we are socialized.

The obvious problem with these putative links between Heidegger's philosophy and politics is that they rest on highly debatable, ultimately unpersuasive, interpretations of Heidegger's early and late philosophy. To claim that the project of *Being and Time* is compromised from the outset by a methodological solipsism that Heidegger inherited from Husserlian phenomenology and that he never relinquished is to rely on an interpretation that is at best a misreading of *Being and Time*, and at worst, simply inaccurate. That it is strikingly out of tune with the views of significant Heidegger interpreters such as Hubert Dreyfus and Charles Taylor, among others, who have refuted persuasively the subjectivistic, monological reading of *Being and Time*, indicates that Habermas's interpretation is an interpretation in need of serious re-evaluation—particularly, by critical theorists.

The arguments of the chapter on Heidegger in *The Philosophical Discourse of Modernity* are based—as is so much else in that book—on a very sharp, and occasionally forced contrast between a series of purportedly failed attempts to break out of the subject-centered paradigm of modern philosophy, on the one hand, and Habermas's paradigm of linguistic intersubjectivity, on the other. But in the case of Heidegger (as in the clearer case of Hegel), this contrast depends on treating differences between *distinct* approaches to intersubjectivity as differences between subject-centered and intersubjective paradigms. Linguistic intersubjectivity, in Habermas's sense, does not exhaust the possible forms of intersubjectivity, or the possible relations between subjectivity and intersubjectivity, and between intersubjectivity and the world.[4] In any case, the salient differences between Heidegger's undertaking in *Being and Time* and Habermas's own project do not turn on the difference between subject-centeredness and intersubjectivity: "So far as Dasein *is* at all, it has being-with-one-another as its kind of being (*die Seinsart des Miteinanderseins*)" (BT 163/125).

Both Habermas and Heidegger offer valuable and insightful ways to approach the problem of intersubjectivity. But because their approaches do not share the same orientation or the same goals, they each focus on quite different *binding* media. Heidegger focuses on semantic media, on how something comes to be mutually intelligible, and Habermas on justificatory media, on how something comes to be mutually acceptable. Central to Heidegger's approach to intersubjectivity is the semantic and ontological notion of world disclosure; central to Habermas's is the epistemic and moral notion of context-transcendent justification. A second crucial difference concerns their respective construals of the relation between intersubjectivity and the availability of an objective world shared in common. For Habermas the world is opened up *through* relations of intersubjectivity, through the dialogical constitution of an intersubjective space shared in common (CA 218). For Heidegger, on the other hand, relations of intersubjectivity presuppose rather than constitute an objective world shared in common.

Dasein is equiprimordially being-with others and being-among entities encountered in the world. The world within which these latter beings are encountered is . . . always already a world that one shares with others. It is only because Dasein is antecedently constituted as being-in-the-world that one Dasein can existentielly communicate something factically to another; *but it is not this factical existentiell communication that first constitutes the possibility that one Dasein shares a world with another Dasein.*[5]

From Heidegger's standpoint, Habermas is making the same mistake as representationalist metaphysics in failing to see that the "world" precedes our speaking, thinking, and acting.[6] Nonetheless, despite these differences, both Heidegger and Habermas understand themselves to be responding to various forms of modern skepticism. Heidegger, especially the later Heidegger, is primarily worried about the threat to our social practices posed by nihilism—by the leveling of meaning, by fragmentation, and by the loss of cultural orientation—and so he is preoccupied with the creation and preservation of intersubjectively disclosed meaning and possibility. Habermas is primarily worried about the threat posed by relativism and contextualism to cognitive and moral universalism—especially to a universalistic conception of justice—and so he is preoccupied with intersubjectively binding *validity*. Thus the third crucial difference between their two conceptions of intersubjectivity concerns the relation of meaning to validity. Is the relation between them a relation of reciprocal interdependence? Or is there reason to grant one some logical or ontological priority? In *The Philosophical Discourse of Modernity* Habermas argues as though he were committed to the reciprocal interdependence of meaning and validity. But, as I will show in part III, he is not committed to defending this more accommodating (and more persuasive) view outside the context of his book-length dispute with Heidegger and other disclosure theorists. Rather, he is committed to defending the priority of validity to meaning (truth to disclosure) against the priority of meaning to validity (disclosure to truth). Any change of commitment would entail extensive alteration of the basic concepts of the theory of communicative action that suppose as much as they reinforce this priority.

Because this third difference is so decisive, and because it can help clarify the second difference, I want to bring it into sharper focus by referring briefly to Habermas's debate with Charles Taylor. According to Taylor, Habermas's theory of communication, and the proceduralist ethics in which it culminates, fails to take account of both Humboldt's and Heidegger's insights into the world-disclosing dimension of language—a dimension that is simply not subsumable under action oriented to reaching mutual understanding. Reaching mutual understanding in language, Taylor claims, presupposes a linguistically disclosed world as the logically *prior* background against which, and in terms of which, communicative action takes place. (Taylor's argument is thus a reiteration of Heidegger's position in *Being and Time*: that "it is not this factical existentiell communication that first constitutes the possibility that one Dasein shares a world with another Dasein.") In his response to Taylor, Habermas concedes that in *"The Theory of Communicative Action* [he] treated somewhat unfairly the world-disclosing function of language" (CA 221). He then goes on to grant Taylor's and Heidegger's point that "language is the constitutive organ not only of thought, but also of both social practice and experience, of the formation of ego and group identities" (CA 221). Having made such an enormous concession to Taylor and Heidegger, one would expect that Habermas would either bring about some rather fundamental changes to his theory or find a way to defend it against the implied theoretical consequences of his concession. Unfortunately, he chooses the second option, following up his concession to Taylor with an accusation—an accusation he directs not only at Taylor but also at all disclosure theorists irrespective of their philosophical and political orientation. This oft-repeated accusation consists of two parts: (1) that Taylor totalizes the world-disclosing function of language and (2) that his view of world disclosure involves a reversion to the self-referential dilemmas of the philosophy of the subject—above all, to the untenable supposition of a world-constituting transcendental subjectivity. This pattern of concession and accusation becomes less and less and informative as it becomes more and more familiar.[7] It is a pattern of response that will be more closely scrutinized in part III.

The claim I am defending in this part of the book is that Habermas has wasted much of his critical energy driving Heidegger's undertaking—the center of which is the idea of disclosure—forcefully but inaccurately into the aporiai of the philosophy of consciousness: the aporiai of Heidegger's thought are not the aporiai of the philosophy of consciousness. A much more fruitful encounter between Habermas and Heidegger would have explored the advantages and disadvantages of their very different conceptions of intersubjectivity, through which an exploration process of mutual correction and mutual enlargement could unfold. Had he treated Heidegger as a proponent of an alternative approach to understanding intersubjectivity, Habermas's attempt to probe the shortcomings of Heidegger's early and late philosophy might have yielded more persuasive critical results. Thus Habermas could have argued more effectively in support of his claims concerning the moral and political shortcomings of Heidegger's philosophy if he had identified as the most glaring weakness of Heidegger's approach, not the lack of a properly intersubjective starting point but, rather, the lack of a sufficiently developed account of intersubjective accountability and recognition. Moreover, by taking Heidegger as a proponent of an alternative account of intersubjectivity that is motivated by a concern with keeping open the realm of meaning and possibility rather than with validity, Habermas could have placed the insights of Heidegger's account in the service of his own. As I have shown above, Heidegger approaches the problem of intersubjectivity from a point logically (and ontologically) prior to it—but without falling back into the philosophy of consciousness.[8] From this alternative perspective it is possible to develop an account of intersubjectivity potentially richer and wider in scope than both Heidegger's and Habermas's. I say potentially richer because the lack of a normatively robust conception of intersubjective accountability and recognition in Heidegger's account blocks the development of its full potential, which that very lack has obscured. In what follows, I plan to make that potential more visible, and show the lines along which it can be developed.

2 Freedom and Intelligibility

The consequences of the conspicuous lack of a normatively robust conception of intersubjective accountability and recognition show up in early and in later Heidegger. In *Being and Time* it shows up in Heidegger's failure to close the normative gaps between one's practical relation to oneself and one's ethical relation to others. The analyses of "resoluteness" (*Entschlossenheit*), of the "self's ability to-be" (*Selbstseinkönnen*), and of "care" (*Sorge*) through which Heidegger lays out Dasein's practical relation to itself are not convincingly connected to the analyses of "being-with" (*Mitsein*), "being-for-another" (*Miteinandersein*), and "solicitude" (*Fürsorge*), through which Heidegger demonstrates the intersubjective conditions of Dasein's freedom *and* dependence. In the later philosophy this same failure shows up in the normative gap between our relation to "being" and our relation to *human* beings. The normative gaps in question are not due to Heidegger's blindness to, or contempt for, the structures of intersubjectivity as such but to a one-sided approach to them. Heidegger made a great discovery concerning the connections between conditions of intelligibility and structures of intersubjectivity. But that discovery could have been all the more significant had he been able to deepen those connections, rendering more visible the ways in which the possibility of social intelligibility and meaning not only supposes a prior pre-reflective disclosure of the world but also the ways in which any reflective redisclosure of the world depends on intersubjective accountability and recognition—on cooperatively achieved freedom and acknowledged mutual dependence.

Although Heidegger did not entirely neglect the ethical relation between self and other, he paid far too little attention to it. As a result the ethical dimensions of intersubjectivity remained in a primitive state throughout the changing course of his thought. One can find traces of what might have been in various texts—for example, in the discussion intertwining care and solicitude in the first division of *Being and Time*. There, he draws a contrast between the two extreme possibilities of "positive solicitude":

It can, as it were, take away "care" from the other and put itself in her position in concern: it can *supplant* her (*für ihn einspringen*). This kind of solicitude takes over for the other that with which she is to concern herself. . . . In such solicitude the other can become one who is dominated and dependent, even when this domination (*Herrschaft*) is a tacit one and remains hidden from her. . . . In contrast to this, there is also the possibility of a kind of solicitude which does not supplant the other, but *clears the way* for her (*ihm vorausspringt*) in her existentiell ability to be, not in order to take away her "care," but rather, to give it back to her authentically as such for the first time. . . . (It) helps the other to become perspicuous (*durchsichtig*) to herself *in* her care and to become *free* for it. (BT 158–159/122)[9]

Audibly echoing Hegel's analysis of the dialectic of slavery and domination in the *Phenomenology of Spirit*, this passage represents one of those altogether rare occasions in which Heidegger actually contributes to enlarging our understanding of how our freedom for self-determination—authenticity (*Eigentlichkeit*) in Heidegger's vocabulary—is both dependent on and facilitated, not just impeded, by our relation to others.[10] Baldly put, our relation to others can be based on implicit or explicit domination, or it can be based on a solicitous cooperation—on a cooperatively achieved mutual realization of authentic freedom. At least in rare passages such as this, Heidegger correctly understands that if freedom is to amount to something more than negative freedom, it will require more than respect for the autonomy of persons, and more than the recognition of the other's claim to self-determination. It will require the recognition that the conditions under which the other and I can realize our freedom are conditions that must be cooperatively established, preserved, and enlarged—conditions for which she and I are responsible, conditions that our placed in our care, to be cared for.

For once in *Being and Time*, the other is not simply an abstraction, an ontologically necessary feature of intersubjective structures of intelligibility. Rather, the other is an ineliminable condition of the realization of my own freedom, and I of hers. The other is not going away. She will always be "there," concretely present even when she is absent. So I can clear the way for the realization of the other's freedom or I can get in the way. We can learn from each other or we can fail to learn—in which case we will fail to realize our freedom because we will have failed to take care of, to cultivate, the conditions under which it could be realized. Coming to see that mutual recognition and accountability are essential conditions of freedom entails coming to see that the necessary conditions of freedom require care and cultivation, and both care and cultivation require the recognition of mutual dependence.

In this all too brief, but highly suggestive passage, Heidegger offers a way of understanding human freedom that is not only close to Hegel's *Phenomenology* but also to Dewey's pragmatism. I take the heart of pragmatism's view of freedom to be a corollary of its view of the cooperative character of successful human activities in general. Of course, cooperation here in no way resembles the more familiar but derivative practice of cooperation based on or constrained by self-interest. It is not something in which we engage in order to achieve some goal external to cooperative activity. In the sense employed by Dewey and other pragmatists from Peirce to Mead, cooperation is not reducible to an instrument or a means to something outside it. Strictly speaking, cooperation is not something that can be instrumentalized at all, since it requires commitment to a process that we can neither control nor direct, least of all, in favor of our self-interest. Genuine cooperation requires that we give ourselves over to a process of moral and cognitive learning that may require a change in how we speak, think, and act.

Cooperation in this sense not only supposes mutual recognition and accountability; it also facilitates the changes in attitude, behavior, and beliefs, the changes in self-understanding, on which the success of cooperative action depends. In this respect "positive solicitude" can be taken as an extension and broadening of the meaning of cooperation as a freedom-facilitating activity. Such cooperation "clears the way" for the other, fostering the conditions under which the other can become intelligible to herself—"perspicuous (*durchsichtig*) to herself *in* her care and . . . *free* for it." Becoming intelligible to herself is essential to her ability both to express and experience her own agency—to express and experience it *as* her own. Cooperation, in the wider sense instanced here, is at once the condition of human freedom and the social form within which it is instituted, preserved, and enlarged. Thus freedom is not just something that we achieve through cooperation; cooperation is that through which we care for and cultivate the conditions necessary to preserving the life of our freedom.

Unfortunately, Heidegger stranded the important insight at the center of his analysis of positive solicitude in the first division of *Being and Time*, and thereby undermined the development of his conception of authenticity in terms of the notion of "resoluteness" (*Entschlossenheit*).[11] When Heidegger lays out the meaning of "resoluteness" in the second division of *Being and Time*, it appears to belong to a quasi-dialogical structure of "call" and "response." Indeed Heidegger regards clarification of the question of "not only *who* is called by the call but also *who does the calling*" as decisive for his ontological interpretation of the "call of conscience" (BT 319/274). Yet the question of "how the one to whom the appeal is made is related to the one who calls" is not formulated in connection with the model of the relation between self and other—from the structure of which it obviously gets its sense in the first place. It is formulated exclusively in connection with the model of one's relationship to oneself. And although Heidegger describes the "call of conscience" as a call that comes "*from* me and yet from *outside and beyond me*" (BT 320/275),[12] he ignores the obvious implications of his description. It does not take much to see that these implications point to the need to bring these two models together into a relation of interdependence; otherwise, we will fail to understand the dialogical component of this "call." Regrettably Heidegger chose to develop the meaning of "resoluteness" one-sidedly, as an openness or receptivity to a "call" whose disclosed meaning should be understood independently of our relation to others. Thus he made monophonic and monological a call that is inherently polyphonic and dialogical. Heidegger then deliberately formalizes the existential-ontological meaning of this "call" so that *all* obligations "which are related to our concernful being with others will *drop out*" (BT 328/283). The "call of conscience" is the call of "care," and it comes from Dasein itself (BT 322/277).

As Heidegger must certainly have realized, this last formulation of the origin of the "call" is ambiguous, referring at once to Dasein as a concrete individual (a self, a subject, a person) and Dasein as such (the "being there" of human being).[13] A purely ontological-existential or formal construal of the "call of conscience" as the call of "care" coming from Dasein itself has a certain plausibility, insofar as it refers to a call that comes from and is addressed to the being of human being. However, the moment we try to think about this "call" ontic-existentielly—to place it in the concrete social life of an individual Dasein—to hear it as a call addressed to us in particular—we are confronted by some serious problems, problems for which Heidegger appears to have no convincing solutions.

The ontological explication of the "call of conscience" does help explain the ontological context of the "call" (the ontological conditions, let's say, of Dasein's possibilities to be or not to be itself). But it fails coherently to illuminate the concrete, socially situated character of the "call," and it fails because Heidegger does not allow the existentiell register of the "call" to be heard intersubjectively as well as intrasubjectively. Were we to hear as selectively as Heidegger himself insists we must, it is extremely unclear just how we could make sense of the "call of conscience" as a call that comes from "outside and beyond me." Given this predicament, one can understand why Habermas and other critics of Heidegger think that *Being and Time* culminates in a solipsistic rather than a "fundamental" ontology, why it fails to break free of the subjectivistic premises of the philosophy of consciousness. Such criticisms could easily have been disarmed if Heidegger had himself listened more openly to the intersubjective register of the "call of conscience." Indeed, if the "call" emanates from me *and* from something outside and beyond me, then Heidegger's decision to suppress that half of the "call" that emanates from outside the self turns out to be inconsistent with and untrue to the phenomenon he is seeking faithfully to describe. The suppression of this intersubjective reference of the call of conscience consists in a denial of dependence—a denial of dependence on the other, and on others.

In the end the whole normative construction of "resoluteness" suffers from Heidegger's insistence on this regressive, self-undermining demand: each individual Dasein must get into the proper relation to itself before it can clear the way for others, before it can become the "conscience" of others. "Dasein's resoluteness toward itself is what first makes it possible to let the others who are with it 'be' in their ownmost potentiality for being, and to co-disclose this potentiality in the solicitude which clears the way and liberates. When Dasein is resolute, it can become the 'conscience' of others" (BT 344/298).[14] Had Heidegger been a better student of Hegel, perhaps he might have conceived of "resoluteness" in a way that did not provoke the following questions: How does Dasein in the singular determine that he is sufficiently "resolute," sufficiently ready to be the "conscience" of others? How can Dasein alone—Dasein as the concrete individual to whom the "call" has been addressed—determine that he has properly heard and authentically answered that which calls him? How can he reassure himself that his "resoluteness toward [him]self" has "let the others who are with [him] be in their ownmost potentiality for being"? How can he tell that the solicitude that follows from his "resoluteness towards [him]self" actually "clears the way and liberates," when the other for whom he is ready to act as a "conscience" is not supposed to figure or participate in what it is that underwrites his readiness to act as *her* "conscience"? How can Dasein alone distinguish between a case of clearing the way for the other and a case of supplanting her? If the point of the discussion of positive solicitude was to show that authentic freedom requires that one must become intelligible to oneself, and that both freedom and self-intelligibility are acquired in relation to others under conditions of cooperative interaction, then Heidegger's soloistic conception of "resoluteness" undermines its own normative standpoint.

The claim that the act of "resoluteness" must precede positive solicitude not only extinguishes the possibility of a nondominating and freedom-facilitating relation to the other; it also places the self-understanding of Dasein at the precarious edge of subjectivism, down which it can all too quickly slide. Pace Habermas, however, we must not draw the much too hasty conclusion that Heidegger's conception of authenticity and "resoluteness" is thereby reducible to subjectivism or decisionism. Heidegger's account of authenticity is unquestionably one-sided and flawed, but there is something very wrong with the widespread habit of treating every attempt to give normative content to one's relation to oneself as unavoidably subjectivistic or solipsistic. Heidegger set out to provide a nonsubjectivistic understanding of one's relation to oneself, and thereby to make up for the lack of attention this relation has received in modern philosophy despite (or because of) its subject-centered orientation. The ideal of authenticity articulated in *Being and Time* succeeded, if only partially, in making explicit the ethical relation to oneself that is the correlate of the moral ideal of autonomy. In this respect—contrary to his own self-understanding—Heidegger did not radically deviate from so much as enlarge (and make less subjectivistic) both Kantian and Hegelian accounts of freedom as self-determination.

For all of its problems, Heidegger's way of formulating one's relationship to oneself illuminates a dimension of our moral lives that moral theory's customary concern with the question of justice has underestimated or misconstrued: the very problem of making oneself intelligible. In Stanley Cavell's view, Heidegger's concern with this practical relation to oneself places Heidegger's thought within the ambit of what Cavell calls "moral perfectionism." This practical relation to oneself is defined not only by questions such as: Who am I? What do I truly want for myself? It is also defined by these more troubling questions: Am I the author of my life? Are these words I use to describe myself my own? Do my actions originate from me or from something alien to me? For Cavell, the force of these questions explains moral perfectionism's "emphasis before all on becoming intelligible to oneself, as if the threat to one's moral coherence comes most insistently from that quarter, from one's sense of obscurity to oneself, as if we are subject to demands we cannot quite formulate, leaving us unjustified, as if our lives condemn themselves."[15] Unlike Cavell, Heidegger leaves unaddressed the question of whether one can become intelligible to oneself independently of one's relation to and one's need of others. Is this really something that one can do all by oneself? And if so, it would seem to require in the sphere of ethical self-understanding a virtuosic act of "genius" more conventionally reserved for the sphere of art. Should we then follow Richard Rorty's suggestion and think of the activity of becoming intelligible to ourselves as "identical with the process of inventing a new language," through which new language we create our new selves in the same way artists putatively create new works of art?[16] The short Hegelian answer to this question is a loud and emphatic No. "Self-consciousness finds its satisfaction only in another self-consciousness."[17] In other words, the reassurance I must seek in order to determine whether I have indeed become less obscure to myself, more capable of formulating the demands emanating from inside as well as from outside me, is to be found only in relation to, not independently of, others.

There are certainly occasions when we will need to find new words to express our new self-understanding, a self-understanding that those very words first make possible. Nonetheless, we will drastically misunderstand this activity if we think of it as equivalent to the ex nihilo creation of works of art. However we might wish to explain the activity by which we find these new words, and by which we let them find us, these words with which we make ourselves intelligible to ourselves will need some form of confirmation and acknowledgment that only others can provide. While my attempts to make myself intelligible must culminate in a self-understanding that ultimately *I* must be able to endorse, such an endorsement, though a necessary and ineliminable condition of self-reassurance, is not a sufficient condition. This is equally the case if I am seeking to reassure myself that my act of positive solicitude on behalf of an other "clears the way and liberates"; otherwise, I would be unable to distinguish clearing the way for the other from getting in her way. It is not just that there is something extremely presumptuous about the idea of becoming the "conscience of others" if others do not actually play a role either in my acts of "resoluteness" or of positive solicitude. It is also that the exclusion of others from these acts would, in practice, obstruct rather than enable my becoming intelligible to myself and thus obstruct, rather than enable, the possibility of the other becoming intelligible to herself.[18]

Like Hegel, Heidegger came to see that the problem of determining whether one's words and actions are genuinely one's own (in Heidegger's vocabulary, the problem of "mineness" [*Jemeinigkeit*]), is a problem that arises only for beings whose world is unavoidably and constitutively a world shared with, as well as inherited from, others. Only because my self-understanding and the words in which it is articulated is intersubjectively constituted—which is to say, only because the words with which I express my self-understanding are received from and shaped in relation to others— can the question of whether they *are* my own, and to what extent they can be reclaimed and made *my* own, becomes urgent, inescapable. (Of course, to speak of "my own" here is not to speak of something that is one's personal property, something that one can possess or copyright. In seeking to recognize oneself in one's words and deeds one is seeking some confirmation of one's agency, not the certification of one's property.)

For Hegel, intersubjectivity is not only the source of the problem of free self-determination; it is also the source of its solution. For this reason Hegel does not approach the question of self-determining freedom exclusively from the standpoint of one's relation to oneself; rather, he begins from a two-sided relation comprising one's relation to oneself, and one's relation to others. For Hegel, freedom consists in this two-sided relation, in terms of which one can "be with oneself in one's other" (*in seinem Anderen bei sich selbst zu sein*).[19] Of course, for both Hegel and Heidegger, self-determination requires more than autonomous judgment and action; it requires that an agent be able to experience her speech and action as her own. But Hegel saw much more perspicuously than Heidegger did that being able to experience one's speech and action *as* one's own depends on a relation of reciprocal recognition between oneself and others.[20] What can count as mine, as freely willed by me, cannot be counted as my own, were it not for others in reciprocal relation to whom I am able to distinguish and confirm that it *is* my own. Additionally "to be with oneself in one's other" involves *self-limitation*. More precisely, it involves *freely* willed self-limitation in relation to the other. In Hegel's view, such self-limitation, as distinct from the Kantian kind, does not culminate in self-alienation or self-repression, since it is only "*in* this limitation" that we can come to recognize, to know ourselves "*as* ourselves."[21] Indeed "freedom consists in this: to be with oneself in one's other, upon whom one depends to be the determinant of one's own self. . . . What we are speaking of here is *dependence"* (*die Freiheit ist eben dies, in seinem Anderen bei sich selbst zu sein, von sich abzuhängen, das Bestimmende seiner selbst zu sein. . . . Hier sprechen wir von Abhaengigkeit*).[22]

This Hegelian approach to intersubjectivity is much more consistent with and much more favorable to Heidegger's account of positive solicitude, and of his view that "[s]o far as Dasein *is* at all, it has being-with-one-another as its kind of being." So, if the emphasis "before all" on becoming intelligible to oneself can be justified, morally and epistemically, its justification will look much less subjectivistic if the task of becoming intelligible to oneself is not comprehended selectively and one-sidedly. For this reason Cavell speaks of the "importance to perfectionism of the friend, the figure, let us say, whose conviction in one's moral intelligibility draws one to discover it, to find words and deeds in which to express it."[23] Supplementing Cavell just a little, I would add that the "friend" is s/he upon whom one must rely not only for inspiration but also for a kind of reassurance that one's words and deeds are genuinely one's own. Only in this way are we able to assure ourselves that our identities, our words, and actions *are* genuinely our own. Reassurance cannot be monological in nature: reassurance has to be dialogical if it is to be reassuring.

Nonetheless, the reassurance we seek cannot be guaranteed by the dialogically mediated recognition of others. *Nothing* can guarantee that. Dialogical and reciprocal relations to others are only a necessary, not a sufficient condition of reassurance. It still requires that an agent reflectively endorse the outcome of such ongoing dialogue; it still requires that she underwrite, that she sign for, that she see herself as enjoined by, its "results". So, while it is the case that both dialogically mediated recognition and my own freely given endorsement are necessary conditions of any possible self-reassurance, they are not sufficient conditions of self-reassurance. Our attempts to reassure ourselves that our words and actions are indeed our own can only be *partially* satisfied. Even under the best social and political conditions, the "satisfaction" we seek will be provisional, subject to recurring normative challenge and self-induced doubt, since we must find "satisfaction" in the place from which the "desire" for it first arises: from the shared life with others where recognition is both conferred and denied, where "satisfaction" can easily turn into or be displaced by "dissatisfaction."

Thus we can take on board the Hegelian insight that only in relations of reciprocal recognition can one justifiably regard one's words and actions as indeed one's own, but we must not give it the final word on the matter. Even if intersubjectivity can be rightly viewed as the solution to the problem of intersubjectivity, the need for a solution is ineliminable. It is ineliminable because the problem of intersubjectivity is ineliminable. Even the most reciprocal relations of recognition can limit, disguise, or block certain freedom-enlarging possibilities. There are no social arrangements, and no cultural practices, that can prevent or eliminate the potential misrecognition built into any act of recognition. Heidegger's perfectionist worries cannot be allayed by appeals to intersubjectivity; intersubjectivity is *also* the ineliminable source of those worries. Put another way, the recognitive structures of intersubjectivity cannot eliminate the worry that our voice may not be truly our own, since it is those very structures, even in their most ideal and egalitarian form, that can make us feel voiceless—not because we do not have a voice but because our voice does not feel as though it is our own. The struggle to overcome our voicelessness, to regain *our* voice once we see that it is our voice itself that is at stake, that is under threat of erasure, is a struggle that cannot be adequately explained, not even motivationally, as a struggle for *recognition*, since it is also and perhaps more fundamentally a struggle *for* or *over* one's voice.[24] In this respect the kind of moral perfectionism that is of concern to Heidegger and Cavell is not merely a matter of "private" self-creation, irrelevant to political life and utterly lacking any "public" value: the struggle for and over one's voice is always already very much a "public" matter, whose positive consequences can both alter and expand relations of intersubjectivity.

Once the "call of conscience" is reconnected to, rather than detached from, positive solicitude—to the "concernful being with others" that "clears the way and liberates"—even the apparent shortcomings of Heidegger's "private" view of "resoluteness" can be developed more fruitfully than first appeared possible. But this will require listening to the "call of conscience" more polyphonically than Heidegger recommends, such that the voice that emanates from me is heard as distinctly as the voice that emanates from outside and beyond me. Put another way: I must not only hear that the "call" is addressed to me in particular, but also that it calls me to go outside and beyond myself—outside and beyond the self that I now am. To go outside and beyond the self that I now am requires listening to, understanding and acknowledging, voices other than the voice I *now* recognize as my own; it requires listening to, understanding, and acknowledging voices different from the ones I am accustomed to hearing. It requires listening not just polyphonically but heterophonically—listening differently to voices that can never be made harmonious within a structure in which universal (consonance) and particular (dissonance) are finally and fully reconciled.

3   *Entschlossenheit* as Disclosure

To dislodge the soloistic and virtuosic residues of Heidegger's concept of "resoluteness," it is necessary to reinstate and clarify its status as a mode of disclosure. If taken as an instance of existentialist decisionism, the essential meaning of "resoluteness" will be missed entirely. By depicting "resoluteness" as a species of decisionism, as the "decisionism of self-assertive Dasein" (WW 198),[25] Habermas evinces the degree to which he has misconstrued the receptive aspect of this mode of disclosure, and misdescribed its volitional/active aspect. In this respect he has been very much misled by a Sartrean reading of Heidegger that forces the volitional aspect of "resoluteness" into the decisionistic framework of Sartre's brand of existentialism.[26]

Certainly this misunderstanding is embedded, mischievously, in the standard English translation of *Entschlossenheit* as "resoluteness," which suggests the power to be decisive, unflinching.[27] The German word for decision is *Entscheidung*, whose literal meaning refers to the act of unsheathing, as in unsheathing one's sword. But *Entschlossenheit* is not synonymous with decision, or decisiveness, or a manly readiness to take action; it is synonymous with *Erschlossenheit*, with disclosure, or disclosedness. "Unclosing" or "unclosedness" would serve as a much more accurate and felicitous translation. It preserves the common semantic origin of both terms in the verb *schliessen*, to close, as well as the characterization of human sense making activities as activities of disclosing meaning and possibility. More important, it draws attention to the receptive character of the activity to which both terms refer. In order not to add one more neologism to a philosophical vocabulary already overpopulated with neologisms, I will henceforth drop the misleading translation and employ the original German term in its place wherever possible. This will help keep the close relation between *Entschlossenheit* and *Erschlossenheit*, "unclosure" and disclosure, and make it more apparent that their opposite is not closure so much as foreclosure (*Ausschliessen*)—the foreclosure of meaning and possibility.

Now that which makes *Entschlossenheit* a distinctive mode of reflective disclosure is its specific orientation to the "call of conscience"—the call to make oneself intelligible. "Conscience gives us 'something' to understand; it *discloses*" (BT 314/269). Thus it is hardly a matter of choosing decisively among distinct, already articulated alternatives. "One would completely misunderstand the phenomenon of *Entschlossenheit* if one should want to suppose that this consists simply in taking up possibilities which have been proposed and recommended, and seizing hold of them" (BT 345/298). The failure to be "unclosed" (as opposed to "resolute") is not the failure to be "decisive," nor is it the inability heroically to will oneself. It is the failure to make sense of one's words and actions in terms of one's life as a whole. For Heidegger this failure constitutes a failure to be receptive to the "call of conscience"—a failure to "unclose" one's framework of intelligibility. Heidegger characterizes such receptivity as a process of "*becoming free for the call*" (BT 334/287). By characterizing it in this way, Heidegger links receptivity to freedom and intelligibility, links being able to reassure oneself that one's words and actions are indeed one's own with being able to make sense of one's words and actions—being able both to recognize and appropriate them *as* one's own.

Since the call of conscience discloses, it calls upon us to make sense of that "something" it discloses. In a sense, the "call of conscience" calls twice: the first time to be given a voice; the second time, to be answered in our own voice. We make sense of the "call" by giving it a voice, and by giving it a voice, we are able to respond to "voices" we did not previously hear as "voices" to whose demands we must reply. Thus receptivity to the "call of conscience" requires not only openness to but also an active engagement with what is to be disclosed, or else there would be nothing disclosed, no "call" to hear, no addressees, and no respondents. So it is essential that receptivity to the "call" should not be confused with passivity, with submitting oneself obediently to an alien authority. Otherwise, any talk of "becoming free for the call" would be meaningless, having little or no connection to freedom in any recognized or acceptable sense. Receptivity does require letting ourselves undergo an experience but not blindly, passively. Receptivity is neither blind nor passive.[28]

In contrast to mindless submission, receptivity calls for an intensification of one's cognitive and affective capacities, not their abandonment. Thus "becoming free for the call" has an entirely different meaning from passive obedience: it means allowing oneself to be unsettled, thereby making it possible to occupy a potentially self-critical, self-illuminating perspective. Since that which calls is likely to (re)introduce us to, or remind us of, our own obscurity, we are exposing ourselves to our failure to render ourselves intelligible to ourselves, and in such a way as to make the experience of that failure the impetus for making sense of ourselves anew. We may thus characterize the response to the call of conscience as an activation of our capacity for self-decentering. Such a capacity is continuous with the capacities for self-reflection and self-criticism; indeed the latter are supervenient upon the former. Making sense of the inadequacy of our current self-understanding in the face of a breakdown in intelligibility does not logically follow from any such breakdown, for there are other ways of "going on," unreflective and uncritically. If the "going on" is to be reflective and self-critical, it will require a capacity for self-decentering experience—the capacity to experience the inadequacy of one's self-understanding as a crisis, to suffer it as an inadequacy for which one must hold oneself accountable.

Moreover, since the "call of conscience" is a call uttered by a voice in expectation of a response, it refers by its very nature to an intersubjective communicative structure of "call" and "response." "Calling is a mode of language (*Rede*)" (BT 314/269), and as Heidegger makes clear throughout *Being and Time*, "language articulates intelligibility" (BT 316/271). Hence a "call" is always a calling by and a calling to: it is always addressed by oneself to another (even when it is self-addressed).[29] Since calling is a mode of language, and since language always involves a speaker and a hearer, it constitutes a relation between speaker and hearer structured by normative expectations. To reiterate, however, those expectations, the demands they make, the normative challenges they issue, are likely to require articulation in words not already at our disposable. These words have to be "found," or they have to "find" us. When we find them, or they find us, we cannot go on as before. That is why *Entschlossenheit* "calls" for sense making and action possibilities that are not already available or discernible: it precedes decision. *Entschlossenheit* brings about—uncloses and discloses—the "authentic" context for deciding and deliberating in such a way as to recognize as genuinely one's own the possibilities (and responsibilities) that the "call of conscience" discloses. "*The unclosing (Entschluß) is precisely the disclosive projection and determination of what is factically possible*" (BT 345/298).

Clearly, what Heidegger is attempting to describe is not a an existential situation that dictates in advance what one's possibilities are, since *Entschlossenheit* involves finding oneself in one's situation as if for the first time: it involves *resituating* oneself.[30] To resituate oneself, one must reorient oneself in light of the new understanding of one's situation, making it possible to "go on" differently.[31] *Entschlossenheit* then requires getting oriented to the call of conscience, and as such, it is a complex act of disclosure, since both the "call" and "response" are a single, continuous act of disclosure, a single, continuous act of making sense of one's possibilities. It is a way of making sense of oneself that will require both a break with the self one was, and a reflective integration of the self one was with the self one can be.

Although *Entschlossenheit* certainly involves "choosing" oneself in light of one's own possibilities, self-choice does not have the subjectivistic meaning that Habermas attributes to it. As the second half of Kierkegaard's *Either/Or* makes clear, "self-choice" is no arbitrary affair. Nonetheless, the language of choice is both misleading and inappropriate, and the trouble to which Kierkegaard has to go to finesse this language is itself telling. Despite the shortcomings of the language in which Kierkegaard states this idea, its import is clear. "Self-choice" is less about choosing than it is about responsible self-appropriation, where what is appropriated is responsibility for one's life history as much as for one's possibilities, responsibility for one's past as much as for one's possible future. In "choosing" oneself, one is both "creating" and "discovering" oneself: by taking responsibility for the self one has become, an individual is at the same time opening up alternative, potentially transformative possibilities for becoming a self that is at once continuous and discontinuous with itself.

The choice . . . makes two dialectical movements at once: what is chosen does not exist and comes into existence through the choice, and what is chosen exists, otherwise it would not be a choice. For if the thing I chose did not exist but became absolute through the choice itself, I would not have chosen, I would have created. But I do not create myself, I choose myself.[32]

The act of "self-choice," however, does not have the individualistic and willful character of Sartrean existentialism, for that act is also an appropriation of transindividual criteria and standards according to which one's life as a whole can be evaluated. For both Heidegger and Kierkegaard, "self-choice" can occur only within a horizon of value and significance, a horizon in light of which certain things appear more worthy than others do.[33] Thus, in choosing oneself, one is also acknowledging that horizon within which Dasein *is* "always already"—acknowledging one's embeddedness in horizons of value and significance, and one's (initial and ongoing) indebtedness to them. The call to "choose" ourselves is "something we ourselves have neither planned nor prepared nor voluntarily performed, nor have we ever done so. It calls, against our expectations and even against our will" (BT 320/275). Decisionism and subjectivism suppose precisely what Heidegger's notion of world disclosure denies and seeks to surpass: the idea that meaning and value are instrumental, and at the disposal of our will.

Just as surely as it is not a matter of decision, *Entschlossenheit* is also not a matter of "self-creation." Kierkegaard's formulation instructively clarifies the degree to which *Entschlossenheit*, as an act of disclosure, is neutral between (self-)discovery and (self-)creation. The goal of *Entschlossenheit* is not the creation of a "new" self; the goal is self-intelligibility. While any successful sense making will lead to a change in self-understanding, such change is not a change one can set as an explicit goal. Despite the claims of at least one strain of cultural modernism, one cannot will oneself to be "new."[34] In other words, one cannot simply decide to exchange one's old self-understanding for a new one the way that one can decide to exchange one's old wardrobe or one's old car for a new one, or one's old "body" for a new one.[35]

To regard a successful change in self-understanding as an act of self-creation is not just to succumb to one of the most seductive of modernist fantasies; it is also to regard the self as an "object," as material, that one can mold according to one's desires. The self's very resistance to our artistic ambitions, its "unwillingness" to cooperate, to be compliant, is not all that speaks against such a conception. To regard the self as material for self-creation is to regard it simultaneously as an instrument and as that which instrumentalizes itself: a self that is both master and slave, owner and owned. Richard Rorty's excessive worries about essentialist conceptions of the self, of the self as something already "there" prior to interpretation, history, language, and culture leads to an unacceptable conception of the self as manipulable material, awaiting an act of "genius" through which the self creates the very criteria by which it is to be judged as successfully self-creating. Kierkegaard's and Heidegger's view is altogether more persuasive, obviating the need to choose between essentialism and nominalism. It is a view that leads out of, rather than back into, the subject/object model.

Of course, there is going to be some degree of change initiated by any act of self-clarification, since any such act will uncover something of ourselves we had not previously understood or known: it will have practical consequences for how we live. If we locate the source of such changes in self-understanding in everyday social practices, in contexts of crisis induced by normative challenges and expectations that arise from our ongoing interactions with others, it will be much harder to regard the possibility of such change as an activity proper to a sufficiently leisured, materially unencumbered, class of individuals, to "artists" of self-creation and self-cultivation. Such change is the result of a painful process of cognitive and moral (re)learning, (re)learning that we can neither initiate nor control by any mere decision of our own. Neither the active nor the receptive aspects of any mode of disclosure are at the disposal of our will: there is nothing *willkürlich* about acts of disclosure. This is as true of the early as it is of the later construal of disclosure. There can be no disclosure without Dasein's participation; on the other hand, neither pre-reflective nor reflective disclosure is at Dasein's disposal. Both forms of disclosure suppose and demand openness and receptivity.[36] Charles Taylor captures nicely the non-subjectivistic and noninstrumental character of Heidegger's understanding of disclosure: it is Dasein-related, but not Dasein-centered or Dasein-controlled.[37]

Our practical identity is ours and ours alone, but not as a thing we possess; it is a project entrusted to us, and placed in our care. We cannot refuse to have an identity of our own; we will have one whether we wish to or not. What matters most is our practical relation to our identity. So what is really at issue here is not one's "identity," strictly speaking but, rather, one's "to be"—one's possibilities to be (or not to be) a certain kind of person, to live a certain kind of life, possibilities to be (or not to be) what we do not yet know. In other words, what is at issue is one's freedom in relation not just to whom one now is but to whom one might be. And it is for this reason, that my "to be," the possibilities of my particular life, the future before me, the past behind me, has the "character of being in each case mine" (BT/68/43). What is "mine" is not something that has the character of property, for what is taken over is not a thing, not an object, not something that can be grasped, manipulated, or fully surveyed. This is why Heidegger discusses the self as a structure of care, or as structured by care: as that for which we (can) care, and (must) take over as care. Looked at in this light, one's possibilities "to be" cannot be objects over which one can dispose. As argued in part I, chapter 4, possibility is no object. "Dasein is in each case already *ahead* of itself (*ihm selbst . . . vorweg*) in its being. Dasein is always 'beyond itself' (*über sich hinaus*), not as a mode of relating to other entities which it is *not*, but as being toward the potentiality-for-being which it is itself" (BT 236/192).

What is in each case mine, then, is the field of disclosed and as yet undisclosed possibilities into which I have been "thrown." The possibilities of self I inherit are, in this sense, the consequence of a collision, not a decision. The expression "thrownness" (*Geworfenheit*) conveys the facticity of this inheritance, this deliverance, of self into circumstances and conditions it has not itself chosen.

Facticity (*Faktizität*) is not the factuality (*Tatsächlichkeit*) of the factum brutum of something present-at-hand, but a characteristic of Dasein's being—one which has been taken up into existence, even if to begin with it has been thrust aside. The "that it is" of facticity never becomes something that we can come across by beholding it. . . . As an entity which has been delivered over to its being, it remains also delivered over to the fact that it must always have found itself—but found itself in a way of finding which arises not so much from a direct seeking as rather from a fleeing. (BT 174/135)

With this last remark Heidegger indicates why it is that the capacity to hear the "call of conscience" is not simply at the disposal of one's will; it depends on an unsettling experience of incapacity—a self-decentering experience of crisis. One cannot choose to have such an experience: it "happens" to one, it "calls" one. It is a "call" I can hear, and to which I can properly respond, when, for some previously unforeseeable reason or circumstances, I am no longer capable of understanding my self, my "to be," in my accustomed, taken for granted way. With Alasdair MacIntyre, we can once again speak of an "epistemological crisis." However, in this case we are not referring in the first instance to a crisis in a tradition of inquiry; we are referring to a crisis in the biographical history or self-understanding of an individual. What initiates such a crisis is a breakdown in the interpretive scheme, the framework of intelligibility, through which an individual had hitherto made sense of herself. In such a crisis we experience that very sense of obscurity, the threat of incoherence, that prompts the fear that we are unable to comprehend and thereby formulate the demands to which we feel ourselves vaguely subject.

From the existential-ontological perspective of *Being and Time*, breakdowns of this kind are an ever-present possibility in virtue of Dasein's kind of being—a being ontologically distinguished by the fact that the question of its own being is always "an issue for it" (BT 32/12). Furthermore it is an ontological feature of Dasein that its "there," its kind of being, is disclosed in anxiety, anxiety that arises when its publicly shared framework of intelligibility breaks down, rendering inexplicable what it had heretofore trusted and taken for granted as the settled significance of its life. Thus, as Hubert Dreyfus puts it, "anxiety reveals Dasein as *dependent upon a public system of significances* that it did *not produce*."[38] And it does this by taking "away from Dasein the possibility of understanding itself . . . in terms of the 'world' and the way things have been publicly interpreted" (BT 233/188). Anxiety unsettles us, not just because it makes the familiar unfamiliarly unresponsive to our sense-making needs but also because it reveals the contingency of our sense-making structures, exposing their permanent "unsettledness" (*Unheimlichkeit*). According to MacIntyre, these are precisely the epistemologically self-conscious conclusions toward which an epistemological crisis pushes any individual who successfully undergoes one:

[T]he first is that his new forms of understanding may themselves in turn come to be put in question at any time; the second is that, because in such crises the criteria of truth, intelligibility and rationality may always themselves be put in question—as they are in *Hamlet*—we are never in a position to claim that now we possess the truth or now we are fully rational. The most that we can claim is that this is the best account which anyone has been able to give so far, and that our beliefs about what the marks of "a best account so far" will themselves change in what are at present unpredictable ways.[39]

As MacIntyre also makes clear, an epistemological crisis is a crisis in human relationships as well, an indication of something gone inexplicably awry in one's relationship with others. Making sense of ourselves is something that we do in relation to others—in relation to their normative challenges and normative expectations. Thus making sense of ourselves requires making sense of those normative challenges and expectations, making sense of how they challenge us, of what they demand of us. Just as much as we need others to make sense of ourselves, we need others to change ourselves, where such change is a consequence of reflective insight.

Once again, however, Heidegger undermines the illuminating power of his own analyses by uncoupling *Entschlossenheit* from Dasein's positive dependence on others and, thus, from positive solicitude. Anticipating somewhat the discussion of *das Man* to come (chapter 4), I want to draw attention to the exclusively negative construal of Dasein's dependence on others that emerges in Heidegger's characterization of *Entschlossenheit*. He describes *Entschlossenheit* as a stance that "signifies letting oneself be recalled from one's lostness in the '(any)one'" (BT 345/299). Dasein "has either projected itself upon possibilities of its own or has been so absorbed in the 'anyone' that it has let such possibilities be presented to it by the way in which the 'anyone' has publicly interpreted things. The presenting of these possibilities, however, is made possible existentially through the fact that Dasein, as a being-with which understands, can *listen* to others. Losing itself in the publicness of the idle talk of the 'anyone', it *mishears* (überhört) its own self in listening to the 'self of anyone' (*Man-selbst*)" (BT 315/270–271).

This one-sided characterization of Dasein's dependence on others is inconsistent with Heidegger's view of positive solicitude and his "constitutive" view of language. Our relationships to others and the public frameworks of meaning and intelligibility through which those relationships are mediated both enable and constrain our possibilities "to be" or "not to be" ourselves. Similarly Heidegger's analysis of the very possibility of intelligibility, of understanding anyone or anything, is a consequence of Dasein's capacity to listen to others. "Listening to (*Das Hören auf*) . . . is Dasein's existential way of being-open as being-with for others. Indeed, hearing (*hören*) constitutes Dasein's primary and authentic openness to its ownmost potentiality-for-being—as in hearing the voice of the friend whom every Dasein carries with it" (BT 206/163).[40] When Heidegger speaks of the possibility of "another kind of hearing" (BT 316/271), it is this that he has in mind. So there is a need distinguish between these two kinds of hearing, both of which are co-present possibilities for any Dasein, and neither of which can be practiced independently of the other. Only because we can "hear" the public way in which things are interpreted can those things become intelligible to us in the first place. But this kind of hearing both makes possible *and* interferes with that other kind of hearing through which we become "free for the call."

Entschlossenheit does not require a total and permanent break from the kind of hearing by which one is absorbed into the "any(one)," since that is no more a real possibility than a total and permanent absorption in it. It does not therefore require one radically to liberate oneself from shared practices of sense making, without which the very possibility of sense making would be lost; rather, it calls for an unclosing relation to this practice, a redirection of one's hearing and a reorientation of one's attention. Thus *Entschlossenheit* makes room for the disclosure of alternative meanings and possibilities, which absorption in the "(any)one" can foreclose. What all this involves, then, is not something that transcends the everyday as the source of intelligibility, for as Heidegger's analysis of social intelligibility demonstrates, we are always drawing on this source even when we are attempting to alter and transform it.

This everyday way in which things have been interpreted is one into which Dasein has grown in the first instance, with never a possibility of extrication. In it, out of it, and against it, all genuine understanding, interpreting, and communicating, all re-discovering and appropriating anew, are performed. In no case is a Dasein, untouched and unseduced by this way in which things have been interpreted, set before the open country of a "world-in-itself" so that it just beholds what it encounters. (BT 213/169–170)

Throughout *Being and Time* Heidegger backslides to a position that is inconsistent with the conclusions toward which its pathbreaking analyses lead. This is understandable to a certain extent, given the radical nature of his conceptual and philosophical innovations. But this reversion to the assumptions from which his analyses break is not just one more case of an original thinker's inability to think consistently in the new terms he has

set; it is also evidence of Heidegger's reluctance to fully accept the intersubjective implications of his analyses. Put more precisely, throughout
Being and Time there is a recurring denial, a recurring suppression, of the
very dependence on others that its analyses demonstrate and explain,
whether they be of "being-in-the-world," of being-with, of language, of disclosure, of positive solicitude, or of *Entschlossenheit*. Both in his early and
in his later work Heidegger never tired of demonstrating the dependence
of our sense-making abilities on inherited frameworks of intelligibility, on
some primary disclosure of the world, ontologically prior to our engagement with it. However, after *Being and Time* he never again made our
complex dependence on others, and so our equally complex obligations
to others, one of his central concerns. The denial and suppression of this
dependence on others is as much a part of the "turn" as anything else
and, perhaps, the real explanation of its necessity. It is time to consider
seriously whether the "turn" from early to later Heidegger was much
more a function of the successful suppression of our dependence on
others than of the avowed need to overcome early Heidegger's residual
subjectivism.

Resisting Heidegger's (and our own) tendency to deny our mutual dependence, we will read *Being and Time* very differently. For example, we will
be able to give a much more generous interpretation of a passage critically
examined above. "Dasein's unclosing *of itself* [previous translation altered]
is what first makes it possible to let the others who are with it 'be' in their
ownmost potentiality for being, and to *co-disclose* [my emphasis] this
potentiality in the solicitude which clears the way and liberates. When
Dasein is unclosed, it can become the 'conscience' of others" (BT 344/
SZ 298). Now it is more apparent than before that getting into that state
of being unclosed, that right relation to one's "to be" is a state that has to
be facilitated by others as much as it has to be desired by the agent herself.
Getting into the right relation to oneself also involves a reciprocal act of
getting into the right relation to others. In both cases, since we are speaking of a mode of disclosure, what is called for is an act of receptivity,
as much to others as to oneself, an act that supposes an acknowledgment of mutual dependence. Now it is possible to read this passage not as
claiming that *Entschlossenheit*, unclosing, must precede positive solicitude
but as claiming that any act of reflective disclosure that "clears the way
and liberates" is necessarily cooperative in character. We no longer need
to be concerned about the apparent presumptuousness of this claim,
since now we are in a position to read it as claim about the normative
continuities between *Entschlossenheit* and positive solicitude. Disclosure

that aims to enlarge the cultural conditions of possibility, and the social conditions of freedom and intelligibility, is necessarily a reflective act of co-disclosure, not a soloistic, monological, and monophonic act of "genius." What it calls for is solicitous cooperation, not individual virtuosity.

Entschlossenheit, as *authentic being-one's-self*, does not detach Dasein from its world, nor does it isolate it so that it becomes a free floating "I". And how could it, when unclosing (*Entschlossenheit*), as authentic disclosure (*Erschlossenheit*), is *authentically* nothing else than *being-in-the-world*? Unclosing brings the self right into its current concernful being-alongside what is ready-to-hand, *and thrusts it into solicitous being with others.* (BT 344/SZ 298, my emphasis in last sentence)

The reinterpretation of key ethical concepts of *Being and Time* that I have thus far proposed raises the question of whether their ethical content possesses any critical potential vis-á-vis Heidegger's politics, and, by implication, the question of whether they allow us to distinguish between better and worse kinds of disclosure (a question to which I will return in parts III and V).[41] One of the primary faults of Habermas's interpretation of *Being and Time* is that it is incapable of identifying anything within it possessing the power to resists its author's manipulations. Determining the degree to which Heidegger's texts resist their political misuse is obviously of some importance to the goal of renewing the critical resources of the German philosophical tradition. It is important to see that the texts possess critical potential vis-à-vis Heidegger's life and politics, vis-à-vis the instrumental relation he took toward them. And it is also important to see that the "ethics of authenticity" sketched out in *Being and Time* is not compatible with just any moral and political institutions—that they are not as *equally* at home in a fascist dictatorship as in a liberal democracy. In fact there is no evidence that the ideal of freedom as self-determination at issue in *Being and Time* is incompatible with the principle of equal respect for all; indeed it must suppose equal respect for all. Thus despite all of its deficiencies Heidegger's ethics expresses an ideal of freedom that can only be realized (once again, contrary to Heidegger's own self-understanding) under conditions of a nonviolent, noncoercive, cooperative form of life—a democratic form of life. If properly developed, such an ethics of authenticity would contribute to fostering the conditions necessary for a radicalization of democratic forms of life in the direction of greater freedom and greater equality.

Unlike the "liberal ironist" who thinks he can neatly separate his private pursuit of autonomy from his public pursuit of intersubjective agreement, the "moral perfectionist" worries about the consequences for democracy under conditions in which everyone has a voice but not a voice of one's own. Rorty's "liberal ironist" doesn't think that such worries should be given a voice in the public life of a democracy: in public discourses, our voices should blend together, not stick out. But even if one is not inclined to regard the politics of recognition as a powerful contemporary articulation of these worries, they are not going to go away any time soon. The need to speak and hear ourselves speak in our own voice is not just a "private" need but fundamental to fostering and preserving the trust on which democracy depends—trusting, for example, that difference and democracy are not irreconcilable. The life forms of democracy would have much to gain and nothing essential to lose from the call to make our lives more intelligible to ourselves, less inscrutable, less of a threat to our moral coherence. If we can respond to that call without becoming deaf to the call of others, that is, without denying or suppressing our dependence on others to make our lives morally intelligible to ourselves, the gain to democratic forms of life will be immeasurable.[42]

Thus far I have tried to put into question Habermas's subjectivistic and decisionistic interpretation of early Heidegger. If the basic thrust of my analysis is right, it also puts into question Habermas's political explanation for the transition between early and late Heidegger. One can understand Habermas's wish to undermine Heidegger's highly exaggerated claims regarding the continuity of his thought, but while there is much less continuity than Heidegger claims, there is much more than Habermas allows. Representing the transition between early and late Heidegger as a politically motivated development during which the accent is displaced from an assertive "decisionism of empty resoluteness" to "the submissiveness of an equally empty readiness for subjugation," requires that *Entschlossenheit* is reducible to decisionism. Not only does it not reduce to decisionism, as a mode of disclosure, *Entschlossenheit* is the complete opposite of decisionism. Similarly the transformation of our stance toward "being," which is the central preoccupation of the later Heidegger, is not reducible to "submissiveness" or a "readiness for subjugation." This is a neat and tidy explanation, but it ignores the continuities between early and later Heidegger's emphasis on openness and receptivity.[43] Once again, this interpretive error is a function of Habermas's misconstrual of disclosure. It is obvious that the more active and volitional aspect of disclosure receded in later Heidegger in favor of its receptive aspect, but it did not vanish altogether. In any case, in both the early and later Heidegger receptivity to sources of meaning outside the self are at the center of his undertaking. He continues to make use of the "call and response" form: the shift is from the call of "conscience" to the call of "being." On this view there is no need to exclude from the account of the transition to the later philosophy the lessons Heidegger learned from his political involvement with National Socialism. These lessons pertain to the nature of historical and cultural change, about which Heidegger was to write very insightfully.

There is nevertheless a moral absence that haunts Heidegger's early and later philosophy. Just as the early work failed to bring together the transformation of one's relation to oneself through a mutual and cooperative transformation of one's relation to others, the later work failed to bring together the transformation of our relation to "being" through a mutual and cooperative transformation of our relation to other human beings. So the problem with the later Heidegger's recommendations concerning our receptivity to "being" is not the problem of a passive openness to anything that comes along. There is undoubtedly a lack of clear, unambiguous normative criteria regulating such receptivity, but that is not the central problem—in any case, it is not clear that this problem could ever be resolved in a manner that would satisfy Heidegger's critics where satisfaction would entail fixed criteria. The central problem is Heidegger's failure to coordinate the stance of receptivity to "being" with a corresponding stance of receptivity to human beings—to their cry of pain, their suffering, to the dehumanisation and destruction of their humanity.

From his very first criticisms of Heidegger, Habermas rightly understood the intrinsically moral nature of this failure: Heidegger preferred to show how we could be "the neighbor of being," not how we could be *each other's* neighbor (WW 199).[44] That this failure shows up in the life as well in the work is surely no coincidence, for the failure is not merely philosophical in nature, it is moral in a much wider sense. What I mean is this: Heidegger's moral failure is a failure not only in relation to others but also in relation to himself. His efforts to make intelligible to himself his involvement with the Nazis fail by the standards of his own ethics of authenticity. They fail because assuming responsibility for one's mistakes, assuming responsibility, self-consciously and self-critically, for the whole of one's life history is a necessary condition of becoming intelligible to oneself. That Heidegger failed to be morally receptive to others is obvious; that he failed to be receptive to the "call" to become intelligible to himself, a need identified and clarified in *Being and Time*, is less so. We are in some sense philosophically indebted to Heidegger's failure in this respect, for it reveals an internal relation not between his philosophy and his politics but between *intelligibility* and *accountability*.

4   Recovering the Everyday

I would like now to return to the second internal connection Habermas claims to have established between Heidegger's philosophy and his politics: the connection between the mandarin *Weltanschauung* and the categorial framework of *Being and Time*. The persuasiveness of this revised account depends on the cogency of Habermas's interpretation of Heidegger's analysis of the phenomenon of *das Man*. Unsurprisingly, what Habermas has to say about Heidegger's analysis of *das Man* fails to convey its strengths, and misinterprets its goals. There is no indication whatsoever that Heidegger is saying something importantly new in this analysis, something that represents an advance both in our understanding of the everyday and of the interconnections between socialization and individuation. Even Heidegger's "scientifically unfiltered diagnosis of crisis" (WW 194) turns out to be of greater value than Habermas is explicitly able to acknowledge. While there is no external evidence to doubt Heidegger's sympathy toward the mandarin ideology or his own elitist self-understanding, what he has to say in the relevant passages of *Being and Time* not only fails to conform to but altogether transcends elitist critiques of the everyday—including his own.

It must be said that worries about the "dictatorship of public opinion" were not exclusive to German mandarins and their ilk. One need only look outside the specific German context of the 1920s and 1930s to find such worries already expressed in Rousseau and, on the other, more democratic side of the ocean, in Emerson and Thoreau. Heidegger's analysis of *das Man* displays no more contempt for "average everydayness" or the "who" of everyday Dasein than is to be found in Rousseau's *Second Discourse*, Emerson's "Self-Reliance," Thoreau's *Walden*, or Mill's *On Liberty*. Even a cursory comparison shows there is no deep disagreement among them on this score.[45] Here in contraposition are Emerson from "Self-Reliance" and Heidegger from the relevant section of *Being and Time*, followed by Mill from *On Liberty*, just for good measure. Note the three-part harmony in the following citations.

Emerson: "Man is timid and apologetic. He is no longer upright. He dares not say, 'I think,' 'I am,' but quotes some saint or sage."[46]

Heidegger: "Primarily my 'I am' is not that of my own self, but that of the others whose way is that of the 'one.' It is primarily from the 'one' and as the 'one' that my 'self' is 'given' to me." (BT, 167/129; translation amended)

Mill: "At present individuals are lost in the crowd."[47]

Emerson: "Insist on your self, never imitate." [48]

Heidegger: "Everyone is the other, and no one is himself." (BT 165/128)

Mill: "Precisely because the tyranny of opinion is such as to make eccentricity a reproach, it is desirable, in order to break through that tyranny, that people should be eccentric. . . . That so few now dare to be eccentric marks the chief danger of the time."[49]

Emerson: "Our reading is mendicant and sycophantic."[50]

Heidegger: "Publicness primarily controls every way in which the world and Dasein get interpreted . . . the way of interpreting the world and being in the world which lies closest." (BT 165/127 and BT 167/129)

Mill: "[The] tendencies of the times cause the public to be more disposed than at most former periods to prescribe general rules of conduct, and endeavour to make every one conform to the approved standard. . . . Its ideal of character is to be without any marked character; to maim by compression, like a Chinese lady's foot, every part of human nature which stands out prominently, and tends to make the person markedly dissimilar in outline to commonplace humanity."[51]

A careful reading of the fourth chapter of *Being and Time* should make clear that Heidegger did not introduce the analysis of *das Man* simply for the sake of a critique of mass civilization: it no more reduces to a mandarin critique of the everyday than *Entschlossenheit* reduces to decisionism. The category of *das Man* is an *Existenzial*; it is used to clarify how our ontological pre-understanding enables (discloses) and constrains (disguises and inhibits) the ways in which we take up our relations to the world and to others. This pre-understanding is disclosed to us *through* everyday practices, which practices are the primary source of social intelligibility. Receptivity plays an ineliminable role here as well, for it is only in virtue of our pre-reflective openness to public practices that there is intelligibility and meaning at all. The everyday practices through which "being in the world" is pre-reflectively disclosed make possible and enfold the massive background agreement that our speech and action draw upon and presuppose. As Hubert Dreyfus has pointed out, this analysis anticipates the later Wittgenstein's talk about agreement in forms of life, and as such, it is continuous with Heidegger's attempt to undermine and supplant the subject-centered orientation of modern philosophy.[52]

It is absolutely necessary to insist that the "one" is not some specifically modern constraint against which Dasein must heroically assert itself if it is to become authentically itself. If Heidegger's view of the "one" is supposed to be a telling example of Heidegger's anti-modernism, it is a very bad one. The "'one'... *belongs to Dasein's positive constitution*" (BT 167/129)—which is why mandarin-like exhortations to overcome the "one" through acts of heroic self-assertion are altogether out of place—even those made by Heidegger in his writings from the 1930s. Nothing so conventionally anti-modern or romantic is called for: "Authentic being-one's-self does not depend upon an extraordinary state (*Ausnahmezustand*) of the subject that is detached from the 'one'; *rather, it is an existentiell modification of the 'one'—of the 'one' as an essential existentiale*" (BT 168/130, translation amended). So long as the "one" belongs to Dasein's positive constitution, authenticity depends on a transformation ("existentielle modification") of the constraints of everyday practice, not upon a heroic escape from them. If the "one" cannot have the final word on the question of the "who" of everyday Dasein (BT 149/114), it is because Dasein's activities can modify the very constraints that make its activities possible. Dasein can redisclose and thereby alter the conditions of social intelligibility. Thus what Heidegger is actually trying to show through the existential-ontological analysis of *das Man* is precisely what Habermas denies he can show: that a relation of interdependence obtains between individuation and socialization. And what is shown gives more depth and more scope to this relation. Yet Heidegger is no less aware than Habermas that there is a crucial difference between "institutionalized" or "obligatory" individuation and a process of individuation that subjects can attribute to their own spontaneous *and* reflective activity.[53] Unlike Habermas, however, he is not advocating an interpretation of authenticity in terms of radical individuality; he is not defining an authentic individual as *einzigartig* (one of a kind)—as "an individual who distinguishes himself from *all* others."[54] Heidegger is in fact critical of such modern conceptions of radical individuality, for they entail practices of "distantiation" (*Abständigkeit*), which he regards—as Rousseau did before him—as one of the internal threats to undeformed everyday practices. (It is not difficult to see the extent to which Rousseau's "amour-propre" is a precursor of Heidegger's "distantiation.")

One of the long-range goals of the *das Man* chapter in *Being and Time* is to make the case for an enlargement of the idea of freedom as self-determination by taking it in a semantic direction. What is being brought to light is the semantic struggle to uncover and transform the meanings unavoidably shaping one's identity and self-understanding. This semantic struggle is just what Habermas's account of "individuation through social-ization" neglects. Heidegger shares with Emerson, the later Wittgenstein, and more recently, Stanley Cavell an interest in exploring the significance of the fact that the words we first speak are words we inherit from others: they are always someone else's words before they are ours. What we inherit, then, is a language that speaks before we do, a "secondhand" language that we need to make our own if we are to claim an identity of our own, if we are to speak in a voice of our own (which does not mean that we speak in a voice *unlike* any other).[55] Heidegger is also quite obviously concerned with showing how everyday practices govern and regulate *what* shows up as significant and relevant in ways that are not transparent and immediately accessible. The concern is with how everyday practices constrain what can show up as significant and relevant, how they can obstruct or mislead our interpretative efforts, how they can discreetly colonize the logical space of possibility. There is no totalizing identification of the everyday with mass civilization here: the aim of Heidegger's analysis is to demonstrate the ontological and not just sociological conditions under which we become speakers of a language, any language. This sets him apart from his fellow mandarins, and from Horkheimer's and Adorno's critique of "mass culture as mass deception." But not this only, for Heidegger's concern with the *leveling* of everyday practices is guided primarily by an interest in recovering the everyday, rescuing its semantic resources from daily degradation. This concern is, of course, entirely consistent with Heidegger's claim that everyday practices are the sources of meaning and intelligibility. If like pragmatism and the later Wittgenstein one thinks of everyday practices as the primary sources of social intelligibility, one will naturally be very concerned about their openness to meaning and possibility, and their ongoing disfiguration by homogenizing and totalizing tendencies within them.

We can have a more productive relation to Heidegger's early and later philosophy when we recognize this concern, and reject Habermas's claim that Heidegger scorned the everyday in favor of the "extraordinary." In so far as Heidegger's distinct philosophical contribution is the illumination of a phenomenon that is at once both extraordinary and mundane, Habermas's claim is once again the mistaken consequence of a one-sided and inconsistent understanding of that phenomenon. We must also be wary of following Habermas to the conclusion that Heidegger's critique of everyday practices reduces to the expression of an anti-modern or anti-Western stance. Heidegger's concerns—in their best and in their worst form—are as modern and Western as any. Habermas often suggests that there is something in Heidegger's thought that is fundamentally alien to Western modernity, and thus creates an image of Heidegger as an exotic outsider (*Aussenseiter*) (PT 145). This image is good for the Heidegger industry, but not good for understanding Heidegger or the German philosophical tradition. There is certainly no reason to give either Heidegger's positive or negative analysis of everyday practices the final word; rather, we need only recognize that his undertaking is part of a larger rescue attempt requiring additional resources, resources that Heidegger's texts alone are not in a position to provide. Habermas—contrary to *his* self-understanding—shares with Heidegger the goal of restoring the vitality and integrity of everyday practices. He approaches this goal by rescuing the potential for rationality latent in everyday practices of reaching agreement. When this potentiality takes a reflexive shape, when communicative reason takes the form of "discourse," it subjects to rational testing and criticism not only our shared beliefs and practices but also the assumptions on which these beliefs and practices rest. This way everyday practices can be both corrected and renewed. On its own, however, this approach is inadequate to its task: it needs to be conjoined with rather than opposed to Heidegger's, and that is because the background assumptions of everyday practices need also to be reflectively disclosed before they can be properly thematized and criticized.

Thus it is not enough for beliefs and practices to be publicly tested and criticized. Heidegger's analysis of *das Man* darkens the meaning of publicity (*Öffentlichkeit*); it shows that even the most public procedures of evaluation and criticism will be invisibly constrained and not just enabled by their languages of evaluation and interpretation. This follows from the Heideggerian/Wittgensteinian insight that we cannot render fully explicit the massive background of shared beliefs and practices no matter how public our procedures: this background resists (or withdraws from) a completely objectifying grasp. Given this, any talk about the "end of ideology" will always be premature, since that expectation is based on the illusion that through the proliferation of public discourses the "lifeworld would gain a singular transparence" (TCA2 145).

[The] everyday way in which things have been interpreted is one into which Dasein has grown in the first instance, with never a possibility of extrication. In it, out of it, and against it, all genuine understanding, interpreting, and communicating, all rediscovering and appropriating anew, are performed. In no case is a Dasein, untouched and unseduced by this way in which things have been interpreted, set before the open country of a "world-in-itself" so that it just beholds what it encounters. The dominance of the public way in which things have been interpreted has already been decisive even for the possibilities of having a mood—that is, for the basic way in which Dasein lets the world "matter" to it. The "one" prescribes one's state-of-mind, and determines what and how one "sees." (BT 213/169–170)

This insight into the way in which the 'everyday way in which things have been interpreted' affects all our sense-making activities does not have to take a skeptical direction. Rather than using it to support some practice-crippling version of linguistic historicism or dismissing it as counter-Enlightenment ideology, we might more wisely put it to use in the name of a richer and more complex understanding of public discourse and of the structures of intersubjectivity. With this understanding we will not only be able to see but also to take into account the ways in which publicity both sheds light on, and withholds light from, our shared beliefs and practices. There is no point in inviting, *ad infinitum*, another skeptical critique of reason in order vainly to purify public reason.

Heidegger belongs to a group of romantic philosophers and poets, made up more of "poets" than of philosophers, who believe that we have drastically underestimated the degree to which the integrity of everyday practices, including our most cherished critical practices, depend on semantic resources that we cannot simply replenish at will.[56] The depletion of the semantic contents of cultural practices and traditions poses a threat to the quality of public practices of criticism and justification, for they too are dependent on and nourished by these same semantic contents. According to this "romantic" tradition of thought, there has been a widespread failure to appreciate the degree to which the semantic resources of the everyday, including those necessary for critical discourse, are endangered by the leveling of meaning, and by homogenizing and totalizing cultural practices.[57] It is easy enough to engage in *das Manish* critiques of democracy, taking the degradation of everyday practices and the depletion of semantic resources to be a function of democratic forms of life, of modern life *tout court*. Such critiques typically confuse the destructive powers of capitalist modernization with the as yet unrealized possibilities of democracy. This has been said before, and it will need to be said again. What needs to be added to the defense of democratic forms of life is a richer account of the everyday practices that constitute (or are needed to constitute) them. Such an account would draw on, rather than ignore, the insights of Heidegger's analysis of *das Man*. If our human forms of life, democratic or otherwise, are not to become decrepit or rigid, if they are to remain open to new meanings and alternative possibilities, they will always be in need of renewal—always. It is a virtue of democratic forms of life—ideally, if not in practice—that the possibility of such self-renewal is incorporated into the normative self-understanding of democratic culture if not in the normative framework of its institutions.

Over the years, Habermas has occasionally recognized the degree to which the semantic resources necessary for undeformed everyday practices are threatened, if not already on the verge of exhaustion.[58] But his idealized construal of the process of rationalization, the "reflexive liquefaction of traditions," gives the impression that it can provide a substitute for, or serve as a communicative barrier to, the ongoing experience of fragmentation and the loss of meaning. As Charles Taylor puts it, Habermas "elides the experiential problem (of "the loss of meaning, fragmentation, the loss of substance in our human environment and our affiliations") under the public, as if the two could be solved for the price of one."[59] Habermas's own critique of capitalist modernization describes this "experiential problem" in a way that makes it seemingly obvious that a two for the price of one solution is simply not on.

For centuries capitalism has lived off the fat of pre-bourgeois traditions. . . . But under the conditions of an extensively rationalized lifeworld, the spent contents *can no longer be regenerated qua contents of tradition.* Thus in the most capitalistically developed regions, these are approaching the point of exhaustion. And the imperatives of an autonomized process of economic growth and the administrative controls of a hopelessly overburdened bureaucracy cut through the detritus of eviscerated traditional forms of life, encountering at the exposed foundations the communicatively structured life forms themselves. From this perspective, one perceives the danger of a systemically induced destruction not only of life forms nourished on tradition *but of the communicative infrastructure of any humane form of life* [my italics]. (SS 16)

Although they precede by a few years the publication of *The Theory of Communicative Action,* it is easy enough to read off these remarks the thesis of the "colonization of the lifeworld" that figures so prominently in the second volume of that work. As is well known, this thesis plays a very important role in Habermas's diagnosis of the pathologies of modernity, in particular, in the diagnosis of the dangers posed to the Enlightenment project by unchecked capitalist modernization. The "imperatives of autonomous subsystems [i.e., economic and bureaucratic imperatives] make their way into the lifeworld from the outside—like colonial masters coming into a tribal society—and force a process of assimilation upon it" (TCA2 355). Thus, to the extent that the communicative mechanisms of social integration are assimilated to mechanisms of system integration, the symbolic reproduction of the lifeworld is cut off from the cultural and semantic resources on which it depends. There is no need here to go into the details of Habermas's conceptual distinction between system and lifeworld in order to grasp the consequences of a culturally and semantically impoverished lifeworld: "consumerism and possessive individualism, motives of performance, and competition gain the force to shape behaviour. The communicative practice of everyday life is one-sidedly rationalised into a utilitarian life-style; this . . . shift to purposive-rational action orientations calls forth the reaction of a hedonism freed from the pressures of rationality" (TCA2 325).

Given the extent to which Habermas's diagnosis of modern social pathologies incorporates the semantic degradation and cultural impoverishment of everyday life, one would expect that he would provide some account of how modernity might recover its semantic resources. One would expect that he would have something to say about how it might renew its cultural traditions or rescue valuable cultural contents whose possible renewal is deeply threatened. One would also expect that he might have something to say about what role philosophy might play under such conditions of semantic degradation. But no such account is provided, since Habermas is of the view that "philosophy has forfeited its contact with the extraordinary" (PT 51), and this it must forfeit if it is not willing to forfeit the cognitive achievements made possible by releasing itself from the grip of its metaphysical past.

Philosophy, even in its postmetaphysical form will be able neither to replace nor to suppress religion as long as religious language is the bearer of a semantic content which is inspiring, and even indispensable, for this content eludes (for the time being?) the explanatory force of philosophical language and continues to resist translation into reasoning discourses. (PT 51)

One must wonder about the fate of everyday life and everyday practices if Habermas's conclusion were warranted. It would seem that Habermas has not fully grasped the implications of his own diagnosis. If "[e]veryday consciousness is robbed of its power of synthesis" and "becomes fragmented" (TCA2 355), it can hardly be expected that everyday consciousness can recover its power to synthesize, can overcome its fragmented state, without the cultural and semantic resources whose depletion or exhaustion is the cause of its diminished powers of synthesis and the cause of its fragmentation. There is no justification given or sought as to why the communicative practice of everyday life can depend only on that kind of contact with the "extraordinary" provided by religious language; nor is there any explanation of what can be gained from such contact when its content eludes the clarifying and critical power of philosophical language, and resists translation into the languages of reason.

Habermas arrives at this rather pessimistic conclusion by misconstruing the nature of the "extraordinary," falsely opposing it to the everyday, by unduly limiting the scope of philosophy, and by discounting the transformative power of reason, claims I will elaborate and defend in parts III through V. Here I wish only to reiterate that Habermas's one-sided concern with the conditions of justice at the expense of a concern with the conditions of intelligibility and possibility not only undermines the potential of his theory of modernity but also exposes the shortcomings of his understanding of everyday practice. He is unable to provide a convincing account of how everyday communication can (eventually) "stand on its own two feet," once fully rationalized and fully posttraditional in nature, once "the interconnection of cognitive-instrumental elements with moral-practical and expressive elements, which obtained in everyday practice before it was rationalized . . . [are] retained at a higher level of differentiation" (TCA2 329). There is something like a leap of faith required here. Actually there are two leaps. One leap involves the belief that the very same processes of rationalization responsible for their erosion will replenish (eventually) the spent semantic and cultural resources. "The rationalization of a lifeworld is measured by the extent to which the rationality potentials built into communicative action and released in discourse penetrate lifeworld structures and set them aflow" (BFN 98). The possibility that the rationalization of the lifeworld is a process that can set lifeworld structures adrift as much as aflow (that there may be no way of theoretically deciding in advance whether it is a case of one or the other) is not taken as seriously as it should.

The other leap of faith follows from the first: the belief that public reason can correct the one-sided rationalization of everyday life *as though* its own power of synthesis were not imperiled by semantic degradation and cultural impoverishment. This leap of faith requires a view of the rationalization of the lifeworld as one that only enhances but never compromises the rationality potential of everyday communicative action—as though the reason latent in communicative action is impervious to the semantic degradation and cultural impoverishment of the lifeworld—as though it were in the lifeworld but not of it.

Both of these leaps of faith have their conceptual foundation in Habermas's strict separation between the right and the good, between questions of justice and questions of meaning, between the abstract form of communicatively structured lifeworlds and the cultural contents of any particular lifeworld. Habermas thinks of these distinctions not just as positions in an (unsettled!) argument about the meaning of modernity but as constitutive of its indisputable cognitive achievements. In this respect Habermas reproduces an error often made by Hegel, taking the cognitive content of his philosophical position as being identical with the cognitive content of modernity. That this strict separation cannot be maintained follows logically from Habermas's theoretically and empirically rich diagnoses of the "social pathologies" of modernity. It is very difficult to see how it can be intelligibly maintained if we are to comprehend and criticize the various means by which the totalizing and homogenizing practices of capitalist modernization threaten "the communicative infrastructure of any humane form of life." What sense can we give to the idea of a humane form of life if we cannot index it to some normatively compelling idea of what it means to be a human being?[60] And how could we possibly determine what a humane form of life could be if the semantic and cultural resources on which a compelling answer to this question depends are constantly eroded and rarely renewed?

Habermas often concedes that "without the support of the sociopolitical culture, which cannot be produced upon demand, the forms of communication adequate to practical reason cannot emerge" (BFN 489). Once he makes this concession, however, it is not clear what normative and critical status the rationalization of the lifeworld retains. What normative and critical standards does it provide if the "rationality potential built into communicative action and released in discourse" is unable to "penetrate lifeworld structures"? Here again we face a recurring dilemma: how is "discourse," communicative reason in its most reflexive and self-critical form, going to be effective if it is itself dependent on semantic resources that it is unable to replenish? This dilemma is certainly not favorably situated by a view of the lifeworld that is supposed to be the source of the solution to the problem it has created, but that in the end proves to be as semantically impoverished and incapacitated as those reflexive practices it was to support.

Given the scope of the problem I have described, it should now be clearer that the needs of democratic forms of life cannot be met by communicatively structured, discursive procedures of justification alone—no matter how reflexive they may become. Alternative possibilities of meaning and action need to be disclosed if the activities of justification are to go beyond the current boundaries of possibility—if they are to move within larger horizons of significance and relevance than these boundaries currently allow. In so far as reasons are always couched in a vocabulary, and in so far as possibility is a function of vocabulary, the need for new or alternative vocabularies of evaluation and understanding will always arise. Social reality will need to be disclosed anew, again and again—not in some "extra-mundane" realm but within everyday practices, through which practices the contents of cultural traditions are renewed. This entails that everyday practices need to be renewed, their semantic resources recovered, and it means that the everyday must be theoretically and practically reclaimed rather than taken for granted (as that which is taken for granted).

If we are to rescue the semantic and cultural resources necessary to a flourishing everyday practice, we will require much more than public or communicative reason is able to provide—no matter how publicly or communicatively mediated it is. The public use of reason is a necessary but insufficient condition of rescuing everyday practice. Concomitantly, the public or communicative use of reason is a necessary but insufficient condition for opening and preserving the very spaces, the "clearings," in which public reason can flourish. Of course, one can respond in good Habermasian fashion with the suggestion that communicative or public reason must be open to semantic and cultural innovation, to alternative ways of speaking and acting. From the perspective of public reason, however, these sorts of activities are viewed as *external* to reason, not as initiated *by* reason. And so they must be viewed, since public reason is construed procedurally. In other words, the normative content of public or communicative reason is identical with the rationality of its procedures. However, normative procedures, such as those that ensure the right of all those affected by a moral or political or legal norm to assent or withhold assent from the norm in question, do not answer our need for richer sources of intelligibility than we currently possess, our need to see what is at issue in this or that political or legal norm in larger horizons of significance and relevance, our need to go beyond the current boundaries of possibility.

5   "To Make Conscious a Murky Reality"

The preceding considerations were meant to shift attention from Habermas's unsuccessful attempt to establish internal links between Heidegger's philosophy and his politics to problems within Habermas's own philosophical project. I have tried to show that his failure convincingly to establish these internal links points to larger problems that are directly connected to the shortcomings of his response to the issues raised by the idea of disclosure. These problems show up even in Habermas's attempt to support his claim that Heidegger's philosophy was the victim of a "scientifically unfiltered diagnosis of crisis." In "Work and *Weltan-schauung*," Habermas everywhere alludes to the "lasting insights" of Heidegger's critique of reason—to "critical insights which have not been superseded even today" (WW 202/195). Yet Habermas also claims that in the very period in which Heidegger was producing these "lasting insights" his thinking had contracted "a dark alliance with scientifically unexamined diagnoses of the times" (WW 193). Moreover Habermas argues that the post-1929 Heidegger "strayed into the regions of a thinking *beyond* philosophy, *beyond* argumentation itself" (WW 202); strayed into "a sublime, primordially operative domain that is removed from all empirical (and ultimately all argumentative) grasp" (WW 193).

If this is indeed the case, Habermas needs very much to explain how a thinking that strayed into regions "*beyond* philosophy, *beyond* argumentation,' and 'removed from *all* empirical . . . grasp" can produce insights that he also claims "have not been superseded even today". He needs very much to answer the question not only *how* Heidegger could produce such insights, but also how—given the regions into which his thinking strayed—Habermas (and we) came to have access to them. And he is very much obligated to clarify the status of a critique of reason that is capable of producing "lasting insights" but that must nonetheless be held in the utmost suspicion on methodological as well as on moral and political grounds. Moreover it very much requires some reflection on how it is that we are to engage in and make sense of our attempts to think anew from a new stance. Habermas's rejection of Heidegger's thinking because it goes beyond the established boundaries of philosophy and argumentation would seem to preclude the value and validity of *any* attempt to think anew from a new stance, to stray beyond the already familiar and accepted modes of philosophical argument. I don't think Habermas would welcome this implication, but it is one that is a recurring feature of his attitude towards disclosure and to the new as such (examined in part V, chapter 1, below).

This way of interpreting Heidegger's thinking, whatever its philosophical merits, has the wholly undesirable consequence of reinforcing, and unintentionally endorsing, an image of Heidegger very dear to Heidegger himself (and to uncritical Heideggerians). That is the image of Heidegger as a "magician," a dark "genius," with an uncanny power to snatch philosophical gold from the surging waters of the Rhine. This is certainly a conclusion that cannot recommend itself. By exaggerating the discontinuity between earlier and later Heidegger, and by exaggerating the discontinuity between Heidegger and the German philosophical tradition, Habermas adds to rather than explodes Heidegger's "aura." And it commits him to a position that his own engagement with Heidegger's texts belies: that Heidegger's texts are beyond evaluation and criticism.

The implications of this unwelcome conclusion do have the advantage, however, of exposing the assumptions governing Habermas's conception of philosophy, argument, and reason. Heidegger's later philosophy does present a host of difficulties that conventional forms of philosophical presentation and inquiry do not, but these are hardly beyond the reach of standard hermeneutic practices of clarification—otherwise, we would be in no position to talk about *insights*. So it is not so much that Heidegger's thinking moves into regions beyond philosophy and beyond argument, but rather, that it moves beyond Habermas's narrowly procedural conception of philosophy and argument. There is no room within a procedural conception for the practice of reflective disclosure, and the idea that there can be normative criteria by which to assess such a practice will seem rather queer, if not completely unintelligible. And that is why Habermas is unable ultimately to distinguish between what is actually insightful and what is merely ideological in Heidegger's fusion of *Zeitdiagnose* with an ontological critique of reason. He is unable do make this distinction because he has failed to address systematically the question of just what makes one *Zeitdiagnose*, one reflective disclosure, *better* than another.

In the late 1970s, at a time before the issue of world disclosure had become an issue, Habermas took up the question of whether *Zeitdiagnosen* were capable of producing any insights at all. Appropriately enough, it was on the occasion of the publication of volume 1,000 of *Edition Suhrkamp*, a collection of essays edited by Habermas and devoted to *Observations on "The Spiritual Situation of the Age."* Given the time-diagnostic purpose of this collection, one would expect that this question might receive sustained and serious attention. This proves not to be the case; still, what Habermas did have to say about the peculiar activity of *Zeitdiagnose* is of some value. For one, he grants that there is "a diagnostic core" to social-scientific analyses and philosophical theories, and recognizes that they define the perspective from which the diagnosis of the *Zeitgeist* must proceed. Nonetheless, the impression Habermas conveys is that the activity of *Zeitdiagnose* involves something of an indulgence for any self-respecting intellectual. Anyone who seriously engages in this interpretive activity with the intention of saying something useful about how things now stand in the world cannot hide "the subjectivity of the gesture with which the author seeks to pull together the richly pleated garment of existing realities—with which he attempts to locate a more than merely subjective unity in the latter's multiplicity" (SS 5). The possibility of insight is compromised right from the start, claims Habermas, by the assumption that a diagnosis of the times can completely illuminate the social totality, as though the philosophical critic enjoyed a uniquely privileged access to the totality as a whole. "Undaunted by the traps the social sciences could set, he dares to confront the totality directly" (SS 3). One need only substitute "undaunted by the traps the social sciences could set "with" unfiltered by any knowledge of the social sciences" (WW 188), to see how effortlessly this remark is transferable to Habermas's critique of Heidegger in "Work and *Weltanschauung*."

But the significance of this remark resides most of all in the fact that it brings together in one concise statement Habermas's two main objections to the activity of *Zeitdiagnose*: (1) that it proceeds without proper social-scientific methods of inquiry and testing and (2) that it is based on the assumption that individual philosophers can confront the totality directly. Taken together, these two objections draw the limits that any *Zeitdiagnose* must respect if it is not to slide into subjectivism or enter into dark alliances with suspect ideologies. It would seem, then, that contrary to my claim above, Habermas does offer criteria for deciding between better and worse *Zeitdiagnosen*. However, it would be a mistake if we were to take these objections as providing adequate criteria, let alone, the right kind of criteria. For example, if we look at whether these objections apply to reflective disclosure, we find that we can quickly dispense with the second objection. Heidegger's view of disclosure altogether precludes the idea of interpretive *Zeitdiagnosen* that can confront the totality directly. We can never have direct access to the totality as such, for whatever of it we can make explicit depends logically on that totality, on an implicit background that is never within our means to survey completely or render fully explicit. In this respect Heidegger would readily concur with Habermas's second objection, but he would disagree with Habermas's rather hasty conclusion that the practice of *Zeitdiagnose* is unavoidably subjectivistic and utterly lacking the fallibilistic consciousness that distinguishes the social and natural sciences.

Zeitdiagnosen, like practices of reflective disclosure in general, are interpretive practices self-consciously constrained by the hermeneutic circle: they are fallibilistic and antisubjectivistic from the outset. In so far as these interpretive constraints are respected, it is not clear what kind of traps the social sciences can lay for unwary practitioners of *Zeitdiagnose*; indeed it is not clear just what the first objection really amounts to, for when pressed, it simply collapses into the second. If *Zeitdiagnosen* are understood as practices of disclosure that are fallibilistic by definition, it is not obvious what they additionally stand to gain from the social sciences in this respect. Of course, it goes without saying that a great deal might be gained from co-operation with the social sciences, and that such cooperation should be fostered and encouraged; however, whatever might result from such cooperation, the contribution of the social sciences to the practice of *Zeit-diagnose* is not going to consist in correcting for the lack of a fallibilistic orientation. Nor is it going to consist in a "value-free" methodology for evaluating world-disclosing *Zeitdiagnosen*—a social-scientifically guaran-teed immunity to ideology (against which even the social sciences, as Habermas is aware, cannot be immunized).

The objections Habermas raises are based on a very selective and very narrow range of sample *Zeitdiagnosen*. He cites as evidence of the intellec-tually unsound nature of this undertaking the naïve, immodest, and ulti-mately futile attempts of Luckacs and Jaspers to illuminate the totality as a whole, either in the name of the class struggle or of a critique of modern civilization. Though their way of engaging in *Zeitdiagnose* hardly exhausts its actual and possible practice, Habermas does not hesitate to consign the practice to the past: "All this has become obsolete. What has not become obsolete, however, is the duty of intellectuals to react with partiality and objectivity, with sensitivity and incorruptibility, to movements, develop-mental tendencies, dangers, and critical moments. *It is the task of intellec-tuals to make conscious a murky reality*" (SS 3, my emphasis). No sooner does Habermas consign the practice to the past than he places himself in a very familiar predicament. To say that it is the "task of intellectuals to make conscious a murky reality" appears very close to saying that it is the task of intellectuals to engage in world-disclosing diagnoses of social reality. Making conscious a murky reality sounds like a decent enough definition of disclosure—sounds a lot like a "bringing-forth (*Hervorbringen*) of some-thing concealed in unconcealment (*Unverborgenheit*)," to use Heidegger's more ponderous language.[61]

If making conscious a murky reality is an essential duty of critical intel-lectuals, should we not be able to say something about what counts as a successful instance of a murky reality made less murky? Habermas's pro-vides only negative examples of *Zeitdiagnose*, and has nothing to say about any of those that have produced insight. Without some normative cri-teria—by which I do not mean fixed criteria—of distinguishing between better and worse *Zeitdiagnosen*, and without some account of how this practice could either be improved or rendered obsolete by the social sciences, Habermas is in no position to back up the claim that Heidegger's "diagnosis of the times" is suspect because it did not meet social-scientific standards of inquiry and testing. Instead, he is left with the unenviable conundrum of how to explain the "unscientific," nonrational production of "lasting insights"—a conundrum that arises because of Habermas's reluctance to accept the world-disclosing role of philosophy, to acknowledge it as necessary and legitimate response to the need to think anew from a new stance. For Habermas any such acceptance leads unavoidably to an "aestheticization" of philosophy, to a philosophical practice that is directed away from "innerworldly" problems and thereby disconnected from learning processes initiated by an engagement with the challenges such problems pose.

This brings us to the most fundamental philosophical difference dividing Habermas from Heidegger, a philosophical difference that gets played out in terms of an opposition between reason and disclosure. As I have already urged elsewhere, we must reject the terms of this opposition.[62] A great deal of what Heidegger wrote does provide Habermas with more than adequate warrant to support the claim that Heidegger did not have an ear for reason-giving speech (begründende Rede), particularly if we do not press too hard the question what reason can mean. But Habermas, for his part, does not have an ear for the plurality of voices in which reason can speak, which plurality is too quickly subsumed by the merely *procedural* "unity of reason." The plurality of voices in which reason speaks is not subsumable by or reducible to any procedural unity of reason: the normativity of procedures is but *one* of the voices in which reason speaks. And so it is the central thesis of this book that any conception of reason that cannot recognize the activity of disclosing the world anew as one of reason's own is not just deeply flawed; it is blind and self-alienating. It casts to historical contingency and to nonrational forces one of modernity's most esteemed ideals: the self-conscious and self-critical transformation of our social practices and our cultural self-understanding.

III Another Voice of Reason

1 A New Orientation for the Critique of Reason

No book has publicly defined the identity of recent critical theory as much as *The Philosophical Discourse of Modernity*. And none has made more apparent its difficult and uncomfortable relation to the German philosophical tradition. In many respects this text sets the terms under which the German philosophical tradition may be inherited: what may be continued, what discontinued. The question, of course, is whether the terms are rightly set, set to enable rather than thwart the renewal of critical theory. This question can also be put in the following way: Does this interpretation of critical theory make it more receptive or less receptive to its calling?

As he has done so often before in the context of other critical debates, Habermas masterfully reconstructs the "philosophical discourse of modernity," identifying the intransigent, ambivalent source of its understanding of modernity: the philosophy of the subject.[1] From this identical source, argues Habermas, issues not just the rather confident and optimistic picture of modernity characteristic of the Enlightenment but also the increasingly skeptical and pessimistic picture of modernity characteristic of our own time. Part of the overall aim of Habermas's reconstruction is to expose and explain the ineliminable aporiai into which the philosophical discourse of modernity has repeatedly been led—ineliminable because they inhere in the premises of the philosophy of the subject. Since he aims to reconstruct, and not just deconstruct, the philosophical discourse of modernity, Habermas also identifies those of its normative features deserving of retrieval. Although he claims unequivocally that the paradigm of philosophy of the subject is exhausted, he is also convinced that its normative content can be retrieved and successfully reformulated in terms of the paradigm of linguistic intersubjectivity. If approached in the way Habermas suggests, the philosophical discourse of modernity can be unblocked, and rather than reiterating the same old insights, it can become the bearer of new insights.

The lectures comprising *The Philosophical Discourse of Modernity* revolve around two rather elaborate arguments, both of which take narrative form. With the *first* of these, Habermas traces the apparently unavoidable grief that comes to any inquiry that begins from the premises of the philosophy of the subject. Reminiscent of Hegel's procedure in the *Phenomenology of Spirit*, this argument shows how irresolvable paradoxes and anomalies arise whenever knowledge, particularly self-knowledge, is modeled exclusively on the knowledge of objects, through which modeling reason is rendered identical with the activities by which human beings represent and objectify what they encounter in the world. By regarding correct representation and, thereby, successful intervention in the world as constitutive of the distinctively human relationship to the world, "Occidental self-understanding" becomes the perpetrator and victim of its own self-misunderstanding.

As long as Occidental self-understanding views human beings as distinguished in their relationship to the world by their monopoly on encountering entities, knowing and dealing with objects, making true statements, and implementing plans, reason remains confined ontologically, epistemologically, or in terms of linguistic analysis, to only one of its dimensions. The relationship of the human being to the world is cognitivistically reduced: Ontologically, the world is reduced to the world of entities as a whole (as the totality of objects that can be represented and of existing states of affairs); epistemologically, our relationship to that world is reduced to the capacity to know existing states of affairs or to bring them about in a purposive-rational fashion; semantically, it is reduced to fact-stating discourse in which assertoric sentences are used—and no validity claim is admitted besides propositional truth. (PDM 311)

In any philosophical paradigm modeled on the knowledge of objects, the subject must relate to itself both as something distinct and as just one more object encountered in the world. Self-objectification is the confounding outcome of the subject's attempt to render itself theoretically and practically perspicuous *as a subject*, since it must bend "back upon itself as object, in order to grasp itself as in a mirror image" (PDM 18). Rather than becoming more perspicuous to itself, the subject finds that its attempts are blocked by its very status as one more object in the world—albeit, an object with some puzzling features. Thus it "renders itself at once opaque and dependent in the very acts that are supposed to secure self-knowledge and autonomy" (PDM 55). Self-knowledge becomes equivalent to self-alienation, autonomy to self-repression. So, to the extent that "reason is grounded in the principle of subjectivity" (another term of art for the philosophy of the subject), it will display ineliminable repressive features, since those features turn out to be structural properties of the "principle of subjectivity" itself.

As long as the basic concepts of the philosophy of consciousness lead us to understand knowledge exclusively as knowledge of something in the objective world, rationality is assessed by how the isolated subject orients himself to representational and propositional contents. Subject-centred reason finds its criteria in standards of truth and success that govern the relationships of knowing and purposively acting subjects to the world of possible objects and states of affairs. By contrast, as soon as we conceive of knowledge as communicatively mediated, rationality is assessed in terms of the capacity of responsible participants in interaction to orient themselves in relation to validity claims geared to intersubjective recognition. (PDM 314)

Of the two arguments that structure *The Philosophical Discourse of Modernity*, this first argument—let's call it the metacritique of subject-centered reason—is by far the most successful. While the context in which it is deployed is new, the argument itself is not. It is a recapitulation of the argument of *The Theory of Communicative Action*, transposed from the relative sobriety of social theory to the rather heady atmosphere of post-structuralist and postmodernist critiques of the universalistic claims of modern reason. Most of the attention that this book has received has been devoted to this argument as an interpretive and evaluative frame for coming to grips with the most recent skeptical challenges to modern reason and to the Enlightenment project.

Habermas's metacritique of subject-centered reason is not just directed at the methodological solipsism that characterizes the philosophy of consciousness from Descartes to Husserl. Much more encompassing in scope, its goal is to expose as instances of a degenerating philosophical paradigm the failure of various prior and contemporary attempts to break free of the subject-centered premises of modern philosophy. It is no accident that the transition to Habermas's paradigm of mutual understanding is proposed in the penultimate lecture, since its appearance there is essential to the narrative structure of the lectures. Above all, the metacritique of subject-centered reason consists of a nuanced and dialectical defense of modern reason out of which emerges a potentially nonobjectifying, nonrepressive conception—one might even say, a *vision*—of reason. This is the most valuable part of the book, not least because of its positive suggestions for how to (re)inherit the philosophical discourse of modernity initiated by Kant and Hegel, a discourse particularly central to the tradition of German critical theory.

To be sure, the claim that self-alienation and self-repression is an unavoidable consequence of any relation to self in which the subject relates to itself as to an object is hardly new. As Habermas points out, this claim was already ably defended in Hegel's earliest criticisms of the Enlightenment's excessively narrow, unavoidably authoritarian interpretations of subjectivity, criticisms reiterated many times since, most forcefully from within the German tradition. Additionally Hegel had established the fatal connection between the modern understanding of subjectivity grounded on knowledge of objects and the repressive dimension of reason. Habermas's proposed shift of the theoretical paradigm "from knowledge of objects to mutual understanding in language" is also not entirely new, since the execution of such a shift was also the central motive of Hegel's program. The transition from "consciousness" to "self-consciousness" in the *Phenomenology of Spirit* is likewise intended to demonstrate the necessity of reconceiving the relation between subject and object, mind and world, in terms of the relation between mutually recognizing subjects.[2] This shift from a subject-object to a subject-subject model will entail placing the problems of truth, objectivity, freedom, justice, and the like, within a theory of intersubjectivity (or, if one prefers Hegel to Habermas, a philosophy of "spirit").

Between Hegel's time and our own, however, the concern with redefining reason in terms of a "vision" of human emancipation and flourishing, a rather grand enterprise to be sure, has been forgotten, buried, or abandoned. This is due partly to the radically original conception of reason proposed by German Idealism, one that goes completely against the grain of the predominantly epistemological construal of rationality as a medium or instrument of knowledge.[3] But it is also due to deflationary pressure, pressure that forces reason to downsize considerably its scope and power. Today anyone attempting to renew the attempt to think of reason as an agency of individual and cultural transformation will appear naïve, a little softheaded, and hopelessly romantic. For in addition to the powerful hold that the epistemological-cum-instrumental picture of reason maintains over our philosophical imaginations, the appeal of reason as an agency of radical social change, as the vehicle of emancipatory projects, has lost its romance. We are more inclined to associate the "romanticism" that fuels such projects with irrationalism and the metaphysical yearning for absolutes than with the idea of human emancipation and flourishing. In effect, what we have witnessed during the course of the last century is the drain of utopian energies from the idea of reason, energies that once propelled the realization of reason within a vision of human emancipation and freedom.

Habermas's position in this philosophical history of reason is not as obviously or characteristically romantic as Hegel's, since he has made clear that he rejects the more immodest metaphysical claims of German Idealism. And although he has proposed a detranscendentalized (but not deflationary) conception of reason, his position remains distinctive, and unique. In contrast to contemporaries such as John Rawls and Hilary Putnam, whose views of reason, especially practical reason, are close to his own, Habermas remains attached to an ideal of reason that is genuinely, if not explicitly, romantic. He has, in his own way, kept the romance with reason alive. Only someone as romantically attached to reason could mount as magnificent a defense of reason against the onslaught of skeptical attacks arising from within his own tradition, particularly by theorists influenced by Nietzsche and Heidegger. Unlike many of his Anglo-American contemporaries, Habermas did not rest content with offering pithy dismissals of postmodernist and poststructuralist "continental" thinkers; he intervened in the heady debates about the fate of modernity with a book-length set of lectures of considerable philosophical and historical depth.

Unlike Kant and Hegel before him, Habermas has the added burden of having to contend with more than a century of intensifying skepticism toward reason, a skepticism whose cogency relied on the historical effects of a barbarous century as much as on compelling philosophical arguments. Under such circumstances a thinker who is as historically and sociologically informed as Habermas will not find especially welcome the call to defend even a very modest vision of reason against its ubiquitous skeptical challenges. Only someone who still believed in reason, who preserved his faith in reason as a self-educating medium, as a palpable force in human history, a force possessing its own retraceable history (of success and failure), would be willing to respond to such an onerous call.[4]

But besides offering an appropriately modest version of the idealist vision of reason, what does Habermas actually contribute to the philosophical discourse of modernity that is new, that is more than a skilfully rewoven fabric of insights, however venerable, already famously expressed by *die Liebhaber und Verächter der Vernunft*? To this particular debate, Habermas has contributed something significant: "a *new orientation* for the critique of reason" (PDM 312). Although he accepts the full force of the critique of subject-centered reason from Nietzsche and Heidegger to Foucault and Derrida, Habermas does not accept its conclusions concerning the potential of modern reason. According to Habermas, their analyses lead to the conclusion that there is no other way out of the aporiai of the philosophy of the subject, no escape from the repressive effects of modern reason, except by appeal to an ambiguously and vaguely articulated "other of reason." Apparently this variously articulated "other" acts as a placeholder for all that reason excludes: "dreams, fantasies, madness, orgiastic excitement, ecstasy . . . the aesthetic, body-centred experiences of a decentred subjectivity" (PDM 306).

By contrast, the new orientation for the critique of reason Habermas proposes is made possible by a very different diagnosis of Western "logocentrism"; rather than attributing responsibility for the various pathologies of modern social life to an *excess* of reason, Habermas attributes responsibility to a *deficit* of reason (PDM 310). It is not a matter of too much logocentrism, but of not enough. Marshaling an insight of dialectical thought, Habermas insists on grasping both sides of the historical process through which quite different dimensions of reason are suppressed and divided.

Subject-centred reason is the *product of division and usurpation,* indeed of a social process in the course of which a subordinated moment assumes the place of the whole, without having the power to assimilate the structure of the whole. Horkheimer and Adorno have, like Foucault, described this process of a self-overburdening and self-reifying subjectivity as a world-historical process. But both sides missed its deeper irony, which consists in the fact that the communicative potential of reason first had to be released in the patterns of modern lifeworlds before the unfettered imperatives of the economic and administrative subsystems could react back on the vulnerable practice of everyday life and could thereby promote the cognitive-instrumental dimension to domination over the suppressed moments of practical reason. The communicative potential of reason has been simultaneously developed and distorted in the course of capitalist modernisation. (PDM 315)

Drawing once again on this dialectically inflected insight of critical theory, Habermas has succeeded in considerably weakening any critique of reason that proceeds one-sidedly, leaving unaccounted the very ironic circumstance he vividly describes here and elsewhere. It is not just the insight common to Marx and Horkheimer that reason is capable of sustaining humane as well as inhumane forms of life; it is also the insight that the possible humanity or inhumanity of any form of life will depend on *which* aspects of reason, and *which* configuration of those aspects, the members of that form of life embrace. It is this insight, then, that serves as the justification for Habermas's conceptual and polemical distinction between the "radical critics of reason" (a.k.a. Nietzsche, Heidegger, Foucault, et al.), on the one hand, and the tradition of the Young Hegelians (in which he places himself), on the other. And it is this insight that allows

Habermas to do what the radical critics of modernity are apparently unable to do: to put the bounce back in the "dialectic of enlightenment."

2   The Metacritique of Disclosure

The proposed new orientation for the critique of reason is not, however, what is most significantly new about Habermas's intervention in *The Philosophical Discourse of Modernity*; what is most significantly new is to be found in the second argument of the lectures, providing the real key to the philosophical drama enacted in it. This second, largely unsuccessful argument, is a response to the multifaceted challenge posed by Heidegger's notion of world disclosure, renewed with considerable success in Michel Foucault's genealogical and archaeological inquiries, Jacques Derrida's deconstructive enterprise, Cornelius Castoriadis's revamped praxis philosophy, Richard Rorty's neo-pragmatism, and Charles Taylor's ontological critique of naturalist epistemology. It is from the response to this challenge that Habermas's lectures receive their urgency, their sense of mission, and much of their polemical bite. One could say that in the 1980s the challenge of world disclosure awoke Habermas, if not from a "dogmatic slumber," then from a certain complacency. Suddenly a term of art rarely (to my knowledge, never) employed in Habermas's pre–*Philosophical Discourse of Modernity* writings became a ubiquitous part of his vocabulary, and by extension the vocabulary of contemporary critical theory.[5]

Even if I am right to claim that Habermas has misconstrued the nature of this challenge, there is no question that he comprehended its seriousness. Not only did it directly challenge his "postmetaphysical" attempt to establish the *context-transcending* power of reason, it represented an increasingly influential form of skepticism arising from within his own tradition—from that very part of it that demands "critical, indeed distrustful, appropriation." And so, it is into this second argument, the *metacritique of disclosure*, that Habermas poured most of his considerable polemical and philosophical energy.

In order to support my claim that it is really the second argument that constitutes the heart of this book, I would like to run together a number of citations from different chapters of *The Philosophical Discourse of Modernity*. I wish first to show that it is the skeptical implications of world disclosure that most concern Habermas throughout the book, and second, that the identical criticisms reappear in different contexts, and in the assessment of different theorists, reiterating over and over again, the same points, the same worries. But also I want to dispense with one of these recurring criticisms right off the top. Habermas repeatedly claims that recourse to the idea of disclosure involves a tacit reversion to the figures of thought of transcendental philosophy. Just as in the early Heidegger "solipsistically posited Dasein once again occupies the place of transcendental subjectivity" (PDM 150), in the later Heidegger, "the *productivity* of the creation of meaning that discloses a world passes over [from Dasein] to *Being* itself" (PDM 152). This same criticism is made against the later Heidegger's view of language, renewed by Taylor, among others: "The world-disclosing function of language is conceived on analogy with the generative accomplishments of transcendental consciousness, prescinding, naturally, from the sheerly formal and supratemporal character of the latter" (PDM 319).

As I argued previously in part II, Habermas is unable to defend this claim, because it rests on a fundamental misunderstanding of what disclosure means, the problems it was meant to overcome, and dissolve. It is on account of this misunderstanding that Habermas places the idea of disclosure in the unreceptive and alien framework of the philosophy of consciousness. Because Habermas's regards the philosophy of consciousness as "the basic figure of thought used in the philosophy of the subject" (CA 218), he treats them as synonymous, the aporiai of one being identical to the aporiai of the other. "If the subject relates to itself at the same time as it knows its objects, then it encounters itself in the double position of being both a single empirical entity in the world and as the transcendental subject facing the world as a whole. It finds itself in the position of being one amongst many and as one against all. . . . Between these two positions of the subject there is no space left for the symbolically prestructured, linguistically constituted domains of culture, society, and socialised individuals" (CA 218). Obviously this criticism does not apply to Heidegger's notion of disclosure, or to his view of human beings as disclosers, since it is just this "symbolically prestructured, linguistically constituted domains of culture, society and socialised individuals" the notion of disclosure was meant to reveal, and explain (as Habermas occasionally concedes).

I want to focus now on what constitutes the more central criticisms supporting the second argument, criticisms that reveal the skeptical worries that motivate them. As I already indicated at the close of part I, Habermas claims that in their attempts to provide an account of semantic, normative, and cultural change, Heidegger and other disclosure theorists absolutize linguistic world disclosure. Thereby they devalue the problem-solving and action-coordinating functions of language and reason, devalue every-day practice, and devalue the cognitive claims of philosophy. In order to bring out both the content and homogeneity of the these criticisms, I have organized them into recurring leitmotifs that appear again and again across various contexts. In the following sequence, they are aimed, in order, at Heidegger, Derrida, Rorty, Foucault, Castoriadis, and, finally, at anyone who wishes to draw on and develop the notion of disclosure.

The luminous force of world-disclosing language is hypostatized. It no longer has to *prove* itself by its capacity to throw light on beings in the world. Heidegger sup-poses that beings can be opened up in their being with *equal* ease by *any* given approach. He fails to see that the horizon of the understanding of meaning brought to bear on beings is not *prior*, but rather, *subordinate* to, the question of truth. (PDM 154, my emphasis)

[F]or Derrida, linguistically mediated processes within the world are embedded in a *world-constituting* context that *prejudices* everything; they are *fatalistically* delivered up to the unmanageable happening of text production, *overwhelmed* by the poetic-creative transformation of a background designed by arche-writing, and condemned to be provincial. An aesthetic contextualism blinds him to the fact that everyday communicative practice makes learning processes possible (thanks to built-in ideali-zations) in relation to which the world-disclosing force of interpreting language has in turn to *prove* its worth. (PDM 205, emphasis added)

According to Rorty, science and morality, economics and politics, are delivered up to a process of language-creating protuberances *in just the same way* as art and phi-losophy . . . [T]he Nietzschean pathos of a *Lebensphilosophie* that has made the lin-guistic turn beclouds the sober insights of pragmatism; in the picture painted by Rorty, the renovative process of linguistic world-disclosure no longer has a *counter-poise* in the *testing* processes of intramundane practice. (PDM 206, added emphasis)

It is these [Heidegger's epochal understanding of "being" or Foucault's "formation rules for a given discourse"] that are supposed to *first* make possible the meaning of entities and the validity of statements with the horizon of a given world or of an established discourse Both also agree that world horizons or discourse formations undergo change; but in these changes, they maintain their *transcendental* power over whatever unfolds *within* the totalities shaped by them. (PDM 254, added emphasis)

[The] concept of language used by Castoriadis permits *no* differentiation between meaning and validity. As with Heidegger, the "truth" of semantic world-disclosure also founds the propositional truth of statements; it *prejudices* the validity of lin-guistic utterances generally. As a result, intramundane praxis cannot get learning processes going. (PDM 330, my emphasis)

Speaking subjects are either *masters* or *shepherds* of their linguistic systems. Either they make use of language in a way that is creative of meaning, to disclose their world innovatively, or they are always already moving around within a horizon of world-disclosure taken care of for them by language itself and constantly shifting behind their backs. . . . No matter whether this metahistorical transformation of linguistic world views is conceived of as Being, differánce, power, or imagination, and whether it is endowed with connotations of a mystical experience of salvation, of aesthetic shock of creaturely pain, or creative intoxication: What *all* these concepts have in common is the peculiar *uncoupling* of the horizon-constituting productivity of language from the consequences of an intramundane practice that is wholly *prejudiced* by the linguistic system. *Any* interaction between world-disclosing language and learning processes in the world is *excluded*. (PDM 318–319, my emphasis)

The recurring criticisms and worries manifest in these and many other identically phrased passages in the modernity lectures, and in a number of subsequent texts, consist of three basic objections: (1) Throughout its various applications, all those who employ the notion of world disclosure proceed on the assumption that the understanding *of* the world disclosed by language (and everyday practices) possesses a transcendental power over what happens *in* the world. Thus ontology dictates history: one can only undergo (ecstatically) the meaning of this or that understanding of being; one cannot reflectively resist it or transcend it. The prior disclosure of meaning horizons overwhelms everyday practices, setting firmly in advance the boundaries of cultural possibility. (2) Given this assumption, any disclosure of the world would seem to preclude the very possibility of learning, since what can be learned in the world is dictated in advance by the prior understanding of the world operative in any given historical context. That would mean that there can be no interaction between world disclosing language and learning processes that is not already hardwired in the relevant language or social practice. (3) Finally, all disclosure theorists from Heidegger to Foucault, Rorty, Derrida, Taylor, and Castoriadis make the same mistake: they forget that a world-disclosing language or world-disclosing practice is not prior but subordinate to the question truth (or validity). World-disclosing language or practice has to be tested against the world it is supposed to illuminate.

The cogency of these and related criticisms will themselves be tested throughout this part of the book. To anticipate a little, I will argue that all of these criticisms fail, often by their own lights. Indeed Habermas's metacritique of disclosure turns out to be rather incoherent, weakening rather than strengthening the case for a "new orientation for the critique of reason." To strengthen the first argument of the modernity lectures, we need to rethink the notion of disclosure, approaching it not as one more skeptical challenge to reason, to philosophy, and to the finer ideals of

modernity, but as an occasion and as a resource for normatively reformulating our conception of them.

3 Invoking the "Other" of Reason

The two arguments that comprise *The Philosophical Discourse of Modernity*
were meant mutually to reinforce one another. By expanding the meaning
of reason, the first argument is supposed to undercut critiques of reason
that seek to convict modern reason as inherently exclusive, generating an
"other of reason" by what it excludes. Although Habermas's first argument
succeeds in showing that reason is not inherently exclusive, his own model
of communicative reason fails to meet its own standards for a nonexclu-
sionary alternative to "instrumental" or "subject-centered" reason.
Habermas did manage to enlarge the meaning of reason by expanding the
bases of intersubjective justification and by locating the sources for such
an expansion within everyday practice itself. Rightly contesting the logo-
centric confinement of reason to the assertoric use of language and to
propositional truth, he showed successfully that a pragmatic theory of
meaning can open truth-like dimensions of validity in connection with
the rightness of norms and the truthfulness of expressions. This is a considerable, but not unchallengeable, achievement. However, the expanded
conception of reason that this produces cannot do all the work Habermas
wants it to do. Certainly, it does not "dissolve the symptoms of exhaustion" that Habermas detects in the so-called philosophy of the subject
(PDM 296). The change to the paradigm of linguistic intersubjectivity does
not dissolve so much as induce once again the symptoms of exhaustion
besetting every conception of reason that restricts reason to its preferred
dimension, be it to the knowledge and control of objects or to intersubjective procedures of justification (whether contextualistically or univer-
salistically conceived). And that is why, as we will see, "symptoms of
exhaustion" reappear again and again in Habermas's argument against
world disclosure, an argument that fails largely because of the narrowness
of the conception of reason on which it depends.

  To preempt an objection that can be raised about the fairness of my treatment of Habermas's response to the challenge of world disclosure, I should
like to acknowledge that Habermas's decision to focus on its skeptical
implications was not entirely unwarranted, for those very implications
were often emphasized by Heidegger and other (not all) disclosure

theorists, particularly Foucault, Derrida, and Rorty. However, in the same dialectical move that allowed him to rescue the potential of reason from its specific, one-sided incarnation in subject-centered reason, he could have also rescued the rational potential of disclosure. This more accommodating and more philosophically consistent move would have prevented communicative reason from entering into a hostile relation with its own "other"—an "other" entirely of its own making. Habermas's inclination to treat the intellectual attraction to the idea of disclosure as part of, as continuous with, a fatalistic or ecstatic "refuge in something wholly Other" (PT 8) is evidence of a unjustifiable narrowness in Habermas conception of reason, and an exclusionary tendency that is supposed to be the distinctive characteristic of subject-centered, not communicative, reason.[6]

The metacritique of subject-centered reason identifies as the central mistake of the deconstructive critique of reason the tendency to conceive of reason solely in terms of the model of exclusion. In that model reason appears as a subjugating power that excludes and represses all that is not identical with itself. The model of "exclusive reason" represents the activity of reason as inherently, as inimically, opposed to all that is "other" to reason. According to Habermas, this image of reason not only presents a distorted image of what reason is (and can be); it also presents a distorted image of reason's "other."

Only if reason shows itself to be essentially narcissistic—an identifying, only seemingly universal power, bent upon self-assertion and particular self-aggrandizement, subjugating everything around it as an object—can the other of reason be thought for its part as a spontaneous, creative power that is at the ground of Being, a power that is simultaneously vital and opaque, that is no longer illuminated by any spark of reason. Only reason as reduced to the subjective faculty of understanding and purposive activity corresponds to the image of an *exclusive* reason that further uproots itself the more it strives triumphantly for the heights, until withered, it falls victim to the power of its concealed heterogeneous origins. The dynamism of self-destruction, in which the secret of the dialectic of enlightenment supposedly comes to light, can only function if reason cannot produce anything from itself except that naked power to which it actually hopes to provide an alternative, namely the *unforced force of the better insight*. (PDM 305, my emphasis, trans. altered)

Reworking a distinction central to Kant and German Idealism, the distinction between *die Vernunft* and *der Verstand*, reason and the understanding, Habermas argues from the standpoint of a differentiated, normatively enlarged conception of reason (*Vernunft*), one that is irreducible to subject-centered reason (*Verstand*). Rather than reclaiming the non-instrumental dimensions of practical reason latent in everyday life, the radical critics of reason neglect them in the name of an aestheticized "potential for excitement, stylized into the other of reason" (PDM 307). To Habermas, the appeal of this aesthetically stylized "other of reason" is such that it produces a devaluation of the everyday in favor of the "extraordinary." And this results in the neglect of precisely those elements of everyday life that signal its breakdown, its engulfment in a crisis manifest not only in forms of social and cultural disorientation but also in a breakdown of human relationships. In other words, the aestheticized "other of reason" is allowed to obscure the presence of a more genuine "other," whose natural home is the world of the everyday, not the extraordinary. Thus the "other of this self-inflated subjectivity is no longer the dirempted totality, which makes itself felt primarily in the avenging power of destroyed reciprocities and in the fateful causality of distorted communicative relationships, as well as through suffering from the disfigured totality of social life, from alienated inner and outer nature" (PDM 306).

Notice the contrast that Habermas draws here between two distinct construals of the "other of reason." On the one side, we have the "other" represented in "dreams, fantasies, madness, orgiastic excitement, ecstasy . . . the aesthetic, body-centered experiences of a decentered subjectivity"; on the other, the "other" that arises from the "dirempted totality, which makes itself felt primarily in the avenging power of destroyed reciprocities and in the fateful causality of distorted communicative relationships." Implicitly, what this argument draws attention to is the way in which reason generates different kinds of "others," depending on whether its concept is derived from the subject-object model (i.e., subject-centered reason) or from Habermas's model of linguistic intersubjectivity (i.e., communicative reason). It would seem that the "other" of subject-centered reason is necessarily "aesthetic" in character—which, for Habermas, is synonymous with an orientation to the extraordinary, and to a preoccupation with limit experiences of one kind or another, experiences of ecstasy, whether induced by madness or chemical agents or Dionysian ritual. The other of "communicative reason," by contrast, remains soberly in the world of the everyday, and strictly oriented to the problems ("the palpable distortions") of everyday life; therefore it can have a genuine connection to reason which the "other" of subject-centered reason (by definition) cannot have.

That a shift of paradigm from the philosophy of the subject to linguistic intersubjectivity will generate a different other of reason and a different relation to reason is certainly plausible enough. Less plausible, however, is the expectation that the shift to a model of intersubjectivity

will eliminate the self-alienating and repressive aspects of reason characteristic of subject-centered reason. Although Habermas claims to have overcome the hopeless attempt to purify reason of all that is empirical and
historical, he has preserved the idea that reason can be purified of all traces
of violence.[7] The governing assumption seems to be that if we derive our
conception of reason intersubjectively, the unwanted traits and effects of
subject-centered reason will vanish, since the knowledge defining relation
is not between subject and object but between mutually cooperating subjects. Is Habermas entitled to this assumption? I do not think so. When
we look more closely at the "other of the dirempted totality," we find that
it is no "other" at all. What it amounts to is nothing more than the theoretically specifiable blockages or constrictions of the practice of communicative reason, blockages and constrictions that are not themselves—as in
the case of subject-centered reason—an ineliminable property or attribute
of communicative reason itself. In other words, from within its own normative standpoint, there can be no "other" to *communicative* reason,
strictly speaking. But that is just what communicative reason generates by
relegating disclosure to the domain of the "wholly other," the wholly aesthetic "other." With this move, reason is once again cut off from communicating with its "other," through which communication reason might
learn from its "other."[8]

Thus contrary to his own intentions, Habermas ends up making the same
mistake that he so skillfully identified in the radical critics of reason. And
that mistake arises from a rather selective appropriation of the normative
content of communicative reason—an idea of reason that consists (or
should consist) of more, much more, than the rationality of its procedures.
As a result the concept of communicative reason reverts to an exclusive
model of reason, entangling itself (if not quite as tightly) in similar conceptual dilemmas. The insightful intervention into the philosophical discourse of modernity is thus unnecessarily undermined, rendering less
compelling the "new orientation for the critique of reason." So long as
current conceptions of reason remain exclusionary, why abandon the old
critical orientation? Why, indeed, if the old orientation can still do so
much work.

Habermas recognizes that a successful change of orientation, and thus a
successful change in the meaning of reason, will need an equally consequential change in the way in which subjectivity relates to itself. Consistent with Habermas's own explanation of the "principle of subjectivity,"
only a promising change in the subject's possible relation to itself will create
sufficient conceptual and normative space for the renewal of reason and

the reformulation of the "project of modernity." But here too, Habermas fails to go far enough. Certainly he is right to locate the source of many of the unsolvable puzzles of the philosophy of consciousness in "the objectifying attitude in which the knowing subject regards itself as it would entities in the external world" (PDM 296). Once this observer's perspective is privileged (epistemically and ontologically), subjectivity cannot but reify its relation to others and to itself. "The transcendental-empirical doubling of the self is only unavoidable so long as there is no alternative to this observer perspective; only then does the subject have to view itself as the dominating counterpart to the world as a whole or as an entity appearing within it. No mediation is possible between the extramundane stance of the transcendental I and the intramundane stance of the empirical I" (PDM 297). But once we substitute the observer's perspective with the perspective of the participant a very different relation between the subject and itself, the subject and other subjects becomes possible. "Then ego stands within an interpersonal relation that allows him to relate to himself as a participant in an interaction from the perspective of alter. And indeed this reflection undertaken from the perspective of the participant escapes the kind of objectification inevitable from the reflexively applied perspective of the observer. Everything gets frozen into an object under the gaze of the third person, whether directed inwardly or outwardly" (PDM 297).

The problem with Habermas's intersubjective alternative is not, in the first instance, a problem with the intersubjective perspective that he introduces but, once again, with a premature restriction of possible self/other relations, itself an expression of an unnecessarily suspicious attitude toward "otherness." Habermas's excessive worries about the "wholly other" overwhelm his analysis of the exclusive model of reason, leaving unthought the proper relation between reason and its other. What is unthought, above all, is the role of receptivity—what an earlier generation of critical theorists (Adorno, Horkheimer, and Benjamin) tried to grasp in terms of the concept of "mimesis"—receptivity to the claims of the "other" (be it a person or a "thing," a subject or an object).[9] The suspicion that the "other of reason" is employed primarily for the skeptical purpose of undermining the claims of practical and theoretical reason is not unwarranted— not altogether. Again, there are plenty of now familiar instances where it is put to use in just this way. Nevertheless, there is good reason to regard the normative significance of the "other" to consist of considerably more than its skeptical or "ecstatic" employment. A new orientation for the critique of reason needs a noninstrumental as well as nonskeptical relation to the "other." Moreover there is a need to reclaim the "other," to question its status as the radically incommensurable "other" of reason, access to which supposedly requires initiation into a "nonrational," nonargumentative discourse, an "extraordinary" discourse.

Heidegger and Foucault want to initiate a *special discourse* that claims to operate *outside* the horizon of reason without being utterly irrational . . . Reason is supposed to be criticizable from the perspective of the other that has been excluded from it; this requires, then an ultimate act of self-reflection that surpasses itself, and indeed an act of reason for which the place surpasses itself, and indeed an act of reason for which the place of the *genitivus subjectivus* would have to be occupied by the other of reason. Subjectivity, as the relation-to-self of the knowing and acting subject, is represented in the bipolar relationship of self-reflection. This figure is retained, and yet subjectivity is supposed to appear only in the place of the object. (PDM 308)

Once again, exaggerated worries about the skeptical and "ecstatic" appeal to reason's "other" get in the way of seeing alternative possibilities, one of which requires far greater attention to the role of receptivity. The radical decentering of the subject described by Habermas need not appear as absurd or counterintuitive as he makes it out to be. What he is describing is a process of decentering, an openness or receptivity to the other, that culminates, at least to begin with, in a radical shift of perspective from the position of the "subject" to that of the "object." Because Habermas's model of intersubjectivity involves such a complete break with the subject-object model, it leaves no room for rethinking the relation between subject and object, person and thing, in terms not already based on objectification or instrumentalization. In taking the position of the "object," the "subject" is not abandoning its subjectivity (or responsibility); that follows only from the premises of the standard subject-object framework. Rather, the "subject" is engaged in a mimetic or receptive act through which it can encounter the "object" in nonobjectifying, noninstrumental way, putting itself in a position where it can see itself through the "object's" eyes.[10] This does not require an "ultimate act of self-reflection," as Habermas claims. It requires receptivity, an opening up to the "object," not bending back upon it, as to one more object of possible subsumption under a rule of one kind or another.

Approached in this way, the other can retain its "otherness," but without becoming irretrievably, unapproachably "other." Were its own "otherness" wholly inaccessible to it, the subject would not be able to see itself and would not be able to encounter itself, in a new, previously unforeseeable way. The resistance of the object's "otherness" to subsumption under a concept or a rule is not the function of an epistemological gap between subject and object—talk of gaps is entirely inappropriate here. What is actually at issue here is the difference between old and new, actuality and possibility, between what is possible today and what may be possible tomorrow. Talk about gaps in knowledge makes sense only against the background of metaphysical realism. If we reject that picture, itself a consequence of treating the knowledge of objects as the model of all knowledge, the discussion changes to the question of how to understand the difference between old and new, actuality and possibility. Since the new or possibility cannot be objects of knowledge (in the standard sense), we are speaking here of a different kind of relationship to "objects" of this kind, whose intelligibility demands an enlargement of logical space, reconfiguring the inferential relationships that currently obtain so that we can make room for new "objects."

Even if Habermas does not directly address the question of the normative relation between reason and its "other," leaving unanswered the question of what that relation should be, there are certain normative implications in his discussion of the other generated by the model of exclusive reason. At the very least, reason must not suspend or close off communication with its other. This, however, does not say very much about what reason can do to foster a less defensive, more open relationship to its "other," whereby it would able to recognise itself *in* its "other"—to recognize itself as it should be, not as it is. The question that must be asked, then, is whether procedural reason, intersubjectively formulated, can succeed where subject-centered reason failed. Is a procedural conception (and its application in practice) as open to its "other," open to self-education through its "other," as its normative self-conception demands? (How else are we to assess reason's capacity for self-education if not by how it responds to its "other"?) Or does it, as I will argue, enter into the wrong kind of relation to its "other," conceptually suppressing its dependence on its "other"?

Consider once again Habermas's rejection of the exclusive model of reason. To conclude that reason is reducible to "naked power," consisting of nothing more than calculation, prediction and control, it would be necessary to demonstrate that from its own activity reason cannot produce the *"unforced force of the better insight."* This phrase must give pause to anyone familiar with Habermas's conceptual vocabulary, since one would have expected the sentence to close with the much more common phrase, the "unforced force of the better argument." This by no means trivial substitution is to be explained by the context in which it appears—but not by that alone. It is also an implicit admission that reason amounts to more than argument. Although argument can be the bearer of rational insight, it is not the only bearer. If we are to avoid formulating reason too narrowly, we must be careful not to identify reason with argument too closely, particularly when we tend to define argument too narrowly. If we accept a procedural conception of reason and argument, we'll simply repeat the mistakes committed by subject-centered reason in failing to hear other voices of reason not recognized by the dominant understanding of reason as voices of reason.

Such a broader, more encompassing recognition of the plurality of voices in which reason speaks and might one day speak (in voices not now imaginable) has implications for philosophy's own self-understanding. Although conventional argument may be the most common medium of philosophical discourse, it is not the only medium of philosophical insight. We cannot say in advance what form "the unforced force of the better insight" will take; we cannot know in advance how, and in which voice, reason will speak. But we can say that in whatever voice reason speaks, it is very much in philosophy's interest to listen, and, when necessary, to learn to speak differently.

Regrettably Habermas has been seduced by the apparent capacity of a procedural conception of reason to reunite at the formal level the unity of reason forever lost at the substantive level. But the selective attention accorded to reason's procedural voice has dulled the philosophical ear's sensitivity to the diversity and multiplicity of reason's voices. That is too high a price for the alleged formal unity of reason. To restore these voices, to lend them an attentive ear, we must give up the dream of unification, as appealing as it is; instead, we should promote a pluralistic idea of reason that can do without the need for formal and substantive unity. The "disunity of reason" need not represent a skeptical defeat for reason; rather, it can be the beginning of something new, opening a new page in the history of reason. Unlike Habermas, I think that disclosure can play a central role in that history, reshaping the meaning and practices of reason in a direction that will require a genuinely "new orientation for the critique of reason." To make good on that claim, I will need to engage in a metacritique of my own—a metacritique of Habermas's critique of disclosure.

Whether he is responding directly to Heidegger's conception of disclosure or to post-Heideggerian reworkings of this notion, Habermas's critique of disclosure is remarkable for being consistently inconsistent. It is comprised of three overlapping argument strategies: an *aestheticizing*, a *debunking*, and an *annexing* strategy, each of which respond to different aspects of the challenge world disclosure poses. The first two strategies are evasive in nature; only the third strategy directly confronts the challenge of disclosure, making a promising, if unsuccessful, attempt to engage productively with the "other" of communicative reason, acknowledging rather than discounting their interdependence. I will discuss each of these strategies along with their various implications and consequences at some considerable length. After showing how and why they fail, I shall develop an internally consistent and more promising account of disclosure in parts IV through VI, rendering more perspicuous, and (I hope) more compelling, its possibilities for enlarging (one might say, transfiguring) the meaning of reason and, thereby, renewing the project of critical theory.

4   The Aestheticizing Strategy

From Nietzsche through Heidegger to Derrida, Habermas discerns a series of increasingly radical attempts to aestheticize language, everyday practice, and philosophy by assimilating them to the world-opening, world-transforming power of practices of disclosure. Such an assimilation would collapse the difference between logic and rhetoric, between normal and "poetic" language, between problem-solving and meaning-creation, and between the everyday and the "extraordinary" (*das Außeralltägliche*); it would prejudice and rhetorically overdetermine everyday communicative practice (constituted by the Yes and No positions that agents take in relation to criticizable validity claims), and, it would allow the action-coordination function of language to disappear behind its world-disclosing function. Rather than allowing disclosure theorists to aestheticize language, everyday practice, and philosophy, Habermas aestheticizes disclosure.

The object of this strategy is to confine disclosure to the cultural site or, speaking Weberese, to the value-sphere that Habermas argues is "proper" to it: art and literature. When released from demands for justification internal to proper everyday practices, art and literature can go about creating "autonomous" worlds of meaning that release subjects from their ordinary routines, and from everyday modes of perception and action: validity-based speech and action, speech based on reasons, goes on holiday. When housed within its own cultural domicile, where it is both marginalized and domesticated, our contact with the "extraordinary" can contribute to, but not seriously disturb or threaten, the well-ordered sober rhythms of everyday life. "What Nietzsche calls the 'the aesthetic phenomenon' is disclosed in the concentrated dealings with itself of a decentred subjectivity set free from everyday conventions of perceiving and acting" (PDM 93).[11]

Interpreting the challenge posed by the phenomenon of disclosure in this particular way gives Habermas another opportunity to find a place for art in the Kantian/Weberian architecture of his theory of rationality and modernity, an opportunity that he much too hastily exploits. His earlier proposal for integrating art into his system by reference to a specifically *aesthetic* validity claim had to be withdrawn in the face of Albrecht Wellmer's telling criticisms.[12] In terms of Habermas's own theory, an aesthetic validity claim cannot be identified with or connected to any one of the basic validity claims: truth, rightness, or truthfulness. As Wellmer put it, in art all three of those claims "intermesh." Following this internal correction, Habermas tried to connect art to disclosure, making it the paradigm case of that phenomenon. In the new proposal, art and literature are no longer distinguished from science and morality by reference to a distinctive type of speech-act and corresponding validity claim, but by their meaning-creating, world-illuminating performances. Once reformulated in terms of their world-disclosing roles, art and literature can be reincorporated into the theory of rationality and modernity. Just as the cultural action systems of science and morality "administer *problem-solving capacities*, the enterprises of art and literature similarly administer *world disclosing capacities*" (PDM 206, trans. amended).[13]

As a matter of fact the enterprises of art do not administer such capacities, not least, because disclosure is not a capacity that can be "administered." One can be taught problem-solving skills, artistic methods of various kinds, but world-disclosing capacities are not isolable and objectifiable in the way that problem-solving skills and methods are.[14] There is no empirical methodology for learning how to disclose a world: it is not an artistic technique or skill that can be transmitted as such techniques and skills are daily transmitted in art schools, music schools, and the like. As an empirical hypothesis, Habermas's suggestion is nothing more than a stab in the dark. To prove such a hypothesis, one would have to show that the activity of disclosure translates into an aesthetically distinct form of knowledge that could be acquired and transmitted in the same way objectifiable knowledge in general is acquired and transmitted. I do not see how that could ever be shown, since what we are talking about is not a kind of knowledge, or even a kind of doing, that is objectifiable and formalizable. We are most certainly not talking about implicit, rule-governed knowledge that can be reconstructed the way that the rule-governed use of language can be reconstructed (or rule-governed speech and action generally): disclosure is *not* a rule-governed form of speech and action. (If one thinks of reason as the exercise of an essentially rule-governed ability, then in one's response to the phenomenon of disclosure one will be forced either to make it conform to rule-like behavior or to treat it as an "unruly" and, therefore, as a nonrational activity. Habermas more or less goes back and forth between these two possibilities, possibilities dictated by his proceduralist outlook and sensibility.)

The way that Habermas conceives of the distinction between problem solving and world-disclosing capacities renders unintelligible the very idea of an empirical test of this "sociological" hypothesis. On Habermas's view, only problem-solving discourses "specialized in questions of truth and justice" are indexed to "innerworldly [everyday] learning processes" (*PDM*, 339); unlike morality and science, art is a "value sphere" that is not indexed (at least not directly) to everyday learning processes, or to any one of the basic validity claims Habermas claims are necessary for initiating such processes. Indeed, according to Habermas's theory of modernity, art has torn itself loose from morality and science, and from everyday practice, in order to constitute its very own cultural sphere of value (*PDM* 90–91)—which is more or less a characterization of art as a value sphere that is "unbound" from the world, as having had to turn away from the world in order create an independent sphere of value for itself. But if disclosure is not *learnable* in the relevant sense, if it is not embedded in a "rationalizable" body of knowledge, but rather displays the "contingency of genuinely innovative forces," it is as hard to see *how* an independent value sphere could *contingently* come to be constituted by world-disclosing capacities as it is to see *what* these capacities are, and *how* they are to be "administered."[15] In short, the very idea of an independent sphere of value organized around the world-disclosing practices of art and literature is incoherent.

In a rare attempt seriously to engage with a work of art or literature, Habermas offers a reading of Italo Calvino's *If on a winter's night a traveller* . . . , a text Habermas reads (rather literally) as a failed attempt to erase the difference between reader and author, fiction and reality, and the everyday and the extraordinary, to erase these essential differences by incorporating them into the production of the text itself. In this aestheticizing interpretive strategy we find two of the central leitmotifs of Habermas's objections to disclosure, regardless of who proposes it, and in what context:

(1) that those who draw upon this idea can't but absolutize or totalize it, and (2) that disclosure seductively directs our attention away from the everyday to the extraordinary, and thereby erases the difference between the everyday and the extraordinary, and between problem solving and meaning-creation.

> In this longing to strip away all that is subjective ... two things are expressed: the genuine experience of the process of world disclosure, or the linguistic innovation that allows us to see with other eyes what happens in the world: but also the desire to *overdraw* this aesthetic experience, to totalize the contact with the extraordinary, to absorb the everyday. Everything that piles up as problems in the world, that is resolved or is left undone, is supposed to be reduced to a mere function of the opening of ever newer horizons of experience and of different ways of seeing things. (PT 216)

This analysis also reveals the general assumptions guiding Habermas interpretation of art and literature. The first is that aesthetic experience in general is largely *ecstatic*—it noncognitively decenters the subject of experience, exemplifying a type of decentering that can have cognitive implications or effects but is itself not "cognitive." Second, ecstatic experience transports us out of the everyday, out of the ordinary, into the realm of the extraordinary, a realm that breaks free of "everyday conventions of speaking and acting," breaks its relation to everyday ("innerworldly") learning, and so offers a momentary transcendence of the mundane. "Explosive experiences of the extraordinary have migrated into an art that has become autonomous" (PT 51). Third, however much ecstatic states of experience open our eyes to new ways of seeing, new horizons of possible meaning, their eye-opening character is inadequate to genuine problems that pile up "in the world." To think of them as offering potential solutions to problems in the world is to erase the difference between what is proper to the extraordinary and what is proper to the everyday. These assumptions constitute what I call the *ecstasis model* of art.[16] Anyone familiar with the aesthetic theories of Schopenhauer and the early Nietzsche will notice how congruent are Habermas's assumptions about aesthetic experience with their noncognitive view of art as constituting another "world," far removed from the mundane world we habitually inhabit, liberated from "everyday conventions of speaking and acting." It is no wonder, then, that he has such great difficulty finding a place for art in his theory of rationality, and a place for disclosure in his theory of the lifeworld. From the very outset, it is placed outside the everyday lifeworld in an "extraordinary" sphere of its own, thus making intractable, the problem of how to reconnect it to the lifeworld.

This second failure to reincorporate art into his system not only casts art adrift from reason (once again, because through no fault of its own art fails to conform to a concept of reason external to it); it also exposes a certain hastiness to shove aside rather than properly confront the challenge that the various aspects of world disclosure pose. Not only is he unable to close the gap between his theory of rationality and his theory of modernity, Habermas is also unable to place the activities of disclosure *in the world*, and so unable convincingly to make the connection between learning and disclosure. As a result Habermas soon came to see the inadequacy of this aestheticizing move, conceding that practices of disclosure cannot be contained within aesthetic contexts and thereby easily neutralized as a skeptical threat. The capacities for disclosure and problem-solving, disclosure and critical reflection, come in a bundle, or not at all; they cannot be neatly separated from one another, for, at the very least, they are radically interdependent. Surprisingly, this concession is announced in connection with a critique of Peirce, a critique which charges Peirce (and, by implication, Habermas himself) with failing to see that our interpretive efforts, our social practices, and our attempts at self-understanding can suffer from semantic blocks or semantic exhaustion to such an extent that they end up breaking down. "They can get moving again when, in light of a *new* vocabulary, the familiar facts show themselves in a different light, so that well-worn problems can be posed in a completely new and more promising way. This *world-disclosing* function of the sign was neglected by Peirce" (PT 106).

With this cautious but highly consequential concession a number of significant implications follow, implications that go far beyond what Habermas intends. One implication is that meaning-creation and the disclosure of cultural possibility are *internal* to everyday practices, *internal* to "innerworldly learning." The force of this implication is such that it requires—but, unfortunately does not motivate—Habermas to take back what he asserted on page after page in *The Philosophical Discourse of Modernity* and subsequent texts; namely that disclosure is a species of "extraordinary" experience *removed* from "innerworldly problems"; that meaning-creation and the disclosure of possibility is a nonrational, "contingent" event that "in our day has largely retreated into aesthetic precincts" (PDM 321). Of course, what is required is much more than simply taking back fallacious claims such as these; what is required is a wholesale revaluation of the role of disclosure in everyday practices, in philosophy, and in reason.

5   The Extraordinary Everyday

Habermas's philosophical attitude toward the everyday reflects the general redirection of Western culture's attention from otherworldly to inner-worldly concerns in the wake of the Reformation. We can speak here of an inversion of cultural priority culminating in an "affirmation of ordinary life"—in a "hallowing of life not as something which takes place only at the limits, but as a change which can penetrate the full extent of mundane life."[17] This new orientation to the everyday found its way into philosophy with the primacy accorded to practical reason by Kant, and with the various ways the primacy of practice was articulated by the Young Hegelians, American pragmatism, the early Heidegger, and later Wittgenstein, the combined and ongoing influence of whom has made this orientation a commonplace of contemporary philosophical inquiries.

It is well known, of course, that Habermas is emphatically committed to the primacy of the practical, and especially the primacy of practical reason. But I think there is good reason to regard his frequent appeal to the everyday as rather partial and selective. In light of his criticism of Peirce, for example, Habermas's tendency to identify disclosure with the extraordinary, with what is inimical to the everyday, is not just strikingly inconsistent: it is conceptually and empirically false. The opposition between the extraordinary and the everyday derives its intelligibility from the assumption that it is a secularized version of the opposition between sacred and profane, between that which can be translated into the speech of reason, and that which is untranslatable, since it is "wholly other" to reason.[18] But if everyday practice is prone to epistemological crises, if its sense-making power is subject to recurrent breakdowns in face of recalcitrant interpretive challenges, and if it "can get moving again" only "when in light of a *new* vocabulary," the familiar facts show themselves to be quite different, then it is pretty clear that the success of everyday practice depends on the world-illuminating, problem-solving power of disclosure. Moreover it is equally clear that what is being illuminated lies *within* the sphere everyday life: the extraordinary face of the "familiar facts" and "familiar things"[19] with which we must daily contend.

Once we do away with the misleading identification of problem solving with everyday practice and disclosure with the extraordinary, it will be all that much easier to recognize the dialectical interdependence between problem solving and reflective disclosure, the everyday and the extraordinary. Once we separate the extraordinary from the sacred, from what is inimical to the ordinary, we will be in a better position to see that we are dealing with interlocking processes, interpermeating phenomena. Of course, this will not be so surprising to serious readers of Heidegger and Wittgenstein, and to readers of Freud and Cavell. Looked at from their angle of vision, the tendency to treat disclosure as inimical to the everyday represents a turn away from, rather than a (re)turn to, the everyday.

From the standpoint of pragmatism, Heidegger, and Wittgenstein, the history of philosophy can be told as a history of evasion of the everyday and the ordinary.[20] Looked at closely, Habermas's appeal to the everyday does not go down far enough to the site that he claims philosophically to occupy, from which he claims to speak. He too evades the everyday—despite his appropriation of pragmatism (not by coincidence, also selective), and this evasion is ironically a function of an inattentiveness to the presence of the extraordinary in the everyday. Ultimately Habermas's appeal is not to the everyday so much as to normative rules and procedures: it is an appeal that selectively abstracts from, rather than (re)turns to, the everyday.

If we are fully to appeal to the everyday, our appeal must not be based on the assumption that the everyday is something we already know, something with which we are already on secure footing, simply because it is that with which we are most familiar. If Cavell's reading of Wittgenstein is right (as I believe it is), the everyday is not what we already "know." "Since we are not returning to anything we have known, the task is really one . . . of turning. The issue then is to say why the task presents itself as returning—which should show us why it presents itself as directed to the ordinary."[21] To get reoriented to the everyday, to get reoriented to that with which we are daily familiar, to what we share in common, is to get oriented to what we do not yet *know*. It is to orient ourselves to an "eventual" everyday, distinct from but not altogether alien to our actual one, an everyday we would encounter as though for the first time. The everyday is indeed where we find ourselves, but we must first *refind* ourselves there, for though we are "thrown" into where we "always already" find ourselves, we are "thrown for a loss."[22] To refind ourselves there where we have always been requires that we disclose the everyday anew, in all its extraordinary ordinariness.

So rather than steering the phenomena and practices of world disclosure into a sphere remote from everyday life, critical theorists need to conceive of everyday life and practice differently. Restoring the integrity of everyday practice, enlarging the conditions of its possible practice, involves considerably more than the linguistic coordination of action in relation to "validity claims geared to intersubjective recognition," it also involves an enlargement of the realm of meaning and possibility. Otherwise, everyday practice is not in a position to resist the homogenizing and totalizing effects of capitalist culture, effects that have preoccupied the critics of modernity from Rousseau to Heidegger and Adorno. Moreover, lacking meaning-creating and possibility-disclosing resources, everyday practice is not in a position to solve intractable interpretive problems. For as Habermas concedes, such problems are symptoms of the need for a new vocabulary, in light of which problems can be reformulated in a more promising way—or, more radically, in light of which old problems can be dissolved and entirely new problems can be generated, problems that turn around "the fixed point of our real need."[23]

Since everyday practice cannot be insulated against epistemological crises, we are in need of a much richer conception of everyday life and practice, and such a conception must begin by rejecting all approaches that immunize the everyday against the extraordinary, just as it will reject all approaches that devalue the everyday in favor of the extraordinary. There is no need to deflate the extraordinary in order to let disclosure into the realm of everyday practice, but there is a need to retrieve the extraordinary *for* everyday practice, to refind and reclaim it *in* everyday life. Not only Heidegger and Wittgenstein but also the classical pragmatists, Dewey, James, and Mead had just such a rejuvenated everyday practice in view.[24] All approaches that seek to divide the extraordinary from everyday practice start out from the assumption that they are mutually and irreconcilably opposed: but even a *profane* conception of everyday practice cannot do without the extraordinary. Even at its most *unheimlich*, as Freud and Kafka have shown us, the extraordinary is much closer to home than we are accustomed to believe, which explains why it is so unsettling to be unsettled by that with which are familiar, but do not "know."

Whether we turn to anthropological, historical, or phenomenological studies, we find that everyday practice cannot do without breaks and punctuations, breaks and punctuations that make possible experiences of collective solidarity and history, that open up spaces for reflection and critique, and that give meaning and shape to everyday life. Certainly there are better and worse ways to relate to these breaks and punctuations, just as there are better and worse kinds of breaks and punctuations. Yes, indeed, there are different ways to affirm the ordinary and everyday, different ways to make it extraordinary. It is equally to the point to say that the capitalist everyday, an everyday whose rhythms of work and consumption are dictated by the imperatives of money and power, actively erase the presence of the extraordinary within the ordinary, actively displacing it from the everyday, turning it contrary to the everyday, and fixedly identifying the everyday with sobriety, joyless sacrifice, and boredom. All this reinforces the idea that the extraordinary is extramundane, that which one finds across the border dividing the *Außeralltägliche* from the *Alltägliche*, the latter being the realm of industrious sobriety or anomic listlessness, the former, the realm of easily consumed ecstatic or "extreme" experience. It is a relation to the everyday that arises not from the need to mark the ordinary with each moment of the extraordinary lying expectantly within it but, rather, from the "need" to reproduce an opposition and hostility between the ordinary and extraordinary, the everyday and extramundane.

Consider how very common is the suppression of the extraordinary ordinary, for example, in the birth of a child. The process of cultural leveling that is so much the concern of Rousseau, Nietzsche, Mill, Heidegger, Adorno, and others, actually begins at birth. At least in most parts of the developed world, whether one looks at the environment of the hospital in which children are born or the (internal and external) pressures upon parents to get right back to work, to impose upon their daily lives the appearance, if not the reality, of a smooth transition from their previous life to their new one, as though nothing really extraordinary happened, one can observe the unquestioned suppression of the new, of novelty, of the extraordinariness of human natality.[25] Is there anything more extraordinary than the ordinary birth of a new human being. Just because "it happens all the time," we are inclined to think it less extraordinary than it is.[26] As Arendt suggests, it is not the fact that humans die that is most distinctive about human life; it is that they are born. That peculiarly human distinctiveness arises from the possibility of beginning something new, interrupting and possibly redirecting the course of events that have taken on the character of inexorable, unchangeable necessity. It is this distinctively human "faculty" that reminds us that though we must die, we "are not born in order to die, but in order to begin."[27] As Dewey puts it: "Each individual that comes into the world is a new beginning; the universe itself is, as it were, taking a fresh start in him and trying to do something, even if on a small scale, that it has never done before."[28]

But the culture of modernity is paradoxically a culture that is open and closed to novelty, open and closed to the extraordinary. Hence it is crucial to grasping the nature of modernity's openness to novelty that we become critically attentive to which kind of novelty, to which experience of the extraordinary, it is actually open—or closed. That we have become so comfortably accustomed to the opposition, to the mutual hostility between the ordinary and the extraordinary, signals not only the degree to which we have misunderstood everyday practices, but also of the degree to which our everyday practices have gone awry. Thus a more appropriate response to the multifaceted challenge of world disclosure requires reconnecting the everyday and the extraordinary, showing how the extraordinary is *internal*, not inimical, to the integrity of everyday practices, and thereby initiating not just a turn to but also a refounding of the everyday.

6   World-Disclosing *Arguments*?

The aestheticizing response to world disclosure was not only meant to immunize the everyday against the extraordinary, it was also designed to prevent the contamination of an ascetically procedural conception of philosophy. For Habermas, the "postmetaphysical" turn in modern philosophy, in part, a consequence of the spectacular success of modern science, requires a commitment to procedural rationality: it requires trusting solely in the rationality of procedures (PT 35) and mistrusting the metaphysical need to limn the rational structure of the world, to identify reason with nature or with history.

Rationality (*Rationalität*) is reduced to something formal insofar as the rationality (*Vernüftigkeit*) of content evaporates into the validity of results.[29] The latter depends upon the rationality of procedures one uses in trying to solve problems—empirical and theoretical problems for the community of inquirers and for the organised scientific enterprise, and moral-practical problems for the community of citizens of a democratic state and for the system of law. The order of things . . . no longer counts as rational; instead, what counts as rational is *solving problems* [my emphases] successfully through procedurally suitable dealings with reality. (PT 35)

Of course, this procedural concept of reason imposes upon philosophy an equally ascetic concept of its own practice. "Philosophy has to implicate itself in the fallibilistic self-understanding and procedural rationality of the empirical sciences; it may not lay claim to a privileged access to truth, or to a method, an object realm, or even just a style of intuition that is specifically its own" (PT 38). If philosophy fails to respect these "postmetaphysical" limits on the scope of its activity, it can easily backslide into metaphysics or seek refuge in the irrational. According to Habermas, the philosophical projects of Heidegger, the later Wittgenstein, Adorno, and Derrida, count as characteristic instances of the latter (PT 37). As with all others who were seduced by the idea of disclosure, these philosophers seem to be motivated by an understandable, but unjustifiable, antiscientism.

This motivation lies behind various attempts from Nietzsche to Rorty to justify a world-disclosing role for philosophy. Were philosophy to succumb to this temptation, it would be forced to surrender its cognitive claims: "it would either have to resign itself to the role of aesthetic criticism or itself become aesthetic" (JA 74). If it is to remain a rational enterprise, let alone the guardian of rationality, philosophy must prove its cognitive accomplishments "through procedural rationality, ultimately through the procedure of argumentation" (PT 38).

Habermas's point supposes, obviously, that what goes by the name of the aesthetic is not entitled to cognitive claims. His claim is just as obviously question begging in other ways, and strikingly dissonant with remarks he has previously made concerning the power of aesthetic experience to insightfully alter "our cognitive orientations and normative expectations."[30] In this present context it is glaringly inconsistent with what he has rather begrudgingly conceded in his essay on Peirce: *the problem-solving power of a new vocabulary is not reducible to procedural rationality but dependent on its world disclosing success.* Since there are no procedures or empirical methods for disclosing the world, the cognitive component of reflective disclosure is not one that can be extracted from the rationality of any procedure or method. Moreover, if problem solving is supposed to be the definitive postmetaphysical task of philosophy, and if the role of world disclosure is irreplaceable for solving the kinds of intractable problems typical of epistemological crises, then there is much more to rationality and problem solving than a strictly procedural conception can accommodate. These self-woven webs of inconsistency entangle Habermas in a most unwelcome dilemma: either disclosure is an indispensable facet of a larger conception of rationality than his procedural conception allows, or it is perforce turned into the other of reason.

Rather than resolving the tension that his consistently inconsistent response to disclosure has created, Habermas's subsequent writings intensify it. One finds him reverting to the aestheticizing strategy, repeatedly claiming that world-disclosure oriented philosophers aim simply "to achieve effects which in the first instance resemble aesthetic experiences" (TK 88). And it is in the very nature of such "world-clarifying, world-disclosing, world-transforming" activity that its analysis is "not directed with a view to everyday (*innerweltliche*) practices. It is not directed to actual problems *in* the world, nor does it initiate learning processes in response to challenges posed *by* the world" (TK 89). Yet, when once again Habermas releases the phenomenon of disclosure from its aesthetic straitjacket, he claims that the creation of meaning, the enlargement of conditions of possibility, is actually triggered by "the pressure of accumu-lating problems", that, indeed, the actual resolution of such problems points to "a feedback relation between world disclosure and epistemolog-ical crises" (TK 43).

Deepening the incoherence of the entire aestheticizing strategy is the attempt to exclude "world-disclosing argument" from the realm of prop-erly philosophical argument. In reply to Karl-Otto Apel's different inter-pretation of the scope of discourse ethics, Habermas objects to Apel's claim that philosophy not only can clarify the "moral point of view" but also explain "what it means to be moral" (JA 79). In Habermas's view, this is a much too metaphysical conception of philosophy, demanding of philoso-phy that "which cannot be achieved through argumentation." The desire to be moral can be "awakened and fostered" in one of two ways: on the one hand, by socialization into a form of life that complements univer-salistic moral principles; on the other, "by the world-disclosing power of prophetic speech and in general by those forms of innovative discourse that *initiate better forms of life and more reflective ways of life*—and also the kind of eloquent critique that enables us to discern these indirectly in works of literature and art. World-disclosing arguments that induce us to see things in a radically different light *are not essentially philosophical arguments*" (JA 79, my emphasis).[31]

What is here of particular interest in Habermas's reply to Apel is the con-torted acknowledgment that moral and cognitive progress requires, *over and above* what can be achieved by arguments that meet the test of pro-cedural rationality, world-disclosing discourses and practices that enable "us to see things in a radically different light" (JA 79).[32] World-disclosing arguments have the power to "initiate better forms of life and more reflec-tive ways of life," yet they operate outside the philosophical boundaries set by a procedural conception. Philosophy, it seems, must refrain from playing this world-disclosing role, even when, in doing so, it is producing moral and cognitive insight, or the conditions necessary for such insight!

Obviously commitment to philosophical proceduralism exacts a heavy price. If applied strictly, the proceduralist criterion of what counts as philo-sophical argument would turn much of what is powerful and compelling in the German tradition, and the inquiries of all those from early critical theory to Michel Foucault and Charles Taylor, into "aesthetics"—in the pejorative sense. While this dramatically enlarges the field of aesthetics, in itself not a bad thing, especially considering how much the field gains thereby, it does require accepting a definition of argument so obviously narrow that we would be forced to reject as *rational* arguments, as *cogni-*

tive achievements, some of the most significant (but by no means uncontroversial) argument forms of modern philosophy:

1. To accept such a narrow definition of argument would mean rejecting transcendental arguments, for careful consideration shows that they have a disclosive as well as a logical structure. Part of what makes this form of argument so controversial is its disclosive features, features that are hardly incidental to its logical cogency. Such arguments begin from a set of shared and largely unquestionable background assumptions, moving by a series of regressive steps to conclusions about certain conditions of intelligibility and possibility indispensable to the sense or coherence of those very assumptions.[33] Unlike deductive arguments, transcendental arguments cannot assume that the logical space necessary to rendering visible the inferential relations between the premises and the conclusions *already* exists; rather, their success depends on the degree to which they can expand existing logical space in order to make room for the conclusions to which they lead. And they can do so only by giving richer and richer articulations of the assumptions from which they begin and the conclusions to which they lead. This is one reason why disclosure should not be confused with or reduced to the rhetorical use of language; why it is not a matter of redirecting the attention of a potential audience by some pragmatic effect or another.[34] What disclosure does within transcendental argument involves uncovering and re-articulating the shared background assumptions from which the argument proceeds, thereby providing a better—a richer and deeper—account of that shared background.

Insofar as the assumptions in question are part of the background conditions of everyday practice, they remain unthematized; to bring them into focus, one must disclose them. Thus the controversy that transcendental arguments can generate in this respect has to do with the adequacy of the descriptions and articulations of the background conditions of everyday practice upon which transcendental arguments depend—that is, with the success of their world-disclosing features. (They are more typically controversial when the antiskeptical thrust of their conclusions is attached to an ironclad conceptual necessity—as is the case with Apel and, occasionally, Habermas—a conceptual necessity that might have embarrassed Kant himself.) [35]

2. It would mean rejecting dialectical arguments, for they too have an essentially disclosive feature that also allows them to reach conclusions stronger than the premises from which they began. Like transcendental arguments, dialectical arguments must also expand the normative space of

reasons to make perspicuous the background assumptions that lead to one-sided and, therefore, unstable self-understandings and practices. And like transcendental arguments, dialectical arguments from Hegel to Adorno are necessary to philosophical inquiries that seek to make sense of phenomena that fall outside our current logical space, our current horizon of possibility. In contrast to transcendental arguments, however, dialectical arguments are *future-directed* and *future-dependent*. For example, the persuasive power of Hegel's dialectical critique of ancient (aristocratic) and modern (negative) conceptions of freedom in the *Phenomenology's* justifiably famous chapter on recognition rests on Hegel's rich descriptions of how the self-understandings and practices that grow from the premises of such conceptions break down and get entangled in self-induced crises. But it rests all the more on the persuasiveness of the possible form of freedom that his dialectical argument projects onto the future, a form of freedom whose "validity claim" can only be confirmed in a future different from the past, a future in which that possible form of freedom can be reflectively tested under epistemically appropriate conditions.

3. The procedural conception of argument would mean rejecting philosophical narratives that, through the use of hermeneutic arguments and creative redescriptions of prior practices and cultural paradigms, reconstruct how we came to have the practices that we have, how we came to be the kind of beings that we are, having the pre-reflective commitments that we do, preoccupied with our particular concerns and anxieties. And, it would mean rejecting the search for new vocabularies, new paradigms, new interpretive frameworks, as a genuinely philosophical and, therefore, as a genuinely *rational* activity. If applied strictly the proceduralist criterion of what is and what is not a "philosophical" argument would mean treating as merely "aesthetic" arguments some of the most interesting "arguments" in Kant's three critiques, the *Phenomenology of Spirit*, *The 18th Brumaire*, *The Genealogy of Morals*, *Being and Time*, *The Quest for Certainty*, *Negative Dialectics*, *Philosophical Investigations*, *Truth and Method*, *The Order of Things*, *The Philosophical Discourse of Modernity*, and *Sources of the Self*. This outcome would not only dramatically enlarge the field of aesthetics; it would make it impossible to think of aesthetics in the same way again, rendering Habermas's aestheticizing strategy otiose. More to the point, the disclosive impetus of these argument forms arises from a circumstance they share in common, namely the need to respond successfully to a now familiar problem: the problem of how to "argue" against a bewitching philosophical picture, against an ontology that has not only colonized philosophical thought, but "the common sense of our civilisation."[36] How

does one argue with a picture, an ontology, or a way of seeing? How can argument break its spell? What are the implications for reason and the rationally motivating power of argument if it cannot?

Obviously this is not the kind of challenge for which conventional argument (deductive or inductive) based on demonstrative proof is adequately prepared, since that kind of argument aims at the direct refutation of a target that takes the form of a fully explicit position. But the target in question, whether a philosophical picture, an ontology, or understanding of being, does not take the form of a fully explicit position, and so is not open to direct refutation. Now, if argument and criticism are to play a rational role at all, they will need to proceed indirectly, disclosively, uncovering and exposing the background cultural understanding (ontological presuppositions, etc.) that supports the current "common sense" of philosophy and of our civilisation. By redisclosing this background understanding, bringing it into focus in a way not seen before, an argument of this kind can reveal the incoherence within this background understanding, making it possible to explain why it is prone to its particular kinds of crises, thereby weakening its grip, its hold on us. But this philosophy cannot do by being "completely opposed to common sense," by creating as much distance as possible from the everyday, for it is precisely because of its proximity to the everyday, within whose precincts it can knowingly move around, that philosophy is able reflectively to redisclose the background understanding of the everyday.

Whether we are aiming at ontologies of disengagement, the metaphysical bewitchment of everyday language, or subject-centered reason, we are taking aim with a form of indirect argument that does not already have an intelligible position in inferential/logical space: it must insert itself into that space, displacing and reorganizing existing inferential relations to make room for new ones. Through this self-inserting move, it makes its own intelligibility possible, and casts the prior inferential relations in a new light. Thus what we are speaking of is a form of argument that must create the logical space—indeed that is its virtue—within which its intelligibility and critical potential can be assessed. For instance, one could not possibly refute something called the "philosophy of consciousness" or "instrumental reason" directly, for there is nothing like a fully explicit position to refute: to refute it, one must uncover it by indirect, often laborious, means.[37]

Once again, it should be stressed that an argument of this kind arises from a palpable need, from the "pressure of accumulating problems," and not from the wish to display philosophical virtuosity (although the latter might come in handy). It arises from the need to make sense of a break-down or crisis of some kind, a need for reorientation when we find our-selves in circumstances where we do not know how to "go on" in our customary way. Wittgenstein described philosophical problems as having the form: "I don't know my way about (*Ich kenne mich nicht aus*)"[38]—which is to say, "I'm disoriented, I don't know where I'm going or how to go on—I'm unsure of myself." Given that the term "crisis" was originally used to name a physical breakdown calling for medical intervention, and given that Wittgenstein is a "crisis thinker," his "therapeutic" conception of phi-losophy, philosophically tracing our disorientation back to its source, should come as no surprise. "The philosopher's treatment of a question is like the treatment of an illness."[39] As Stanley Cavell has persuasively argued, Wittgenstein's critique of philosophy is continuous with his cri-tique of culture. This dual-track critique is highly characteristic of "world-disclosing argument" in philosophy. Since the basic premise behind this kind of philosophical "argument" is that philosophy articulates (rather than creates) the background understanding of the culture of which it is a part, it is not infrequently the case that those who are drawn to philos-ophy join the critique (and possibility) of philosophy with the critique (and possibility) of culture.[40]

There is a further feature of world-disclosing argument that requires explicit thematization: it draws on the resources of the cultural background it critically illuminates. It follows from a world-disclosing conception of argument that the cogency of nondemonstrative arguments depends on the background of intelligibility and meaning from which, ultimately, lin-guistic utterances get their sense and point. Arguments that fail to disclose the background only presume it; failing to respect their dependence on that background they fail critically to engage with it, fail to illuminate it. Hence it is a form of argument that does not rely on culture-independent criteria or on counterfactual, context-transcending idealizations. Its con-ditions of possibility are identical with the historically disclosed cultural conditions of possibility that constrain and enable its activity, constrain and enable its success. In other words, the possibility of its success is a function of *critical intimacy* with its culture rather than critical distance from it. This need for critical intimacy is what I take to be the normative injunction contained in Nietzsche's prescient claim: "What is familiar is what we are used to; and what we are used to is most difficult to 'know'—that is, to see as a problem; that is, to see as strange, as distant, as 'outside us.'"[41] Put into my own terms, it is through critical intimacy that we achieve the right kind, and the right measure, of critical "distance." We can thereby encounter our own strangeness, our own otherness, *this* side of everyday life and practices. No philosophical critique can be worthy of the name if it fails to be disclosive. In discounting the philosophical content of world-disclosing argument, the procedural conception of rationality exposes the severely restrictive, cramping limitations of a myopic view of reason and argument.

I would like now to compare, somewhat obliquely to begin with, my world-disclosing conception of philosophical argument to Habermas's procedural conception. Aligning himself with a venerable antipaternalistic tradition of moral philosophy, Habermas ascribes to everyday practices an educative power that far exceeds what can be achieved by moral argument. In the following passage, notice in particular the gap opened up between moral argument and moral practices, between argument procedurally conceived, and the pre-reflective, philosophically unproblematized work of everyday practices:

We learn what moral, and in particular immoral, action involves *prior* to all philosophizing; it impresses itself upon us no less insistently in feelings of sympathy with the violated integrity of others than in the experience of violation or fear of violation of own integrity. The inarticulate, socially integrating experiences of considerateness, solidarity, and fairness shape our intuitions and provide us with better instruction about morality than arguments ever could. (JA 76)

Reiterating a point already made by Kant in the *Groundwork of the Metaphysics of Morals*, Habermas demonstrates his own unease about any conception of philosophy that takes on the paternalistic function of moral expert, usurping the educative role already played, evidently quite adequately, by everyday moral practices. Yet the worry seems somewhat unwarranted given the educative limitations attributed to moral argument. If everyday practices and everyday experiences offer "better instruction about morality than arguments ever could," it is hard to see how philosophy in the person of the moral philosopher could ever get a sufficient foothold in everyday life to operate as a moral expert, and so hard to see how the worry could ever arise. Certainly the sociological evidence to support it is slim at best. On the other hand, the implication of this assertion easily leads to a conception of argument, and of reason, much weaker than Habermas would wish explicitly to defend: it is only because he wishes to permeate his conception of philosophy with his commitment to proceduralism, setting as firmly as possible philosophy's "postmetaphysical" limits, that this unwelcome implication appears at all.

Looked at just a little more closely, we can see just how bizarre is the outcome of Habermas's proceduralist conception of reason and philosophy. On the one hand, we have the preceding assertion that the educative power of everyday life is superior to that of moral argument. From this assertion, however, unwanted doubts are set loose concerning the very capacity of reason to shape or alter our moral beliefs and judgments. With just the slightest pressure applied, they can be used to support a contextualist view of reason and argument, even a deflationary, unreservedly naturalistic construal of reason—precisely the opposite of what Habermas intends. Applied at another point, pressure can expose the very deep split between reason and everyday practice that follows from this proceduralist outlook. This, in turn, produces another undesirable outcome, undermining the normative appeal to the everyday, to the lifeworld, central to Habermas's conception of philosophy and his reformulation of critical theory. But as I argued in the previous section, that appeal is already both partial and intermittent, and it is partial and intermittent because it is the consequence of a suppressed theoretical implication: reason's *positive dependence* on—not just its immanence in—everyday practice.

Doubts about the educative limits of argument can also be pressed in another direction. The concession to the educative power of everyday life renders much more salient reason's positive dependence on everyday practices, which, for the sake of continuity, can be designated generally as reason's positive dependence on its putative "other." Thus, by ascribing an educative power to everyday practice, Habermas illuminates, however unintentionally, the *interdependence* between the cogency of reasons and the formative power of everyday practices. Now this is similar to the point Aristotle made long ago: a moral subject has to be in a certain kind of state, an ethically receptive state, itself an achievement of everyday ethical practices, before she can recognize a certain range of ethical reasons as cogent, and as binding on her—which is to say, the cogency of reasons, their bindingness, depends on a historically shaped *culture of reason*. Encompassing plural practices of reason broader than either a procedural or a naturalistic conception can accommodate, it is a culture of reason that we can regard, in good Hegelian fashion, as a historical achievement and as an ongoing and open-ended historical process.[42]

For Heidegger and Wittgenstein, as for Cavell and Putnam, culture and objectivity, facts and values, are hopelessly entangled.[43] To a certain extent, Habermas also accepts this entanglement—but not its hopelessness. For Habermas there is a way out—rather, a way up: context-transcending idealizations or presuppositions of speech and action derived from a Peircian picture of truth-tracking inquiry. What this escape route amounts to, ultimately, is a denial of dependence, and an assertion of independence from cultural conditions of intelligibility and possibility.

In so far as the critical exchange of reasons presupposes a culture of reason on which the intelligibility and cogency of reasons depends, the interdependence between reason and everyday practices, reason and its "other," seems to be very tight indeed. The interdependence which I mean here is quite dissimilar to the kind implied by Habermas when he talks about a form of life needing to complement or meet "halfway" the universalistic moral principles he derives from his procedural conception of communicative reason. Habermas is actually speaking of a possible (fortuitous? planned?) *convergence* of reason and form of life, not of interdependence. The question that Habermas does not adequately confront is the question of what happens when the culture of everyday life fails to meet procedural reason "halfway." What happens when everyday practices become disoriented, when their sense-making power breaks down, when they appear unable to provide better moral instruction than philosophical arguments ever could? What happens when the culture of reason becomes deeply divided, fragmented, uncommunicative?

There is considerable agreement among a diverse group of crisis thinkers that under such circumstances we require some new interpretation, some new vocabulary, by which we may see our familiar problems in a new light. This much Habermas has already conceded, and at the same time he has acknowledged that any enlargement of the space of reasons, and thereby the cultural conditions of possibility, is not a matter of rational procedures. But where does that leave reason? Where does it leave argument? If the answer is to come from a procedural conception, it will not be satisfactory or reassuring, since the enlargement of logical space, the self-education of reason, will depend on the "contingency of innovative forces" or "prophetic speech"—hardly something ascribable to reason procedurally understood, or to reason embodied in the interpretative accomplishments of social actors, or to the self-conscious activity of the "participants themselves".

7   The Debunking Strategy

As with the aestheticizing strategy, the debunking strategy is a response to the skeptical implications of disclosure, focusing largely on attempts by disclosure theorists to explain historical and cultural change in terms of ontological change. The primary skeptical worry arises from the way in which change of meaning and belief threaten to outrun validity (justification) and undermine agency. The primary targets of Habermas's debunking strategy are Heidegger's *Seinsgeschichten* and Foucault's genealogies, influential models of "critical history" (in Nietzsche's sense) that track the formation and transformation of ontological frameworks, worldviews, cultural paradigms, and epistēmes. These critical histories track changes in "what counts as a thing, what counts as true/false, and what it makes sense to do."[44] In other words, they are world-disclosing investigations of the ontological presuppositions and historical preconditions that constitute different historical epochs, cultural paradigms, understandings of being, and forms of life. So they are principally concerned with the emergence of new cultural "criteria," to employ a Wittgensteinian term of art—"criteria" that constitute as well as render intelligible new "things," new truth candidates, and new ways of speaking and acting. Such investigations not only focus on radical discontinuities in cultural practices and radical shifts of meaning horizons; they *also* shed light on how we might understand ourselves as agents of change, as participants in cultural and historical, change that doesn't simply happen to us but is facilitated by us. The kind of agency that is illuminated here is not one that flows from the activity of justification, since it involves much more than taking a Yes/No position on this or that validity claim.

The debunking strategy updates Habermas's standard bag of arguments against the philosophical practice of time-diagnosis; however, he could not be as dismissive as he was a decade earlier when he could treat Lukacsian and Jasperian styles of *Zeitdiagnosen* as intellectually discredited and passé. He could only recycle so much of those arguments against Heidegger and Foucault; for his new targets Habermas needed some new arguments. These new arguments are aimed at the "ontological difference"—Heidegger's most prized philosophical innovation. According to Habermas, such ontologically guided investigations as Heidegger's and Foucault's assume that an ontological difference exists between the "constitutive understanding *of* the world" disclosed by language, and "what is constituted *in* the world" (PDM 319/my emphasis). Habermas claims that this interpretive device by its very nature uncouples the "constitutive understanding of the world" from "what is constituted in the world." That putative uncoupling makes it rather easy to reduce the results of Heidegger's and Foucault's critical histories to the claim that changes in ontology, disclosed by and sedimented in language and cultural practices, succeed one another independently of what human beings learn from their interactions with one another and with the world. That would mean that human history would assume the form of predestined fate, unfolding inexorably within the antecedently fixed horizons of meaning set by the most recently disclosed ontology.

While the texts of Heidegger (and one infamous interview), Foucault, Castoriadis, and Derrida lend themselves to Habermas *reductio ad absurdum*, it is at best a caricature. Heidegger certainly does claim that neither large-scale nor small-scale changes in our self-understanding or our social practices are simply at the disposal of our will, and moreover that acting on this assumption envelops us all the more deeply in nihilism (of course, the lessons of his engagement with National Socialism play a decisive role in shaping this view).[45] But he is far from asserting the self-refuting view that ontologies determine in advance our self-understanding, our practices, and our possibilities *independently* of what we may say or do. To say that we cannot make fully explicit, fully transparent, our ontological pre-understanding of the world, to say that we cannot objectify and master it, because our theoretical and practical activities depend on it, is *not* the same as saying that we are at the mercy of metahistorical transformations of worldviews that we can only undergo but not resist or criticize.

The debunking strategy exaggerates to the point of distortion Heidegger's already exaggerated account of the degree to which changes in ontologies can take place behind our backs. Yes, Heidegger went on and on about how our ontological pre-understanding constrains and limits our speech, thought, and action, but he had all the more to say about how it also enables them, just as one would expect of a thinker predisposed to transcendental figures of thought. Habermas focuses one-sidedly on the ways in which meaning-horizons disclosed by a given understanding of the world are said to limit or constrain our social practices, our truth claims, and our agency. He has given altogether insufficient attention to Heidegger's equally vigorous attempts to show that its own possible self-transcendence is a *necessary* condition of any disclosure of the world, any horizon of meaning, any *Lichtung* or "clearing," any social practice, a necessary feature of its "opening" *and* "concealing" structure. After all, it was Heidegger who claimed that possibility is ontologically higher than actuality, a claim that is hardly surprising, since the diagnostic work of crisis thinkers is guided and enabled by the disclosure of possibility. Habermas's assertion that Heidegger's view of such change excludes "any interaction between world-disclosing language and learning processes in the world" is simply wrong— but that is not all that is wrong about it.

Habermas's generally dismissive attitude toward ontological explanations of cultural change are also a function of the view that such "idealist" explanations are inferior to "materialist" explanations of change because, unlike the former, a materialist explanation "takes into account a dialectical relationship" between world-disclosure and learning. As we saw in part II, Habermas objects to ontological explanations because they are apparently not open to social-scientific testing, and rest on an "esoteric" knowledge open only to "initiates." By now we have sufficient grounds to find this criticism less than compelling. The same is true of the second criticism: that world-disclosing interpretations and explanations direct our attention away from actual problems and human suffering "in the world." According to Habermas, Heidegger simply "ontologizes" genuine problems and suffering (PDM 139). Rather than illuminating them, he transports them to an inaccessible extra-mundane realm, access to which everyday cognition and discourse is barred: the "thinking that uses the ontological difference must claim a cognitive competence beyond self-reflection, beyond discursive thought" (PDM 136) With this claim we return to a line of criticisms first opened up by the young Marcuse, and reiterated by critical theorists ever since. And what we find, once again, is a panoply of criticisms whose plausibility owes more to the irrefutable moral shortcomings of Heidegger's life than to the shortcomings of his ontological approach. There is *no* reason given to support the claim that the "thinking that uses the ontological difference *must* claim a cognitive competence beyond self-reflection, beyond discursive thought." In fact, no convincing evidence is presented that anyone (Foucault, Taylor, Hacking, Heidegger, or anyone else) employing its interpretive and explanatory potential actually makes such a claim. It is hard, indeed, even to imagine someone seriously making that claim, and defending it—even Heidegger.

Habermas does point accusingly to Heidegger's claim that "All refutation in the field of essential thinking is foolish,"[46] a claim that seems to provide all the required backing. But the problem with taking this as sufficient justification for Habermas's assertion is that it preempts the question of what Heidegger is actually claiming, and that turns out to be rather different from what Habermas takes it to be claiming. To say that "all refutation in the field of essential thinking is foolish" is just to say that *direct* refutation of ontologies, understandings of being, conditions of intelligibility, is misguided: we cannot refute conditions of intelligibility, since they are themselves neither true nor false. What we can do, however, is critically disclose their hold on us, on our understanding of our possibilities, making it possible to transform our relation to them. Critical disclosure is indirect, not direct "refutation." As I argued in chapter 6, this is the reason why we so very much need world disclosing arguments, without whose weak illumination we could not get at those conditions of intelligibility discursively.

Looked at very closely and open-mindedly this "materialist" criticism of ontological explanation simply crumbles. Nevertheless, throughout *The Philosophical Discourse of Modernity* we find a running battle between materialist and ontological forms of explanation, a battle neither side can win for the simple reason that they are complementary forms of explanation, mutually supplementing one another. While a strictly materialist explanation can give us a detailed account of the processes of capitalist modernization, tracking their palpable and demonstrable consequences, it is not yet an adequate account. For example, a materialist explanation cannot offer a sufficiently adequate (nonpsychological) explanation of what makes these processes appear inexorable, why they capture almost all of the available logical space, making them seem like the only intelligible possibility for us, why they bewitch, why they captivate. For such an explanation we also need to understand the ontological presuppositions of these processes, palpable but not so easily demonstrable, if we are successfully to criticize and alter them.

Now this point follows logically from Habermas's own conception of the lifeworld as both a semantic and cultural resource, on the one hand, and as the bundle of social practices it makes possible, on the other. It is not enough to provide a materialist account of those practices, as important and essential as such an account is; we need also to provide an account of their conditions of intelligibility and possibility, without which we could not really make sense of them. They stand in a symbiotic relationship to one another. And for that reason an ontological explanation *also* requires supplementation by materialist explanation. The young Marcuse was certainly right about that, but rather than trying to coordinate those two essential forms of historical explanation, critical theory took the shortcomings of Heidegger's life as confirmation of the philosophical shortcomings of critical ontology, stranding Marcuse's suggestion until the emergence of intellectual conditions more conducive to its reappraisal.[47]

An opposition between materialist and ontological styles explanations is neither necessary nor productive. The pre-reflective background understanding of the world that such notions illuminate, an understanding lodged in and made accessible by everyday practices, is clearly an understanding that can be investigated both synchronically and diachronically. Habermas himself does both: the synchronic investigation of the lifeworld is used as an antiskeptical move to counteract the skeptical possibility of massive dissensus; the diachronic investigation is used to provide a history of reason in terms of the "rationalization of the lifeworld"—an increasing reflexivity concerning traditions and social practices as a consequence of increasing demands to test and justify them. Leaving to the side the question of whether the very idea of a "rationalization of the lifeworld" is defensible, there seems to be no reason to oppose those two forms of explanation, and every reason to regard them as interdependent, interlocking types of explanation. Thus, to assert of Heidegger, Foucault, and others, that their "thinking ... must claim a cognitive competence beyond self-reflection, beyond discursive thought" is not just to ignore this symbiotic interrelationship but also to ignore (or forget) that when dealing with ontological presuppositions, we are not dealing with items subject to the rational procedures of empirical research, since the empirical data is not directly available or directly demonstrable. Just because our access to such presuppositions is necessarily indirect and interpretive, just because it is not an undertaking that is assimilable to conventional social science, that hardly justifies wholesale dismissal of an indispensable medium of historical interpretation and explanation. To invoke Aristotle once more, why must we subject constitutively different kinds of inquiry to standards of evaluation quite foreign to them, particularly when we cannot "go on" without the weak illumination they provide?

Any fundamental change in our ontological pre-understanding, however it may come about, will affect or alter what counts as a thing, what counts as true/false, and what it makes sense to do—that is, there will be a change in the conditions of intelligibility, conditions that are *also* conditions of possibility. But the very idea of an isolated, self-enclosing horizon of meaning or ontological pre-understanding that fixes in advance what subjects may learn or do, is incoherent—as incoherent as the very idea of a conceptual scheme.[48] Heidegger was as aware of this as Davidson or Gadamer. (The philosopher who provided so much insight into the hermeneutic circle was not the methodological naïf that Habermas sometimes makes him out to be—a political *naïf* yes, but not a methodological one.) Yet, in order to deflate Heidegger's approach to historical and cultural change, the debunking strategy must suppose the correctness of this interpretation of the ontological difference as a species of ontological dualism, entailing ontologically distinct worlds (as in the usual misreading of Kant's distinction between the transcendental and the empirical).[49] This utterly reductive reading of the ontological difference is all the more peculiar in so far as Habermas also assumes just such a difference in his notion of the lifeworld. Here are some typical formulations:

Communicative actors are always moving *within* the horizon of their lifeworld; they cannot step outside of it. As interpreters, they themselves belong to the lifeworld, along with their speech acts, but they cannot refer to "something in the lifeworld" in the same way as they can to facts, norms, or experiences . . . . The lifeworld is, so to speak, the transcendental site where speaker and hearer meet. (TCA2 126)

The horizons of our life histories and forms of life, in which we always already find ourselves, form a porous whole of familiarities that are prereflexively present but retreat in the face of reflexive incursions. (PT 16)

However, if Habermas also grants that this background understanding cannot be mastered or objectified, cannot be rendered in fully explicit terms, then Habermas's criticism cannot be aimed at the ontological difference itself, since he pretty much accepts the Heideggerian and Wittgensteinian descriptions of it. He is just as committed to the idea that we must suppose some kind of "transcendental" difference between the "constitutive understanding of the world" and "what is constituted in the world," and he is just as aware that you can't relate or refer to "something in the lifeworld" the way that you can to "facts, norms, or experiences." This particular criticism of the ontological difference turns out to be a red herring. What most worries Habermas is not the ontological difference per se but the way the likes of Heidegger and Foucault have put it to use in their respective critiques of modernity and reason. So that which Habermas finds objectionable is the way in which it is deployed to demonstrate an *asymmetrical dependence* of social learning upon world-disclosing language, "what is constituted in the world" upon the "constitutive understanding of the world."

For Habermas this demonstration seems to involve a denial of the obvious: that social practices are engaged in an "ongoing test" of the ontological presuppositions that holistically structure a given understanding of the world, the consequence of which test can affect or alter those structures, weakening their grip on social practice. Habermas prefers to think of this interaction between social learning and world disclosure, what is constituted in the world and the constitutive understanding of the world, as also involving a relation of asymmetrical dependence, but with the positions reversed. As we will soon see in my analysis of the annexing strategy, Habermas is sometimes divided between this view and a more conciliatory one that posits a symmetrical dependence between social learning and world disclosure. What remains constant, however, is the inclination to treat the critical use of the ontological difference as a pernicious skeptical challenge, a use that contrasts sharply with Habermas's antiskeptical construal of the lifeworld's background understanding as a bulwark against massive dissensus.

But is the thought that our practices and forms of life are asymmetrically dependent on some prior understanding of the world that can never be fully overcome so utterly unpalatable? It is indeed an unsettling thought, but it is neither unlivable nor unwarranted. After all, it is entirely consistent with the general direction of decenteration that has been the consequence of two centuries of radical critique. Albrecht Wellmer offers a handy summary of this multiple, far-reaching process: it consists of a psychological decentering of the desiring subject (Nietzsche and Freud), a linguistic decentering of the speaking subject (Wittgenstein and Heidegger), and a philosophical decentering of the rational subject (Adorno and Horkheimer, Foucault).[50] In each case we are compelled to give up an egocentric, hence narcissistic, conception of ourselves as masters in our own "house," as masters of linguistic meaning, and masters of our reason. But if we are not masters of our desires, our languages, and our reason, how are we to understand ourselves as accountable agents? To what do we ascribe our agency?

The problem for all those who wish to make use of the idea of the ontological difference, the idea that we always already find in ourselves in a pre-interpreted world of meaning upon which we always already rely as a source of intelligibility and for orientation, is the problem of how to assert our "independence" from it—how to distinguish our "independence" from our "dependence." Habermas, for example, would like to dam up the unwanted or unpalatable implications of this idea with his notions of context-transcending validity and nonlocal justification. On this view, our "independence" as autonomous agents is achieved only through learning processes enabled by an orientation towards truth-like validity claims that submit our ontological pre-understanding to an "ongoing test," forcing it to prove itself "against the world." But the idea of the ontological difference has a momentum of its own, and it is not so easy to dam up: once you accept its premises but not its conclusions you are forced repeatedly to reinforce the dam. Rather than exploring alternative conceptions of agency more congruent with those premises, and truer to the process of self-decentering in which we are already caught up, we get entangled in a perfunctory repudiation and denial of dependence. And so we end up defining our independence in opposition to the sources upon which it draws. Must we conceive our agency in opposition to our inherited conditions of intelligibility? Would it not be worth our while to find another way to transform their limitations and constraints, a "transcendence" that draws generously upon, rather than completely opposes, the sources of intelligibility and meaning?

8   The Annexing Strategy

Of the three strategies shaping Habermas' argument, only the annexing strategy engages constructively with the phenomenon of disclosure, treating the challenge it poses as an occasion to demonstrate the capaciousness and flexibility of communicative reason. Habermas goes so far as to offer a positive, if underdeveloped, proposal for linking disclosure to learning processes in terms of a "reciprocal interaction" (*Wechselwirkung*) or "mutual interplay" (*Zusammenspiel*) between meaning and validity, disclosure and truth. I will refer to this as the *reciprocal interaction* thesis. The most remarkable feature of this thesis is just how much it implicitly concedes to the notion of disclosure, and just how little of what is conceded impacts on Habermas's procedural conception—"reciprocal interaction" ends when it begins to threaten the stability of its basic concepts. Put in the vocabulary of Piaget's theory of learning, communicative rationality "assimilates" but does not "accommodate" its "other." Assimilation without accommodation precludes the decentering effects necessary to any genuine learning process. In the end the annexing strategy reverts to a homeopathic strategy: by taking the poison in diluted form, its aim is to immunize (not transform) the procedural model.

The reciprocal interaction thesis stipulates: (1) that "world disclosure and proven praxis in the world mutually presuppose one another," (2) that "meaning-creating innovations are . . . intermeshed with learning processes," and (3) that both meaning-creation and learning processes "are so anchored in the general structures of action oriented toward reaching understanding that the reproduction of a lifeworld always takes place *also* by virtue of the productivity [the critical and innovative success] of its members" (PDM 335). These three stipulations are quite clearly in conflict with the intentions of the aestheticizing and debunking strategies. They preclude an aesthetic segregation of world disclosure, and undercut the attempt to draw a sharp distinction between meaning-creation and learning processes, between disclosure and problem solving. On the basis of the reciprocal interaction thesis, world-disclosing practices are *necessarily* situated within everyday practice, not on the side of the "extraordinary." Moreover they must necessarily be regarded as *accountable* accomplishments through which agents reflectively reproduce their lifeworld.

Thus far the implications of the reciprocal interaction thesis point in the same direction as my own suggestions concerning how disclosure ought to be interpreted. They point the way to an enlarged conception of reason (and, by implication, to an enlarged conception of agency). But, once again, this way is blocked by a narrowness with respect to what reason can mean. In the same moment as the opening appears, it is closed. Although the reciprocal interaction thesis promises much more than it is allowed to deliver, it does provide Habermas considerable wiggle room, giving him the opportunity more convincingly to acknowledge that our social practices, our cultural traditions, and our identities suppose a linguistically disclosed pre-understanding of the world. For example, in his reply to Charles Taylor, he endorses, in qualified form, the latter's account of the world-disclosing capacity of language.

Using Humboldt's work, Taylor demonstrates how every language opens up a grammatically prestructured space, how it permits what is in-the-world to appear there in a certain manner and, at the same time, enables interpersonal relations to be regulated legitimately as well as making possible the spontaneous self-presentation of creative-expressive subjects. "World disclosure" means for Taylor, as for Humboldt, that language is the constitutive organ not only of thought, but also of both social practice and experience, of the formation of ego and group identities. (CA 220)

On the face of it, this acknowledgment amounts to nothing more than an updated restatement of Habermas's concept of the lifeworld as constituting the background and resource for the communicative reproduction of the lifeworld. Habermas is sufficiently convinced of the value of Heidegger's concept of the "world" and its corresponding concepts in classical pragmatism and in later Wittgenstein, that he has no particular difficulty in endorsing this qualified view of world disclosure. But the reciprocal interaction thesis goes much further, leaving unsustainable the conceptual distinctions between language as a medium of action coordination and as a medium of world disclosure, between its problem-solving and meaning creating "functions," distinctions central to the theory of communication action. If Habermas were really committed to the reciprocal interaction thesis, he wouldn't bother with the following criticism of Derrida, which depends on just those unsustainable distinctions.

Linguistically mediated processes such as the acquisition of knowledge, the transmission of culture, the formation of personal identity, and socialization of and social integration involve mastering problems posed by the world; the independence of learning processes that Derrida cannot acknowledge is due to the independent logics of these problems and the linguistic medium tailored to deal with them. . . . These learning processes unfold an independent logic that transcends all local constraints, because experiences and judgments are formed only in the light of criticizable validity claims. Derrida neglects the potential for negation inherent in the validity basis of action oriented toward reaching understanding; he permits the capacity to solve problems to disappear behind the world-creating capacity of language. (PDM 205)

Notice the surface dissonances that are created by juxtaposing Habermas's reply to Taylor with his criticism of Derrida. World disclosure "is the constitutive organ not only of thought, but also of both social practice and experience, of the formation of ego and group identities"; it "enables interpersonal relations to be regulated legitimately as well as making possible the spontaneous self-presentation of creative-expressive subjects." By "contrast," linguistically mediated processes, processes dependent on the action-coordinating function of language, "such as the acquisition of knowledge, the transmission of culture, the formation of personal identity, and socialization and social integration involve mastering problems posed by the world." Independently of any appeal to the reciprocal interaction thesis, however, how is it that these two completely different "functions" of language can perform virtually the same tasks? The "contrast," such as it is, depends entirely on depriving world-disclosing language of the capacity to master "problems posed by the world" and, thereby, to initiate learning. By drawing that "contrast," Habermas goes against all three stipulations of the reciprocal interaction thesis. If "world disclosure and proven praxis in the world mutually presuppose one another," if "meaning-creating innovations are . . . intermeshed with learning processes," and if both meaning-creation and learning processes "are so anchored in the general structures of action oriented toward reaching understanding that the reproduction of a lifeworld always takes place *also* by virtue of the productivity of its members," the sharp contrast between the world-disclosing and action-coordinating functions of language becomes untenable. Habermas's persistent attempts to drive a conceptual and normative wedge between aspects of language that he concedes are dialectically interconnected vitiate his constant criticism of disclosure theorists for allowing the "problem-solving capacity of language to disappear behind its capacity for world disclosure" (CA 222). If these capacities are tightly intermeshed, if they are mutual suppositions of one another, this criticism is idle. On the other hand, the reciprocal interaction thesis can be turned against Habermas for subordinating the world disclosing capacity of language to its problem-solving capacity, rendering opaque both the dependence of the latter on the former and their dialectical interdependence.

As accommodating as its impulses might be, the reciprocal interaction thesis is ultimately subject to the demands of Habermas's theory of meaning, which postulates "an *intrinsic* connection between meaning and validity" (PDM, 320). Understanding and evaluation are so closely identified that to understand the meaning of an utterance (or speech act), one must know what makes it *acceptable* (i.e., the conditions that must obtain to determine whether it is true or right). Given everything that has already been said about disclosure, it should be obvious why such an account of the relation between meaning and validity, between understanding and justification, is simply, totally, inappropriate to the phenomenon of disclosure. Jay Bernstein has already pointed out how the idea of taking a Yes/No position toward a validity claim supposes that one is responding to a *determinate* claim.[51] But that does not apply to the case of innovative claims, new meanings, new interpretations, to new styles of reasoning. When we are dealing with the sufficiently strange, when we are trying to understand and assess innovative claims and new vocabularies, we cannot take Yes/No positions toward them, since the conditions that would make a world-disclosing claim acceptable or unacceptable do not yet obtain. We could only take Yes/No position toward an innovative claim if we *already* know its acceptability conditions (in Habermas's truth-conditional sense of acceptability).[52] Moreover, as Mead and Dewey show, under conditions of crisis the "object" to which one would be taking a Yes/No position has disintegrated, and until such time as it has been "reconstructed" in new form, a form not knowable in advance, there is nothing determinate toward which we can take a Yes/No position. Since what is at stake is not a determinate claim that *already* occupies an explicit position in a public space of reasons but rather an articulation of possibility, its confirmation or verification is radically future-directed and future-dependent. Thus any disclosive articulations of possibility promise a horizontal not a vertical transcendence of our current self-understanding and practices—a transcendence that can be realized and assessed only in historical time and in conformity with the sense of responsibility that arises from modernity's relation to time. So it turns out that the "truth" of disclosure "is that of an indeterminate possibility, of conceiving of the practice continuing on differently."[53]

Similarly James Bohman argues that the connection that Habermas postulates between meaning and validity is much too strong to accommodate world-disclosing claims. Drawing on Ian Hacking's reworking of Foucault, Bohman shows that what is at issue in such claims is not "truth" but "truth-candidacy"—that is, possible truth-candidates whose intelligibility and possibility depends on the emergence of "new styles of reasoning."[54] In such cases the cultural conditions of intelligibility and possibility are co-extensive with one another: "what counts as a thing, what counts as true/false, and what it makes sense to do" will be inseparable from the "styles of reasoning" by which they so count. Communication breakdowns or epistemological crises make us aware of the extent to which current conditions of intelligibility also mark the boundaries of possibility. That is why the resolution of such breakdowns and crises is in need of a new vocabulary or new style of reasoning. Since possibility is a function of vocabulary, only a new vocabulary or new style of reasoning can expand the logical space of possibility, by which expansion something previously unintelligible can become intelligible.

However, it would be a mistake to think of disclosure only in terms of truth-candidacy; the fixation on "truth" draws attention away from the role of disclosure in facilitating new interpretations of "what counts as a thing" and of "what it makes sense to do." It can facilitate revaluations of what is good, worthy, of what is higher and lower, and of what it means to be a human being. It can also awaken new social hopes and new normative expectations. All of this involves learning, but "what learning amounts to here is not learning about some given domain but learning about how we can, and must, conceive of ourselves and our possibilities for acting."[55] On such occasions, learning is initiated by calls for a change in our self-conception, a change of sensibility, and so, a change of orientation from one set of possibilities to another. If we treat this call as a call for a collective change in sensibility, we can connect it to a point made by Dewey in *The Public and Its Problems*. To the extent that our existing political institutions and social practices limit our action possibilities, it may not be enough to reform them so that they can meet newly arising needs; we might have to form a new "public," bringing about a change in self-conception and collective sensibility at the same time as we bring about a reform of our political institutions. In this respect Dewey seems to have anticipated Castoriadis, having worked out "the normal case of the political from the limit case of the act of founding an institution" and forming a new public. Unlike Habermas, but just like Castoriadis and Arendt, Dewey thinks of the act of founding an institution and forming a new public not as a limit case of the political but as the *normal* case of the political, the ultimate test case of democratic political institutions and practices.

To form itself, the [new] public has to break existing political forms. This is hard to do because these forms are themselves the regular means of instituting change. . . . That is why the change of the form of states is so often effected only by revolution . . . By its very nature a state is something to be scrutinised, investigated, searched for. Almost as soon as its form is stabilized, it needs to be remade.[56]

Habermas's skeptical worries about disclosure continually get in the way of full acknowledgment of its connection to learning, to need-responsive cultural change and innovation. As I claimed earlier, and in part I as well, the fact that this kind of learning is not controllable, that it outruns rational evaluation regulated by adherence to normative rules and procedures, arouses both anxiety and antipathy: whatever is not subject to rational control or subsumption under rules must be cognitively and morally unruly, and so cognitively and morally suspect. Thus, although Habermas has conceded over and over again that disclosure enables the kind of learning without which we cannot get over intractable problems and recurring crises, he insists on restricting social and cultural learning to practices of justification. "These learning processes unfold an independent logic that transcends all local constraints because experiences and judgments are formed *only* in the light of criticizable validity claims" (PDM 205, my emphasis). If that were indeed the case, the need for new vocabularies and styles of reasoning that open up the space of possibility and intelligibility would never arise, since the "independent logic" of such learning processes, being self-maintaining and self-regulating, could never encounter any contextual limits, could never breakdown, could never get entangled in crises. But we know that is definitely *not* the case.

All the talk of "reciprocal interaction" and "mutual interplay" notwithstanding, the commitment to the priority of validity to meaning remains steadfast. The disclosure of meaning and possibility is "not prior to, but rather subordinate to, the question of truth" (PDM 154). Over and over again Habermas remarks that new interpretations of the world must be "tested against" the world. And over and over again Habermas's discussion of disclosure evinces the worry that the rational conduct of everyday life and the normative order of society will be overrun by the "anonymous hurly-burly of the institutionalisation of ever new worlds" (PDM 330), as though the institutionalization of new worlds, the formation of new publics, was a capricious, arbitrary process completely unrelated to emerging needs "in the world." In response to the worry that meaning will outrun validity, Habermas tries to corral meaning. This attempt is reminiscent of attempts in the philosophy of science to come up with a "logic of discovery," to offer, in response to Kuhn, a "rational and principled change of meaning," where "rational" and "principled" refer to independent criteria by which change of meaning can be assessed.[57] But such attempts, whatever they are responding to, variously seek to remove the threat of the new, seek to neutralize the future. I have already suggested that new disclosures can be retrospectively and comparatively evaluated according to whether they make possible "better forms of life and more reflective ways of life." But what it means to say "better" cannot be fixed in advance: "better" will have to be, at least *partially*, disclosure-relative. Otherwise, we would have to exclude new possibilities altogether—we would have to foreclose the "novelty of the future."

9   The Test of Disclosure

The entire thrust of the argument against disclosure can be compressed into the claim that "meaning cannot absorb (*verzehren*) validity' (PDM 320; trans. altered). But this claim amounts to much less than Habermas thinks it does. There is a completely uncontroversial sense in which it is true— which is to say, a sense in which it is trivially true. It adds nothing to the reciprocal interaction thesis. On the other hand, and here we move onto much more contested terrain, validity cannot absorb meaning. This claim is entirely consistent with the reciprocal interaction thesis. Alerting us to the dangers of a truth-fixated conception of meaning (out of concerns not dissimilar to Nietzsche's and Heidegger's), John Dewey concluded that "truth [validity] is but one class of meanings."[58] Meaning is "the wider category." Truth/validity has jurisdiction within its own class of meanings, but its jurisdiction by no means extends over the entire range of human meaning. There is an "ocean of meanings to which truth and falsity are irrelevant,"[59] for example, new meanings, new interpretations, new styles of reasoning. Truth and falsity are irrelevant for this particular class of meanings, not because they are by definition beyond the reach of evaluation and justification but because they are beyond the reach of our current practices of evaluation and justification. Insofar as they can enlarge the cultural conditions of intelligibility and possibility, they "create" the conditions under which their "truth"—that is, the possibilities they disclose— can be tested and verified.[60]

Language not only has the capacity to coordinate action in the world, it has the capacity to transform the world. A "constitutive" view of language as proposed by Humboldt, Heidegger, and Taylor, takes into account how "language introduces new meaning in our world, letting "the things that surround us become potential bearers of properties."[61] This world-disclosing aspect of language can be very vexing; it can also be liberating. It is vexing because, as Taylor points out, "it makes possible its own content."[62] To say that is to say that "language opens up the domain of meaning it encodes." Now that seems to imply that meaning outruns validity, that it is, in some controversial sense, self-verifying or self-justifying, and that is vexing. For the same reason language is liberating, since it is in virtue of its world-opening and world-transforming capacity that we are able to emancipate ourselves from rigid meanings and the current space of possibility. But the course of such emancipation is not something over which we can exercise direct control, since world-disclosing language is not language we can instrumentalize. If we are dealing with something that is neither directly controllable nor directly instrumentalizable, how is it to be "tested against the world"? After all, the very idea of a test supposes some degree of control over the conditions under which it is carried out. Moreover, given what we are dealing with, what would it mean to "test" an innovative claim or new vocabulary against the world? If the "world" in question is what language itself opens up and upon which it confers intelligibility, what kind of test must we devise? Are we stretching the meaning of "test" here?

Beyond vague references to the requirement that any new meaning be "tested against the world," "confirmed," or "checked" by social practice, Habermas never stipulates what such a test actually involves. On occasion, however, he does assert that this test is both "ongoing" and extremely successful, an assertion that reveals the degree to which he is committed to the priority of validity to meaning, since the success of this "test" seems to be a foregone conclusion.

In communicative action, which requires taking yes/no positions on claims of rightness, and truthfulness no less than reactions to claims of truth and efficiency, the background knowledge of the lifeworld is submitted to an ongoing test across its entire breadth. To this extent, the concrete a priori of world-disclosing language systems is exposed—right down to their widely ramifying ontological presuppositions—to an indirect revision in the light of our dealings with the intramundane. (PDM 321)

One cannot but wonder how Habermas has arrived at this confident assessment. Recall that Habermas has conceded repeatedly that the "world" as a holistically structured background understanding disclosed by language is not fully surveyable. Now, if that is the case, how can one ever be in a position to know that this background has been tested "across its entire breadth," particularly, when one also holds that we cannot refer to "something in the lifeworld" in the same that we can refer "to facts, norms, or experiences"? Would the success of such an exhausting "test" not entail that the entire lifeworld background has been made fully explicit? And wouldn't that thereby dissolve its status as background, as that "porous whole of familiarities that are prereflexively present but retreat in the face of reflexive incursions"? That implication becomes unavoidable when

Habermas further claims that practices of justification *expose* the "a priori of world-disclosing language systems . . . right down to their widely ramifying ontological presuppositions." One would think that such extensive exposure would bring about the disintegration both of the holistic nature and "transcendental" status of "world-disclosing language." But one cannot at the same time claim, at least, not without self-contradiction, that world-disclosing language is the "constitutive organ not only of thought but also of both social practice and experience, of the formation of ego and group identities" *and* that one can get around it, expose it right down to its "ontological presuppositions." Once unpacked, this set of overreaching claims reveals a view of validity as capable of coming level with meaning, ultimately, as capable of absorbing meaning entirely. But that too is not a position that Habermas can hold without massive self-contradiction. If validity-oriented learning processes reach an impasse, if they break down and can get going again only with the emergence of a new vocabulary, new interpretation, or new style of reasoning, then validity-oriented learning can never get level with meaning, can never absorb meaning. Quite the contrary, if it is to secure its own success in the world, validity-oriented learning will always depend on meaning, on an "ocean of meanings" that encompasses much, much more than its particular class of meaning.

Alongside this indefensibly strong conception of validity's relation to meaning, is a somewhat weaker conception, a conception in which the "test" of disclosure is guided by the assumption that it is not "a matter of the world disclosing power of . . . language, but of the innerworldly success of the practice it makes possible" (PDM 154). In this case it sounds like the "test" of disclosure is of a pragmatic nature, leaving open the possibility that the outcome is not already a foregone conclusion. Whether this is in fact what Habermas has in mind is not clear, since he is himself not clear about what would count as "success." John Dewey's view of the matter was much more definitive and consistent: the only kind of "test" new meanings confront is a pragmatic one, at once experimental and holistic.

A newly acquired meaning is forced upon everything that does not obviously resist its application, as a child uses a new word whenever he gets a chance or as he plays with a new toy. Meanings are *self-moving* to new cases. In the end, conditions force a chastening of this spontaneous tendency. The scope and limits of application are ascertained *experimentally* in the process of application.[63]

There are three features of Dewey's pragmatic "test" that I would like to emphasize. The first is the claim that "meanings are self-moving to new cases." This is another way to state Taylor's point that language "makes possible its own content." To understand that "language opens up the domain of meaning it encodes" is to recognize that meaning is "self-moving." Not just any new meaning is self-moving; only truly disclosive meanings are self-moving—meanings that let "the things that surround us become potential bearers of properties." Now that does not mean that self-moving meanings do not encounter any resistance. As Dewey points out, and here we come to the second feature, current "conditions force a chastening of this spontaneous tendency." Our current social practices will both absorb and resist the new meaning, but that resistance is not going to be of a kind that is of an orderly or conclusive nature, checked against social practice from a stable standpoint outside it. No matter how far the new meaning moves itself, "the scope and limits of [its] application are ascertained experimentally in the process of application." With this assertion we come to the third feature of Dewey's conception. There can be no "formal" test for new meanings; they can only be tested experimentally, *in the course of application.* That means, of course, that there is a considerable degree of indeterminacy built into the test, which further entails that the outcome is necessarily provisional. In so far as it is pragmatic, such a test is neither final nor definitive. Some meanings may be resisted for the wrong reasons; some new meanings may take a long time to catch on. After a time some particular meaning that was greeted with more resistance than it could sustain may need to be retrieved from the background into which it faded when more receptive conditions emerge. Since the test of possibility depends on future verification, since it unfolds in time ideally under appropriately reflective conditions of evaluation, the possibility in question is not tested against the world as it is, but as it might be, and, then, only when it might be other than it is. Any new disclosure of meaning and possibility is *underdetermined* by the "world."[64]

Taking a more narrowly methodological view of the matter, we can render a little more precise Habermas's unduly ambiguous formulations of what would count as testing disclosure "against the world." Given the phenomenon, any "test" of meaning will be a test against an already disclosed "world" of meaning in which it may or may not find a place; thus any such test will take place within, and be constrained and enabled by, the hermeneutic circle. Habermas tends to regard the hermeneutic circle as static and constraining, as a horizon of meaning inherently resistant to self-critical practices, but that is because of his false conception of meaning horizons as closed systems of meaning rather than as self-opening and self-closing horizons of intelligibility and possibility. He supposes that any testing that takes place within the hermeneutic is going to be inconclusive, since within a form of life or horizon of meaning it is not possible to identify a "clear-cut difference between the validity of an utterance and its social acceptance." Accordingly he finds fault with both Wittgenstein's and Heidegger's view that the only kind of "test" available to us must take place within the hermeneutic circle; otherwise, they argue, the test would be question-begging, viciously circular. Habermas does not accept that argument and so accuses them both of promoting a view of language and social practice that asserts the priority of meaning to validity.[65]

In the context in which this criticism is made, Habermas cites a passage from Wittgenstein's *On Certainty* that echoes Heidegger's discussion of the hermeneutic circle in part one of *Being and Time* (BT 194–195/152–153), and takes it as evidence of the degree to which both Wittgenstein and Heidegger exclude interaction between "linguistic knowledge" and "knowledge of the world." But that claim ignores what Heidegger, Wittgenstein, and, more recently, Davidson have gone to great lengths to demonstrate, namely that there is no reliable, non–question-begging way to distinguish knowing a language from knowing one's way around the world, and hence when we are dealing with deep disagreements, or with the sufficiently strange, any test of one against the other, of "linguistic knowledge" and "knowledge of the world," will be both pragmatic and holistic in character. Wittgenstein is right: "All testing, all confirmation and disconfirmation of a hypothesis takes place already within a system. And this system is not a more or less arbitrary and doubtful point of departure for all our arguments: no, it belongs to the essence of what we call an argument."[66] All that needs to be qualified is that here "system" does not mean a closed system, for that is just the idea of language Wittgenstein seeks to repudiate, a view of language in which the possibility of meaning is to be explained by a system of fixed linguistic rules (or the deep structure of language) or by fixed conventions of use. Linguistic understanding is possible not because meaning is fixed (from inside or from outside language games); understanding is possible because meaning is open-ended, not closed. That is why breakdowns in understanding occur when some meanings become rigid and inflexible.[67]

Nonetheless, Habermas is right to claim that Heidegger and Wittgenstein promote a view of language that accords priority to meaning over validity; however, he is wrong to claim that according priority to meaning excludes the possibility of self-critical practices, excludes learning. By ignoring or misconstruing a whole range of self-decentering learning processes, Habermas is forced to defend a much narrower range of learning processes against a largely fictitious enemy: closed systems of meaning.

He gets into this predicament in the first place because he subscribes both to a procedural conception of reason and argument and to a conception of language as a rule-governed system. Thus he misses the extent to which testing within the hermeneutic circle is genuine testing, testing through which the activity of making explicit background assumptions and beliefs by disclosing them anew, bringing them into focus in a different light, exposes them to possible criticism and revision.

If the test of disclosure has to be pragmatic, both experimental and holistic in nature, the idea of an independent test of disclosure proves to be incoherent. But if that idea is incoherent, so is the idea of a "cognitive" function of language (problem-solving, action-coordinating) that is (relatively or absolutely) independent of its world-disclosing "function."[68] Thus, if it were consistently applied, the reciprocal interaction thesis forces one to abandon a cognitivistic conception of language. But does that mean that we must do without epistemic or normative criteria for distinguishing successful from unsuccessful disclosure? Again, the answer we must give is Yes and No. The only "criteria" of successful disclosure that we can offer are as follows: (1) that it be capable of enlarging the cultural conditions of meaning, through which (2) it facilitates the resolution of epistemological crises, by which, (3) it can open up the future and potentially revitalize modernity's relation to time. However, these are not just criteria of successful disclosure; they are criteria of disclosure *überhaupt*. As "criteria" of disclosure they not only define the activity of disclosure, they define one of the central (if not most central) activities of modern reason.

When we interpret the relation between meaning and validity in terms of the reciprocal interaction thesis rather than the other way around, a different picture of meaning and reason emerges. First of all, it leads to a more comprehensive conception of meaning that includes the practices by which the realm of meaning (and therefore of possibility) is enlarged and transformed. Second, when it concerns "how we can, and must, conceive of ourselves and our possibilities for acting," there can be no learning without disclosure, and no disclosure without learning, from which it follows that the relation between meaning and validity is both *interdependent* and *radically open-ended*. However, we must also go beyond the reciprocal interaction thesis in order to recognize the *asymmetry* between meaning and validity and, therefore, the priority of meaning to validity: meaning is the wider category. This is no cause for skepticism about the possibility of self-decentering, self-critical, learning processes. If the "internal connection between meaning and validity" were indeed "symmetrical"

(PDM 335), genuine novelty would not be possible. Habermas is simply mistaken to think that the priority of meaning to validity "prejudices the validity of linguistic utterances generally." That could only be the case if language were a closed system of meaning rather than an opening/closing horizon of meaning. Indeed it is the "ocean of meaning" that makes possible the wealth of differentiated uses of language, and the very possibility of justification. The practice of raising and criticizing validity claims is dependent on the availability of an excess of meaning, a normative surplus of meaning, without which the practices of justification could not get going in the first place. But that also means that the more scarce our semantic resources, the more endangered are our practices of justification: like the rest of our cultural practices, they are not semantically self-sustaining.

Let me amplify this point by referring to an important critic of the Piagetian model of learning, the model of cognitive learning to which Habermas largely subscribes. For Lev Vygotsky, the problem with the Piagetian approach is that it focuses on "independent problem solving"— that is, it measures and classifies discrete developmental stages of learning by taking account what the young are capable of when they are left to their own devices. By contrast the "zone of proximal development" is what we discover when we take account of what children are capable of when they are able to draw upon wider cultural resources. It consists of "the distance between the actual developmental level as determined by independent problem solving and the level of development as determined through problem solving under adult supervision or in collaboration with more capable peers."[69] Such accomplishments made possible by "loans of consciousness" allows Vygotsky to claim that "the only 'good' learning is learning which is in advance of development"[70]—that is, learning that leaps ahead of the kind reconstructed by Habermas's favorite hybrid sciences as "independent logics of development." One can think of Vygotsky's "zone of proximal development" as the cognitive analogue of Gadamerian traditions, Heideggerian horizons of meaning, or Wittgenstein forms of life. In each case, what we are talking about is the dependence of nonalgorithmic learning processes on our "readiness to use culturally transmitted knowledge and procedures as prostheses of mind. *But much depends upon the availability and the distribution of those prosthetic devices within a culture.*"[71] As Jerome Bruner correctly points out, we are speaking of a kind of learning that we cannot take for granted, that is not "hardwired" either in our brains or our social practices. Our success in cooperatively solving problems of an apparently intractable nature depends on the availability and the distribution of "prosthetic devices," "loans of consciousness," "devices," and "loans" made available and distributed by "a cultural tradition that ranges across the whole spectrum, not just the fruits of science and technology." This circumstance should make us all the more ready to preserve the semantic contents of tradition, and innovatively and self-critically to replenish them. The asymmetry between meaning and validity is not an impediment to learning but its very condition.[72]

IV The Business of Philosophy

1 Philosophy: Overburdened or Shortchanged?

As the discussion of world-disclosing argument in part III, chapter 6, made clear, the answer to the question of what counts as a philosophical argument more or less defines what philosophy is—what it does, what its business is. Therefore a great deal is at stake in the answer we give: if the answer is too broad, it is hard to see what is distinctive to philosophy; on the other hand, if it is too narrow, the definition of philosophy becomes sectarian, exclusive.[1] The procedural conception to which Habermas subscribes commits the second error, restricting philosophy to a definition of argument so narrowly professional as to be unphilosophical. A history of philosophy that employed a procedural criterion of what counts as philosophical argument would be a very short, colorless history—a history without much of a history to speak of. The critical theory tradition would not be the only one left out of such an improbable "history" of philosophy. The restrictiveness of the procedural conception is such that one wants to say, "if world-disclosing arguments are not philosophical arguments so much the worse for philosophy."

Fortunately philosophy has not been as unaccommodating, as sectarian, as its typically "professional" or "specialized" self-conceptions make it out to be. Why, then, must the activity of philosophy be defined so narrowly? What can be gained from a procedural conception that is not already an unquestionable part of philosophy's self-conception? After all, is philosophy really in danger of being separated from the practice of argumentation, from the critical exchange of reasons? Is anyone seriously proposing that the history of philosophical arguments—their strengths and weaknesses—is not worthy of study? If so, is anyone really listening? It would be hard to imagine anything called philosophy that did not employ arguments of various sorts to generate insights of various sorts. So, if philosophical insight is not generated *only* by argument procedurally understood, why exclude the means by which such insight can be generated from the sphere of properly philosophical activity? Mustn't there be something philosophically wrong with a conception of argument that would be forced to describe as unphilosophical—as a series of merely aesthetic effects—the intellectual achievement of Wittgenstein, Heidegger, Adorno, and others? Again, one is tempted to say, so much the worse for philosophy. A critical theorist, especially someone with Habermas's demonstrated interdisciplinarity, should be the last one to adhere to an exclusive or proprietary conception of philosophy. What is it that Habermas is trying to guard against by insisting on such a sectarian conception of philosophy?

Well, if world-disclosing arguments were accepted as *essentially* philosophical arguments, at the very least a legitimate part of the business of philosophy would involve the practice of disclosure. For reasons discussed already in varying degrees of detail, this possibility is a source of considerable worry for Habermas. It threatens to transform philosophy from a "problem-solving" to a "world-disclosing" activity, thereby bringing about its dissolution: philosophy "would have to resign itself to the role of aesthetic criticism or itself become aesthetic." Once again, however, it is hard to see just what the rational basis of this worry amounts to, since a more capacious, more pluralistic conception of philosophy could accommodate both the world-disclosing and problem-solving roles of philosophy: neither role would have to dominate, making one or the other philosophically definitive.[2] But that harmonious solution would leave untouched the unwarranted assumption that world disclosure and problem solving are mutually exclusive, an assumption that dominates Habermas's thinking despite his various concessions to the effect that they are dialectically related to one another, most apparently under conditions of epistemological crisis.

Nonetheless, consistently inconsistent, Habermas continues to claim that a world-disclosing role for philosophy would bring about its demise. Why is that? It is because philosophy would have to give up its role as the "guardian of rationality," because it would overburden itself with meaning-generating tasks for which it lacks the semantic resources and the cultural authority, and because it would risk becoming the self-serving vehicle of havoc-wreaking charismatic figures, "world-disclosing" *Führern*—a dreaded combination of Heidegger and Hitler rolled into one. But clearly, this latter possibility is notional at best. As Habermas rightly noted a couple of decades back, "master thinkers have fallen on hard times" (MC 1). Today we can say a little more than that: the age of *le maître penseur* has passed. We have not only left it behind, the distance between that age and ours is growing. Habermas, Foucault, Derrida, and the rest of that extraordinary group of intellectuals that came to prominence in the 1960s, are the last generation of master thinkers. As they themselves helped make abundantly clear, the conditions that made their mastery possible no longer obtain. Among the most obvious of these: the hypercomplexity of contemporary modernity; the "strange multiplicity" of cultures confronting one another in a time horizon of contemporaneous noncontemporaneity; the intense media and academic scrutiny that easily turns "master thinkers" into celebrity intellectuals; and, not least, the impact of feminism on the division of labor in the family making scarce the time that the autonomous male thinker could once take for granted as his own "free time."

It is no longer possible for us to treat as urgent Nietzsche's question as to whether today "greatness" is still possible, because as Habermas recognized, we now have a broken relation to "greatness"—not just to the "great men" who preceded us, but to the very idea of "greatness," and "great men." To be blunt: we've come to see that "greatness" isn't all it is cracked up to be. *Pace* Nietzsche, "greatness" has not become a victim of the leveling effects of "democratization" and "modernity," as a consequence of which it has morphed into "the cult of celebrity." "Greatness" has "disenchanted" itself, unmasked itself. One can only guess at the cultural possibilities that might arise for an age prepared to part with the very idea of "greatness," and of "great men," possibilities whose realization will depend on the capacity of "ordinary" citizens unreservedly to cooperate with one another, to clear the way for one another, and daily do "extraordinary" things together.

Habermas's reason for believing a world-disclosing role for philosophy would overburden it with unfulfillable tasks is most clearly stated in "Remarks on Discourse Ethics," the central chapter of *Justification and Application.* Just preceding his aforementioned reply to Apel, Habermas's assesses the plausibility of Charles Taylor's modern ethics of the good within which Taylor reserves an important place for world-disclosing argument, and a world-disclosing role for philosophy. To Habermas, both Taylor and Apel, however different their starting points, wrongly overburden philosophy by expecting from it an answer to the "existential question concerning the meaning of being moral."[3]

But a postmetaphysical philosophy is too belated to perform the one task, the awakening of moral sensibility, and is overtaxed by the other, that of overcoming moral cynicism. . . . For moral despair requires an answer to the fundamental ethical question of the meaning of life as such, of personal or collective identity. But the ethical-existential process of reaching an individual self-understanding and the ethical-political clarification of a collective self-understanding are the concern of those involved, not of philosophy. In view of the morally justified pluralism of life projects and life forms, philosophers can no longer provide on their own account *generally binding* directives concerning the meaning of life. In their capacity as philosophers, their only recourse is to reflective analysis of the procedure through which ethical questions *in general* can be answered. (JA 75)

On the face of it, this position seems entirely congruent with the claim that philosophical argument has little impact on moral education, a role more suitably and ably performed by everyday practices. By restricting its activity to the normative analysis and design of the procedures by which ethical questions in general are settled, philosophy is doing what it purportedly does best when it respects its "postmetaphysical" limits. What those questions are *about* is not, evidently, the concern of philosophy. In other words, it can only be concerned with the *way* in which the questions are answered, not the questions, and not the answers. Does this sound a little puzzling? It should, since it removes from the range of philosophy's concern such questions as the question with which our study began—the question of the proportion of continuity and discontinuity of the forms of life we inherit and pass on. How can, why should, philosophy remain uninvolved, if not unconcerned, when such questions as this are at issue—and not only because of the way they touch on the question of what reason is, what it is capable of, but because of the way they touch on the question of what philosophy is, what it is capable of.

Of course, Habermas could say that he is by no means suggesting that philosophy should not be concerned with these particular kinds of "ethical" questions (as opposed to questions of justice); all that he is saying is that philosophy has no jurisdictional authority over such questions: they are to be left to the participants themselves. But who ever suggested otherwise? Once again, is there any evidence to the contrary? Is philosophy really sticking its uninvited nose into the affairs of the lifeworld? Does it anywhere in the modern world possess a Platonic or pope-like authority on existential-ethical or ethical-political questions that needs to be curtailed? Contrary to his various claims about philosophy's "postmetaphysical" situation, Habermas sometimes writes about philosophy as though it posed the same threat to the lifeworld as those expert cultures (e.g., science, law, medicine) against whose incursions the lifeworld must be defended—by philosophy!

Notice, too, that Habermas presumes that philosophy's capacity to awaken moral sensibility or to respond to moral despair would necessitate having definitive answers to questions such as the meaning of life, on the putative basis of which it could issue "generally binding directives" stipulating how it should be lived. But this worry seems just as baseless as the political worry, since it supposes, impossibly, that the question of life's meaning could be settled once and for all. Obviously definitive answers to this question are not forthcoming, and never will be. At least this much we have to grant to Heideggerian ontology: human being is distinguished by the fact that its own being is in question for it, a question for which there is no final, insuperable answer. By raising the bar so high, however, Habermas does succeed in making the suggestion that philosophy can play a world-disclosing role sound more than a little presumptuous and pointless, but that suggestion has a lot more going for it if, instead, we lower the bar to a height appropriate to, consistent with, the purpose and limits of world-disclosing practices.

Once we do that, we see that it is not at all obvious that philosophy is too belated to perform the task of awakening moral sensibility, of sensitizing us to the hidden or suppressed aspects of our moral lives. This it has always done, and sometimes very well. The critical illumination of the lives we live with our concepts (Putnam)—our concepts of the person, of freedom, of justice, and so on—has always been a part of philosophy's role in our culture. For such an undertaking to be successful, it is by no means necessary that philosophy be in a position to offer generally binding directives as to how we should live our lives. Indeed it is contrary to the activity of disclosure to offer directives of any kind: it can only aim at the disclosure of alternative possibilities—facilitating alternative ways of understanding ourselves and our practices and, with a little luck, the emergence of alternative practices. At the very least, disclosure resists the foreclosure of possibility, offering critical reminders that the way things are now is not the way things have to be. So it is not clear what sense "belated" can mean in this context. In any case, whatever and whenever alternative possibilities are disclosed, the question of whether they are genuine possibilities for us is indeed *for us* to decide, after suitably appropriate reflection and experiment. Acknowledging philosophy's occasional power to illuminate our lives does not necessarily license it to prescribe how they should be lived.

Likewise an effective response to moral cynicism hardly requires an answer to the question of the meaning of life. It does require, however, the presence of meaningful alternatives to the current moral and social order. Cynicism thrives where the cultural space of possibility is fixed, where possibilities appear exhausted and resignation to the current order appears to be the only intelligible response. We cannot expect philosophy (or any other cultural practice) to defeat moral cynicism or, for that matter, moral scepticism: neither cynicism nor scepticism, nor the experiences that give rise to them—disappointment, injustice, cultural alienation, meaninglessness, wanton destruction of human life and the natural world—can be stamped out once and for all. Philosophy cannot play the role of cultural superhero, but a modest world-disclosing role appropriate to its power of *weak illumination* is certainly not beyond its reach, especially when successful reaching means finding or defending some other way of going on not currently in view. To repeat, whatever the suggested alternative, it is not philosophy that determines its viability but those to whom it is addressed, those to whom it is offered for reflective consideration. Philosophy is just one more voice in this conversation. But the question *of* philosophy's voice—in which voice philosophy should speak, and when it should speak—is, of course, *the* question.

2   Guardian of Rationality? Defender of the Lifeworld?

The rather baseless worry that playing a world-disclosing role would overburden philosophy turns out to be part of another unstated worry—namely that philosophy would thereby sacrifice its cultural authority. For Habermas, philosophy's cultural authority is conditional upon the success with which philosophy is able to (1) assimilate itself to the procedures of the empirical sciences, trusting solely in procedural rationality, and (2) honor its obligations as "the guardian of rationality" (MC 19). Understandably Habermas takes it for granted that the cultural authority of science is the appropriate model of cultural authority for philosophy to emulate. So it comes as no surprise to find that he thinks the cultural authority of philosophy depends largely on its capacity successfully to engage in the business of science—to contribute to objective but fallible knowledge.

One of the problems with trying to derive philosophy's authority from the authority of science, however, is that it makes philosophy's authority (such as it is) derivative, just like the rationality of its procedures. This particular problem is exacerbated by Habermas's claim that philosophy "must now operate under conditions of rationality it has not chosen" (PT 18)—conditions brought about by the successful application of the procedures of the empirical sciences. But if philosophy finds itself bound to conditions of rationality not of its own making, and if the sciences set the conditions and standards of success for procedural rationality, philosophy's guardianship of rationality is rendered redundant, if not entirely pointless. Any changes in the conditions of rationality will be changes in relation to which philosophy has little say or role to play—in which case, philosophy would seem to be a most unlikely candidate for playing the role of guardian of rationality. Indeed, if there is one task a "postmetaphysical" philosophy is too belated to perform, it would be the task of safeguarding rationality, for philosophy would arrive on the scene much too late to be of any use. (Yet it is by no means self-evident that the *procedural* rationality of the sciences has any need of such a guardian, especially since on Habermas's own view that particular form of rationality has successfully institutionalized itself in the modern world, and established itself as the standard bearer for the rationality of all inquiries.)

Recall that the "postmetaphysical" condition of philosophy is such that it must not only abandon its foundationalist ambitions, it must also renounce any claims to "a privileged access to truth, or to a method, an object realm, or even a just a style of intuition that is specifically its own." Although somewhat excessive, this admirable humility is hard to square with the ambition to play the role of *the* guardian of rationality. Moreover it is hard to see upon what philosophy can base its claim to the guardianship of rationality. Clearly, Habermas's self-limiting "postmetaphysical" gesture is meant to break with the Kantian conception of philosophy, the cultural role of which is to show science, morality, and art to their proper place and to set for them the proper limits of their activity. Once philosophy gives up its unjustifiable claim to know "something about knowing which nobody else knows so well,"[4] as Rorty so aptly puts it, philosophy loses its epistemological-cum-judicial authority over the rest of culture.

So what qualifies philosophy to be the guardian of rationality after it has lost any right to its foundationalist claims? While Habermas is happy to part with epistemological foundationalism, he is far from ready to give up another distinctively Kantian ambition: to reformulate and defend the "unconditional" element of reason in universalizable claims to validity. If this project is still feasible, it presents philosophy with another basis for justifying its claim to be *the* guardian of rationality, since what it is now claiming to guard is not, apparently, contingent upon conditions and events over which it has little say or control. In this case what it is claiming to be guarding is that element of reason that is transhistorical and transcultural, guarding it, for example, against the rampant relativism and contextualism characteristic of the humanities and the social sciences since the "cultural" or "postmodern" turn. This now looks to be the salvageable basis of philosophy's cultural authority: to the extent that it can show the presence of the unconditional in everyday communicative practice, it justifies its claim to the guardianship of rationality. Well, almost, since philosophy's capacity to show the unconditioned depends entirely on the success with which its partner sciences can substantiate philosophy's claims (otherwise, its claims would be strictly metaphysical).

Considerably attenuated, then, the Kantian conception of philosophy can be renewed by being reconceived postfoundationally and split into two different roles: philosophy as "stand-in" (*Platzhalter*) and as "interpreter." This division of roles is reminiscent of Kant's like-minded division of philosophy into the scholastic (*Schulbegriff*) and cosmopolitan (*Weltbegriff*) concepts of philosophy.[5] The scholastic concept incorporates philosophy's scientific ambitions, its self-understanding as an indispensable component of the scientific enterprise in virtue of its epistemically self-defining methods and procedures. The cosmopolitan concept incorporates philosophy's connection to the totality, its self-understanding as an irreplaceable source of cultural orientation and cultural diagnosis in virtue of its culturally self-defining capacity to educate human beings about the "essential ends of human reason." Habermas's division of roles is similar in form but not, obviously, in content. In the role of "stand-in," philosophy plays a much more modest role in the business of science, supplying universalistic hypotheses for appropriate empirical testing. As is well known, Habermas singles out as most promising the possible partnerships with the "reconstructive sciences," sciences whose goal is to reconstruct the rule-governed bases of speech and action. But here again, one wants to ask just what it is that philosophy can bring to such a partnership—besides a stubborn belief in the practical power of the unconditioned—when "it may not lay claim to a privileged access to truth, or to a method, an object realm, or even just a style of intuition that is specifically its own." Is philosophy's view of itself as enjoying a special relation to the sciences anything more than a piece of its scientistic self-misunderstanding, an apparently inexpungible residue of its metaphysical past?

Certainly such partnerships as Habermas proposes should be encouraged, and not just between science and philosophy but also between science and the humanities in general, and between science and the arts. Only someone suffering from an extreme anti-scientism could fail to the see the potential value of such partnerships, especially when both partners are open to mutual edification. But why should philosophy be entitled to claim for itself a special or privileged relation to the sciences? If it brings nothing of its own to the partnership, if its own "scientific" credentials are derivative, why should its partnership with science be definitive of one of its basic roles in culture? Do the sciences really need philosophy—any more, say, than they need art or literature—to play this particular role? Has philosophy had any success playing it? The available answers are not conclusive, not least because all those research programs extolling such partnerships, be they of the reconstructive or naturalistic variety, have yet to deliver the promised goods (although not for lack of financial support). A far less inconclusive aspect of these partnerships is philosophy's continuing dependence on the cultural authority of the sciences to justify its "cognitive" claims. Does that mean philosophy cannot claim an independence or autonomy of its own? Upon what could its autonomy be based if philosophy has indeed nothing of its own to offer?

The shortcomings of the procedural conception of philosophy are even more telling when we turn to the other cultural role philosophy is assigned to play—the role of lifeworld interpreter. It is in this role that philosophy displays its connection to the social totality, but here too, the role is more modestly conceived than it is in Kant's cosmopolitan concept. Chastened by the fallibilistic consciousness of the sciences, all that philosophy can do in this role is to critically illuminate some local region of the lifeworld but not the social totality as a whole. Ideally it will engage in the pressing task of mediating between expert cultures and different regions of the lifeworld. "What remains for philosophy, and what is within its capabilities, is to mediate interpretively between expert knowledge and an everyday practice in need of orientation.... For the lifeworld must be defended against extreme alienation at the hands of the objectifying, the moralizing, *and* the aestheticizing incursions [*Durchgriffe*] of expert cultures" (PT 17–18) The question that arises here as before, is just what qualifies philosophy for this (not inessential) role. The question, as Habermas acknowledges, is not impertinent. "What in the world . . . gives the philosopher the right to offer his services as a translator mediating between the everyday world and cultural modernity with its autonomous sectors when he is already more than busy trying to hold open a place for ambitious theoretical strategies within the system of the sciences? I think pragmatism and hermeneutics have joined forces to answer this question by attributing epistemic authority to the community of those who cooperate and speak with one another" (MC 19).

The answer given here is not just highly indirect and ambiguous: it more or less sidesteps the question, leaving its implications wide open. That mediation between expert cultures and the lifeworld is a pressing problem is obvious; that philosophy, above all, is qualified to perform this task is much less so. According to Habermas, philosophy is well suited to play this mediating role "by virtue of its intimate, yet fractured relation to the lifeworld" (PT 39). One must ask: fractured as opposed to what? Is it possible to have any other kind of relation to the lifeworld, supposing that the extremes of either total absorption or total alienation are not live(able) options? Is there a cultural practice or form of inquiry that is not related to the lifeworld in a broken, fractured way? Even the most mundane everyday practice is not fully absorbed into the lifeworld's taken for background schemes of intelligibility; otherwise, it would resemble an automaton, not an all too human practice. Ethnomethodology and phenomenology have demonstrated just how reflexive are everyday practices—even at the most mundane levels of speaking and acting. There is no sharp break between the kinds of reflection operative in everyday culture and what goes in philosophy—intensification, yes, persistence and systematicity, yes, but no sharp break. But then what makes philosophy's relation to the lifeworld uncommonly, even uniquely, intimate? Is its claim to a privileged intimacy anything more than an unexamined presumption?

[T]he lifeworld is always already intuitively present to all of us as a totality that is *unproblematized, nonobjectified,* and *pretheoretical*—as the sphere of that which is daily taken for granted, the sphere of common sense. In an awkward way, philosophy has always been closely affiliated with the latter. Like it, philosophy moves within the vicinity of the lifeworld; its relation to the totality of this receding horizon of everyday knowledge is similar to that of common sense. And yet, through the subversive power of reflection and of illuminating, critical, and dissecting analysis, philosophy is *completely* opposed to common sense. (PT 38, my emphasis)

It is not clear to me how philosophy can be *completely* opposed to common sense if it is itself nourished, for better and for worse, by what nourishes common sense. Also unclear is how the common sense of philosophy can be so radically different from and superior to the common sense of our civilisation, without presuming a power of insight to which it should not be entitled. Even when we oppose common sense, we draw from it, and our opposition is one that aims to return to common sense what is currently missing from it. We return to common sense bearing new words to share with one another.

Were the stance of complete opposition to be sustained constantly and consistently, it would lead to the extreme state of alienation from the lifeworld's resources—from invaluable "common sense" so wisely revealed in Cervantes's *Don Quixote*. When philosophy is completely opposed to common sense, it can make itself look as completely ridiculous as Don

Quixote, which is just how Quixote looks when he refuses to listen to his "vassal" (the vessel of common sense), Sancho Panza, and instead willfully denies the constraints of the everyday and his dependence on its available schemes of intelligibility. To deny those constraints (in a fit of pique or in a fit of scepticism) is to risk madness.

After another glance at the previously cited passage, it looks as though Habermas is sneaking through the back door what he has refused entry through the front. Implicitly attributed to philosophy is an unspecified but privileged kind of "knowing," or a privileged access to the totality, permitting philosophy to roam about the lifeworld without risk of being corrupted or diverted by "common sense". But how can that be if "[e]very instance of problem solving and every interpretation depend on a web of myriad presuppositions. Since this web is holistic and particularistic at the same time, it can never be grasped by an abstract, general analysis" (MC 10). How can Habermas endorse the pragmatist's emphasis on "the webs of everyday life and communication surrounding our cognitive achievements" (MC 9), and construe those cognitive achievements as won in complete opposition to "common sense"? To what, then, does philosophy owe its "subversive power of reflection and of illuminating, critical, and dissecting analysis"? Why is philosophy the lucky beneficiary of such subversive critical power? If philosophy's "critical power" arises from its assimilation to the procedural rationality of the empirical sciences, it is not clear why it has any special claims to intimacy with the lifeworld. One would expect that whatever intimacy with the lifeworld it *might* have previously enjoyed, that intimacy would no longer be possible once philosophy assimilates itself to the procedural rationality of the sciences—the very model of an expert culture totally alienated from the lifeworld.

Of course, Habermas is well aware that the derivative rationality of philosophy's procedures cannot begin to explain the source of its subversive critical power if philosophy's purported intimacy with the lifeworld is not convincingly demonstrated. But given the avowed awkward nature of this intimacy, it will not be so easy to offer a convincing demonstration. In its awkwardness philosophy displays, once again, its traditionally suspicious and alienated relationship to the everyday, an expression of philosophy's fear of becoming absorbed by the everyday, lost in it, and hence the talk of awkwardness, hence, too, the awkward way it walks about the lifeworld like one who lives as an exile in his native land. Such apparent awkwardness belies the claim to intimacy and close affiliation. In fact its relation to the lifeworld is not one of critical intimacy but of *self-alienated* critique. Even at its most intimate point of contact, a procedural conception of philosophy alienates itself from that on which its own practice depends. What can be illuminated by self-alienated critique? What can philosophical arguments illuminate when their world-disclosing potential is both denied and proscribed? Certainly not the *heimlich* and *unheimlich* aspects of the everyday, the co-presence of which renders suspect the comforting and misleading account of the lifeworld as the sphere of what is mainly taken for granted, what is "unproblematized, nonobjectified, and pretheoretical."[6] Since philosophy has no right to presume the trust of the lifeworld to act as its interpreter, especially given its divided loyalties, how will philosophy earn that trust?[7] After all, the philosopher is not a common sight in the lifeworld; he is more often out of sight (and when in sight, just as often out of place or out of sorts).[8] If Wittgenstein, Heidegger, and pragmatism are right, philosophy has not yet caught sight of the common, and so, is not yet ready, not yet fit, to "dwell in the common"—let alone, to offer unsolicited advice.[9]

Instead of going awkwardly about the lifeworld as an internal exile who can neither return to it nor leave it for good, why can't philosophy walk about the lifeworld more often, and less awkwardly? This is a question Thoreau, a nonprofessional philosopher and an avid walker, might have asked. As it turns out, he recommended a particular kind of walking, a more relaxed, less self-alienated, but by no means uncritical way of walking, which might serve as a model for philosophy. He describes it as a *sauntering* kind of walk, the walk of someone who is on a very particular quest: to reclaim the "Sainte-Terre," the holy land of the common, the extraordinary everyday we all share.[10] We have no other land, no other home, that can be more our own. Can philosophy walk itself, as well as talk itself, back to the everyday, to a place where "having no particular home," it is "equally at home everywhere"?[11] If philosophy wants more than a suspect intimacy with the lifeworld, it will have to find that place; it will have to risk returning to that topos that is no place (Utopia) we now "know," a place where displacement is an ever-present possibility, making our returning a continuous task, a continuous quest. In other words, it will require of philosophy much more than offering its services as interpreter or translator on the lifeworld's behalf, for that offer may well be seen as part of the problem, rather than its solution.

Note the paradox. Philosophy is supposed to leave to the participants themselves the hermeneutic clarification of ethical-existential and ethical-political questions; otherwise, it turns into a meddling, moralizing expert (JA 75, 76). At the same time it is supposed to speak on behalf of the lifeworld (PT 17–18), defending it against the extremely alienating effects of expert culture. Note also how the role has changed from interpreter to defender, from translator to attorney. But defending the lifeworld against the unwelcome interventions of expert cultures is not the same as acting as its interpreter. In a court of law the role of attorney and interpreter are quite distinct, not ambiguous. In the role of interpreter, philosophy ostensibly represents both parties in need of mediation and translation. In the role of defender, it cannot but represent the interests of the lifeworld. The more it is scrutinized, the more this whole mixed-up conception of philosophy as "stand-in" and "interpreter" appears to be the product of an expert-culture mentality, exhibiting that mentality's tendency to think in terms of highly specific "specializations" and roles within an insufficiently examined division of labor. Contrary to his stated intentions, Habermas has not completely let go of the Kantian ambition to have philosophy play the role of *Platzanweiser*, arrogating to itself the authority to inform expert cultures when they trespass upon the lifeworld, and thus reserving the right to put them back in their proper place. Yes, it is a dirty job, and somebody's got to do it, but why does that somebody get to be philosophy?

In his social theory Habermas describes the process of the rationalization of the lifeworld as a process by which the once substantive unity of reason divides into three independent aspects: cognitive-instrumental rationality, moral-practical rationality, and aesthetic-expressive rationality, each of which is institutionalized into a corresponding sphere of culture—science, morality, and art. Since *The Theory of Communicative Action* Habermas has struggled to grasp both the independence *and* interdependence of these three aspects of reason: both their difference and their unity. This is not just a theoretical problem, since Habermas's diagnosis of the pathologies of modernity rests on the claim that only an "*uninhibited* and *balanced* interpenetration" of the cognitive, moral, and expressive dimensions of reason—at the level of everyday life and practice, and not only at the level of expert cultures—can effectively remedy those pathologies (CA 225). But he has not yet managed to avoid the problem first brought to light by Martin Seel—the problem of how to emphasize their independence without sacrificing their interdependence.[12] The more the formal independence of these three dimensions is emphasized, the more urgent and intractable the problems of mediation appear to be, both among the various expert cultures and between those expert cultures and the lifeworld. Yet, if the cognitive necessity of their independence is not sufficiently emphasized, if it turns out to be an illusory necessity, then the whole differentiation of reason thesis loses its centrality and diagnostic explanatory power.

By contrast, within the lifeworld, within everyday life and practices, the three aspects of reason persist in a state of integration and interdependence: they do not split neatly apart into their corresponding discourses and forms of argumentation. "In everyday communication, cognitive interpretations, moral expectations, expressions, and evaluations cannot help overlapping and interpenetrating. Reaching understanding in the lifeworld requires a cultural tradition that ranges across the whole spectrum, not just the fruits of science and technology" (MC 18). If that is the case, then we need to ask which of these two manifestations of modern reason is more fundamental, and more endangered. Is it the interlocking and interpenetrating rationality of the lifeworld, inescapably dependent on the available semantic and resources of cultural traditions? Or is it the independent and compartmentalized rationality of expert cultures alienated from the lifeworld? If it is the former, philosophy will also have to guard, which is to say, actively preserve and renew the cultural resources on which lifeworld practices depend (including its own).

As we will soon see, the implications of these question rebound on the question of the role philosophy is supposed to play as interpreter/defender of the lifeworld. In the role of interpreter philosophy is supposed to help "overcome the isolation of science, morality and art and their respective expert cultures," joining expert culture knowledge to the "impoverished traditions of the lifeworld" but without "detriment to their [the expert-culture's] regional rationality" (MC 19). In this mediating role philosophy is supposed to act as the exoteric filter through which the esoteric knowledge of expert cultures is transferred to the lifeworld, thereby decreasing the distance between expert cultures and the lifeworld, and replenishing its impoverished cultural traditions. But does this proposed role actually have a chance of being played? Its plausibility requires (1) that philosophy actually has direct, unmediated access to the contents of expert cultures—namely that its access to that expert culture knowledge is of such intimacy that philosophy itself doesn't require its own mediator, and that science—contrary to postempiricist philosophy and history of science—is a highly unified rather than a highly disunified field of knowledge, and (2) that the meaning of these contents is determinate, unambiguous and uncontested within the expert cultures themselves.

Of course, the challenge philosophy faces is not just that of translating esoteric fallible knowledge into some exoteric form. Before it can even begin to translate, it must make sense of a bewildering array of hypotheses that are contested, unstable, and in a constant state of revision.[13] So the question of interpretation and translation becomes potentially overwhelming: What to translate, and on the basis of what criteria? And who might be in the fortunate position of having the competence to check the translation, since translation will not typically be from one established language to another, but from an evolving, unstable expert dialect to a multiplicity of lifeworld languages. The lifeworld does not speak one language, let alone one dialect.[14] That brings us to one further requirement: (3) that philosophers are not only highly competent speakers of the various expert dialects but also competent speakers of the multiplicity of languages in use within the culturally pluralistic lifeworld/s of modernity, able to translate smoothly from one set of languages to the other. But that would also suppose that the languages of philosophy are sufficiently capacious, flexible, endowed with adequate semantic resources in order to accommodate within themselves the contents transferred from expert cultures and, moreover, capable of considerable semantic innovation so that those contents can then be rendered intelligible in the most (but how to decide?) appropriate target languages of the lifeworld.[15] But that is not all, for what has to be transferred is not just the "contents," but also the particular "style of reasoning" on which the intelligibility of those "contents" depend.[16] Finally, (4) it would require that philosophers could be educated in such a way that they would become equally intimate with the various languages of science and the many dialects of our pluralistic lifeworld, and that philosophy is (or can be) institutionally positioned at the borders between expert cultures and the lifeworld to perform this translating/mediating function, without philosophers themselves turning into a special class of mediation experts, thereby reproducing the problem for which they represent the solution.

I take it as obvious that philosophy as it is now practiced cannot meet all these requirements (if any one of them). Were it one day able to do so, it would be *truly* extraordinary. Apparently Habermas's conception of philosophy has its own self-overburdening implications to worry about.[17] And that does not even include the added burden of defending the lifeworld against "extreme alienation at the hands of the objectifying, moralizing, and aestheticizing incursions of expert cultures."[18] Now that role, however it is to be played, still requires an answer to the question of which rationality philosophy should be guarding: the procedural rationality of the sciences or the integrated rationality of the lifeworld?

As I mentioned earlier, it is not self-evident that the procedural rationality of the sciences needs a guardian, and by taking on that role, philosophy does little more than make itself redundant. Well, what about guardian of the unconditioned element of reason? According to

Habermas's analysis, nobody is more capable of playing that role than philosophy, so long as it is prepared to test its claims in the fallibilistic spirit and empirical framework of the sciences. Here too, however, there is the question of just what philosophy has to offer—given the total poverty of its means—to sciences already engaged in discovering the universalistic bases of human speech and action. And what would be the fate of philosophy as the guardian of rationality were those investigations to end inconclusively, surely not an unthinkable or entirely implausible possibility? Conversely, would the fate of philosophy look any better if those investigations indeed proved successful? In either case, what would there be left for philosophy to do?

The question of whether philosophy should be the guardian of the procedural rationality of the sciences or the integrated but endangered rationality of the lifeworld cannot remain unanswered. Does philosophy wish to be the redundant guardian of expert-culture rationalities or the defender of the threatened lifeworld? Given Habermas's claim that "[e]veryday life . . . is a more promising medium for regaining the lost unity of reason than are today's expert cultures or yesteryear's classical philosophy of reason" (MC 18), it would seem to decide the issue in favour of the lifeworld. But to say that everyday life "is a more promising medium for regaining the lost unity of reason" is more than slightly misleading, since by Habermas's own analysis the "lost unity of reason" pertains only to the differentiated culture of experts not to the lifeworld, within which the different aspects of reason remain both integrated and threatened by the alienating incursions of expert-culture rationalities.[19]

It was in response to the potentially most alienating of all such incursions, that Habermas recently intervened in the debate on genetic engineering. To Habermas's mind, quite rightly, the new genetic technologies "make a public discourse on the right understanding of cultural forms of life in general an urgent matter. And philosophers no longer have any good reasons for leaving such a dispute to biologists and engineers intoxicated by science fiction."[20] Once again, Habermas has been awakened from a "dogmatic slumber," this time in connection with his altogether too restrictive conception of philosophy. Most surely philosophers should be part of "a public discourse on the right understanding of cultural forms of life in general," and most surely this is "an urgent matter," but there were *never* any good reasons for philosophy not to participate in any discourse concerning the right understanding of cultural forms of life. In making an exception in this instance, Habermas exposes what is wrong with the proceduralist conception. Not only that, however, he also re-exposes the problem I have been discussing all along: if philosophy has nothing of its own to contribute to such a discussion, just what does it have to say that is worth saying, worth hearing?

Notice that what Habermas calls for goes far beyond what the procedural conception stipulates for philosophy in its role as interpretive mediator between expert cultures and the lifeworld. Philosophy is not just being asked to play a mediating role; it is expected to have a say in determining the *"the right understanding of cultural forms of life in general."* Now that calls for a great deal more than what Habermas's procedural conception allows: it calls for critical illumination of what it means to be a human being. And this is precisely what Habermas seeks to illuminate through his analysis of the "ethical self-understanding of the species." So in thematizing what is at stake in the "future of human nature," Habermas is attempting to reflectively disclose the ethical self-understanding of the human form of life and what threatens dramatically and fatefully to alter it by the normatively unregulated (i.e., market regulated) application of genetic technologies. So the answer to the question, What philosophy can contribute to a public discourse on the right understanding of the human form of life is nothing more and nothing less than its weak power of illumination, its capacity for reflective disclosure. To the extent that it can exercise that capacity effectively, what it has to say is most definitely worth saying and worth hearing.

Habermas's impressive intervention in the genetic engineering debate shows that philosophy has a more important responsibility than to act as the "guardian of rationality"; that more important responsibility is to hear itself called, now more than ever, to speak in the name of the human. And as Habermas acknowledges, to be able to do so requires normative concepts and arguments that ascetic construals of morality and justice are unable to provide. Both are too narrowly conceived to capture the "intuitive self-descriptions that guide our own identification *as human beings—* that is our self-understanding as members of the species."[21] To articulate that self-understanding Habermas had to go "beyond procedural questions of a discourse theory of morality and ethics" (JA 176), which he previously maintained circumscribed the limits beyond which philosophy must not go. Those limits were supposed to keep the time-responsive philosopher from running "up against the limits of his own historical situation," and thereby "make room" for critical theory. But contrary to his intentions, and as his intervention in the genetic engineering debate shows, the ascetic conception of "moral theory" and of "philosophy in general" that Habermas has advocated does not "make room" for, but rather stands in the way of, a critical social theory (JA 176), rendering it mute, speechless.

Pace Habermas, consciousness of the "limits of our historical situation" not only constrains what we can say, it also enables what we can say. If we don't "listen" to our own time, if we do not run up against its limits and transgress them when we must, we will fail to be responsive to our time and so fail to bear the responsibility that modernity's relation to time imposes upon us. How will we be able to justify ourselves to the future if we do not speak up now in the name of a *human* future? By speaking in the name of a human future, Habermas has helpfully (if unintentionally) exposed the cost of adhering to a proceduralist conception of philosophy. But that is not all that his timely intervention has exposed; it has also exposed the normative and critical limitations of a sharp distinction between morality and ethics, and between justice and the good life. And this he does when he acknowledges that the priority of justice to the good life "must not blind us to the fact that the abstract morality of reason proper to subjects of human rights is itself sustained by a prior *ethical self-understanding of the species*, which is shared by all *moral persons*."[22] Now that acknowledgment not only acts as a check on the priority of justice to the good life, it fundamentally reverses that priority, since it implicitly admits that our conceptions of morality and justice are sustained by and are dependent on a *prior* background understanding of what it is to be a human being. Moreover to draw upon the normative content of that understanding, to critically resist the alienating incursions of expert cultures, is to redisclose it. This means that when philosophy is faced with the question of how to continue our human form of life, the question of the right understanding of cultural forms of life, it cannot revert to standard forms of philosophical analysis and argument: it must proceed disclosively. For it is not enough simply to offer reminders of what it means to be a human being; philosophy must do what it can to speak in the name of the human, disclosing and redisclosing the meaning of human being in the face of all that threatens it—including those expert cultures which claim to *know* the human.

3   Philosophy's Virtue: Knowing When to Speak

Habermas's intervention in the genetic engineering debate reveals the limitations of his conception of philosophy. As proposed, the interpreter role is inapt, for we will surely not close the gap between expert culture and everyday life by creating another class of experts. Moreover, if the lifeworld is in need of orientation, *so is philosophy*, since just as much as everyday practices, philosophy depends on the resources of "a cultural tradition that ranges across the whole spectrum [of cognitive, practical, and aesthetic rationality], not just the fruits of science and technology." When such cultural traditions are themselves in crisis or disoriented, there is no epistemologically safe or neutral place to stand. The fruits of science and technology, no matter how successfully (nonincursively) transferred to the lifeworld (by whomever), will hardly be sufficient to remedy the problems repeatedly and continuously thematized by the philosophical discourse of modernity since its inception.

As Habermas's own social-theoretical diagnosis makes clear, it is not access to or lack of knowledge, strictly speaking, that is the cause of the various pathologies of modern life; it is a *deficit of rationality*, most palpably felt and suffered in the lifeworld (where else?). A deficit of rationality is not the same as a deficit of knowledge. Making appropriate use of fallible knowledge is only one aspect of rationality. To speak of reason, in the sense of a more comprehensive understanding of human rationality, is to speak of a capacity to make sense of ourselves and the world through sense-making practices that are, at best, the consequence of cooperatively achieved understanding and interpretation. This is particularly true when our sense-making practices break down or become disoriented, making us unsure of how to go on, or to where. Under such circumstances there is no already available "knowledge" upon which we can draw in order to solve our sense-making crisis, for that knowledge is part of what is in crisis, along with the perspective/s in light of which we apply it. But since we are aware—after more than two centuries of reflection and criticism—of the place where the crisis is most deeply felt, and where the resources necessary for its solution are most endangered, namely everyday life and the cultural traditions on which it depends, it would seem obvious that it is this same place from which the call for philosophy will come—the place out of which the need for philosophy arises.

As I suggested in part I, this is not a need to which philosophy is already in a position to respond. The need that gives rise to philosophy also instructs philosophy about its own need—about what philosophy is itself in need of, if it is properly to respond to the need which gives rise to its own activity. To reiterate, philosophy receives its concept of itself from the need/s of its time, and it is from the quality of philosophy's response to the need/s of its time that it can be in a position to act responsibly as an agency of critical enlightenment. "Philosophy's virtue is responsiveness. What makes it philosophy is not that its response will be total, but that it will be tireless, awake when the others have all fallen asleep. Its commitment is to hear itself called on, and when called on—but only then, and only so far as it has an interest—to speak."[23]

Cavell's variation on the young Hegel's idea that philosophy's responsibility to its own time is a function of its time-responsiveness adds a further layer of complexity to the relation between philosophy and its own time, a layer that is concerned with the long-standing problem of philosophy's presumptuousness—which is, of course, the question of its cultural authority, the authority of its voice. Philosophy's self-education not only requires hearing itself called; it requires hearing *when* it is called to speak. The point Cavell is making is that philosophy ought not to speak first, since it does not *yet* know what to say, or, for that matter, how to say it. In this construal of philosophy, its role is determined by its position as the respondent, as the second speaker.[24] As the respondent, it occupies a position analogous to the position of the child first learning to speak, and so finds itself in a situation analogous to a scene of instruction. When learning to speak our mother tongue, or any other tongue, we speak second. From the position of the respondent, philosophy discovers that the nature of its business is not determined by it alone but rather by something that it (willingly, receptively) inherits, as a child inherits a language and culture. That discovery seems to involve a continual rediscovery of not only what to say when called upon to speak but also how to speak, and in what voice. And so it constitutes the task of philosophy as a task of re-inheritance—that is, as a task that is concerned with the proportion of continuity and discontinuity in the forms of life it inherits and passes on.

Recognizing the need for a more modest and more dialogical approach, James Tully has drawn on the normative and epistemic ideal of "reciprocal elucidation" to reconceive the relation between philosophy and the lifeworld. Although the relation is worked out primarily in connection with the role of political philosophy, his Foucauldian view of political philosophy as a "critical activity" is one that is practically indistinguishable from critical theory's understanding of its own activity and calling.

Political philosophy as a critical attitude starts from the present struggles and problems of politics and seeks to clarify and transform the normal understanding of them so as to open up the field of possible ways of thinking and acting freely in response. These investigations are addressed to political philosophers and scholars in related disciplines, and they are tested in the multidisciplinary discussions that follow. However, insofar as they do throw critical light on contemporary struggles over oppressive practices of governance, they are addressed to the wider audience of citizens who are engaged in the struggles and seek assistance from university research.

This is a communicative relationship of reciprocal elucidation and mutual benefit between political philosophy and public affairs. On one hand, such studies throw light on the features of the practice in which a problem arises and becomes the site of struggle and negotiation, enabling the participants to become more self-aware of the conditions of their situation and the range of actions available to them. On the other hand, the experiments of the participants in negotiating, implementing, and reviewing concrete changes in practice provide a pragmatic, concrete test of the studies and their limitations. By studying the unanticipated blockages, difficulties, and new problems that arise in the cycle of practices of freedom—of negotiations, implementations, and review—political philosophers can detect the limitations and faults of their initial account, make improvements, and exercise again, on the basis of the new problems, this permanent critical *ethos* of testing the practices by which we are governed.[25]

Among the advantages of Tully's proposal is that it is much more democratic, much more concrete, and much less presumptuous. The interaction between philosophy and the lifeworld is conceived of as genuinely reciprocal, epistemically and politically. To the extent that we are all participants in the process of Enlightenment (in Kant's and Foucault's sense), we are all guardians and defenders of the lifeworld, for ultimately we are the ones in whose care the lifeworld has been placed. So, instead of assigning itself the overburdened role of guardian/defender/translator of the lifeworld, philosophy needs to think of itself as its natural ally, ready to speak *with* rather than speak *for* the lifeworld. By waiting to speak second, and by choosing to speak with, not for, the lifeworld, philosophy makes more compelling and more believable its (re)turn to the everyday. And by drawing its orientation from the need/s of the lifeworld, philosophy most surely speaks "with an interest," since it explicitly links its own fate to the fate of the lifeworld. Everyday life is not just "a more promising medium for regaining the lost unity of reason than are today's expert cultures" (MC 18), it is the *only* medium in which the "need of philosophy" can be heard and answered.

Since cultural crisis and disorientation can engulf philosophy no less than the lifeworld, philosophers and "laypersons" are all in the same boat, seeking through cooperative means to make sense of problems that have become unintelligible, intractable. In such a circumstance the critical activities of philosophers are coordinated with lifeworld struggles for self-determination and self-illumination, forming a feedback relationship that reciprocally alters the way both parties "go on" with their activities. When philosophy renews its relationship to the lifeworld guided by the idea of reciprocal elucidation, it aims at horizon-fusing dialogues among *equal* participants, making no special claims to "knowledge," since knowledge is not primarily what is at issue. What *is* at issue is the disclosure and realization of possibilities for going on with our practice more reflectively, cooperatively enlarging the space of freedom as we cooperatively enlarge the space of possibility.

However, we do not need to add that philosophy has nothing of its own to offer to cooperative partnerships of this kind. Philosophy need not be *excessively* humble about what it brings to its dialogical exchanges with the lifeworld. True, philosophy has no special access to truth nor any special truth-tracking methods or intuitions: its "postmetaphysical" inheritance does not include anything so special. Nevertheless, as Putnam points out, "it does inherit a field, not authority, and that is enough."[26] It is enough, because that field consists of an inestimably rich history of critical reflection on the lives we live with our concepts. If philosophy has anything of its own to offer, it is the resources of this inherited field. In this respect philosophy is not particularly different from the humanities and the arts, from which it has too often struggled vainly to separate itself. It is a sense-making practice, making sense of the changing look and outlook of humanity. When it abandons its scientism (as well as its anti-scientism), philosophy remains an important sense-making practice—but devoid of any self-importance.

4   Cultural Authority

What cultural authority can philosophy enjoy when it identifies itself with the humanities rather than with the sciences? Perhaps the more appropriate question is whether philosophy should even seek to speak with the voice of "authority." If it is to enter into a relationship of reciprocal elucidation with the lifeworld, a relationship based on genuine cooperation, it must give up its aspiration to cultural authority in favor of a more modest aspiration: to play a vital role in clarifying and criticizing everyday life and practices in partnership with those whose life and practices they are. Such an aspiration is entirely compatible with "attributing epistemic authority to the community of those who cooperate and speak with one another." But, of course, that authority would not be philosophy's property but an outcome of the quality of its cooperative alliance and communication with the lifeworld.

However, this is not the only candidate conception of professional philosophy and its future. We have been speaking about philosophy in the singular, rather than in the plural, ignoring for the time being the fact of the disunity of philosophy: the disparate and diverse activities, projects, and exemplary achievements of philosophy cannot be unified under one conception of the "discipline." Most certainly family resemblances abound, as do family differences, but there is no overarching unity. Many in the profession would agree with Habermas when he asserts that "philosophical thought originates in reflection on the reason embodied in cognition, speech, and action; and reason remains its basic theme" (TCA1 1). But what counts as *the* reason embodied in cognition, speech, and action is very much contested in contemporary philosophy, which is deeply divided not so much between "analytic" and "continental" philosophy as between naturalistic and nonnaturalistic approaches to cognition, speech, and action. Of course, by "naturalism" I'm referring to various attempts to reduce agency, mindedness, reason, and the realm of the normative to causal laws, appealing to whatever currently trendy science facilitates such reduction—be it cognitive science, cybernetics, sociobiology, evolutionary psychology, and so forth. In my view, the antagonism between these two approaches represents a much deeper, much more fateful split within philosophy than the philosophically (but not politically) superficial split between "continental" and "analytic" philosophy.[27]

Philosophy's traditional identification with science may explain its resistance to identifying itself as one of the humanities, but that identification also evinces a reluctance to identify with its own humanity, preferring the "view from nowhere" to the view from the merely human. Today the strength of its identification with science can be seen as originating not just in philosophy's scientistic self-misunderstanding but also in a brute desire for self-preservation. It is hardly a coincidence that naturalistic approaches in philosophy stand a much better chance of institutional survival in a time when the legitimacy and value of the humanities are being undermined not so much by self-crippling forms of relativism and scepticism (although they too play a role), as by the insidious commercialization of the university, forcibly accelerated by neo-liberal and neo-conservative regimes, themselves willing agents of market forces. As a result there is now the risk, eloquently stated by Bernard Williams, "that the whole humanistic enterprise of trying to understand ourselves is coming to seem peculiar ... to a point at which any more reflective enquiry may come to seem unnecessary and archaic, something that is best preserved as part of the heritage industry."[28] The risk is such that philosophy cannot afford to take its own future for granted: it is as endangered as any other of the lifeworld's cultural traditions. The more philosophy identifies with the lifeworld, and with the merely human, the more it is endangered. But the more philosophy identifies with the merely human, the more able it is to respond to what threatens the human.

Unlike contemporaries such as Hilary Putnam, Bernard Williams, Stanley Cavell, Charles Taylor, and Richard Rorty, Habermas is unwilling to accept the idea that philosophy is *just* one of the humanities, and not essentially linked to the empirical sciences. The philosophers I have just mentioned do not see the point of prying philosophy apart from the humanities, from art, literature, and culture; they do not see what can be gained, besides artificial purity, by insisting that philosophical argument is incomparably different from forms of argument employed in the humanities (PDM 210). This is partly because they do not think philosophical argument eventuates in definitive solutions to problems in the way that science sometimes does: when there is something genuinely at stake concerning our human form of life, there are no knockdown, non–question-begging arguments. Furthermore they would be suspicious of the attempt to define philosophy in procedural terms, since those terms presuppose a conception of problem solving inherited from the sciences, a conception for which a problem can have only a single correct solution. But it is far from obvious that problem solving in this sense is what defines distinctively philosophical cognition. Can one tell the recent history of philosophy as a story of solutions to such textbook modern "problems" as the mind-body problem, the problem of the external world, and the problem of other minds? Have these "problems" been solved? If so, why are so many professional philosophers (and their graduate students) still trying to "solve" them? Given the impact of pragmatism, Heidegger, Wittgenstein, et al., can one even regard these "problems" as problems in the scientifically relevant sense?

So in what sense does philosophy "solve" problems? What does it mean to say that philosophy solves problems through "procedurally suitable dealings with reality"? The question presupposes an unproblematic notion of problem solving. And that is the problem. The procedural conception of philosophy espoused by Habermas (and not only Habermas!) incorporates an inappropriate notion of problem solving. Though deeply influenced by the practical orientation of American pragmatism, Habermas has not really let that tradition's highly original reconceptualization of problem solving sink deep enough into the philosophical roots of his thinking. Whether we turn to Mead or Dewey, we encounter an account of problem solving that is not just congenial to the idea of world-disclosing argument and a world-disclosing role for philosophy, it is itself a world-disclosing conception of problem solving. For pragmatists like Dewey, cultural practices do not individuate themselves by specializing in problem solving (science and philosophy), on the one hand, and world disclosure (art and literature), on the other: problem solving and world disclosure not only presuppose one another, in the most critical phase of that activity they are *indistinguishable* from one another.

As with the early Heidegger and the later Wittgenstein, pragmatists took a radically anti-Cartesian view of problems, regarding them as arising from genuine rather than artificial experiences of doubt, from paralyzing blockages, interruptions, breakdowns, and crises, putting into stark relief the inadequacies of our previously taken for granted ways of making sense. To find some way to "go on" again means not just making adjustments to new realities, it means newly reorganizing the habits on which our sense-making practices depend: "Habits become negative limits because they are first positive agencies."[29] The process by which old habits (practices, institutions, traditions, languages) are transformed into new ones is a process in which reflection, criticism, and semantic innovation are intertwined. This much Dewey and Mead understood much better than Peirce. They did not need to have their attention drawn to the "world-disclosing function of the sign." More important, they drew our attention to how the "solution" to experiences of crisis and breakdown not only remakes our world, but, perforce, our own selves as well.

The kaleidoscopic *flash* of suggestion and intrusion of the inapt, the unceasing flow of odds and ends of *possible objects* that will not fit, together with the *continuous collision* with the hard, unshakable objective conditions of the problem, the transitive feelings of effort and anticipation when we feel that we are on the right track and substantive points of rest, as the idea becomes definite, the *welcoming and rejecting*, especially the identification of the meaning of the whole idea with the different steps of its coming to consciousness—there are none of these that are not almost oppressively present on the surface of consciousness during just the periods which Dewey describes as those of *disintegration and reconstitution* of the stimulus—the object. . . . If there is ever a psychical feeling of relation, it is when the related object has not yet risen from the underworld. It is under these circumstances that identities and differences come with *thrills and shocks*. . . . And it is in this phase of the subjectivity, with its activities of attention in the solution to the problem, i.e., in the construction of the hypothesis of the new world, that the individual qua individual has his functional expression or rather is that expression. . . . It is equally evident that it is not the individual as "me" that can perform this function. *Such an empirical self belongs to the world which it is the function of this phase of*

*consciousness to reconstruct. The selves of our scientific theory are part of the data which
reflection brings to us.* . . . Furthermore, *one of the results of the reconstruction will be a
new individual as well as a new social environment.* . . . It is evident that in this state
of reflection it is impossible to present the elements out of which the new world is
to be built up in advance, for disintegration and analysis of the old is as dependent
upon the problem that arises as is the reconstruction. It is equally impossible to
state the form which the world will take in advance. (my emphasis)[30]

In these penetrating observations, Mead delineates a processual picture
of "problem solving" as an existential and cognitive struggle with "data"
that is at once disintegrating and reconstituting, "data" that includes the
very self that is engaged in making sense of it. Such a picture of problem
solving is equally appropriate to science, morality, and art, but not one
typically identified either with science or morality. Nowhere in this
account can one find justification for differentiating these "enterprises"
into their distinctive cultural ghettos according to the "form" of their
respectively unique problem-solving or world-disclosing practices. The
picture presented here is one in which innovation and reflection, reflection and receptivity, the tension between a disintegrating old world and
an emerging new world, between a disintegrating old self and an emerging new self, constitute a whole. The "thrills and shocks" are as much a
part of a scientist's, a philosopher's, or a composer's experience of problem
solving, as they are of a caregiver's, a plumber's, or a detective's. But they
are also indicative of the way in which "problem solving" fully involves
and affects not only our rationality but also our sensibility, our subjectivity. In as much as the *selves of our theory are part of the data*, any solution
to the problem will depend on a decentering of the self, and the emergence of a new self, possessing the capacity to integrate its old and new
worlds, its old and new selves. Subjectivity is not erased or withdrawn: it
enters into the definition of the problem and, when met with success, into
its solution. Since we are not dealing with deductive or inductive styles of
reasoning (which are truth-preserving, not possibility disclosing), we
cannot know in advance what form the new self or new world will take.
As Ian Hacking has pointed out, there are no procedures or methods for
discovering or dealing with a whole new range of possibilities: "Understanding the sufficiently strange is a matter of recognising new possibilities for truth-or-falsehood, and of learning how to conduct other styles of
reasoning that bear on those new possibilities."[31]

To Ian Hacking's reflections on the need for new "styles of reasoning"
when confronting the "sufficiently strange," we can add the correlative

need for *new forms of sensibility*—on the need for a new "I" that makes possible a new "me."[32] Note that in this alternative conception of problem solving, the exercise of full rationality necessarily involves the exertion of full sensibility. Note also that in Habermas's procedural conception of philosophy there is no place for such an exertion of philosophical sensibility culminating in a transformation of subjectivity. This absence is particularly curious when it marks a critical theorist's conception of philosophy, since the aim of critique is not just the critical transformation of the "object" of critique but also of the subjectivity of the critic. Nietzsche regarded the practice of philosophical critique as an "art of transfiguration": to engage in it is to engage in changing oneself. Wittgenstein held a similar view of philosophical activity: "Work on philosophy is ... a kind of work on oneself. On one's own conception. On the way one sees things. (And what one demands of them)."[33] In one of his last interviews, Foucault also gives us an indication of the fuller exploration and transformation of sensibility that philosophical critique involves: "I am not interested in the academic status of what I am doing because my problem is my own transformation. . . . This transformation of one's self by one's own knowledge is, I think, something rather close to the aesthetic experience. Why should a painter work if he is not transformed by his own painting?"[34] Why should a critic engage in critique if she is not willing to risk and foster her own self-transformation? Indeed, is it even possible for one seriously to engage in critique without bringing about a change in one's life, a change in who and what one is? The point is that a transformation of sensibility is inseparable from the life of critique: it is not something one lives at work but not at home, in public but not in private—it is not a "specialty." To reprise Mead, the self that is involved in the activity of critical theory is part of the theory's data; whatever "solution" is arrived at, it should not leave that self unchanged.

In some recent comments concerning the value of Stanley Cavell's romantic conception of the philosophical life, Putnam praises Cavell's insistence on just this point: transforming sensibility is as rational an undertaking as transforming belief. "Philosophy is not only concerned with changing our views, but also with changing our sensibility, our ability to perceive and react to nuances."[35] Contrary to its typical treatment among contemporary critical theorists who take their philosophical orientation from Habermas, this transformation of sensibility is not reducible to a self-regarding "aesthetics of self-making," and therefore easily dismissible. Rather, it simultaneously involves the critical assessment of one's culture and oneself—involves that is, an unending learning process, an education in which the phases of criticism and transformation are intertwined.

In philosophizing, I have to bring my own language and life into imagination. What I require is a convening of my culture's criteria, in order to confront them with my words and life as I pursue them and as I may imagine them; and at the same time to confront my words and life as I pursue them with the life my culture's words may imagine for me: to confront the culture with itself, along the lines in which it meets in me. This seems to me a task that warrants the name of philosophy. It is also the description of something we might call education.[36]

Cavell's talk of philosophical critique as a task that requires confronting my "culture with itself, along the lines in which it meets in me" is one more way to give substance to the idea of "critical intimacy" I delineated earlier. It is a task that not only requires intimate knowledge of my culture but also a critical understanding of the intimacy I share with my culture, particularly, since I may need to break with my culture to inherit it and pass it on differently. This conception of critique is also a conception that does not take for granted what philosophy is, and what there is still left for it to do: the question of the business of philosophy remains open, problematic. This romantic self-consciousness, a function of modernity's relation to time, is not something that philosophy ought to suppress or ignore, for it defines philosophy's own historical situation, and does so in the same way that it defines the historical situation of other cultural practices, most obviously, art and literature. It also imposes on philosophy a more historically reflexive attitude not only toward its theories and statements but also toward its principal mode of communication: writing.

5   Philosophy's Kind of Writing

A comparison between Habermas and Putnam on whether, and to what extent, philosophy is a kind of writing, or is its writing, proves instructive, particularly since Putnam is a philosopher who in many respects is close to Habermas in temperament and style—much closer, say, than Cavell or Derrida. Here is Putnam: "If I agree with Derrida on anything it is this: that philosophy is writing, and that it must learn now to be a writing whose authority is always to be won anew, not inherited or awarded because it is philosophy. Philosophy is, after all, one of the humanities and not a science."[37] Now Habermas: "Significant critics and great philosophers are also noted writers. Literary criticism and philosophy have a family resemblance to literature—and to this extent to one another as well—in their rhetorical achievements. But their family relationship stops right there, for in each of these enterprises the tools of rhetoric are subordinated to the discipline of a *distinct* form of argumentation" (PDM 210).

Habermas's reference to the "discipline of a *distinct* form of argumentation" supposes that the question of what philosophy is, the business it is in, is settled, not open. Moreover it supposes that this question *can* be settled. But that would mean philosophy is not subject to the pressure that modernity's relation to time imposes on other cultural practices and cultural traditions, forcing them to keep open, unsettled, the question of what they are, and how they are to "go on." What Cavell shares with Heidegger, Wittgenstein, and Adorno, among others, is the thought that the question of what philosophy is, just as the question of what art is, has now become a self-defining feature of its (possible) practice. The fact of its historical circumstances compels philosophy to ask this question, a question that turns out to be as unsettling as it is unanswerable. Rather than the "distinctive" employment of common rhetorical devices (metaphor, simile, irony, hyperbole, etc.), it is their peculiarly modern(ist) historical situation that first allows the family resemblances shared by philosophy and literature to stand out.

Habermas goes to great lengths to limit, to hold at bay, the kind of considerations that have prompted the likes of Cavell and Derrida to regard philosophy as a kind of writing whose success as philosophy depends on *its* kind of writing and involves, of course, much more than what is conventionally understood as philosophical argument. For Habermas, on the other hand, its writing should not be what is distinctive to philosophy, since that would open the door to world-disclosing argument aiming at the transformation of sensibility, at new possible discourses and practices. And that would mean that philosophy is no longer be able to define itself strictly in terms of the rationality of its procedures. But drawing attention to the dependence of philosophy on its kind of writing is hardly an endorsement of the claim that philosophy and literature are indistinguishable, ostensibly because they employ and depend on identical rhetorical devices. The claim is not that philosophy is a form of literature, and therefore subject to the same canons of criticism. Rather, the emphasis on philosophy as a kind of writing consists of a belated acknowledgment that both literature and philosophy are subject to the same historical pressures, pressures that can be released, if only to a limited degree, through an exploratory or experimental writing that illuminates the nature of its own philosophical activity and its existential fragility.

No better example comes to mind than the many-voiced text of Wittgenstein's *Philosophical Investigations*. Of course, there are many such inimitable, unrepeatable texts in the history of philosophy, texts that are inseparable from their kind of writing (Hegel's *Phenomenology* is obviously another, but so is Descartes's *Meditations*). That there are philosophical texts that are inseparable from their writing does not entail that philosophy's kind of writing is to be judged, or can adequately be judged, by the standards of literature. Whatever its merits *as* literature, philosophy is not reducible *to* literature. (Conversely, whatever its merits as philosophy, literature is not reducible to philosophy.) Philosophical texts such as these aim, not surprisingly, at disclosing alternative possibilities for philosophy and for human forms of life. Unlike literature and art, philosophy does not operate in the medium of appearance or fiction. Its medium is argument—in the very broad, nonsectarian sense that I have been proposing.

Once we recognize that world-disclosing argument is properly philosophical argument, a second family resemblance between philosophy and literature stands out, and that is their shared world-disclosing purpose. *Pace* Habermas, what distinguishes philosophy from literature is not that the former is a problem-solving enterprise while the latter is a world-disclosing enterprise—this is an untenable and incoherent distinction, since there is no way to separate world disclosure from problem solving in the relevant instances: they are interdependent activities, operating on one and the same cognitive continuum. There is just as much, if not more, so-called problem solving in the arts as there is in philosophy. In fact the histories of music and architecture can be told as histories of solved problems in ways that the history of philosophy cannot, not least, because the relevant problems are widely accepted *as* solved by their practitioners. Nothing but ignorance of what goes on in literature and the arts can conclude that they are less "cognitive" than philosophy. To assert that is to be in the grip of the "third dogma of empiricism," which as Albrecht Wellmer has argued, is most visibly present in the sharp boundary persistently drawn between rationality and the imagination.[38]

Given that art and literature demand more of our full rationality and full sensibility than philosophy typically does, they may well be more, rather than less, cognitively demanding, more, rather than less, rational. Peter Dews makes the very pertinent point that unlike expert cultures (science, law, morality) that are constituted by specializing in one aspect of reason, art and literature preserve the lifeworld's integrated rationality without sacrificing their reflexivity: "Knowledge of the world and moral insight are intrinsic features of the work of art."[39] (This point connects with Wellmer's point that the different aspects of rationality are intermeshed in works of art with the point that those same aspects are integrated in everyday speech and action.) Were one inclined to rub it in, one could make a strong case for how much more attuned to the everyday have been art and literature than has been philosophy, how much more they have illuminated "the prose of the world," and how much philosophy owes to art and literature for its own illumination of the everyday.[40]

As I said before, what does distinguish the world-disclosing activity of philosophy from that of literature is that it takes place in, is made possible by, a *different* medium—the medium of argument, rather than the medium of fiction or appearance. In each case the medium is distinctive of that practice, self-defining by virtue of its particular constraints and particular possibilities. That is all the difference there is, but it is nonetheless quite a difference, for each medium in which is variously disclosed the familiar things with which we daily contend, requires its own medium-specific response. There is indeed an important difference or two between literature and philosophy, but as far as this issue is concerned, the issue of philosophy's kind of writing, the difference between philosophy and literature lies in the medium in which, if I may say it, problem-solving disclosure takes place. The idea that art and literature specialize in world disclosure while philosophy and science specialize in problem solving is just a variation on the hoary idea that the former are products of imagination while the latter are products of reason. To repeat, I am claiming that it is the medium in which problem solving and disclosure take place that is decisive, not the fallacious distinction between (cognitive) problem solving and (noncognitive) world disclosure.

Certainly one of the "virtues" of the procedural conception is that it disburdens philosophy of the existential concerns about how it might be re-inherited and continued, concerns that famously obsessed Wittgenstein, Heidegger, Adorno, and Derrida. Hence the narrow identification of writing with rhetoric (as though it were reducible to the latter), and of its subordination to a distinct form of argumentation (as though one could know in advance what one had to say, needing only to hit on the right words to say it), relieves philosophy of the pain of thinking about and finding a voice of its own, a voice that is not the voice of the "expert" who at once claims authority and disclaims the expertise upon which it could be based.

Thus it is one of the "advantages" of the procedural conception that it does not leave philosophy vulnerable to that agonizing struggle with its own identity, the struggle over which voice is its "own" voice, a struggle that used up so much of the intellectual energy of those who have taken that question seriously, knowing it was going to remain an unsettling, unanswerable question.

6   Two Kinds of Fallibilism

Recall that Habermas attaches great importance throughout *The Philosophical Discourse of Modernity* to the phenomenon of modernity's relation to time, acknowledging that the "vitality" of the philosophical discourse of modernity "has had to be constantly renewed" by world-disclosing cultural interpretations that once again open up the horizon of possibility (PDM 13). Now a procedural conception can hardly make sense of, let alone engage in, this kind of endeavour. It seems that the commitment to a procedural conception of philosophy excludes as *distinctively* philosophical, the very activity most necessary for renewing the vitality of the philosophical discourse of modernity. For philosophy to be responsively and responsibly modern in the sense common to Kant, Hegel, Foucault, and Habermas, it requires of philosophy much more than incorporating the fallibilistic consciousness of the sciences. It requires incorporating modernity's relation to time.

The two are complementary, but quite distinct. The former consists in the recognition that the warranted assertability of any truth and rightness claim may not be ensured against future disconfirmation: any claim justified today may need to be revised or withdrawn in light of new evidence, new arguments, and new experiences. The orientation to the future that a fallibilistic consciousness establishes is essentially *negative*, notional—open only to the possibility of disconfirmation. If an agent has good reasons to believe *p*, she does not look to the future in hopeful anticipation of reasons to reject *p*, for such an orientation would not be consistent with what it means to have good reasons for believing *p*. On the other hand, the orientation to the future that modernity's time-consciousness establishes is essentially *positive*, expectant— involving an openness to and a hopeful anticipation of a future different from the past. It is only in virtue of this positive relation to the future that allows the future to function as a horizon of possibility and as a source of pressure, intensifying our attunement and our responsiveness to present possibility.

The fallibilistic consciousness of the sciences needs to be evidence-responsive, not time-responsive. Moreover modernity's relation to time possesses its own distinctive "fallibilism." This "fallibilism" arises not from methods or procedures open to disconfirmation and to new evidence; it arises from the historical self-consciousness that modernity's relation to time fosters. It brings to awareness the degree to which our interpretations, valuations, our practices, and traditions are temporally indexed. And because of this awareness, we are compelled to incorporate a "diagnosis of the times" into philosophical thought (PDM 54).

Just about anything that looks solid today may crumble and melt away, whether it is because of unforeseeable events that force us to rethink things from the ground up or because of the emergence of new interpretations, valuations, and practices that, equally unforeseeable, force us to reconsider our old ones, either transforming or suspending them. Richard Rorty coined an exceedingly apposite phrase for this distinctive form of fallibil-ism—the recognition of contingency. It consists in the recognition that things could have been otherwise, and because things could have been otherwise, things do not have to remain as they are. The way things are now, is not the way things have to be. Emerson made use of the time-honored image of the circle to convey the same message: 'every action admits of being outdone. Our life is an apprenticeship to the truth, that around every circle another can be drawn.'[41] Thus the recognition of contingency, the recognition "that around every circle another can be drawn," expresses both the "fallibilism" particular to modernity's relation to time and the openness to the future (and the past) equally particular to it.

In the end, the question of whether philosophy can or should be a world-disclosing activity is moot, since for some time now philosophy has engaged in its own kind of world-disclosing activity. As Dewey recognized, "the articulation and revelation of the meanings of the current course of events is the task and problem of philosophy in days of transition."[42] Doubtless, we are living in days of transition. These are modernity's kind of days, days with which we are altogether familiar. This is pretty much the point of Habermas's discussion of Hegel's concept of modernity in the opening pages of *The Philosophical Discourse of Modernity*. So he is once again inconsistent in his treatment of an insight that he contends is as essential to the practice of philosophical critique and illumination as it is to the understanding of what it means to be modern. Thus it is not a question of whether philosophy should articulate and reveal the meanings of the current course of events; it is a question of whether philosophy can continue to do so, whether it can do in the future what it has done in the past. Certainly it is hard to imagine how philosophy could have a future if were not able to illuminate, however weakly, the meaning of the current course of events, events that define our days as days of transition. In other words, it is much too late in the day for a procedural conception to regulate (if not rule out) what philosophy already does. World-disclosing arguments need not pretend to some privileged access to truth, for they are not about truth in the ordinary sense but about enlarging the realm of meaning and possibility, facilitating the emergence, the birth or rebirth, of "better forms of life and more reflective ways of life." Nor do such arguments seek to disclose the social totality in one shot, since that is a possibility the very idea of disclosure denies.[43] As with any interpretive act, world-disclosing interpretation anticipates Gadamerian "completeness"—anticipates, not achieves. No interpretation can achieve completeness. All disclosure is partial, and falliblistic, in both senses of fallibilistic I have discussed.

As Habermas has acknowledged, world-disclosing practices are no more the property of philosophy than they are the property of art or of any other expert culture. They depend on capacities with which we are all endowed in varying degrees of reflexivity, capacities that are essential to understanding, criticizing, and renewing everyday practices essential to our agency. All that distinguishes philosophers from nonphilosophers is that the world-disclosing capacities in question are embedded in and supported by a culturally specific (but not culturally circumscribed) tradition of inquiry and critique that has acquired a significant level of reflexivity about the employment of concepts and the individual and collective lives we live with them. If we take Heidegger seriously, we might wish to say that we are disclosers *before and after* we are knowers, more primordially disclosers than knowers, and of course, that characterization goes altogether well with the primacy of the practical, giving priority to speaking and acting rather than knowing. In any case, the world cannot be disclosed or redisclosed merely by the application of fallible knowledge.

As I hope to have shown, no good reasons can be adduced for critical theory to accept the limitations imposed on it by a procedural conception of philosophy that reduces its role, on the one hand, to that of a normative engineer designing the better procedure for testing the validity of generalizable norms and, on the other, to that of a mixed up go-between offering "mediation" to the disoriented lifeworld and its alienating expert cultures. Habermas can't help himself to the Hegelian insight that "the modern consciousness of time exploded *the form* of philosophy" (PDM 53) and, at the same, propose (as fully and adequately modern) a procedural conception of philosophy that proceeds as though the *form* of philosophy has remained intact—as though philosophy can go on as before, as though it were not obligated to be time-responsive, as though time did not imprint itself upon its activity and its self-conception, making the *form* of philosophy a never-ending problem *for* philosophy.

V   Alternative Sources of Normativity

1 Disclosure, Change, and the New

Throughout my critical analyses of both Habermas and Heidegger, I have been exploring alternative sources of normativity in light of which we may re-envision the project of critical theory. In what follows I would like to bring more sharply into focus how these alternative sources of normativity can redefine the practice of critical theory once it is liberated from an altogether confining proceduralism and from an unjustifiably narrow interpretation of the German philosophical tradition. Envisioning a richer and more pluralistic critical theory, I will elaborate in greater detail how we can rethink our notions of reason, agency, and change as continuous with the disclosure of possibility and the capacity to initiate a new beginning. As we will see (in chapters 2 and 3), I am placing the capacity for receptivity and self-decentering in an unusually prominent and central normative position.

Approached in the right way, Heidegger's life-long preoccupation with the problem of beginning anew, a problem that he considered continuous with the problem of how to "receive" our inherited ontological frameworks, can enrich considerably both our understanding of cultural and normative change and our understanding of the role that our own agency can play in facilitating such change. Once we see that the usual dismissive and debunking criticisms simply miss what is valuable in Heidegger's reflections on change and agency, we can have a more perspicuous view of them. It simply is not the case that Heidegger's position entails that ontology completely dictates history, as though there were *no* interaction between world disclosure and everyday practice, between pre-reflective and reflective disclosure. In fact Heidegger's position can be made consistent with the reciprocal interaction thesis. Treating the ontological difference as though it were a self-refuting denial of human agency allows Habermas to sidestep the real issue that divides him from Heidegger, and from all those for whom the notion of disclosure plays an essential role in understanding historical and cultural change.

That issue concerns the role that disclosure plays, reflective and pre-reflective disclosure, in facilitating normative and cultural change. It concerns the kind of practices that enable such change, and the kind of agency such change demands. In the end it comes down to the issue of whether there are other sources of normativity and other media of social and cultural learning that enable a freer, more open relation to the cultural conditions of intelligibility and possibility that we inherit and pass on. Because the proceduralist paradigm can only make sense of learning processes indexed to practices of justification, to taking Yes/No positions on criticizable validity claims, it is unable to make sense of how agents themselves can enlarge the realm of meaning and possibility, accountably initiating the kind of normative and cultural change that leads to "better forms of life and more reflective ways of life."

Although Heidegger's account of disclosure as a practice that facilitates a new beginning greatly enriches our understanding of change and agency, it is nonetheless marred by two egregious errors. First, as I have already argued in part II, he neglected to coordinate the question of how we might transform our relation to our pre-reflective understanding of the world with the question of how we might transform our relation to one another. Put another way, he failed to connect the normativity of disclosure with the normativity of intersubjectivity. Like Habermas, he failed to see that the two are mutually interdependent. The question of how we might transform our inherited ontological frameworks and the question of how we might transform our relation to one another normatively suppose one another, not only because separating them would preclude the possibility of nonviolent, noncoercive transformation. Moreover we cannot make sense of either intersubjectivity or disclosure without relating the dependencies of one to the dependencies of other; otherwise, we end up, as Heidegger and Habermas have, with conceptually truncated accounts of each.

Second, Heidegger mistakenly identified disclosure with truth, treating the formation and transformation of epochs, worldviews, and, generally, any enlargement or alteration of the conditions of intelligibility and possibility, as self-regulating and self-constituting "truth-events" (*Wahrheitsgeschehen*). He never recognized the depth of the first error, but rather belatedly, he came to recognize the depth of the second. He came to see that by fusing disclosure to truth, he conflated the conditions by which meaning and possibility are enlarged with the truths they enable. "To raise the question of *aletheia*, of disclosure as such, is not the same as raising the question of truth. For this reason, it was inadequate and misleading to call *aletheia* in the sense of opening, truth."[1]

It took Heidegger roughly forty years—between *Being and Time* and *Zur Sache des Denkens*—to see this. Why? Is it simply because he had failed to notice that he had made a basic error in transcendental argumentation?[2] It does look that way, but it is hard to understand how someone so steeped in transcendental argumentation, someone who is himself an important innovator in this form of argument, could make such an error. The beginnings of a better explanation can be found in the essay in which Heidegger acknowledges his mistake, "The End of Philosophy and the Task of Thinking." In the same part of the text where he notes his mistake, Heidegger also offers a clue as to its cause. "*Aletheia*, disclosure thought as the opening of presence, is not yet truth. Is *aletheia* then less than truth? Or is it more because it first grants truth as *adequatio* and *certitudo*, because there can be no presence and presenting outside of the realm of the opening?"[3]

The clue to Heidegger's mistake is found in the question of whether *aletheia*, disclosure, is less or more than truth—ontologically less or more. In Heidegger's view, that which "first grants the possibility of truth" is ontologically higher than truth itself—this is more or less the substance of the claim that possibility is ontologically higher than actuality. It was also Heidegger's view that because the Western philosophical tradition had not taken account of the ontological difference, having assimilated "Being" to "beings," it was unable to recognize the transcendental difference between the constitutive understanding of the world and what is constituted in the world. This prompted Heidegger to "correct" the tradition's ontological one-sidedness. So he proposed a change in the meaning of truth, redefining it in terms of disclosure—in terms of that which first grants the possibility of truth in the customary or derivative sense of truth as correspondence or well-justified belief. Thus Heidegger's mistake is a consequence of overreaching and overcorrection: having discovered something extremely significant about the ontological and epistemological conditions of truth he tried to make that which had been long suppressed and neglected the "foundation" for a radically new view of truth. This is altogether a shame because this misplaced ambition got in the way of a far less objectionable goal, namely to accord to cultural conditions of intelligibility and possibility the philosophical significance and dignity that the tradition accords to truth. This other goal is indeed a worthy one, for it redirects philosophical activity from its fixation on the question of truth to the question of how to understand and initiate changes in the conditions that not only make new truth-candidates possible but also new forms of agency.

Habermas, Tugendhat, and others, are certainly right to point out that by conceiving disclosure as some kind of "truth-event," Heidegger precludes the question of justification (validity). But this criticism is guilty of its own kind of distortion, treating Heideggerian disclosure as entailing "the imperative force of an illumination compelling one to one's knees" (PDM 255). This dramatically overstated objection just takes for granted what it has failed to prove: that disclosure is "raised above any and every critical forum," that the world can be disclosed "with equal ease by any given approach" (PDM 154). Heidegger certainly made a drastic mistake by running disclosure together with truth, but his interpretive and critical practice did not proceed as though it were impossible to criticize or justify one disclosure from the standpoint of another—otherwise, his critique of modernity would have been totally incoherent, incapable of contributing "lasting insights."

It is not at all Heidegger's view that every disclosure, every new beginning, is as good as every other. As I've tried to show, once one accepts that disclosure is a type of problem-solving activity whose success is measured by its problem-solving power, this criticism simply crumbles. As does the criticism that on Heidegger's view of disclosure, all we can do is passively accept, not criticize or transform, our inherited ontologies. For example, in *The Question Concerning Technology*, Heidegger argues that if we continue to understand and represent "technology" as an instrument, we will continue to misunderstand our relation to it, both the problems it alleviates and the dangers it introduces. Heidegger's ontological reinterpretation of technology obviates the need to choose between the two currently available positions toward technology: either as something we master or as something that masters us. Thus his later reflections on technology are best understood as seeking a way to overcome the "fate" that accompanies our technological understanding of the world by clarifying what is fatal about it—and much of what is fatal about it is thinking that we have to respond to technology either as something that we control or as something that controls us. Either we intervene by taking the appropriate measures, or we face the possibility of becoming enslaved by that which is supposed to serve us.[4] From *Frankenstein* to *The Matrix*, art and popular culture have played out this anxious scenario in various ways, some of which come closer and closer to everyday experience. But Heidegger's analysis of the modern technological understanding of being is one that tries to disclose another possibility, and that possibility involves rethinking how we "receive" our understanding of being, a possibility that will be explored in detail in the next chapter. For now, all that needs repeating is the point that there would not be any reason for Heidegger to explore such an alternative—whatever its value—were he committed to the view that we must simply submit to whatever ontological pre-understanding we contingently inherit.

Now had Heidegger come to appreciate the depth of the first error, he might have seen that to talk about how *we* receive our understanding of being is necessarily to talk about not just how we become more receptive to "being," but also more receptive to one another. For the kind of change in our relation to our inherited understanding of the world that Heidegger envisioned, is a kind of change that requires a complementary change in our understanding of one another. It requires, in short, a recognition and acknowledgment of our dependence on one another that is co-extensive with the recognition and acknowledgment of our dependence on our pre-reflective understanding of the world. And if Heidegger had more fully appreciated the depth of the second error, he might have also noticed that we can't meaningfully talk about "the opening" that makes our various truth claims possible, without talking also about how *we* must work at keeping the "opening" open by our cooperative acts of disclosure and receptivity—and so, once again, must talk about what kind of relations to one another make that "opening" stay open—open to openness itself. If Habermas erred in anchoring truth and objectivity in relations of intersubjectivity alone, that error cannot be corrected simply by disclosing the prior dependence of relations of intersubjectivity on conditions of intelligibility. Rather, the dependence has to be understood as mutual and as mutually enabling (as well as mutually entangling).

Even though these two errors significantly weaken Heidegger's account of disclosure, they do not negate the potential of Heidegger's suggestions concerning how we might redisclose our ontological frameworks, by which redisclosure we might open up the possibility of less deformed and less distorted social practices, and thereby facilitate a new beginning for ourselves. Open-minded interpretation of *Being and Time* reveals that much of what Heidegger has to say about fate (*Schicksal*), destiny (*Geschick*), and temporality (*Zeitlichkeit*) in the second division of *Being and Time* is rather close to Habermas's own reflections on the normative implications of modernity's relation to time. This is by no means a coincidence, for Habermas's reflections are indebted both to Heidegger's and to Nietzsche's "Dionysian messianism."

Guided by Nietzsche's second "untimely meditation," Heidegger tries to develop the normative connections between modernity's sense of possibility (its orientation to the novelty of the future) and its sense of responsibility (its obligations to the past). Thus he offers a critical-interpretive position in which "the future-oriented gaze is directed from the present onto a past that is connected as prehistory with the present, as by the chain of continual destiny." Yet, despite the close proximity of their views of modernity's time-consciousness, Habermas's debunking strategy points Heidegger's "future-oriented gaze" in the direction of an "apocalyptic expectation of a catastrophic entry of the new" (PDM 134). Assimilating Heidegger's reflections on beginning anew to apocalypse and catastrophe not only distorts Heidegger's "Dionysian messianism," it empties the idea of reflective disclosure of all normative content, as if all that mattered were an "ecstatic" new beginning stripped of any evaluative questions concerning better and worse disclosures of the world, better and worse ways to begin anew. Even before we begin to evaluate this or that newly disclosed possibility, we already have at the very least an inchoate awareness of these limitations. So our future-oriented gaze is already guided by a consciousness of present crisis, and of the need for alternative possibilities that can answer our needs. That is why, as Habermas came finally to acknowledge, we depend on the problem-solving power of reflective disclosure to overcome the limitations of our current conditions of intelligibility and possibility, limitations that hem in our agency and frustrate our sense-making activities.

That Habermas's negative attitude toward Heidegger's "Dionysian messianism" originates in the truly catastrophic history of twentieth-century Germany is easy enough to see and understand. And, of course, it is also shaped by the historically justified worry that massive cultural and political change carried out in the name of some determinate utopia will turn out to be catastrophic indeed. As discussed in part I, chapter 2, we are understandably hesitant to endorse a new stance, to support a new beginning, which, because it is genuinely new, is not only "unfamiliar to us" but also "uncontrollable by us." The obvious advantage of Habermas's attempt to treat the orientation to validity claims as the primary engine of social and cultural change is that it is change that is both familiar to us and controllable by us. Change that is regulated by the rationality of justificatory procedures is change that cannot overwhelm us, catch us by surprise, or make unexpected demands on us. It is change we can master, change we can direct, at a pace we set. But this is a very restrictive notion of change and of agency, restrictive because it reduces the scope and possibilities of change that we can indeed ascribe to our own agency. The only other kind of change this view allows is change that displays the "contingency of genuinely innovative forces," the paradigm of which is an aesthetic model of change exemplified by modern art (the rationality of which is construed as defective at best). So, on the one hand, we have the possibility of procedurally regulated change, and, on the other, change that depends on brute contingency. We can comfortably live with the latter kind of change because it is safely confined to the domesticated aesthetic sphere of cultural value—a sphere of private, not public value (as Rorty likes to put it).

This is not just a highly restrictive model of change and of agency; it is also a defensive one. And it is not hard to see that the basic concepts of the theory of communicative action have internalized this restrictive and defensive view of change and agency: they can accommodate only so much discontinuity, only so much of the new. However, it must be said that Habermas's suspicious attitude towards the new is hardly unique; on the contrary, it reflects the general view of the Western philosophical tradition since Greek antiquity. Given its perennial antipathy toward all that is changeable and transient, it is hardly surprising that modernity's relation to time shattered "the *form* of philosophy." To Nietzsche and Emerson, Western philosophy's suspicious attitude toward the new betrays a conservative cultural attitude: "What is new . . . is always *evil*, being that which wants to conquer and overthrow the old boundary markers and the old pieties; and only what is old is good."[5] "The new statement is always hated by the old, and, to those dwelling in the old, comes like an abyss of skepticism."[6] As a consequence the claims of the new are typically met with an unwelcome response largely because of their unsettling ability to shake up our taken for granted beliefs about ourselves and about the world, opening up an "abyss of skepticism," threatening disorientation.

The sense of the new to which Emerson and Nietzsche allude is clearly not the new as it is typically understood today. It is not something one can simply will, not something that can be manufactured or consumed, not something that is inimical to the everyday, and not something that can be reduced to the desire for unbounded self-invention. It is a conception of the new that needs to be distinguished from, and defended against, contemporary culture's drunken infatuation with the promise of limitless freedom, whether it be through the consumer-driven reorganization of our daily life, the various ways we are encouraged to remake our "plastic" bodies,[7] or through the ecstatic escape from the constraints of a life shared with others.[8] Increasingly it is getting harder for us to think of the new, of alternative possibility, any other way—much harder than it was for Emerson and Nietzsche. After witnessing more than a century of what can be done in the name of the "new," we are justifiably wary of it. But that is not all the new can mean, not all the new can promise. As I argued in part I, it is by no means necessary to think of the new as requiring the annihilation of the old nor is it necessary to think of it as opposed to the everyday or the ordinary. That opposition is itself the problem, and in our time it is played out in the continuous degradation and trivialization of the everyday, which in turn distorts and mystifies the extraordinary. The crazed fascination with celebrity, with "reality TV," and with "extreme" forms of recreation, the endless consumption of distance-shrinking and time-compressing technologies, reflects an insatiable desire for the "new" as for the ideal narcotic. But we should not let this hugely seductive and hugely successful instrumentalization of the promise of the new obscure or distort the idea of the new as a critical response to the old, as that which arises out of a genuine rather than an artificial need, and as that on which the intelligibility of our own agency also depends.[9]

Any genuine new beginning disclosed in response to obdurate problems in the world for which currently available possibilities are inadequate will be subject to intersubjective judgments concerning better and worse, right and wrong, temporary and more lasting ways, of going on with our practices. Yet in almost every instance Habermas treats suggestions for reinterpreting human agency in terms of practices of disclosure as recipes for disaster, regardless of the political orientations of the philosopher making them. And that is because Habermas's understanding of what such practices involve is manifestly influenced by an uncritical (though widely accepted) interpretation of Kant's "aesthetics of genius," according to which semantic and cultural innovation is a process that is neither rational nor reflectively accessible to the innovating "agent." This is especially evident in Habermas's response to Castoriadis's attempt to reformulate Heidegger's view of disclosure as a basic concept of social and political theory. For Habermas, this is just one more example of how disclosure theorists aestheticize everyday practices, and aestheticize processes of normative and cultural change:

Castoriadis works out the normal case of the political from the limit case of the act of founding an institution; and he interprets this in turn from a horizon of aesthetic experience, as the ecstatic moment erupting from the continuum of time when something absolutely new is founded. . . . The social process consists in the generation of radically different forms, as though it were a demiurge setting itself to work in the continuous creation of new social models embodied in ever different exemplary ways—in short, the self-positing and ontological genesis of ever new "worlds". (PDM 329/trans. altered)

The claim that Castoriadis cannot connect the process of disclosing the world anew to the activity of accountable individuals but must ascribe it to "being" or to "society," as though to the normatively unconstrained power of a meaning-creating genius or irrational meaning-creating force (PDM 330, 332/PT 41) indicates just how much the "aesthetics of genius" governs Habermas's view of semantic and cultural innovation, semantic and cultural change, that is not directed or overseen by practices of justi-fication. As with the construal of the extraordinary, the "ecstatic moment" in which the new erupts "from the continuum of time" is here completely opposed to, and inimical to, the everyday. The "normal case of the polit-ical" can never incorporate the extraordinary, thereby positioning the new as necessarily the ecstatic "other" of the everyday, and, therefore, as nec-essarily the "other" of reason. The idea that the reflective disclosure of pos-sibilities that can initiate a new beginning, a different and hopefully better way of going on with our practices, is ruled out from the start because there is no room for a conception of disclosure as a cooperative activity that takes place (and can only take place) on the level of everyday practice. Being suspicious of what is new, because it is unfamiliar to us and uncon-trollable by us, we rule out this possibility. As I argued in part II, chapter 2, reflective disclosure is always an act of co-disclosure, a matter of coop-erative activity, not a matter of virtuosity or "self-positing." And coopera-tive activity is no more controllable and instrumentalizable than the disclosure of possibility. We can't draw upon the normativity of the new unless we facilitate its appearance by cooperative acts of disclosure. The more cooperatively a new possibility is disclosed, the more realizable the possibility disclosed, for it is disclosed under the same conditions as the conditions under which it would have to be noncoercively and reflec-tively endorsed.

Regarded from a view of semantic and cultural innovation not in the grip of Kant's "aesthetics of genius," and from a view of agency and change not in the grip of proceduralism, the idea that the disclosure of possibil-ity can facilitate a cooperatively achieved new beginning for ourselves will not seem "out of the ordinary" at all; in fact it will seem odd *not* to regard it as one the most fundamental and most necessary of all concepts of social and political theory. That is most certainly how Hannah Arendt under-stood it, which is why it is the basic concept of her theory of action, the core of her view of freedom. For Arendt, freedom needs to be understood as "the freedom to call something into being which did not exist before, which was not given, not even as an object of cognition or imagination, and which therefore, strictly speaking, could not be known."[10] Indeed the central category of social and political thought may be *natality*, the distinctively human capacity to initiate a new beginning, because we ourselves "are new beginnings and hence beginners."[11] On this view of freedom, human beings can experience their freedom as their own only in so far as they can initiate a new beginning for themselves through which they break free of something oppressive and debilitating in their relationship to one another, to their institutions, or to their commonly shared world. Moreover this public space of freedom can be preserved as a public space of freedom only so long as "new beginnings are constantly injected into the stream of things already initiated."[12] This in turn depends on our ability freely to disclose alternative possibilities, "to call something into being which did not exist before, which was not given, not even as an object of cognition or imagination, and which therefore, strictly speaking, could not be known."

It was just this novel connection between the new and freedom that the revolutions of the eighteenth and nineteenth centuries revealed and at the same time suppressed. That connection is clear enough when we identify the revolutionary act not with "rebellion and tearing things down," but with "founding anew and building up."[13] In *On Revolution* Arendt criticized the way in which the American Revolution was one-sidedly institutionalized in the new republic: "there was no space reserved, no room left for the exercise of precisely those qualities which had been instrumental in building it. And this was clearly no mere oversight, as though those who knew so well how to provide for power of the commonwealth and the liberties of its citizens, for judgment and opinion, for interests and rights, had simply forgotten what actually they cherished above everything else, the potentialities of action and the proud privilege of being beginners of something altogether new."[14]

The lesson that Arendt draws from this is that the possibilities and potential of democracy cannot be sufficiently grasped in justice or rights conceptions of democracy such as those articulated by Habermas or Rawls: something crucial is missing. Unlike Rawls and Habermas whose normative orientation is not to freedom but to justice, Arendt thinks that the institutionalization of basic rights—that is, as negative and positive liberties (private and public freedoms)—are a necessary but insufficient precondition for establishing a public space of freedom. Of course, there can be no democratic "self-government of the people" without the institutionalization of individual rights, and their continual revision and reinterpretation in the medium of democratic discourse. But even deliberative models of democracy do not touch on what concerns Arendt, namely how to constitute and preserve a public space of freedom so as to make a permanent and ineliminable element of democracy, cooperative acts of "founding anew and building up." Her primary concern was with the question of how to bring about a fundamental change in what we take democratic politics to be, such that we come to understand that so long as we view "founding anew and building up" as a "limit-case" of democratic politics, then we'll have to accept a state of paralysis and arrested development as the "normal case of the political" in our democratic form of life.

In a recent discussion of the significance of Arendt's views of freedom and revolution to democratic theory, Albrecht Wellmer states the point in the following way:

[T]he inherent goal of what Arendt calls revolution is an institution—an institutionalization—of freedom, which can only emerge from the common *willing* of people who begin to act in concert and thereby *transform* their common world and create a space of public freedom. *On the other hand*, the internal correlation of "revolution" and "institution" also means, that a performative and inventive element belongs to the very preservation of republican institutions, so that . . . the spirit of revolution becomes something like a condition of the permanence of republican institutions . . . [I]nasmuch as the institutions of public freedom become a common *project*, their preservation and re-invention becomes an end-in-itself, through which the problems of "rights" and "justice" will be seen in a new light, or . . . focused in a new way.[14]

Arendt thus belongs to that group of crisis theorists who recognize that the (never to be taken for granted) capacity to begin anew and so found anew our own traditions, practices, and institutions is essential to the success of any democratic form of life. Because they have incorporated modernity's relation to time into the basic concepts of social and political theory these are theorists who are able to draw upon sources of normativity unavailable to proceduralists. Without these sources we cannot open up the future by disclosing alternative possibilities for ourselves. When we cannot do that, when we are, so to speak, prepared to work within an already given range of possibilities, we render otiose the idea of critique, the idea of critical democracy, the idea of change that we can attribute to and that expresses our own agency.

It cannot be seriously suggested that Habermas's model of critical theory is politically conservative, but I would like to suggest that it is conservative about possibility. In my view, Habermas's model of critical theory has absorbed far more of the right-Hegelian account of modernity than a viable critical theory can support. It has made critical theory far too respectful of

the facts of social complexity, "facts" that are treated quasi-transcenden-
tally in the way that Kantian critique treats the limits of knowledge, as
though social critique consisted only in identifying but never transgress-
ing "necessary" limits. Just as Kant's critique of knowledge must already
know more than it can allowably presuppose, a critical theory that claims
to know the limits of social change, must also know a great deal more than
it can allowably presuppose—namely the limits of possibility. But how
could one ever be in a position to know the limits of possibility? How could
one know what our possibilities are if possibility is not an object of knowledge? A one-sided focus on the question of the normative order of society
reduces modernity's need for self-reassurance into a question of the legitimacy of its political institutions. As a result the question of normative and
cultural change that answers the need for "ethical-political" reassurance,
the need to enlarge the realm of meaning and possibility, has been woe-
fully neglected. The price for this neglect is resignation to already available possibilities:

Philosophy, working together with the reconstructive sciences, can only throw light
on the situations in which we find ourselves. It can contribute to our learning to
understand the ambivalences that we come up against as just so many appeals to
increasing responsibilities within a contracting space of possibility. (PT 146/trans.
altered)

The resignation voiced here may sound like tough-minded realism, free
of pathos and nostalgia. But if we have learned anything about the nature
of possibility, it is that it is not an object about which we can make fact-
like claims. Possibility is not something whose conditions of possibility
(historical or transcendental) we can fully and explicitly state; it is not
something that can be empirically surveyed and demarcated. That is one
of the reasons why a new possibility catches us by surprise—we didn't
expect it, we didn't see it coming. A newly disclosed possibility always
exceeds what is given to us by our current understanding of ourselves and
our current historical circumstances. It always exceeds, semantically and
ontologically, what is. That's why the disclosure of alternative possibilities
is absolutely crucial to the success of our attempts to initiate "better forms
of life and more reflective ways of life."[16] Resignation to "a contracting
space of possibility" registers, if only implicitly, the abandonment, the
very premature abandonment, of modernity's consciousness of time as a
normative resource for critical theory. And so, unknowingly, what is
announced is not the need for a realistic acknowledgment of the constraints within which we must continue the project of critical theory but,
rather, its end. The moment critical theory resigns itself to working within

"a contracting space of possibility" it effectively disconnects itself from modernity's relation to time, and dissolves itself. For in that moment it accepts the exhaustion of possibility and the foreclosure of the future; it accepts a restrictive conception of agency, and forgets the human capacity to enlarge the cultural conditions of possibility and initiate a new beginning. The "end" of critical theory is the logical outcome of a commitment to a procedural conception of philosophy and a right-Hegelian view of modernity's possibilities.

If critical theory is to have a future worthy of its past it must resist resigning itself to already available possibilities for thought and action. And it can do so by exploring in cooperative collaboration with its addressees, models of historical, cultural, and normative change that elucidate—at the level of everyday practice—how our own agency facilitates (or can facilitate) such change. (The right-Hegelian emphasis on the "facts" of social complexity must not trump the left-Hegelian emphasis on social change that responds to our genuine needs.) If we are to regenerate our confidence and hope, whose regeneration requires counteracting the contraction of our possibilities, we need to understand much better than we currently do just how practices that disclose the world anew facilitate "better forms of life and more reflective forms of life." Otherwise, it is one short step from resignation to fatalism.

2   Receptivity, Not Passivity

Now if any philosophical outlook can be said to be fatalistic, it is Heidegger's. Unfortunately, Heidegger's putative "fatalism" has too often served as the distorting lens through which we have read his writings on disclosure and the problem of beginning anew. Certainly this reading is essential to the success of the debunking strategy, portraying Heidegger's ontological analyses as laying the groundwork for a passive submission to mysterious, anonymous powers. "The propositionally contentless speech about Being has ... the illocutionary sense of demanding resignation to fate. Its practical-political side consists in the perlocutionary effect of a diffuse readiness to obey in relation to an auratic but indeterminate authority. ... The rhetoric of the later Heidegger ... attunes and trains its addressees in their dealings with pseudo-sacral powers" (PDM 140).

Here again, we have a criticism whose apparent cogency owes more to Heidegger's flirtation with Nazism than it does with the content of

Heidegger's philosophical views. We can make benign use of notions like "fate" and "destiny" without endorsing a submissive relation to what is, and which use is in accord both with the fallibilism of the sciences and with the fallibilism of modernity's relation to time. It is now a widely accepted premise of critical inquiries in the humanities and social sciences that our self-understanding and our practices are shaped by social and historical processes that take place "behind our backs." Although they take place "behind our backs," these processes can be made visible, if not as a whole and not all at once. Like Marx, Habermas holds the view that human beings make history but not under conditions of their own choosing. What Heidegger adds to this view of history is the idea, rather controversial, to be sure, that the self-conscious transformation of our inherited historical conditions might depend more on how we *receive* rather than on how we *make* our history—which is to say, that it might depend on how we recognize our dependence on, rather than on how we assert our independence from, our history. Because this view directs our attention to an important but largely misunderstood source of normativity, it deserves serious consideration rather than immediate dismissal.

Before it can be taken seriously, the connotations of receptivity, connotations that appear to involve a denial of autonomy and agency, also need critical scrutiny. One of those connotations involves associating—actually conflating—receptivity with passivity and with submissiveness. (That this connotation has been associated with distinctively "feminine" characteristics is, of course, not irrelevant to the generally dismissive response that greets talk of receptivity and openness.) It is not wrong to link Heidegger's emphasis on receptivity to the "fatalism" of his philosophical outlook, but the items to be linked are not at all what Heidegger's critics take them to be. Our background understanding, our inherited ontology, may indeed have something fatal about it. The term "fatal" need not refer to an *inescapable* fate. Rather, it can refer to the consequences of a distorted or one-sided understanding of the central concepts with which we live our lives—concepts like reason, truth, knowledge, freedom, authenticity, technology, and modernity. From Hegel to Adorno and Taylor, similar "fatalistic" things have been said in connection with the "fate" that is inscribed in the narrow modern understanding of freedom as negative freedom, and of reason as "instrumental reason." All that such views hold is that our self-understandings and cultural practices are obsessively or compulsively oriented toward certain possibilities more than others, and as such they exhibit a fate-like, but not necessarily unchangeable, character. That is not to say that bringing about a change in that character is going to be easy, a matter of simply deciding to bring about the desired change once we see the need for it.

Consider Benjamin's oft-cited parable about the "fatal" character of progress, "The Angel of History." The image of the entangled angel unable to intervene in the accelerating process of destruction in which it is caught and which it is forced to witness powerfully conveys the sense of helplessness and powerlessness induced by a historical process that seems irresistible and unstoppable, and thereby undermines our confidence in ourselves as agents. Now the intent of Benjamin's parable was not to induce fatalism about the future of humanity. But it does alert us to the alarming degree to which we experience progress, particularly scientific and technological progress, as unstoppable, carrying us along to where we know not. Typically we try to ride out the storm, enduring "progress" as it sweeps unimpeded through "homogeneous empty time." We have not yet "stopped" or even slowed down this seemingly independent process, possessing the power to dictate the nature and tempo of our lives, and, worst of all, to erase the presence of alternative possibilities for going on differently. This certainly makes progress feel fatal, giving it the appearance of a supra-human agency sucking all of humanity into a "destiny" not of its own choosing. And this is what renders ironic the claims of the Enlightenment, forcing us to ask "whether we can survive its solutions." Maybe we human beings do make our own history, even if not under conditions of our own choosing, but these conditions have become such that we can't but give our "consent" to almost every scientific "breakthrough," every technological "advance," even when we are filled more with dread than excitement about the future they will bring, a future we did not ask for, nor one which answers our genuine needs. So, to draw attention to what is fatal, perversely fatal, about what we call "progress" or "technology," is not to surrender to it. Heidegger no more welcomes passive submission or blind obedience than Benjamin does. He does suggest the need to listen more patiently, more attentively, to that which "calls" us: *listen*, not obey (Heidegger distinguishes clearly between one who listens, a *Hörender*, and one who obeys, a *Höriger*).[17] Like Benjamin, Heidegger is drawing attention to the fact that we *already* obey—that we have already submitted passively to progress, to modern technology, to modern capitalism, and done so without actually listening to what it is that calls, that beckons, that seduces. The suggestions made in connection with hearing, listening, receiving, are all suggestions that propose a reflective kind of listening, a receptivity that becomes reflexive about its own activity. What is being proposed is therefore nothing like blind submission to fate, but rather, a way by which we might become more attuned to our pre-reflective understanding of the world, to our inherited ontologies, and to our historical circumstances, and thereby open up a freer relation to them.[18]

Literature and psychoanalysis have shown us how a certain kind of character is going to encounter a corresponding set of situations and problems, problems that will have the form of "repetition-compulsions" because an individual keeps doing that thing he does over and over again, "without wanting to," "without meaning to." Similarly a background understanding will come with its own corresponding range of possibilities, some of which are played out in retrospectively accessible patterns of crisis and breakdown. Is it really to succumb to fatalism, if we say that within our inherited ontologies are deposited cultural meanings and ontological presuppositions that "govern" what we say and do? If it is the case that we are always already drawing upon such meanings and presuppositions in order to make sense of the world, and if the reproduction of the lifeworld necessarily draws on those resources, resources that cannot be exhausted by "learning oriented to validity-claims" since that learning is itself permanently dependent on those resources, then can we not say that our form of life has something "fatal" about it? And, can we not say, can we not acknowledge, that this is a permanent possibility for human forms of life, since a human form of life can never make fully transparent the conditions of intelligibility on which its sense-making practices rely, and thus cannot ensure those practices against determination by unconscious, fate-like processes? That we cannot ensure against such determination, against ever new configurations of power and domination that can arise, serves as an important reminder of the ever-arising need to redisclose the background understanding from which both practices of emancipation *and* practices of domination get their sense.

Once we reformulate the link between receptivity and fate in this way, we are in a better position to see the enlarged conception of agency that Heidegger's reflections on historical discontinuities and cultural change illuminate. Both Heidegger's early and later writing offer a promising starting point for understanding how cooperative, accountable practices of reflective disclosure can facilitate new cultural beginnings, initiate new practices, and found new institutions. In both the early and later writings, agent accountability is not developed in relation to the goal of intersubjective agreement; rather, it is developed in relation to intersubjectively verifiable experiences of epistemological crisis and cultural breakdown—that is, it is developed in response to the need cooperatively to begin anew. However, with their explicit focus on receptivity, the later writings appear to be particularly problematic. Occasionally irritating and not without risky implications, later Heidegger's exploration of receptivity requires critical and open-minded appropriation. His exploration of receptivity does push reflections on agency in an unfamiliar direction, not only decentering but also reconfiguring what it means to be an agent. I say "reconfigures" because it provides a picture of agency that places a great deal more emphasis on receptivity than we are accustomed to, and more than we are generally comfortable with. It does not eliminate activity so much as it makes receptivity active, reflective. Again, it is this unaccustomed emphasis on receptivity that leads sympathetic and unsympathetic interpreters to conclude that on Heidegger's view, all that is left to human agents is passively to submit to whatever ontological changes befall them. As I've already argued, this conclusion obscures rather than explains Heidegger's intentions.

The emphasis on receptivity ought to be interpreted in light of a non-instrumental idea of change, a non-instrumental relation to transformative practice, and that non-instrumental possibility is built into the idea of disclosure, since the idea of change it contains is radically non-instrumental. Reconfiguring agency in terms of the demands of receptivity opens up a different perspective on transformative practice, making it possible to think of human beings as cooperative facilitators rather than as heroic creators of new disclosures and new beginnings. This suggestion might help free us from the mistaken idea that new disclosures and new beginnings are the work of some artistic 'genius', human or otherwise, and free us from the subjectivistic effects this idea has had on our conception of agency. To make sense of that suggestion, it is necessary to undo the damage done by conflating receptivity with passivity, particularly, the idea that being receptive is akin to being mindless, to being in state of unmindedness. Due to this association it is easy to equate Heidegger's talk of receptivity to 'being' with an unminded receptivity to anything that comes along—for example, seductive but morally repugnant ideologies. However, careful examination of what receptivity involves, ultimately dissolves this misleading association. Passive submission to fascist ideologies is not to be explained by too much receptivity, but by too little; the success of such ideologies depends on closed, not open minds. It depends on one group of human beings becoming unreceptive to another group of human beings—unreceptive to their reasons, to their suffering, unreceptive to their humanity. Fascism and totalizing thinking of any kind encourages and demands listening only to one voice, and listening only in one way excluding other voices and closing, rather than keeping open, the logical space of possibility. In short, it is a form of thinking that eliminates, not fosters, receptivity.

If receptivity should not be confused with passivity, then what is it, exactly? Rather than explicating this idea by referring immediately to Heidegger's writings, I want first to show its centrality in the work of some other thinkers, thinkers whom it is not so easy to dismiss as attempting to make philosophically respectable a morally suspect idea. I return once again to the writings of Emerson and Cavell. In the following excerpt from the late essay, "Experience," Emerson describes the nature and role of receptivity in the illumination of everyday life, finely elucidating how everyday acts of disclosure are enabled by receptivity:

> Do but observe the mode of our illumination. When I converse with a profound mind, or if at any time being alone I have good thoughts, I do not at once arrive at satisfactions, as when, being thirsty, I drink water, or go to the fire, being cold: no! but I am at first apprised of my vicinity to a new and excellent region of life. By *persisting* to read or to think, this region *gives* further sign of itself, as it were in flashes of light, in sudden discoveries of its profound beauty and repose, as if the clouds that covered it parted at intervals, and showed the approaching traveller the inland mountains, with the tranquil eternal meadows spread at their base, whereon flocks graze, and shepherds pipe and dance. But every insight from this realm of thought is felt as initial, and promises a sequel. *I do not make it; I arrive there, and behold what was there already.*[19]

Emerson's remarks prompt us once again to do what professional philosophy is disinclined to do—to treat the claims of receptivity seriously. But even when we are prepared to do so, what are we supposed to make of the claim that once "apprised" of "new and excellent region of life" (the lifeworld?), that "region *gives* further sign of itself," when, and only when, we are properly attuned to it? That does sound like a valorization of passivity, if not like "new age" mumbo-jumbo. A second listening can actually prove more informative, telling us something valuable about "our mode of illumination," for whatever it consists in, it does not consist in "satisfactions" of this or that desire, whose satisfaction requires the use of "hypothetical imperatives"—namely that my need or desire instructs me as to what is required for its satisfaction, "as when, being thirsty, I drink water, or go to the fire, being cold." The "mode of our illumination" is such that we do not yet know where we will arrive, for we do not yet "know" the nature of the need that impels us or where it will lead us. To "arrive" there requires something different from arriving at the satisfaction of desires or appetites; it requires *persistence*, a lingering kind of thinking, lingering long enough in thought to allow a previously unvisited region of life (of the lifeworld) to give "further sign of itself," to *"give . . . itself."* What is given is *weak illumination*—partial, incomplete illumination, not overwhelming, knee-buckling, Saul on the road to Damascus illumination. As "initial," as thought and action initiating, weak illumination "promises a sequel," and that promise is, and surely Emerson would have concurred, a promise of happiness—a weak illumination of how things might otherwise be, a weak illumination of the good as a more open, freer relation to an other.

It is, however, the final sentence of this passage that connects Emerson's view of receptivity to Heidegger's: the illumination, the weak disclosure of meaning and possibility, does not involve a "doing" in the way that satisfying an appetite or desire does. *"I do not make it; I arrive there, and behold what was there already."* This is equivalent to saying that I received the illumination; I did not make it happen. Should there be any doubts about what he is getting at, Emerson says it again all the more bluntly: "All I know is reception; I am and I have: but I do not get, and when I have fancied that I have gotten anything, I found I did not."[20] In a commentary on Emerson's "Experience," Cavell treats this assertion as a deliberate inversion of Kant's theory of knowledge, turning it upside down by giving priority to reception.[21] Now the cognitive activity Kant designated as "apperception," the "I think" that must accompany all my mental representations, necessarily involves consciously "taking" some *x* of experience provided by sensibility (receptivity) and spontaneously subsuming it under an appropriate concept.[22] Thus the consciousness of spontaneity underwrites the subject's cognitive accomplishments as accomplishments it can attribute to its own cognitive activity. Receptivity only provides the necessary stuff of experience; making sense of that stuff requires self-conscious epistemic spontaneity: the "I think" is at the same time an "I take," and an "I make." In the place of the 'I think' as a spontaneous "taking as," which reproduces the traditional notion of cognition, of thinking, as a seizing, grasping, clutching activity, Emerson substitutes the "I think" as a spontaneous "receiving as." With this move Emerson is not just displacing the accent from activity to receptivity, he undercuts the distinction, making spontaneous and reflective what was considered passive and compliant.

To state unequivocally that "all I know is reception" is not to revert to mindless empiricism, conceiving the mind as the passive filter through which impressions pass, raw data processed; rather, it is to think of mindedness as requiring exposure to human vulnerability—the vulnerability of a being that can be "marked," "struck," "impressed" by experience, by what it encounters in the world. (Emerson's essay is, after all, an essay of mourning, mourning the death of his young son.) By placing receptivity at the center of mindedness, Emerson evokes a picture of agency as the "willingness" to risk self-dispossession, as a "willing" self-surrender. To reiterate, once more, we do not will our self-dispossession; it is not something we do, it is something we let happen. We *allow* ourselves to be affected by experience, *allow* ourselves to be decentered. It is just this self-decentering learning process that reveals itself when we "but observe our mode of illumination"—a cognitive and moral learning process for which traditional concepts of agency are unsuitable, for there is no spontaneous act of subsumption, no taking an x as an F, no subsumption under moral or cognitive rules. There is simply no x to subsume—whatever "it" is, it just isn't for the taking. "It" can be given, but not taken; received, but not subsumed. Thus the "satisfaction" we seek is not to be had by choosing an appropriate course of action; our need will be "satisfied" only to the extent that we can unclose ourselves, letting ourselves be claimed by something, by someone. This still requires as it expresses agency, for it is something that *I* let happen: *I* am the one who *allows* it to happen. But the "I" here is not the cause of what happens. The "I" only facilitates, it does not directly control what it receives. Receptivity facilitates discovery and self-discovery, since it enables movement from an old to a new understanding ("I arrive there")—enables the enlargement of the realm of possibility, and, at the same time, a transformation of sensibility.

Here is a perfectly "ordinary" example. One day one finds oneself answering to "Daddy" or "Mommy," answering to expectations and demands one had not known before. One's identity literally changes overnight; one has to play a new role for which there is no available script. Nothing can prepare one for the intensity or relentlessness of the new demands to which one must respond; they are exacting, but not exactly the same from one "Daddy" or "Mommy" to another. One can't train for "fatherhood" or "motherhood." There is no method to follow. The change that takes place is as imperceptible as it is sudden, abrupt, marking a discontinuity between who one was the day before, and who one is called to be today (and tomorrow). It didn't happen because one decided that from this moment on, "I am a 'Daddy.'" What happened is not the consequence of a decision, or an act of volition. Nor can one "decide" to be a parent. Yes, of course, one can decide to bring a child into the world, but that is not anything like deciding to be a parent, since one cannot know in advance what that means, what it demands of *oneself*. In saying that one can't "decide" to be a father or a mother, I mean to make the more general point that one can't decide to be decentered, to decenter oneself, to surrender something of oneself: that is a learning process not at the disposal of anyone's will. It doesn't come about as the consequence of any decision. I can't know in advance what *my* child is going to demand of me, or how these demands are going to conflict with "self-regarding" demands that have not been challenged before, at least, not in this way. I can't know in advance how one set of demands will be reconciled with the other, or even if they can be reconciled. I receive my identity as a father *as* I receive this child into the world (*in the way* I receive this child). The child comes into the world bearing its particular demands, demands to which one can respond in various ways, in various degrees of self-dispossession. One does not "make" oneself into a caregiver by following some strict regime of self-making, one "lets" oneself become a caregiver; one lets oneself be claimed, lets oneself be enlarged in ways one could not have foreseen prior to *this* child's arrival into the world. One doesn't make it happen, one either allows it to happen, or one does not allow it. So we can say, in the language of Heidegger's analysis of positive solicitude, that we can clear the way or get in the way of our own self-decentering. One can't completely shield oneself against any experience of self-dispossession, but one can get in the way enough to limit or circumscribe the extent of self-dispossession.[23]

Now it is this talk of "letting it happen" that so irritates defenders of standard notions of autonomy or agency. To "let it happen" does sound a lot like passivity, submission—the very negation of what it means to be an autonomous agent. Set very deep in our notion of autonomous agency is the assumption that agency is a doing, a making things happen, not a letting things happen; a claiming of this or that, not a being claimed by this or that, a determining, not a determined.[24] To identify agency with receptivity does not only seem counterintuitive, it seems morally irresponsible, for it implies that one can let *anything* happen, that one will go along with *whatever* is happening (e.g., a hate-filled ideology). But is this really the case? This implication rests on a false assumption, namely that in becoming receptive to something or someone, our moral and cognitive faculties are totally disabled, leaving our mind unminded. But the stance of receptivity to normative challenges and claims that arise outside us is not a stance in which our cognitive and moral powers are temporarily put on hold. Quite to the contrary, it is a stance in which our moral and cognitive powers are heightened in a dynamic, not suspended, state of judgment—a reflective state of judgment.

Receptivity is neither identical with nor reducible to passivity: it does not refer to a blind openness to whatever comes along. If we "but observe our mode of illumination, we find that receptivity is a thought-filled not a thoughtless engagement with demands that arise outside the self." Illumination "happens" when we linger "somewhere" filled with thought, prepared to surrender something of ourselves, giving in to that which gives itself. This act of self-surrender by no means entails the surrender of our moral and cognitive faculties, nor the surrender of our most deeply held values and beliefs: any of the latter may well be up for grabs, but not all at once. Much of what we most deeply value and believe will stay in place, must stay in place, since the very intelligibility of whatever we encounter requires it. The point is that a complete and total break between old and new self is just not possible, for that would require rendering meaningless the difference between old and new, not to mention the very idea of a self. Our moral and cognitive dispositions enable and constrain what we are receptive to: they can be transformed but not disabled by what we receive.

On the other hand, our moral and cognitive dispositions can impede or block receptivity, constrain more than they enable. This is easier to demonstrate, and that is because, contrary to another fallacious assumption, receptivity involves accountability. It is not uncommon to be reproached either in the intimate sphere (by a friend, spouse, lover, or child) or in the public sphere (by members of minority or subaltern cultures who feel marginalized or misrecognized) for not listening. When this familiar reproach is uttered—"You're not listening!"—we are not being reproached for an acoustical failure; we are being reproached for being unreceptive, for failing to put ourselves in a position to judge justly the rightness or wrongness of some claim. And that failure is a consequence of failing to register a need for acknowledgment, whose register is a precondition of just judgment. Above all, we are reproached for rendering voiceless someone with whom we claim to share a life, leaving them bereft (even if only temporarily) of the power of appeal. Said otherwise, we fail to acknowledge their dependence and, thereby, our own.

Cavell's well-known interpretation of Ibsen's *A Doll's House*[25] offers a compelling example of rendering voiceless those from whom we withhold receptivity, tuning them out instead of tuning them in. It comes down to this: Nora experiences her marriage as a violation of self, as having violated her to such an extent that she wants to "tear herself to pieces." That destructive urge arises from the realization that she has been giving her consent to an arrangement, to an institution, that has rendered her voiceless. Her husband, Torvald, doesn't get what all the fuss is about, and so treats her moral outrage as a case of childish histrionics, as a petulant refusal to understand her place, their place, in the world. "You're ill Nora,

I almost believe you're out of your senses." To treat her as though she were a child, as willfully inducing a state of madness, is, needless to say, blatantly to disregard her urgent need to voice her voicelessness. Torvald can't understand that Nora's reproach is also a self-reproach, can't understand the depth of her painful realization that having "given" her consent to the current institutional order, Nora has endorsed the conditions that silence her; hence Torvald can't understand that her outrage is her voice recovered. But that voice speaks in a language ("I could tear myself to pieces") that Torvald finds unintelligible: it is not a language he speaks nor one he wishes or feels obligated to learn. So he is unable to hear what can be said—for now—only in that language. To hear Nora speak in her own voice, to understand why she must now withhold her consent not just from her marriage, but from the current institutional order (which gives her a place in that order at the cost of self-dismemberment), Torvald would have to hear not only the claims she utters in that voice but also the institutional conditions that make them utterly "nonsensical," unintelligible. Rather than receiving those claims differently, letting his guard down and, thereby, letting himself be affected differently, Torvald treats them as a case of an x that is an F, subsuming them under an already available concept—the "hysterical woman." Had he received those claims differently, had he listened before he subsumed, he could have placed himself in a position to see and understand why they could not occupy an intelligible position in the existing "normative space of reasons," and thereby facilitated their entry into that space by enlarging it. Of course, to enlarge the "normative space of reasons" is also to press for a change in the current institutional order, since the two are interdependent. By intensifying our receptivity to claims that sound unintelligible to our ears, we become more aware of how our languages and social practices establish conditions of intelligibility and possibility, and so more aware not just of what can be intelligibly said or done but also what *can't* be intelligibly said or done. It is our responsibility to determine whether that which can't be intelligibly said or done gets in the way of or clears the way for our mutual freedom.

Can Torvald be held responsible for being unresponsive to a cry of pain? Had Torvald been responsive rather than defensive, could Nora's need for change have been his as well, letting her transfiguration initiate his own? Recalling our earlier analysis of Heidegger's account of positive solicitude, we can regard Torvald's unreceptive response to Nora as its negative instance: "in such solicitude the other can become one who is dominated and dependent, even when this domination is a tacit one and remains hidden from her." This allows us to see the extent to which Torvald's unreceptiveness is an instance of tacit "domination," whether consciously intended or not, undermining Nora's capacity for agency. By contrast, positive solicitude "does not supplant the other, but *clears the way* for her . . . not in order to take away her 'care,' but rather, to give it back to her authentically as such for the first time." Substitute "voice" for "care" and Cavell's analysis of *A Doll's House* converges with Heidegger's analysis of positive solicitude. This convergence allows for an application of the Hegelian notion of recognition as a receptive re-cognition of the other, as involving the cognition of a "familiar" other as for the first time, through which cognition we re-cognize our mutual dependence on one another. Not only are we enjoined to re-cognize the other, we are enjoined to re-cognize ourselves—otherwise, we would not be able to understand what it was that led us to misjudge or to misconstrue the other (e.g., because of previously unnoticed cultural background assumptions or patterns of evaluation). Understood in this way, recognition preserves its connection to cognition—failures of recognition will necessarily be failures of cognition, of just cognition.[26]

3   Self-Decentering

What can Emerson's remarks on "our mode of illumination" contribute to understanding the nature of such moral and cognitive failures? When we place them within a broader and more encompassing "struggle for recognition," we see that what is taking place is a struggle for a different kind of reception, and that entails a re-cognizing of the other. Such a struggle will not only involve a struggle between oneself and another. The act of re-cognizing the other will also involve a struggle with oneself, a struggle in which one's own self-understanding, one's prior commitments and justifications as well as the language/s (of interpretation and evaluation) from which they derive their intelligibility and cogency, will be at stake. That is why such a struggle for re-cognition is at once cognitive and affective, demanding an examination of one's reasons and one's sensibility, and of each in the light of the other. Of course, the willingness to engage in such a demanding and unsettling struggle depends on one's response-ability— the ability to respond to a "call" for re-cognition, for a change in reception. Regarded as part of a larger struggle for re-cognition, failures of receptivity appear more perspicuously as failures of reason.

Receptivity is not just a presupposition of reason, the way, for instance, that the intuitions of sensibility are a condition of the contentfulness of the concepts of the understanding; it is inseparable from the activity of reason, internal to successful learning. In Kant's theory of knowledge, receptivity plays a necessary, but necessarily passive, role. It refers to a *pre-intellectual* openness to the world that is passive and not at our disposal. As is well known, Kant thought of this kind of receptivity as a condition of possible experience. Early Heidegger reformulated it as a condition of possible intelligibility. In both cases this pre-intellectual openness to the world is construed as a condition either for the possibility of experience or for the possibility of something showing up as something in the first place. But there is another sense of openness that figures in the work of Emerson, Heidegger, Adorno, and Cavell, a sense of openness that is neither passive nor constant, but active and reflective. When we're speaking of openness in this sense, we may describe ourselves as suffering from too much as well as too little openness. If we are not open enough, we will be deaf to calls to change our language and our life; if we are too open, we will be unable to call our language and our life our own. While the latter is not a baseless worry, it is the preponderance of the latter that should be our principal concern. The kind of openness to which I refer here is of a kind for which we can be held accountable. In this second sense, openness will figure unavoidably in evaluations of the rationality of a given social practice, institution, or cultural self-understanding as well as the rationality of individual actions and judgments. This ineliminable aspect of reason is simply taken for granted by procedural conceptions of reason. Despite the fact that the Kantian models of practical reason espoused by Rawls and Habermas presuppose a form of self-decentering that follows from an encounter with demanding forms of discursive justification, both the nature and diversity of processes of self-decentering are left drastically unanalyzed.

Habermas's procedural view of practical reason does require "ideal role taking" through which participants in practical discourses are able to decenter their original standpoint—a self-decentering that comes about by taking into account the perspective of all possible others (the universal or generalized "other"). But rather than analyzing the varieties of processes of self-decentering, Habermas proceduralizes one kind of self-decentering, "ideal role taking," treating the capacity to take the perspective of the other in practical discourse as the invariable and predictable outcome of a developmental learning process that makes possible a "decentered understanding of the world" (MCCA 138–140). This creates the very mis-leading impression that we have reached the final stage in the process of self-decentering learning, such that we are now in a position to draw on it to make correct moral judgments. While it is trivially true that we always rely on already achieved levels of moral and cognitive learning, it is by no means the case that we have arrived or can ever arrive at "a decentered understanding" of ourselves or the world that is not in any further need of self-decentering. We are never fully "decentered," for after each decentering we recenter ourselves, seeking a state of equilibrium between our previous self-understanding and our current one. That state of equilibrium will be both reflective *and* unreflective because even at our most reflective we cannot achieve total self-transparency, the best we can do is to keep ourselves open to futher self-decentering, without which we cannot go on learning.

To reiterate, self-decentering is not a learning process at the disposal of our will; it doesn't happen simply because we encounter a new argument or new experience; it supposes a prior openness, a "willing" receptivity to what we encounter, not an encounter that we will. Thus it is a mistake to think that self-decentering can be proceduralized (MCCA 161). That doesn't mean that the demands of discursive justification cannot initiate self-decentering, but it does mean that they can initiate only so much. Moreover what can be initiated by such means is of a narrow and limited range because it draws upon only *one* source of normativity. As important as such a source of normativity is to the self-reflective and self-critical form of social life we want for ourselves, that form of social life cannot be created from or sustained by a single source of normativity, whatever that source may be. For a form of life to be self-reflective and self-critical in the req-uisite sense, it will need plural and richer sources of normativity. In order to draw on such sources, it will also need to trust sources of normativity that are not subsumable under "universalizable" rules or procedures. Not all normativity is rule-governed or rule-like because there are aspects of reason (and agency) that cannot be captured in terms of normative rules. The normativity of receptivity is clearly not something that can be stated or expressed in the form of normative rules, but it is not therefore lacking in reason because it is "unruly."

To make this difference between sources of normativity clearer, I want to contrast two ways of understanding "insight," both what it is and how and it comes about. For Kantian proceduralists like Habermas, "insight" stands for correct judgment, a "cognitive feat" that is the attainment of a truth-like view of a moral problem or moral conflict (MCCA 161–62; JA

174–75). "Insight" is what we arrive at by discursively testing disputed norms against higher order norms of impartiality and universality. In other words, "insight" is analogous to truth, and like truth, it is an explicit and determinate judgment that is the result of a process similar or analogous to the process by which we test truth claims. For hermeneutically inclined thinkers like Gadamer, on the other hand, "insight" does not consist in truth-like correctness that takes the form of an explicit and determinate judgment. Rather, it refers to "an escape from something that had deceived us and held us captive" (TM 356).[27] In this case insight is not a point of arrival but a point of departure. It is an emancipatory experience, freeing us from the grip of a certain way of thinking and acting, opening us up to the presence of alternative possibilities. "Insight" in this sense makes us aware of how our previous way of thinking and acting foreclosed those other possibilities, kept us from seeing things differently.

In both cases "insight" is connected to an experience of self-decentering. On one side, it is connected, as its condition and consequence, to an impartial or objective view of things, and on the other, to an openness to experience that keeps open a freer relation to how we think and act. If the former is primarily oriented to truth and objectivity, the latter is primarily oriented to freedom—the freedom to begin anew. Thus the latter kind of self-decentering is intimately connected to, as its condition and consequence, the reflective disclosure of possibility. This kind of self-decentering is not about overcoming our partial, subjective view of things in order to arrive at the single right answer to a moral problem. It is not about a "transcendence" of our parochial self in order to achieve an impartial or objective view of things; it is about an enlargement of self, opening it up to what it was previously closed (or to what was previously foreclosed). To "escape from something that had deceived us and held us captive," we will need to see things in a very different light; that kind of seeing is what reflective disclosure makes possible. Having escaped from what "deceived us and held us captive," we are now in a position to begin anew in light of new possibilities of thinking and acting.

The design of discursive procedures of justification, no matter how demanding the standards of justification, can only reproduce the *same kind* of self-decentering experience; it cannot bring about other kinds of self-decentering. This limitation is a function of the single normative source from which its kind of self-decentering arises. Like other Kantian proceduralists, Habermas overestimates the degree to which practices of justification, on their own, can initiate self-decentering learning processes. When practices of justification are disconnected from practices of disclosure, and when receptivity is sharply distinguished from reason, self-decentering learning processes cannot get sufficiently anchored in everyday practice. Indeed an experience of self-estrangement equated with the achievement of optimal critical distance is built into the design of justificatory procedures: "When they become subject to judgment from a purely moral point of view, interactions not only emancipate themselves from parochial conventions but also lose the vigorous historical coloration of a particular form of life. Interactions become strangely abstract when they come under the aegis of principled autonomous action" (MCCA 161). Given this characterization, I wonder whether in fact the more "strangely abstract" interactions become, the less susceptible they are to the kind of self-decentering that helps us "escape from something that deceived us and held us captive." Might it not be the case that the more abstract our interactions, the less self-decentering they are capable of, since the more abstract they are, the more artificial their character will be—which is to say, the more removed from the contexts in which genuine self-decentering *can* take place. It is important to ask ourselves in just what kind of evaluative language could these interactions be conducted the moment that they have been drained of all the "historical coloration of a particular form of life"? Who would be the speakers of such a language? What would its conditions of intelligibility be? What if "the historical coloration of a particular form of life" is necessary to the possibility of other kinds of self-decentering? Clearly, what is being imagined here is a wholly artificial context, complete with an artificial language, and an artificial conception of argument that is unduly abstract, cognitivistic, and detached from lifeworld practices. At this estranged level of abstraction, self-decentering turns into a merely *notional* possibility.

By contrast, genuine experiences of self-decentering involve and challenge all of our cognitive and affective capacities, *our whole sensibility*. A purely cognitive decentering through "ideal role taking," would be ineffective even if it were possible; it would be ineffective because it would be free of risk—free of a genuine (not merely notional) challenge to one's own normative perspective. Real self-decentering demands real change, and real change of one's normative perspective is not possible if "role taking" does not incorporate an element of risk. We are not speaking here of something like a skill that one can get good at by repeated practice, like spotting logical fallacies or playing tennis. It is not something we can master; if anything, it masters us. Genuine decentering is genuinely uncomfortable, unsettling, which is why, understandably, it is resisted. And it is resisted because it demands our willingness as much as it tests our capacity to expose and suffer our vulnerability, not just the fallibility of our beliefs. So what we are speaking of is a normative challenge that demands a cognitive *and* affective response to concrete, plural others, through which is initiated a learning process whose outcome can be neither foreseen nor directed. Now this kind of self-decentering is very different from the kind that that proceduralism presupposes: the outcome of this learning process cannot be determined in advance by the normative rules of practical discourses.

Descending back down the rungs of cognitivistic abstraction, we find that everyday discourse and argument are always imbued with "the historical coloration of a particular form of life," making it richer, more complex, messier, unbounded, and much less "impersonal." There is a great deal more at stake in everyday argument: the reasons in play are tied to subjectivity, to sensibility, to who we are and would like to be, and so to the uncomfortable question of whether we might need to change ourselves—to change our habits of thinking and acting, and to change our language. If we can say that in everyday life all aspects of reason interlock and interpenetrate, we can also say that these aspects are imbricated in, and at the same time indexed to, the lives we live, and the historically colored languages through which we articulate our reasons and make sense of our lives. We have no other languages through which we are in touch with what most matters to us. In so far as an openness to reason involves rendering the lives we live receptive to reason, our lives are rendered vulnerable, exposed, which is why so much of everyday argument is taken up with processes of self-clarification and self-understanding, not with refuting skepticism. A life exposed to reason is a life willingly exposed to the reasons of others—and to the lives with which those reasons are interwoven.

The question of how we should conceive of a form a life exposed to the reasons of others has been too much distorted by skeptical worries that arise only from the vain attempt to achieve a view of that life as from a view from nowhere, in particular, the worry that without an alternative to a perspectival view of our lives, our view of ourselves will remain parochial, and our lives provincial. That worry arises only because of a very limited conception of change, a conception that can conceive of only one kind of change, one kind of perspectival shift, one kind of self-decentering. But this is not the only kind of change and decentering available to us, not the only kind we can facilitate and endorse, and most certainly not the only kind we need. Besides, the conditions of deep cultural pluralism reveal the internal limitations of such a restrictive view of change and self-decentering, making it necessary to look to other transformative processes of change, to other sources of normativity. We can make room for other kinds of transformative encounters between self and other, "us" and "them," thereby disburdening an overworked model of change and an overdrawn source of normativity. We can then once again ask the question of whether an expert-culture conception of argument and practical discourse, and therefore an expert-culture conception of reason, is appropriate to, right for, lifeworld practices. Is it not time to return the language of argument to everyday life, to acknowledge rather than alienate the diversity of historically colored voices in which reasoning humans actually speak?[28] And when we do that, do we not then open up the range of possible self-decentering, and so indicate that we are ready to place our trust in what is not familiar to us and what can't be controlled by us?

At this point, another aspect of receptivity's connection to reason needs to be made explicit: its connection to possibility. To see more in things than they are, is to let something, someone, speak to us in a voice we are unaccustomed to hearing or unable fully to understand. Again, we are talking about letting something happen, and for that to happen we need to stop getting in the way of letting it happen. It requires, as Cavell puts it, "stopping to think . . . as if to let our needs recognize what they need. This is a reasonable sense of intelligence—not the sense of applying it but that of receiving it. Reason does not need to make anything happen; as romantics like Friedrich Schlegel, Emerson, and Heidegger like, more or less, to put it, what happens in the world (as with poetry) is always happening."[29] If this is a "reasonable" sense of intelligence, then what reason is cannot be explicated independently of receptivity. To explicate that notion, we have to take notice of what happens when we "let it happen," when we "but observe our mode of illumination." That observance also allows us to see how reason, by its receptiveness, can disclose possibility. Noticing that "what happens in the world . . . is always happening," is not just an inert kind of receptivity, since it also attunes us to what is *not* happening in the world, to what is not allowed to happen, not allowed to speak. It attunes us to the exclusion of other meaningful possibilities.

Returning now to some of late Heidegger's reflections on receptivity, we find that it is just this kind of receptivity that Heidegger has in mind. It is that "mode of illumination" by which we come to notice not only what is always happening but, all the more important, to notice what is not happening, and so to notice what gets in the way of something new happening, what get us in the way of a new beginning. Thus, for Heidegger, the primary critical-normative role of receptivity resides in its being able to attune us to marginalized practices and suppressed possibilities. In the influential essay on technology, Heidegger not only insists on treating modern technology as something entirely new (i.e., as a pre-reflective disclosure of the world rather than as an instrument or tool we can use wisely or unwisely); he also insists on drawing attention to the new dangers it introduces. Distinguishing between threats to nature and human life that arise from the employment of specific technologies (the usual list of suspects) and entirely new threats that arise from "the style of our technological practices" (the "style of reasoning" on which their intelligibility and value depends), Heidegger shows that the nature of this threat is twofold. First, because of its totalizing character, modern technology threatens the pluralism of cultural practices, driving out other cultural practices, other "styles of reasoning," making them anachronistic, peculiar, passé. "Where an ordering-calculating thinking dominates, *it drives out every other possibility of disclosure.*"[30] It is not just other practices, but other *possible* practices that are driven out. Totalizing practices foreclose alternative possibilities. Second, and this is its most distinctive aspect, as a totalizing practice modern technology disguises, occludes, its own disclosedness—"*it conceals disclosure itself.*"[31] Now that, according to Heidegger, is what is most dangerous about modern technology. Because it conceals its own disclosedness, we fail to see what it is we are dealing with, and so fail to respond to it correctly.

If Heidegger is right, then our response to technology has to be very different from what it has been, directed to its disclosedness rather than misdirected by its concealment. After all, if what we are confronting is not an "instrument" (that seems as if it has a mind of its own, ready to enslave those whom it was designed to liberate) but, rather, a pre-reflective form of disclosure, then we had better respond appropriately. Once again, it is a question of how we "receive" this understanding, not how we control or master it; otherwise, we will not really understand the threat it poses. Hubert Dreyfus and Charles Spinosa put it this way: "This threat is not a problem for which we must find a solution, but an ontological condition that requires a transformation of our understanding of being."[32] This condition arises from not listening correctly to what draws us into the technological understanding of being—the "understanding of things and ourselves as resources to be ordered, enhanced, and used efficiently."[33] Of course, we would not have become captive to this understanding were we not "open" to it in the first place; on the other hand, this state of captivity is a function of not being open to it in the right way, of not paying sufficient attention to "our mode of illumination," to our way of receiving an understanding of being. We are not condemned to suffer an inescapable fate. There is another possibility that Heidegger's ontological interpretation of technology discloses. We can seek a freer, more open relation to the technological understanding of being. That possibility involves the kind of transformation of our relation to "being" to which Dreyfus and Spinosa averred, the kind that preoccupied Heidegger. And that depends on the degree to which we can acknowledge both our dependence on our received ontologies, and recognize our own agency in our receptive activity as disclosers.

To some, all this talk of will sound like a resacralization of social practices, the secular equivalent of going to mass, where we hope to receive our "communion" with being. That is unfortunate, but understandable. Nevertheless, one can only hope not to have argued in vain, for it is certainly the case that Heidegger's diagnosis of the danger of modern technology is empirically verifiable. Indeed the danger he noticed half-a-century ago is more apparent to us now than it was then, and it has been increasingly recognized as such. Take the worldwide resistance to genetically engineered crops, for example. That resistance is not to the promising benefits of a new technology but to the totalizing ambitions of the modern technological style. Where resistance is encountered, the agribusiness industry deliberately sows its wild seeds, so to speak, contaminating soils faster than governments can introduce effective legislation. The goal is to make legislation meaningless, by cross-pollinating and polluting the global food supply to such an extent that it is impossible to separate the genetically engineered from the natural food supply.[34] So what we have is not just the emergence of a dominant agricultural practice, but the annihilation of all others, rendering the term "natural food" meaningless. The result: the silent disappearance of alternative possibilities.

Here's another example of disappearing possibilities, possibilities whose disappearance coincides with the disappearance of human voices that once spoke in a language that expressed the 'vigorous historical coloration of a particular form of life:

I used to take a long road trip every year or two. . . . And though I always took along an atlas, I rarely used it. I navigated by radio. You used to be able to do that in America: chart your course by the accents, news and songs streamlining in from the nearest AM transmitter. A drawling update of midday cattle prices meant I was in Wyoming or Nebraska. A guttural rant about city-hall corruption told me I'd reach Chicago within the hour. A soaring, rhythmic sermon on fornication—Welcome to Alabama. The music, too. Texas swing in Southwest oil country. Polka in North Dakota. Nonstop Led Zeppelin, Black Sabbath and Jethro Tull in the Minneapolis–St.

Paul suburbs. What's more, the invisible people who introduced the songs gave the impression that they listened to them at home. They were locals, with local tastes. I felt like a modern Walt Whitman on those drives. When I turned on the radio, I heard American singing, even in the dumb banter of "morning zoo" hosts. But then last summer somewhere between Montana and Wisconsin, something new happened. *I lost my way*, and the radio couldn't help me find it. I twirled the dial, but the music and the announcers all sounded alike, drained, disconnected from geography, reshuffling the same pop playlists and canned bad jokes.[35]

This altogether familiar modern experience of dislocation is instructive, not just because it captures a specific loss at a particular point in historical time in a particular national culture. It is instructive because it identifies what it means to lose one's way, to find that one no longer knows one's way around one's own cultural world. It identifies, to be exact, the degree to which our sense of orientation depends on the availability of distinct local worlds. The more homogeneous and totalizing a single lifeworld becomes the more disoriented, disconnected, become its members. In other words, orientation depends on the presence of a lifeworld rich in distinctive subregions: the more washed out the lifeworld, the greater the disorientation and alienation. Like the "blinding light" of the sun that incapacitates the protagonist of Camus's *L'Etranger*, rendering him unable to make meaningful distinctions, totalizing practices possess the power to wash out distinctiveness as such.

As Dreyfus and Spinosa point out, alertness to the disorienting tendencies of modern technology forced Heidegger to rethink his most prized philosophical innovation: the ontological difference. In a late seminar he came to see that if a plurality of cultural practices and 'styles of reasoning' are to be fostered and preserved, "it becomes necessary to free thinking from the ontological difference."[36] What Heidegger has in mind is the need to change his previously monistic construal of being into a pluralistic one, such that we acquire an increased sensitivity to the presence and endangered state of plural "local worlds"—plural understandings of being not subsumable under a single understanding of being. This late revision is obviously not motivated by a belated recognition of the virtues of cultural diversity; rather, it is a more sophisticated and richer defense of an idea that goes back to *Being and Time*, namely that the very intelligibility of the world, and hence the possibility of becoming oriented within it, depends on everyday practices. To that argument Heidegger adds a new twist, namely that both the intelligibility of the world and our orientation within it depends on the presence of a plurality of everyday cultural practices and a plurality of local worlds. Fostering and preserving a plurality of cultural practices and a plurality of local worlds enables us to resist totalizing practices, totalizing disclosures of the world that conceal their disclosedness. Resistance to totalizing practices also depends on the availability of something that such practices cover up and render scarce: the kinds of self-decentering that only an alternative range of possibilities and alternative sources of normativity can enable. The presence of a plurality of local worlds and cultural practices is not just essential to making sense of the world; it is also essential to keeping the world open to other possible disclosures, enlarging the field and scope of possible self-decenterings, and therefore of possible learning.

In the end, Heidegger's insight into the interdependent relationships between intelligibility, plurality, and possibility forced him to repudiate his own life-long attempt to track *the* understanding of being that has held sway in the West every since those inimitable Greeks. He came to see that attempt as itself in the sway of a totalizing kind of thinking that gets in the way of a much more urgent and important task—the task of tracking and, whenever possible, of preserving rapidly disappearing possibilities. Here, too, his preoccupation with preserving alternative possibilities coincides with Benjamin's worry that "every image of the past that is not recognized by the present as one of its own concerns threatens to disappear irretrievably." Now this increasing concern with the preservation of local worlds and cultural practices renders all the more implausible Habermas's interpretation of Heidegger's "Dionysian messianism" as the "apocalyptic expectation of a catastrophic entry of the new." It is no longer susceptible to the charge that it promotes an expectant anticipation of some grand, large-size disclosure of the world that would once and for all triumph over the Western understanding of being.[37] Any new understanding that is to be fostered, whatever it may be, should *not* be of this kind. We do not want to replace one monolithic ontology with another monolithic ontology. Perhaps this is why later Heidegger so strongly emphasizes the need for small-size disclosure, the disclosure of endangered "local worlds," as the most promising way to prevent the foreclosure of possibility. No redisclosure of the world should colonize the logical space of possibility, which it can do only by foreclosing other possibilities of disclosure and by concealing its own disclosedness. In such a case we would (once again) be dealing with the kind of totalizing practice that modern technology instances. So we can now see more clearly than before that reflective disclosure possesses its own distinctive normative resources for distinguishing between better and worse disclosures, between "good" and "bad" disclosures. For in addition to the normativity it possesses as a problem-solving practice, reflective disclosure makes its own practice possible, makes it reflective and reflectively accessible, by making room for rather than driving out other possibilities of disclosure, and by revealing rather than concealing its disclosedness. Put another way, it lets itself be redisclosed. By disclosing some particular possibility it at the some time discloses the possibility of alternative possibilities, and in disclosing the possibility of alternative possibilities, it discloses its own disclosedness. That makes it a fallibilistic practice in accordance with both kinds of fallibilism explored in part IV, chapter 6. It is thus distinguishable from propaganda and from practices of domination and power: the latter must mask and disguise themselves, and in such a way as to foreclose the disclosure of alternative possibilities.

From early to later Heidegger, whatever else might have changed, the internal connection between receptivity and disclosure remained constant. One can even say that for later Heidegger, receptivity became the key to disclosure, its precondition. The more one understands the centrality of receptivity, the more one is disinclined to think of disclosure as a distinctive cultural practice (e.g., art) or as a distinctive use of language (e.g., rhetoric). Disclosure, both the pre-reflective and reflective varieties, is "always happening" across the breadth of everyday practices and expert culture practices. It is not specific to, or more typical of, any one practice or any one use of language, or any one cultural sphere. By drawing out the connections between disclosure and receptivity, and between receptivity and reason, I hope to have weakened the propensity to conflate receptivity with passivity or submissiveness. I also hope to have exposed the weakness of arguments that claim there is no way to distinguish disclosure from propaganda.[38]

Human beings are sufficiently masters of linguistic meaning to stretch it this way and that in order to achieve a desired effect. The ability to manipulate meaning should not be confused with disclosure: disclosure is a self-decentering learning process, not a technique of persuasion by which we can influence or alter the beliefs or actions of others. To think of disclosure as a function of the rhetorical use of language is to think of it as a tool. Once you think of it as a tool, then you inherit the problem of how the same tool that can be used to initiate moral and cognitive learning can just as easily initiate unjust practices, so you inherit the problem of how rhetorical effects "can disclose both just and unjust worlds."[39] Like any employment of rhetoric, propaganda depends on the self-conscious instrumentalization of meaning. Distinctive to propaganda is that it seeks to deceive, not just persuade, its addressees. But disclosure as I have argued throughout this text is not instrumentalizable. No one can decide in advance that rhetorical trope x is necessary for disclosive effect y, since we can't "know" what y is in advance of its disclosure *as* y. Disclosure is not a technique, a distinctive way of using language over which we can dispose at will, something that can be "administered." Besides, disclosures are always taking place that cannot be explained by or attributed to the "rhetorical" use of language—such as the birth of a child, a family gathering, when we fall in love, when we encounter a bridge that focuses a world (e.g., the old and new bridge of Mostar).

If I have correctly characterized reflective disclosure as continuous with non-instrumentalizable learning, the kind of learning that precludes knowing in advance what it is we are going to learn, and if disclosure is inseparable from problem solving, and indeed the only kind of problem solving that can help us overcome various kinds of epistemological and cultural crises, then disclosure is hardly something that can be assimilated to rhetoric. Furthermore, if self-decentering is a condition of cognitive and moral learning, and if it is something that is not subject to our control, then it is not going to be the kind of "effect" one will seek to achieve if the "disclosure" of unjust worlds is one's goal. The disclosure of an "unjust world" would require the concealment of its disclosedness, and at the same time, an elimination of other possibilities of disclosure—in short, the foreclosure of alternative possibilities.

To draw again on Ian Hacking, making sense of the sufficiently strange requires not just reflectively recontextualizing preexisting meanings and words to bring about some desired effect, it requires a new style of reasoning. It requires not just manipulating old sentences in a new way, but introducing "new sentences, things quite literally never said before."[40] It is part of the claim of this book that disclosure at this level is not a feat of "genius," whether "good" or "evil," but supposes, is radically dependent on, receptivity—on paying attention in a way that lets something new happen, lets something new begin. That is why, no matter the level at which our "genius" operates, we cannot just will a new idea or new practice into existence—no matter how reflective we are, no matter how masterful our command of the medium in which we think, speak, or act.

The very idea that we can disclose an "unjust world" makes no sense if disclosure is continuous with self-decentering learning processes. One can only come to this conclusion if one assumes that the world can be disclosed any which way, arbitrarily, and unconstrained by what already obtains "in the world." But that thought additionally supposes that disclosure is something at our disposal, rather than something that demands receptivity, both the pre-reflective and reflective kind. It also supposes that disclosure is some nonrational, norm-free practice through which supposition it acquires its status as the "other of reason." Worlds cannot be disclosed arbitrarily, or any which way. Disclosure is both a response to the world, and what makes the world available to response. To say that disclosure can disclose "just and unjust" worlds is less a remark about disclosure than it is about the long-recognized capacity of human beings to speak and act in ways that are just and unjust. We do not yet have justice, which is why we worry about the disclosure of unjust worlds. We worry about it not because disclosure is indistinguishable from propaganda but because it is not a controllable source of normativity. But that is precisely one of its normative virtues, part of what makes it irreducible to, distinguishable from, propaganda.

4   The Possibility-Disclosing Role of Reason

I have been arguing that the various shortcomings of Habermas's metacritique of disclosure expose not only the narrowness of a conception of reason that makes reason more or less identical with the rationality of procedures but also the shortcomings of a model of critical theory that draws its normativity from this single source. It follows therefore that the possibility of renewing critical theory will depend—once again—on the possibility of an enlarged and pluralistic conception of reason. And that latter possibility depends on the availability of alternative sources of normativity upon which this enlarged and pluralistic conception can draw. As we have seen, we do not have to roam far and wide to discover such sources: they are at the contested center of the philosophical discourse of modernity. Habermas's reconstruction of this discourse fails to do justice to these sources because they can occupy no meaningful place within his proceduralist conception of reason, and because he regards them as essentially "other" to reason. As it turns out, the narrow identification of reason with justification (*Begründung*) stands in an uneasy relation to Habermas's occasional but significantly more capacious identification of reason with intersubjective learning. I am not referring here to Habermas's evolutionary or developmental model of learning but to an "unofficial" model of learning that Habermas consistently describes as embedded in and made possible by historically conditioned contexts of social life. Unlike the evolutionary or developmental model of learning, this model does not play a prominent role in the theory of communicative action—which is to say, it does not perform any essential explanatory or justificatory function in that theory. But it does enter into the argument of *The Philosophical Discourse of Modernity*, particularly in a few crucial passages, where it is intimately connected to history. When Habermas speaks of reason's relation to history in these passages, it is identified with "suprasubjective and mutually intermeshing processes of learning and unlearning" (PDM 55), or with "a dialectic of successful and unsuccessful mutual understanding" (PDM 324). Whereas the procedural conception of reason is identified primarily with the context-transcending moment of universal validity through which it "triumphs over time" (BFN 14), the identification of reason with self-formative learning processes reveals a much more historical and much less procedural conception of reason—a conception of reason as a time-bound and time-imprinted ensemble of cultural practices in which "learning and mislearning" are "entangled" with one another.

The relation of history to reason [*Vernunftbezug der Geschichte*] remains constitutive for the discourse of modernity—for better or for worse. Whoever participates in this discourse, and nothing about this has changed up to today, makes distinctive use of the expressions "reason" and "rationality." They are used neither in accord with ontological game rules in order to characterize God or being as a whole, nor in accord with empiricist game rules to characterize the dispositions of subjects capable of speech and action. Reason is valid neither as something pre-formed, as an objective teleology manifested in nature or history, nor as a mere subjective capacity. Rather, the patterns sought out in historical events yield *encoded* indicators of unfinished, interrupted, and misguided formative processes that exceed the grasp of any individual's subjective consciousness. As subjects relate to internal and external nature, they reproduce the socio-cultural life-context in which they find themselves. The reproduction of forms of life and life histories leaves behind impressions in the *soft* medium of history that, under the strenuous gaze of clues-seeking trackers [*Spurensuchern*], condense into patterns and structures. This specifically modern gaze is guided by an interest in self-reassurance. Although always frustrated by the risk of deception and self-deception, it nonetheless manages to catch a *glimpse* of configurations and structures by which it *deciphers* self-formative processes in which learning and mislearning are *entangled*. (PDM 392–393, translation altered, my emphasis)[41]

Notice how the relation of reason to history described here is one that admits of a great deal of contingency and indeterminacy. Notice, too, how our current understanding of that relation is said to depend on our ability to decipher fleetingly discernible patterns and configurations of meaning, preserved (for the moment) in the "soft medium of history." That glimpse of "unfinished, interrupted, and misguided formative processes" is revealed only to that "strenuous," "specifically modern gaze." It is the gaze of the "philosophers of modernity," who, like modern day "detectives on the trail of reason in history . . . seek the blind spot where the unconscious nests in consciousness, where forgetting slips into memory, where regression is disguised as progress, and unlearning as a learning process" (PDM 56).

Once again, Habermas invokes the idea of reflective disclosure to describe how we gain access to the presence and absence of reason in history, making more conscious our currently murky reality. The activity of uncovering what has been covered up, disguised, or suppressed is not only a cognitive activity that must decipher encoded, fragmentary, and ephemeral signs of reason and unreason, learning and unlearning. It is a cognitive activity that depends, on the one hand, on a capacity for receptivity, for persistently lingering until such time as one can catch, even if only for an instant, a glimpse of reason in history and, on the other, on the "soft medium" of history in which traces of meaning can be impressed. So we not only depend on disclosure to illuminate, however weakly, the "unfinished, interrupted, and misguided formative processes" in the midst of which we now find ourselves; the disclosure of those processes itself depends on historically disclosed horizons of meaning and possibility. Any glimpse we may receive of encoded formative processes is both enabled and constrained by the very history whose meaning we are trying decipher.

While Habermas is quite right to claim that "history and its interpretation have now become the medium in which cultures and peoples find their self-reassurance" (BFN 96), the reflective appropriation of cultural traditions is not all that guides the "specifically modern" gaze of the philosophers of modernity. The interest in self-reassurance that guides this gaze also embraces the question of what modern reason is and the question of what it ought to be. Around these questions the whole of the philosophical discourse of modernity evidently revolves: they do not admit a final answer. These questions that must be asked again and again follow from the idea of reason as a dialectical process of learning and unlearning. There is no internal teleology, no inexorable "inner logic," guiding this dialectical process, not least because the very notion of what reason is, of what it ought to be, is open-ended and subject to unforeseeable contingencies and possibilities, and so internal to the dialectical process in which it is inescapably entangled. Thus, insofar as what reason means is entangled with the problem of self-reassurance, it is an inherently unsettling question. To pose it in the first place, to set out once again on the "trail of reason in history," is to risk unsettling ourselves, for though we seek self-reassurance, we have to remain open to self-decentering.

As Nietzsche already made clear in his second "untimely" meditation, history and its interpretation is not just a medium of self-reassurance, it is also a medium of self-decentering. As such, it can release decentering effects, effects that impel us to revise our self-understanding and our practices, put in question the nature of the self-reassurance we seek. Here, too, our interpretations of the past are guided by an understanding of our present needs, which, as Nietzsche rightly claimed, is an understanding that is as much shaped as it is enabled by the nature of our openness to the future. Now the kind of openness normatively distinctive of modernity is not supposed to be an openness to just anything the future brings, but an expectant openness, open to the "novelty of the future," open to the possibility of a new beginning. The something new that arrives with the future must be judged by the quality of light it sheds on the present and the past. Since the weak illumination of the present and the past requires that it be interpreted from a "present-open-to-the-future" (PDM 55), the patterns glimpsed, the possibilities disclosed, may vary from one "present-open-to-the-future" to another. This means, of course, that there will be interpretive conflict concerning the meaning of reason in history, for that meaning is cobbled together from unavoidably *partial* glimpses of "unfinished, interrupted, and misguided formative processes," processes whose very nature renders their meaning unstable and direction unclear. Reason cannot stop educating itself about itself. So long as it is time-bound and time-imprinted, its education is continuous with its possible transformation: reason cannot be sufficiently self-critical if it is not sufficiently time responsive.

By contrast, the developmental or evolutionary model of social learning that Habermas derives from the "reconstructive sciences" of Piaget and Kohlberg is altogether different, as is the image of reason (and agency) it projects. The difference can be stated as the difference between a form of learning that is deposited in anonymous "rule systems" and reconstructed from the standpoint of the observer and a form of learning that can be reflectively recapitulated from the standpoint of the participant. For our purposes, a more useful way to state this difference is to state it as the difference between a form of "learning" that follows an independent logic of its own, independent of history and subjectivity, and a form of learning that depends on historically disclosed meaning and possibilities. In the first case, we are talking about "learning" that takes place behind our backs according to an "internal logic" of its own; in the second, about learning that *we* can experience as our own, a process in which we self-consciously participate and in the outcome of which we recognize our own sponta-neous and reflective agency. If we wish to be in a position to identify our-selves *with* our reason, then it is only with this second kind of *learning* that reason should be identified.

Most certainly we should not identify reason with a "learning process" that is impervious to epistemological crises or breakdowns not *already* built into its developmental logic as a predictable transition to the next devel-opmental stage. To construe human reason in terms of this developmen-tal model is therefore to treat the problem of self-reassurance as already solved, or as destined to be solved. But by Habermas's own critical assess-ment, any conception of reason that "solves" the problem of self-reassur-ance by postulating the ineluctable progress of reason in history solves that problem all "*too well*" (PDM 42). This, claims Habermas, is the error of Hegel's hubristic conception of reason as "absolute knowledge," whereby reason takes over "the place of fate and knows that every event of essen-tial significance has *already* been decided. Hegel's philosophy tried to satisfy the need of modernity for self-reassurance only at the cost of devalu-ing present-day reality and blunting critique" (PDM 42).

With these critical remarks Habermas gives the impression that he wholeheartedly endorses the Young Hegelians's critique of Hegel's concept of reason, since it "shoved aside" what mattered most to modern con-sciousness: "the transitory aspect of the moment, pregnant with meaning, in which the problems of an onrushing future are tangled in knots" (PDM 53). Unfortunately, this same constitutive feature of modernity's relation to time is shoved aside by a developmental learning process that has the character of inevitability. This is an inescapable limitation of develop-mental models: one simply can't employ the vocabulary of "inner logic," "logic of development," and "rationalization," however fallibilistically, without implying (or projecting) the inevitability of such developments. Habermas repeatedly uses these highly speculative reconstructions in support of his account of modernity, breaking sharply from the tradition of the Young Hegelians by theoretically envisioning a speculative philos-ophy of history that effectively neutralizes the future, robbing it of its openness and indeterminacy.

This outcome is unavoidable so long as one believes that the problem of self-reassurance or cultural self-confidence is a "problem" that can be solved. To treat it is a problem that admits of a solution is to misunder-stand it, for what we are actually dealing with is not a "problem" but an existential and political condition of modernity, a condition of being modern. We cannot "solve" the problem of self-reassurance without fore-closing the future; however, if we treat it is an existential and political con-dition of being modern, we can transform our relation to it. We can do that by bringing into normative alignment with, rather than detaching it from, modernity's relation to time.

Seyla Benhabib once expressed the worry that Habermas has reformu-lated critical theory in a form that lacks the "utopian potential" that dis-tinguished its earlier incarnations—and justified its existence.[42] Clearly, utopian contents cannot be generated from a conception of reason that displays a developmental logic all its own. Just as clearly, they cannot be generated from its procedural correlate, in which modern reason is iden-tified with the rationality of its procedures. Procedurally construed, com-municative reason fails to provide the promised "new orientation for the critique of modernity" because it cannot let itself be affected by moder-nity's relation to time, which relation is supposed to be constitutive for any such reorientation. As a consequence modern reason cannot be infused with any transformative or utopian contents from historically disclosed sources of meaning and possibility.

The thought that the utopian deficit of critical theory might be made up by the universalistic, time-transcending potential of communicative reason is mistaken in at least two respects. First, it supposes that it can be made up by drawing upon a single source of normativity, and, second, it fails to see that the required utopian content can only be generated through a renewal of modernity's relation to time. A time-transcending conception of reason and of universality cannot revitalize what is time-dependent and time-responsive. To assume that reason must be capable of transcending history, if it is critically to intervene in history, is to divinize the idea of reason. And this divinized reason, invoked in a passage from Peirce that Habermas is very fond of citing, is as "theological" as anything attributed to Benjamin.

The real, then, is that which, sooner or later, information and reasoning would finally result in, and which is therefore independent of the vagaries of me and you. Thus, the very origin of the conception of reality shows that this conception essen-tially involves the notion of a community, without definite limits, and capable of a definite increase in knowledge.[43]

This divinizing description of reason and human community denies our dependence on time as much as our dependence on each other, for it is precisely the "vagaries of me and you" that make the human community human; it is the "vagaries of me and you" that make possible practices that wander and stray from, that depart from our current ways of speaking and acting; that make possible new ways of speaking and acting, new norms and practices, new institutions. If not for the "vagaries of me and you" there would be nothing new under the sun. But, of course, the "vagaries of me and you" are not just what make possible semantic and cultural innovation, they are also the stuff out of which communication break-downs and cultural conflict are made. As I claimed in part II, intersubjec-tivity is both the problem and its solution, but that "solution" can never eliminate the problem that intersubjectivity is. That is why we need always to stress the interdependence between disclosure and intersubjectivity, for our sense-making practices and the "origin of our conception of reality" does not arise from relations of intersubjectivity alone, nor from any ide-alization of them. So we have also to come to terms again and again with the "vagaries of me and you," for without being able to count on each other's goodwill and cooperation, goodwill and cooperation that is facili-tated by nothing other than other acts of goodwill and cooperation, all the self-divinizing talk about an ideal communication community without "definite limits" is just so much bad utopian thinking.

The vision of an idealized intersubjectivity to which Peirce and Haber-mas appeal is a vision that excludes the "vagaries" of human community and human reason—the peculiarities and the eccentricities of human forms of life. But once we subtract the "vagaries of me and you" from human forms of life, are we still speaking about a *human* form of inter-subjectivity? The recognition of our fragility, like the recognition of our contingency, de-divinizes human practices and human community. We are faced with nothing more and nothing less than our shared fragility, the fragility of all that is human, all that is bound to natality and mortality.[44] As Albrecht Wellmer has already argued, the Peircian idea of an intersub-jectivity destined to converge on *the* truth supposes a "state of full trans-parency, of absolute knowledge, of moral perfection—in short, a situation of communication which would transcend the constraints, the opacity, the fragility, and the corporeality of finite human communication."[45] Projected onto human history is a divinizing idea of reason and community that resists full incorporation into the human world, for it is an idea of reason that does not let itself experience "the deficiency of finite existence" but remains "raised above it."[46] Indeed it seems to express dissatisfaction with what is merely finite and human.

Perhaps it is this dissatisfaction that explains the need to attribute to reason the power to "blot out" space and time (PDM 323). This claim repeats, no less immodestly, Kant's claim that reason "is present to all the actions of human beings in all conditions of time . . . but it is not itself in time, and never enters into any new state in which it previously was not; in regard to a new state, reason is *determining* but not *determinable*."[47] But it is just as hard to see how the claims of reason can "blot out" space and time without blotting themselves out, as it is to see how reason can be determining but never determined. This is simply a self-defeating characterization of reason, since, among other things, it involves a denial of the historical and cultural conditions of intelligibility that make possible the self-education of reason.

So why must we characterize reason in this time-transcending way? What lies behind the impulse to *prove* that truth and reason will win out in the end? Considered from this angle, the controversial distinction between "context-transcendence" and "context-dependence" seems to be one more attempt to hoist what is all too human up to the realm of the divine. Subjected to close scrutiny, neither side of this distinction stands up too well. Rorty is right to suggest that the talk of "context-transcendence" sounds suspiciously like "make-believe" transcendence, since one can never be in a position to know whether a currently justified claim actually transcends "all possible contexts" of justification or "all possible, merely local standards of validity."[48]

The notion of "context-dependence" does not look any better. It supposes that which Heidegger, Gadamer, Wittgenstein, Davidson, and others, have given us good reason to reject: the idea of a logically and semantically closed cultural context. It is a notion that requires us to hold a view of the local, the "provincial," even the everyday, as constituted by rules and conventions that are typically taken to have an algorithmic character. This is just one more instance of the general tendency to think of social practices as structured by rules and conventions. But rules and conventions do not sufficiently explain the essentially practical character of human speech and action; if anything, exclusive appeal to such rules and conventions only reifies human practices. Such explanations simply cannot abide the "vagaries of me and you," the vagaries of the human world. If social life is not as rule-governed as we have made it out to be, if its "vagaries" have been too little appreciated and understood, it is very hard to ascribe a special status to practices of justification that sets them apart from other social practices. Habermas simply misconstrues the nature of human practices when he claims that practices of justification are practices not regulated by "social convention" (BFN 15) or "settled custom" (BFN 20). There is no social practice whose meaning is strictly "context-dependent" or strictly regulated by "social convention" and "settled custom." All social practices possess a surplus of meaning, and therefore a "context-transcending" potential, but none possess the power to transcend *all* possible contexts, to escape their dependence on everyday conditions of intelligibility and possibility not of their making. If we are willing to look at our practices with open eyes, the very idea of a practice regulated *merely* by social convention or "settled custom" is incoherent. No social practice can be understood and explained by reference to rules and conventions alone, for explaining their success as practices requires taking account not only the rules they follow or conform to but their capacity for self-criticism and innovation, which capacity is not subject to or subsumable by rules not even "universal" rules of argumentation and justification![49] In this respect there is nothing to distinguish practices of justification from other social practices: human practices are not algorithmic; they are also dependent on "the vagaries of me and you," without which "vagaries" there would be no self-criticism, no self-decentering, no learning. Here again, I would agree with Rorty: the only thing that can transcend a social practice is another social practice. Transcendence, in this case is outward not upward, moving forward to the future and outward to enlarged logical and social spaces. Moreover transcendence, if "transcendence" is still the right word, is not transcendence from the perspective of a make-believe community but an actual community, retrospectively justifying the move from a worse to a better social practice. In other words, the kind of "transcendence" that takes account of the "vagaries of you and me" is of a kind that is always *in* time and space, not outside or beyond them.

Already in his seminal study of Habermas, Thomas McCarthy drew attention to the mutually exclusive ideas of reason competing for Habermas's theoretical allegiance, creating an irresolvable tension between a transcendentally grounded and a historically grounded conception of reason.[50] That tension arises from Habermas's reluctance to part with a conception of reason that, contrary to Habermas's stated intentions, reverts one way or another to "the understanding," *der Verstand*. Whether construed transcendentally, developmentally, or procedurally, it is a conception that aspires to the status of *disinterested* reason. Alongside this conception, or rather, trailing along at some distance behind it, is an alternative conception of reason that is open to its own self-transformation through exposure to historically disclosed sources of meaning and possibility. We could call this an *expressive* conception of reason, since it is one in whose various manifestations we can recognize ourselves and our own agency. This would be a conception of reason that we can make our own, and a conception of reason that can be reconstructed from a plural set of normative standpoints. Habermas worked with such a conception up to *Knowledge and Human Interests* but found it could not be made compatible with the strong conception of "theory" (the successor to philosophy) to which he turned thereafter. That turn to theory refashioned the project of critical theory as a *strenge Wissenschaft*, less bound by or beholden to the historical and existential exigencies of modernity, of being modern.

Although Habermas has never been of one mind about what reason ought to mean, the *picture* of reason toward which he has most often inclined is one that displays some unappealing features. I want now to approach this picture from a couple of angles by carefully attending to the language in which it is drawn. The first feature I want to look at is the depiction of reason's relation to contingency. "Communicative reason is of course a rocking hull—but it does not go under in the sea of contingencies, even if shuddering in high seas is the only mode in which it 'copes' with these contingencies" (PT 144). The image of reason as an impregnable and impermeable "hull" is revealing, for it places reason beyond the reach of self-decentering experience: the possibility of any such experience supposes a mindful openness to historical novelties and contingencies. It supposes the capacity to do more than "shudder" when reason encounters its other. An impermeable "hull" is unreceptive by design, it is meant to shield what is inside from what is outside. But must reason shield itself against all contingency and novelty? Is there nothing to be learned from exposure to them? Can reason learn about itself without such exposure? Put differently: Can that which is impregnable give birth to something new?

Pictured as impermeable and impregnable, reason encounters the open seas of contingency and novelty as fixed and rigid as when Odysseus encountered the Sirens. The acuity of Adorno's characterization of reason's encounter with its "other" remains undiminished. Communicative reason shudders, ecstatically perhaps, but like the mythic paragon of instrumental reason, it is just as incapable of learning from its "other." This image of reason is at odds with the Young Hegelians' time-sensitive understanding of reason. There can be no "dialectic of learning and unlearning" between a "rocking hull" and its "other." That which is impregnable and impermeable cannot have a history, for the material out of which it is made is not sufficiently porous to be marked by the otherness of the "other." As in the case of the rigid, defensive self tempted by the Sirens' song, hull-like reason can brace itself for its encounter with the "other," but it cannot let itself be affected, permeated, or, to speak more carnally, penetrated by the "other"—if it did, it would be sunk.

If having a history and being affected by history is a condition of learning, then that which has no history cannot learn. To say that reason has the capacity to criticize itself is to say that it has the capacity to transform itself: self-criticism and self-transformation mutually presuppose one another. But for there to be a reciprocal interplay between reason's self-criticism and its self-transformation requires that reason let itself be determined, let itself be decentered; otherwise, it could not learn anything new about itself. Of course, in ascribing these self-critical and self-transformative capacities to reason, we are ascribing them to ourselves, for every interpretation of reason implicitly projects some idea of what it means to be a human being and what being human demands of us. Needless to say, the stuff out of which an impermeable and impregnable hull is made is not the stuff out of which beings capable of self-criticism and self-transformation are made.

The second feature of this picture of reason I want to look at concerns the language in which the universalistic claims of reason are characterized. Habermas claims that "the transcendent moment of *universal* validity bursts [*sprengt*] every provinciality asunder" (PDM, 322). I am compelled to ask: Why must the universality of reason be portrayed in this violent language? Why must *every* provinciality be burst asunder? Are *all* provincialities so alike that reason can indiscriminately burst them asunder? Should not *certain* provincialities—such as the semantic resources of traditions—be sensitively preserved and reflectively renewed rather than collectively burst asunder? Most certainly this talk of bursting all provincialities asunder renders meaningless the question of getting right the proportion of continuity and discontinuity in the forms of life we pass on. All we can pass on are the stories of the glorious victories of reason over all that is provincial. The impulse to burst asunder every provinciality exposes an objectivistic stance toward meaning, and a surprisingly subjectivistic idea of reason—subjectivistic because it projects an idea of reason as able to begin radically and independently anew at will, as if without any debt to the past, or dependence on anything outside it. In this respect, but not only in this, it is a picture of reason that is totally incompatible with modernity's relation to time. It is hard to see how the form of life this picture of reason projects is one that could understand itself as obligated to recognize any image of the past as one of its own concerns, no matter how "provincial." After all, every "image of the past" is unavoidably provincial, historically colored by its time and place.

The picture of reason that emerges from this violent encounter with all that is provincial is hardly reassuring, to say the least. First, it implies an insensitivity to particularity, justifying the long-held suspicion that the basic concepts of communicative rationality have been rigged in favor of the universal at the expense of the particular, making quite unconvincing all the talk of a "dialectic" of universality and particularity (since reason cannot be penetrated by particularity). Second, a provinciality-destroying reason is a meaning-destroying reason, since eliminating all that is merely provincial is eliminating all that does not survive the judgment of universal validity. But, as I have argued, and as Habermas has occasionally conceded, even the practices of reason depend for their intelligibility and cogency on sources of meaning embodied in social practices and cultural traditions, the "provinciality" and "particularity" of which is a condition of their being able to embody meaning in the first place. Furthermore a provinciality-destroying reason is a history-destroying reason, since it must stand in a permanently adversarial relation to the past. It can never be in a position to recognize the past as the prehistory of the present, or every image of the past as one of its one concerns. It is a conception of reason that must remain suspicious of all that is provincial, particular, traditional; a picture of reason that is constitutionally incapable of identifying with any of the traditions it is supposed to criticize and renew, and so a picture of reason that is incapable of drawing upon the normativity of modernity's relation to time. Thus it justifiably provokes the worry that it is a conception of reason that, lacking the normative resources for distinguishing between those cultural practices and traditions we wish to continue, and those which we wish to discontinue, will strike indiscriminately at the wrong as well as the right targets, producing a great deal of unnecessary "collateral damage."

Construed procedurally, communicative reason reverts to the "understanding," and hence makes itself into one more variant of "instrumental reason." Rather than rendering that critique of instrumental reason obsolete, communicative reason reinvigorates it: the shift to the paradigm of linguistic intersubjectivity has not yet shaken off the violent element at the core of modern reason. And since it is grounded in the normativity of rules, "in the sense that those pragmatic rules are normative which generally play a constitutive role in the practice of subjects capable of language and action trying to reach understanding about something in the world" (CA 228), communicative reason is an idea of reason that more or less collapses the distinction between *der Verstand* and *die Vernunft* central to the German tradition since Kant.[51] Although he was not himself altogether consistent about it, even Kant realized that reason as *die Vernunft* could not be a rule-governed faculty of mind; otherwise, it could not be capable of disclosing anything new. Reason, as opposed to the rule-governed activity of the understanding, is a *possibility-disclosing* activity, proposing ends that go beyond what is already given empirically or normatively. If it is to be normatively innovative, capable of initiating normative change, reason cannot draw its normativity from the normativity of rules alone, even from those pragmatic rules putatively constitutive of human speech and action. It must "call something into being which did not exist before, which was not given, *not even as an object of cognition or imagination*, and which therefore, strictly speaking, could not be known."

Drawing on the idea of a new beginning, Kant reinterpreted reason (and human agency) in such a way as to make it qualitatively distinct from instrumental or narrowly epistemological construals of reason. In response to Rousseau's critique of instrumental reason, he focused on reason's spontaneous power to initiate something new, to form "an order of its own according to ideas," an order "according to which it declares actions to be necessary even though they have never taken place, and perhaps never will take place."[52] Anticipating Dewey, Heidegger, and Arendt, Kant is not appealing to the normativity of rules but to the normativity of possibility—the possibility of a future different from the past, the possibility of understanding ourselves and the world differently, the possibility of transforming our relation to ourselves and to the world. This particular source of normativity is not at all assimilable to the normativity of rules or "law."[53] And for that very reason it was not good enough for Kant, not good enough as a source of normativity, which prompted his magnificent attempt to make freedom and the moral law identical by showing how we can think of ourselves as both authors and addressees of the moral law. However, independently of its particular strengths and weakness, this endeavour cast a very large shadow over his no less important attempt to redefine reason in terms of its freedom, its capacity, to initiate a new beginning by disclosing alternative possibilities. Of course, this circumstance is a function of Kant's fundamental conviction that freedom could be made compatible with law, since any hint of lawlessness would render freedom normatively and morally suspect. Here again, we have the ever-reappearing worry that whatever is not rule-conforming or rule-governed (because unfamiliar and uncontrollable) must be inherently unruly; if not irrational, then, definitely nonrational, and, hence, nonmoral. Thus whatever it is, being unfamiliar and uncontrollable, it cannot serve as the basis of a morally accountable practice.

Nonetheless, this "romantic" idea of reason as a critically transformative, possibility disclosing medium took on a momentum of its own. It inspired the Young Hegelians and American Pragmatism, and it continues to find resonance today in the work of theorists such as Cavell and Taylor.[54] Reason's capacity to be a possibility-disclosing, beginning-initiating agency depends on its capacity to be time-responsive, receptive to the novelties and contingencies of history. The normative horizon of reason exceeds (and must exceed) the horizon of procedural rationality, exceeds (and must exceed) the horizon of the sciences of knowledge. This much Kant already understood, if not fully appreciated, which is why he distinguished the possibility-disclosing activity of reason from the rule-governed acquisition and exercise of knowledge: "as pure self-activity (*Selbsttätigkeit*)" reason "is elevated even above the understanding ... with respect to ideas, reason shows itself to be such a pure spontaneity and that it far transcends anything which sensibility can provide it."[55] Neither instrumental nor procedural conceptions of reason can grasp how human beings can reflectively and spontaneously initiate something new, can self-critically begin anew, in response to breakdowns and crisis, in response to self-decentering experiences.

Already with this radically new conception of reason, disidentified both from knowledge and from rule-governedness, Kant shows how reason comes to possess its own utopian or transformative potential—it need not be added as an afterthought or conceived as something heterogeneous to reason. From Kant to Habermas, however, it has been far too little understood that this aspect of reason cannot be captured in procedural terms, cannot be accommodated by the normativity of rules, for we are speaking of reason's possibility-disclosing ability, which ability is not rule-governed or rule-enabled. And so the general problem I have repeatedly thematized throughout this book remains unresolved: how to grasp as learning— which is to say, as an activity of reason—those accomplishments through which we acquire new tongues with which to say what cannot be said and new ears with which to hear what cannot be heard, accomplishments through which we overcome epistemological crises, and partial, one-sided interpretations of ourselves and others and accomplishments through which we are able to "go on" learning from our interaction with one another and our interaction with the "world." If we continue to think that learning processes occur "*only* in the light of criticizable validity claims," we will be unable to grasp such accomplishments as an activity of reason. And so long as this is the case, the very practices on which the possibility of "better forms of life and more reflective ways of life" depend will con tinue to show up (at best) as superfluous appendages of communicative reason rather than as essential to the life forms of reason as practices of justification.

It is a fundamental premise of critical theory that the forms of reason with which we most closely identify is fateful for our form of life. The sociohistorical critique of reason carried out in its seminal texts illuminate how we have come to identify so closely with those forms of reason, how they have come unexpectedly to dominate and distort our form of life. If we are to overcome the negative effects of the dominant forms of reason, we need to weaken our attachment to them to make room for neglected, devalued or suppressed forms of reason.

Of course, this whole enterprise supposes a view of human agents as reason-responsive, as reason-resonant, beings. It also supposes that human agents can be receptive to different *kinds* of reasons, and that they possess sufficient freedom to determine which reasons will count as self-determining reasons, which reasons they will let themselves be moved by. Thus it is a view that supposes that human agents have a say in determining which kinds of reasons become authoritative reasons for them: in having such a say, human agents also have a say in the kind of future they wish for themselves, a say in the future of their form of life.

Our relation to reason, more precisely, our identification with reason, is so self-defining that it becomes more or less obvious that *we* are reason. We are reason insofar as we are beings who are prepared, and are expected, to justify our beliefs, actions, and judgment with reasons for which we are epistemically and ethically responsible—reasons whose normative force we can recognize and to which we can willingly assent. More fundamentally, I believe, we are reason insofar as we are able to *change* our beliefs.

We could then say that we are reason to the extent that we can change not only the reason that we use, but also the reason that we are.

Shifting Foucault's famous question "What is this reason that we use?" to the question "What is this reason that we are?" allows me to bring out *the* distinctive feature of the critical theory tradition. That feature consists in its insistence on the possibility of another kind of reason, another way of living reason in practice, which is not merely an abstraction or something impossibly utopian but an actual possibility that we can locate in existing, if marginalized, practices of reason. Of course, all this will sound quite peculiar if you don't already suppose the view that reason has a history, a history that shows certain tendencies and patterns, opening up some possibilities while closing off others. With Hegel, we can say that the history of reason is directional, that some forms of reason come to be dominant, self-determining, so long as we also acknowledge Foucault's point that it is also a contingent history: the form of reason dominant at any one time is "only *one* possible form among others."[56]

If we are successfully to renew critical theory, we cannot squander its Young Hegelian inheritance, its romantic-expressive understanding of reason. We must insist upon the possibility-disclosing role of reason, and not rest content with placing all our critical eggs in the basket of procedural rationality and "context-transcendence." The idea that reason is a world-disclosing practice may well sound strange to the ears of many, accustomed as they are, to leaving such secondary activity (secondary to truth-tracking activity) to the "imagination."[57] But reason does disclose the world, and is always disclosing the world, through its reflective and critical interventions. The discussion of world-disclosing arguments in part III, chapter 5, was intended to highlight this essentially disclosive aspect of reason's activity, rendering less peculiar the thought that "argument" can open up by indirect means the ontological background upon which our sense-making practices rely. As Charles Taylor once suggested, the "task of reason has to be conceived differently: as that of articulating the background, 'disclosing' what it involves."[58] We have no other way of reflectively illuminating our unavoidable dependence on this background without denying and, thereby, distorting it. And we have no other way of "going on" reflectively, self-critically, when our practices break down, when epistemological crises overtake us. Here, too, we depend on the disclosive power of linguistically incarnated reason to shed new light on our circumstances and our predicament, without which we could not make better sense of them.

Disclosure is also intimately related to critique. Indeed, as I will suggest in the final part of my book, critique needs to be reconceived as a practice of reflective disclosure. Right now, I wish only do draw attention to a feature common to both "immanent critique" and reflective disclosure. The feature to which I refer is the way in which both immanent critique and reflective disclosure enable passage from one perspective to another, enable the transition from one self-understanding or one social practice to another. Hegel was the first explicitly to identify the "self-determination" of reason with this transition-enabling activity, transitions chronicled in the *Phenomenology of Spirit*—the book of transitions.

Habermas himself comes ever so close to a similar view of reason's capacity for "self-determination" in an essay defending the "unity of reason." Rejecting as a metaphysical illusion the idea that the unity of reason can be grasped as a totality, he makes the "postmetaphysical" suggestion that "the unity of reason remains perceptible only in the plurality of its voices—as the possibility in principle of passing from one language into another—a passage that, no matter how occasional, is still comprehensible" (PT 117). This suggestion, claims Habermas, obviates the need to choose between two equally unattractive choices: either the objectivistic, one-world ontology posited by metaphysical realism, on the one hand, or the plurality of radically incommensurable worlds posited by relativist contextualism, on the other. Whether Habermas's alternative can preserve the possibility of incommensurability, preserve the possibility of "the sufficiently strange," as a normative challenge to which reason must respond, the still more decisive issue concerns just how Habermas conceives of the possibility of passage or transition from one "language" to another, or from one "voice" of reason to another. By now we should not be surprised to find that Habermas undermines his promising suggestion by construing it procedurally (PT 117). Appeal to the rationality of procedures can by no means "guarantee" the unity of reason in the plurality of its voices: the rationality of procedures is but one of the voices in which reason speaks. A procedural conception of reason is just as incapable of making perceptible the plurality of reason's voices—a motley crew if ever there was one—as it is of explaining the passage from one language to another. It cannot even secure the unity of procedural reason, since the differentiation of validity claims (truth, rightness, sincerity) so central to its self-justification does not produce out of itself a complementary re-unification at any level.

There can be no rules or procedures that can tell us in advance when or how to move from one language to another, or from one voice of reason to another. What is involved is an irreducibly *practical* ability, an ability to make transitions, to open passageways not already open. The opening of passageways that did not exist before, making transitions not possible before, cannot be attributed to the rationality of any procedure, or to any underlying procedural unity of reason. The activity by which such passageways are opened is neither rule-governed nor unruly. But it is an ability definitive of reason as a possibility-disclosing practice. It is this possibility-disclosing power of reason, not its procedural rationality, that renews our confidence in reason just when we are most likely to doubt it—that is, when we confront intractable problems, when our practices of justification or languages of evaluation break down, when we are disoriented, when we find we've become unintelligible to one another or to ourselves. The fact that such passageways can be opened up at all shows that we *can* move back and forth between languages, between old and new voices of reason, and, most important, reassures us that change attributable to our own agency is possible, that things can be otherwise than they are. Perhaps we will one day be sufficiently reassured and inspired to arrange our political institutions and cultural practices in a way that makes them more receptive to the practice of reflective disclosure—that makes them more disclosure facilitating. So long as we continue to construe reason in procedural terms, we will fail repeatedly to recognize the possibility-disclosing activity of reason—fail repeatedly to understand reason as an agency of normative and cultural change. Captive to a procedural picture of reason, we will be forced to surrender to the "contingency of genuinely innovative forces" the very activities and practices through which we self-consciously exercise our reflective and spontaneous agency.

Even today, few critical theorists would question the early Marcuse's idealist claim: "Reason is the fundamental category of philosophical thought, the one by means of which it has bound itself to human destiny."[59] Certainly it would receive Habermas's wholehearted endorsement. However, unlike Habermas, Marcuse did not identify reason primarily with justification, but with freedom: "the concept of reason contains the concept of freedom."[60] Obviously we cannot simply presuppose the meaning of either reason or freedom, but at least in respect of their interconnection, Marcuse and early critical theory remained faithful to the normative conception of reason shared by the Young Hegelians. Although *The Philosophical Discourse of Modernity* begins its narrative reconstruction of that discourse by emphasizing just this reciprocal interconnection between reason and the "freedom of subjectivity," it soon veers away from it, and by the end of the lectures we find once again the usual close identification of reason with practices of justification. The talk of emancipation that distinguished early critical theory up to early Habermas has in the meantime been replaced by talk of justifying claims to validity: the modern "individual, with his irreplaceable yes or no, is only fully on his own under the presupposition that he remains bound to a universal community by way of a cooperative quest for truth" (PDM 347). Gone, then, is the thought with which the lectures on modernity began, the thought identified by the first philosopher of modernity as *the* principle of modernity: "The principle of the modern world is freedom of subjectivity" (PDM 16). In its place Habermas substitutes the thought that the principle of modernity is the orientation to nonlocal, context-transcendent justification, and thus supplants a freedom-oriented conception of reason with a truth-oriented one. Neither social criticism nor cultural innovation can be explained as practices that are definable by a "cooperative quest for truth." What is missing from Habermas's account of modernity is the focus on freedom that rendered visible the "constellation among modernity, its time-consciousness, and rationality" in the first place (PDM 43). Hegel was able to make that constellation visible because he did not disconnect its individual components from one another. It is hardly enough to say "the renewal of traditions depends more and more on the readiness of individuals to criticise and their ability to innovate" (TCAII 146), particularly, if one cannot provide an account of how those same cultural traditions provide resources for social criticism and cultural innovation and if one cannot provide an account of those very activities as activities different from (though not independent of and no less rational than) the activity of justification.

Times of change and transition require corresponding forms of reason (or styles of reasoning). What Hegel envisioned was an idea of reason modeled on an idea of freedom, an idea of reason as the art of making transitions from old to new languages of interpretation and evaluation, an idea of reason as the cooperative disclosure of passageways through which the different voices of reason may pass, and continue to pass. The relevant notion of freedom is neither freedom construed as negative freedom in the sense of freedom from external constraint, nor freedom construed as positive freedom in the sense of freely willed conformity to a principle of action. The relevant notion of freedom draws its normativity from the idea of possibility, from the possibility of beginning anew. We need to reformulate our normative conception of reason in a way that incorporates its possibility-disclosing activity, for it is through that very activity that the relevant connection between reason and freedom becomes visible. What we should be aiming for is a conception of reason that preserves its change-initiating power at the same time as it accommodates (rather than denies) its dependence on history, culture, and language—on semantic and cultural resources not of its own making and not at its disposal. To acknowledge that dependence is also to acknowledge reason's finitude, human finitude. It is to identify reason with the "vagaries of me and you," while drawing upon them self-critically to transform the reason that we are.

VI . . . in Times of Need?

1 An Aversion to Critique and the Exhaustion of Utopian Energies

It is self-evident that the times in which we live have become inhospitable to the practice of critique—especially to self-critique.[1] Closely observed, all models of social and cultural criticism, regardless of normative or method-ological orientation, bear the marks of this inhospitality. What I am speak-ing of is a dimly perceived process of self-restriction and accommodation, at once the outward adjustment to new conditions and an unrecognized expression of normative despair. In short: resignation to the contracting space of possibilities; resignation to the thought that our possibilities might be exhausted, that the future may no longer be open to us, no longer welcoming.

This unfortunate circumstance should not come as a complete surprise, given that so much of the culture of modernity finds itself in the grip of a profound skepticism from which it appears either unable or reluctant to escape. The appeal of this skepticism is difficult to resist in as much as nothing else seems better equipped to make sense of unceasing, ever-more common experiences of disillusionment, devastation, and injustice. Its appeal is such that it cannot be refuted by argument alone—at least, not by standard types of argument.

To regard this deeply perplexing phenomenon as an effect or symptom of "postmodernism" is to give in to a myopic and historically inadequate perspective. This skeptical condition has a long history, a *Wirkungs-geschichte* at least two centuries old.[2] Rather than regarding it as something entirely new or unprecedented, we need to see that it is a highly complex and increasingly resistant strain of skepticism that is itself a creation of and a response to modern forms of life. We need moreover to distinguish the ways in which this skepticism manifests itself as a cultural sensibility from the ways in which it manifests itself as an intellectual position. Of course, the cultural sensibility and intellectual position mutually influence and support one another, but they are not reducible to one another. By "cultural sensibility" I mean the pre-reflective way that a culture allows itself to be affected by historical experience, the interpretive stance it takes—open here, closed there—to what befalls it. While a cultural sensibility in this sense is historically variable, it is not ephemeral or transient. Indeed a half-century or more may pass before a new cultural sensibility becomes discernible, and its effects visible. So it is not enough simply to argue against the theoretical manifestation of such skepticism. When stated as an intellectual position such skepticism is, as Putnam points out, "all too easily refutable," but it lives on "because the attitude of alienation from the world and from the community is not just a theory."[3] And that is why far more than an "intellectual" response is required, demanding some reflection on the role the practice of critique might play in facilitating a change of cultural sensibility.

Once we drop the misleading, historically uninformative opposition between "modernism" and "postmodernism," we will be in a better position to recognize the degree to which both "modernist" and "postmodernist" models of critique have been negatively affected by this pervasive, deceptively subtle strain of skepticism. Thus we will be in a better position to recognize that no model of critique has remained immune to its effects. Perhaps the most palpable of these effects is the pervasive decline of confidence in our social practices, in our cultural traditions and, more generally, in our agency. We might even have lost the power to believe in social progress—the faith that tomorrow can be better than today, not just for the lucky few, but for all. That almost nobody talks about this kind of social progress anymore is understandable, since it is so very difficult to talk about it without being conscious of, without surrendering to, the mocking irony that encircles this endangered idea. Our lately departed twentieth century did not give us much reason to hope for better days to come, and much reason to doubt their very possibility.

The future, for which so much of the old was sacrificed and so much of the new embraced, once had a much broader horizon of possibility, and a much more welcoming visage. To say that an openness to the "novelty of the future," an openness to disruption, discontinuity, and unforeseeable change, is what makes modernity historically distinctive as an epoch and as a form of life is not to say enough. For what had until recently made such openness to disruption and discontinuity sustainable, which is to say, what made it liveable, endurable, was the expectation that the "novelty" to come would be of a kind that answered our hopes and needs. While massive, jarring, relentless, accelerating change continues apace, our experience of such change has altered. It has altered because our relation to the future has altered—perhaps for good.

There was a time, as recently as the 1960s and 1970s (in spite of, as much as because of, all that was then transpiring), when our relation to the future was still marked more by hope and excitement than by skepticism and despair. There was some vague but palpable sense that long unfulfilled promises might soon be fulfilled. When Sam Cooke sang "I know a change is gonna come," he was not just expressing a yearning for change; he was also expressing the still widely shared faith, tested time and again, that a better day would soon dawn, and that we would have a hand in its dawning. We may no longer be capable of such faith in the future and in our own agency. Skepticism and despair seem to have outstripped hope. Understandably, we no longer yearn for it as we once did. We have seen too much change, unwelcome, irrational change, change that does not answer to our hopes and needs, change that makes us feel like patients, not agents.

But, if that is the case, what can we consider ourselves capable of when we experience change as a symptom of our powerlessness rather than as the product of our own agency? What can we now ascribe to our own agency, besides the capacity to make "choices" from a fixed menu not of our own choosing? Is it any wonder that the mood of the times is one of fatalism in the face of apparently irresistible and uncontrollable change?[4] Indeed much of the change we are compelled to undergo appears to be so entirely unmotivated by any genuine human needs that it takes on the character of a cataclysmic natural event that we are powerless to prevent— something akin to earthquakes, hurricanes, floods, and forest fires, wreaking havoc wherever they occur. Events such as "9/11," the growing and unpredictable threats of climate change, the resurgence of old and the emergence of wholly new diseases, the fragility and vulnerability of hyper-complex, interdependent, and massively interconnected financial and technological systems, and the demise of a feeble but not altogether ineffective system of international governance by the imperial ambitions of the world's lone superpower are among the overwhelming indications that the project of modernity—in whatever form we imagined it—is not just out of control but that it may be long past its best before date. We have no idea what catastrophe might befall the planet tomorrow, how widespread or fatal its consequences will be. There is no such thing as "normal" anymore.

Persistent, intractable doubts about the very possibility of moral and political progress cannot leave our practices, traditions, and self-understanding intact, since they are all deeply structured by the anticipation of such progress, whether in the near or distant future. Once the future can no longer function as its placeholder, talk about progress as a genuine rather than merely notional (or merely "technological") possibility will become impossible. A certain degree of openness in our social practices and cultural traditions, a readiness to reflect on previously unquestioned assumptions and to re-evaluate previously esteemed values is a necessary condition of the successful practice of critique. But does that openness not depend on the openness of the future? And does not the openness of the future itself depend on our capacity to envision confidence-regenerating, hope-inspiring alternatives to the current social order?

Today, it seems as though utopian energies have been used up, as if they have retreated from historical thought. The horizon of the future has contracted and has changed both the *Zeitgeist* and politics in fundamental ways. *The future is negatively cathected.* . . . The responses of the intellectuals reflect as much bewilderment as those of the politicians. It is by no means only realism when a forthrightly accepted bewilderment increasingly takes the place of attempts at orientation directed toward the future. The situation may be objectively obscure. Obscurity is nonetheless also a function of a society's assessment of its own readiness to take action. *What is at stake is Western culture's confidence in itself.* (NC 50–51, my emphasis)

With this prescient observation made in an essay published in the mid-1980s, not long after the lectures on modernity, Habermas identified—whether intentionally or accidentally—two necessary (if not sufficient) conditions of the cultural self-confidence of modernity: (1) the availability of utopian energies and (2) the openness of the future. Once these conditions fail to obtain—and they obtain jointly or not at all—we have the preconditions for a crisis of cultural self-confidence. Until the present historical conjuncture, the problem of modernity's self-confidence, its self-reassurance, was continuously re-articulated by "a consciousness of the significance of the present moment in which historical consciousness and utopian thought are fused with one another" (NC 68). But now it seems that we have arrived at a point in the history of modernity when historical consciousness and utopian thought have split apart for the very first time. The significance of the present moment now appears obscure, opaque, because it cannot be connected either to a past from which it derives its difference or to a future from which it draws its orientation. At this point it becomes clearer than ever before just how much our capacity to envision alternative possibilities depends on our expectation that the social conditions under which these possibilities can be successfully realized might one day obtain. But how do we "go on" then, and toward what, when the future can no longer be the bearer of utopian hopes and expectations, when its horizon seems to be contracting, appearing increasingly unreceptive to our future-directed and future-dependent attempts at orientation?

Habermas did not sufficiently develop the diagnostic potential of his extremely perceptive observation. The focus of his attention was not so much on the decline of cultural self-confidence as it was on the demise of the "welfare-state," a demise that signaled the exhaustion of a particular utopia—that of a society based on social labor. But the putative exhaustion of that particular utopia is hardly the most worrisome implication of his observation; most worrisome is the implication that the cultural energies or semantic resources on which the very possibility of utopian thought depends may be exhausted.[5] On the plus side, Habermas regards this turn of events as potentially liberating, since we are forced to abandon the kind of illusion, methodological and otherwise, that arises from imagining utopia as a fully determinate totality. There is much to recommend this point, not least of which is the bitter knowledge that the utopian dreams of modernity all too easily turn into dystopian nightmares. There are also the much-remarked facts of social complexity and cultural pluralism. But are these unavoidable facts to be regarded as impediments to utopian thought, or are they merely the new, potentially enabling constraints under which utopian thought must operate? It is very hard to see how such facts as might productively constrain utopian thought could be the source of radical self-doubt. On the other hand, it is not hard to see how radical self-doubt might become irresistible when the conditions necessary for utopian thought, and thereby, the conditions necessary for cultural self-confidence, no longer obtain.

Once utopian thought is uncoupled from historical consciousness it is most certainly very hard to see how the "utopian content of a society based on communication" can regenerate the requisite self-confidence by relying with sanguine confidence on the utopian promise of procedural rationality.

The utopian content of a society based on communication is limited to the formal aspects of an undamaged intersubjectivity. To the extent to which it suggests a concrete form of life, even the expression "the ideal speech situation" is misleading. What can be outlined normatively are the necessary but general conditions for the communicative practice of everyday life and for a procedure of discursive will-formation that would put participants themselves in a position to realize concrete possibilities for a better and less threatened life, on their own initiative and in accordance with their own needs and insights. (NC 69)

The juxtaposition between Habermas's procedural utopia and his critical diagnosis of the times presented could not be starker, not just because of the obvious disjunction but also because it is allowed to stand unmediated. Only a page before Habermas states that as "utopian oases dry up, a desert of banality and bewilderment spreads" (NC 68).[6] If contemporary consciousness is "bewildered" and "fragmented" by the erosion of semantic contents on which its sense-making activities depend, just what "concrete possibilities" can "participants themselves" realize, "on their own initiative and in accordance with their own needs and insights"? And in relation to what kind of future? There must be some articulable possibilities in which participants can recognise a future they would like to make their own, possibilities around which they can orient their hopes and practices? Moreover such possibilities must be capable of reopening the future, rendering it responsive to our hopes and needs. A future no longer open to our hopes and expectations reinforces rather than alleviates the experience of bewilderment, tightening the grip of skepticism, and deepening the paralyzing sense of cultural exhaustion. It appears that this merely formal image of utopia is itself a symptom of unrecognized resignation, adapting itself to the skeptical mood of the times that Habermas incompletely diagnoses. Does the proceduralist response to this circumstance really discharge philosophy of its obligations to its own time? Is that all there is for philosophy to do? Is that all it can do arrest the decline of confidence and the foreclosure of the future?

A proceduralist view of reason takes it for granted that hitting on the right normative procedures is more or less to solve the problem of cultural self-confidence or trust. There is of course a circular relation between trust and reason. But to claim as Habermas does that the times are such that "Western culture's confidence in itself" is at stake is more or less to declare the poverty of proceduralism. "Our language game rests not on proof or on Reason but *trust.*"[7] As Putnam argues in a Wittgensteinian vein, cultural self-confidence, trust, including trust in reason, is not grounded in reason alone—all the less so in a restrictively procedural conception of reason. Reason can reinforce our trust, and it can undermine our trust; it cannot all by itself generate trust in our cultural practices and political institutions. The need of the times is not answered by a proceduralist conception of reason and philosophy that restricts itself to the question of the right normative procedures for settling questions of truth or justice. What we are faced with, then, is *the problem of how to trust again,* and not just the problem of which norms, which ideals, which practices to trust. And this problem, the problem of learning to trust again, is of course tied up with the problem of how to reopen the future, without which reopening it is practically impossible to regenerate trust and cultural self-confidence.

Let us look at this gap between critical diagnosis and philosophical response from a slightly different angle. This time in connection with a question that has haunted critical theory, particularly in its Habermasian form, ever since it was first posed by Walter Benjamin. Habermas paraphrases it as follows:

> Is it possible that one day an emancipated human race could encounter itself within an expanded space of discursive will formation and yet be robbed of the light in which it is capable of interpreting its life as something good? . . . Without the influx of those semantic energies with which Benjamin's rescuing critique was concerned, the structures of practical discourse—finally well established—would necessarily become desolate.[8]

This question is much more pertinent today than could be foreseen in 1972 when Habermas wrote his sensitive and insightful essay on Benjamin. We are perhaps farther than ever from the day when we can talk about an emancipated human race, but much closer to a situation in which we can see Benjamin's question in a different light. The possibility that must be reckoned with is not quite the one Habermas describes. It is not the Kafkaesque possibility that an "emancipated" human race, having thoughtlessly depleted the semantic contents of its cultural traditions, will find itself incapable of interpreting its achievement as something good, incapable even of understanding the question. The possibility that faces us is not quite as nightmarish as that. If Benjamin is right, we will never have to face that question. What we face is the very real possibility that our attempts to fashion just institutions within the framework of democratic forms of life will be in vain if we proceed as though we can do so without drawing upon and *at the same time* renewing the semantic contents and utopian energies on which they ultimately depend. (All of which supposes, of course, that the human race will survive long enough to retrieve and renew the semantic and cultural contents without which neither justice nor freedom can find a secure place on this earth. We don't have all the time in the world. A "happy ending" is not guaranteed; the expectation of a "timely rescue" not warranted.)

My point is not just that whatever utopia we imagine, it must have substantive content: the notion of a "formal utopia" is an oxymoron. My point is also that the possibility of imagining a utopia with content is a necessary condition of the practice of critique. And that is because the practice of critique, unlike the practices of science or theoretical reason, is not normatively guided by "a cooperative quest for truth." Truth cannot be the goal of critique. Critique does not aim at truth but at the reflective disclosure of possibility, the "truth" or "correctness" of which can be verified, to the extent that possibility can be "verified," only by the addressees of critique in the course of time.[9] In other words, critique is unavoidably "utopian," not in the sense that it depends on the availability of a fully determinate utopia, but in the sense that it depends on the openness and receptivity of the future to utopian thought—to the possibility that things might be otherwise than they are. Put in Habermas's terms, critique depends on the fusion of historical consciousness with utopian thought, without which the disclosure of alternative possibilities would be a hopeless endeavor. But what kind of historical consciousness are we capable of today? To what possible future(s) can it be oriented?

If the contemporary aversion to self-criticism, pervasive skepticism, and the exhaustion of utopian energies together comprise the inhospitable, unreceptive circumstances in which critique now finds itself, they are not circumstances into which it was suddenly thrown. Critique has had a hand in creating them. When Kant proudly and confidently proclaimed that "[o]ur age is the genuine age of critique, and to critique everything must submit,"[10] he could not have comprehended just how radical were the skeptical implications of his claim, for he could not have foreseen just how much would be submitted to unrelenting critical interrogation. Everything imaginable has been forced to submit to critical unmasking—nothing has been spared, nothing left unexposed. Already Nietzsche had an inkling of the consequences of unbridled unmasking, regarding it at as a pathological manifestation of "bad taste," itself the effect of an unbounded "will to truth," the aim of which is to expose everything, to strip naked all that confronts or confounds it.[11] Quite unexpectedly, critique has been much more successful in undermining the hopes of the Enlightenment than in justifying them.[12] It has shaken rather than fostered confidence in our norms and ideals, giving us compelling reason to doubt our capacity to shape the meaning of our individual lives and to determine the appropriate norms of our collective form of life. But in the course of this process of global unmasking, critique has exhausted itself.[13] It has exhausted its critical energies, and depleted its normative resources. Critique is not a self-sustaining practice. It is as dependent on the self-reflective renewal of its semantic and normative resources as any other cultural practice, as any form of life.

Unlike Kant and the *Aufklärung*, we cannot insulate ourselves against self-crippling skepticism by an unshakable confidence in reason: we no longer enjoy the protection of such an effective firewall. Under conditions of normative disorientation, if not normative despair, critique can hardly serve as the "handbook of reason," as Foucault once called it, not intending, perhaps, the ambiguous, ironic, connotations. Our situation is very different. With good reason we are today much more aware that the question of what reason is, what it is capable of, is up for grabs as never before. Since nothing can be immune to critical scrutiny, not even reason, we find ourselves in a situation in which all our normative standards, all our social practices can be placed under suspicion. It is not necessary that they be placed equally under suspicion to engender practice-crippling, hope-disabling doubts. All that is required is that our doubts be persistent, extensive, and deep. If our current doubts were not genuine, then we would be hard-pressed to explain why in the last few decades so much intellectual energy has been spent trying to defend (and revise) our most cherished ideals and norms in response to unrelenting unmasking and intensifying doubts. Yet, for all the energy expended on disarming them, these doubts remain firm. We are not only unsure which of our norms to trust, we have profound doubts about the likelihood of ever finding norms that we can confidently trust, supposing that we can learn to trust again. I do not of course mean norms that we can trust with certainty—that is the very skeptical trap we wish to avoid. Confidence does not require certainty, but it does require a successfully reflective and open relation to our ideals and our practices. Such confidence can do quite well without foundational support so long as the ideals and practices to which it lends itself can facilitate and sustain ongoing self-criticism and self-transformation. Once such confidence is shaken, however, there is no obvious or direct way to restore it. Most certainly it will not be restored by metaphysical or philosophical "guarantees." The existential condition of being modern requires us to live without guarantees, but not without confidence.

Undeniably we have learned a great deal from the insights generated by the practice of unmasking critique, and perhaps we may yet learn something from its self-crippling skepticism. Yet there is no denying that the fruit of two centuries of unmasking critique are decidedly bittersweet. That our ideals, norms, and practices were in need of unmasking is more than clear enough; what is not at all clear is just what can take their place. If we cannot espouse or uphold them as before, how do we go on from here? We now have a much better idea of how we got here. But where are we going? In the name of what? What new or refashioned ideals, norms, and practices might re-inspire confidence in the possibility, the hope for, a future different from the past? Our culture, most obviously our high culture, has become highly adept at contemplating its own demise, having become understandably but obsessively concerned with "the end of history," "the end of art," "the end of philosophy," "the death of the subject," and so on and on. Are we more capable of imagining our own end than of imagining a new beginning for ourselves? Do we no longer know, have we forgotten, how to begin anew? Have we forgotten how to make use of our one "miracle-working faculty"?[14]

2   Disclosure as (Intimate) Critique

In the face of such inhospitable circumstances, the very circumstances in which the need for critique is greatest, the question naturally arises as to whether critique is still possible. Just what is critique capable of, practically speaking, when it is as dependent on the openness of the future and on cultural self-confidence as our other practices? If it is to remain a viable cultural practice, we need to reconceive its role, making it more responsive to these new circumstances. It is my thesis that the possibility of practically effective critique depends on the success with which it can meet the challenge of reopening the future, enlarging the space of possibility, and thereby, restoring cultural confidence—a task without end. In order to reopen the future, critique must once again facilitate the fusion of historical consciousness with utopian thought. If it is to do that, it must reconceive itself as a possibility-disclosing practice, for that is just what critique is at its hope-inspiring best. As Dewey once put it, the "disclosure . . . of possibilities that contrast with actual conditions is the most penetrating criticism of the latter that can be made."[15]

Indeed we can say more than that. The disclosure of possibility is not just essential to critique; critique and reflective disclosure are practically indistinguishable, and that is because they are structurally homologous. Take the case of the most common form of critique, "immanent critique." As exemplified in the work of its finest exponents from Marx to Adorno, and from Nietzsche to Foucault and Derrida, it is a disclosive practice, revealing the background assumptions, ontological, epistemological, political, and so forth, that are hidden within a text, a cultural practice, a political institution. As a disclosive practice, critique makes conscious a murky reality, "discloses each image as script," and "teaches us how to read from its features the admission of falseness which cancels its power and hands it over to truth."[16] But successful critique depends not just on showing that

x is a disguised effect of y, which effect in turn requires the exclusion or repression of r. For this to be shown in the first place, critique needs to find the new normative stance, the new interpretive perspective, in light of which what is familiar is defamiliarized, seen again, as if for the first time.

Reconceptualizing critique as a practice of reflective disclosure corrects the tendency of immanent critique to aim at (or to presuppose its own) "truth," for it precludes the very idea of a final unmasking. To reiterate, the background understanding on which we pre-reflectively rely is not something that can be exposed as a whole, not something that we can render fully explicit. Nietzsche, no slouch at unmasking, was well aware that truth did not remain truth when, *per impossibile*, all the veils are lifted.[17] The background is an ontological condition of the possibility of any human sense-making practice. The misguided goal of total unmasking has distorted and undermined the disclosive character of critique. Habermas correctly detects a "purist" element in the idea of total unmasking but fails to detect the purist element in his proceduralism, preserving the idea of a final agreement grounded in the unforced force of *the* better argument. But such a conception is just as ill suited to serve as the basis of critique, for as I have already asserted, truth (conceived as consensus or as convergence or as a final unmasking) should not (indeed cannot) be the goal of critique. Rather, the goal of critique should aim at the self-decentering disclosure of meaning and possibility. Otherwise, critique will continue to be swamped by the usual list of familiar, intractable dilemmas, dilemmas that arise, for example, from the conditions of cultural pluralism, the ever-present possibility of reasonable disagreement, and the various obstacles to underwriting the epistemic superiority of the critic vis-á-vis her audience. In so far as the practical insights of critique disclose genuine possibilities for us to "go on" differently, they can have the status of "truth-candidates," but not "truth." Although the possibilities critique discloses is subject to a reflectively appropriate form of testing by those to whom it is addressed, as I argued in part III, chapter 9, the relevant test of those possibilities will be pragmatic, at once holistic and experimental, future-directed and future-dependent. Ultimately the test of any newly disclosed possibilities is the degree to which they can initiate self-decentering learning that makes a cooperative new beginning possible.

By reconceiving the practice of critique as a possibility-disclosing practice, critical theory would also gain a very different perspective on its own history. According to the now canonical view of its history, Frankfurt School critical theory began in the 1930s as a fairly confident interdisciplinary and materialist research program, the general aim of which was to connect normative social criticism to the emancipatory potential latent in concrete historical processes. Only a decade or so later, however, having revised the premises of their philosophy of history, Horkeimer and Adorno's *Dialectic of Enlightenment* steered the whole enterprise, provocatively and self-consciously, into a skeptical cul-de-sac. As a result they got stuck in the irresolvable dilemmas of the "philosophy of the subject," and the original program was shrunk to a negativistic practice of critique that eschewed the very normative ideals on which it implicitly depended. Of course, it takes more than adherence to a purportedly exhausted philosophical paradigm to get stuck in the deeply skeptical picture of modernity outlined in *Dialectic of Enlightenment*: Horkheimer and Adorno got a lot of help from the once unspeakable and unprecedented barbarity of European fascism. Still, so the official story goes, to get out of this skeptical picture, we need not await a merely fortuitous change in our historical circumstances, but we do need some well-marked *Ausgang*, showing the way out of the ever-recurring nightmare in which Enlightenment hopes and Holocaust horrors are fatally entangled. This "exit" would have to lead to an alternative picture of our situation, giving the course of human history some much needed maneuvering room, and modernity another chance to fashion a different narrative for itself. Then perhaps we might once again be able to believe that the "unfinished project" of modernity could have a happy ending after all, finally and deservedly redeeming its many broken promises.

As we know, the requisite *Ausgang* was provided by Habermas's intersubjective reformulation of the Enlightenment's cognitive and moral universalism. Once reformulated in intersubjective terms, the whole picture of reason and modernity looks different, for now we can confidently distinguish the reason that we use to objectify and master all that we encounter, from the reason that we use to reach a communicatively mediated agreement with others. When we replace the objectifying attitude of the third person with the performative attitude of the second person, we fundamentally alter our basic orientation to other human beings, opening up a space of social interaction free of strategic orientations and relationships of power. And so we can bring to an end the philosophical nightmare in which the Enlightenment and Holocaust are inverted mirror images of one another. Adorno and Horkheimer did not choose this option, having succumbed to an "uninhibited skepticism" toward reason. Had they more successfully resisted its appeal, critically examining rather than uncritically accepting its premises, claims Habermas, they could have laid "the normative foundations of critical theory so deep that they would not have been disturbed by the decomposition of bourgeois culture that was then being enacted in Germany for all to see" (PDM 129).

A great deal is packed into this astonishing claim. First, it encapsulates the official history of critical theory, according to which *The Dialectic of Enlightenment* represented, along with the subsequent writings of Horkheimer and Adorno, a disastrous deviation from the original program of critical theory. Second, it indicates that the narrative genre of this history is that of the "epic," in which is recounted the (ultimate) triumph of critical theory over the Siren song of skepticism (after a few initial shipwrecks). Third, it reinforces the image of reason as an impermeable "rocking hull" that cannot be penetrated by history, by contingency, by experience—capable of intervening in history without being deformed by it. And fourth, though less obviously, it identifies critical theory with the acquisition of theoretical knowledge, which kind of knowledge Horkheimer and Adorno are accused of renouncing (TCA1 385).

Parsing the claim into its different aspects may help explain how it is that Habermas could make such an astonishing claim in the first place. Not only does Habermas commit himself to a form of normative foundationalism, he renders historically *invulnerable* his favored source of normativity. It is tantamount to claiming that "Even if history conspires against us, we can at least reassure ourselves with the thought that we got our norms right, that we've got the right norms." It is arguable, of course, whether the skeptical stance taken by Horkheimer and Adorno in *Dialectic of Enlightenment* was indeed a critical failure. It could be argued that at the very least it was an authentic critical response to the times in which they lived, a response that is possible if and when one lets oneself be affected by historical experience. For some, to be "affected by historical experience" can mean only to succumb passively to whatever comes along, to the currently available schemes of intelligibility. My discussion of receptivity tried to show that we can think of being "affected by historical experience" in a very different way—as the condition of seeing things differently, of being able to redisclose the world by drawing not from some source outside history but from a plurality of sources within it. A normative position that prevents itself from being "affected by history" will not only be viewed as an "inauthentic" response to that history but also as cognitively disconnected from it. The possibilities of response are not exhausted by appeal to unshakeable "normative foundations," on the one side, and succumbing to "uninhibited skepticism," on the other. We do not have to choose between them. The history of critical theory, the story of its "deviations" and of its return to itself, will certainly be very different once we think of critique as a possibility-disclosing rather than as a truth-tracking practice.

What is at stake here is the question of what kind of enterprise critical theory should be. There is certainly a deep ambiguity in its name, an ambiguity that manifests itself in a constant tension between two largely incompatible ways that critical theorists understand their undertaking. The original Horkheimerian program and Habermas's reformulation of it in the theory of communicative action represents one side of this tension. Critical theory is here understood as a critical *theory*. It is thought of as a knowledge-generating theoretical enterprise with "practical intent." On this view of critical theory, it is easy enough to say that with *Dialectic of Enlightenment* Horkheimer and Adorno renounced the goal of theoretical knowledge. But if we understand critical theory not as a critical *theory*, but as a critical *practice*, then that criticism misses the mark. For then the change in the self-understanding of critical theory instanced by *Dialectic of Enlightenment* is not so much a deviation from the original program as it is a break with the theoretical conception of critical theory. It remains a theoretically guided enterprise, to be sure, and one that must be theoretically inventive, but it is not an enterprise whose goal is to produce a single comprehensive social theory that generates theoretical knowledge about society.

The conception of critique as a possibility-disclosing practice I have been proposing attempts to resolve the tension between these two views in favor of the view of critical theory as a methodologically and normatively pluralistic critical practice. The key to its practical success will lie in its ability to disclose alternative possibilities, possibilities that suppose the kind of openness and responsiveness to the world that I have been exploring throughout this text. A change of perspective, a new interpretive language, and the disclosure of alternative possibilities all depend first and foremost on the practical abilities and practical knowledge of agents. Successful critique depends on the practical ability to see more in things than they are, and on the ability to articulate that "more" in some new way; it does not first depend on an increase in theoretical knowledge about those things. Said otherwise, critique supposes a capacity to "suffer" the world, to "bear" it, to bear it as a burden and as one bears a child, to bear it so as to make a new beginning possible. (One may fail to do so; one may miscarry. But there is no shame in that.)

Reconceiving critique as possibility-disclosing practice also allows us to think of critique as much more intimately related to its objects. The long-standing appeal of rules and procedures as a neutral source of moral and epistemic normativity owes its longevity and power to the belief that successful critique supposes optimal critical distance from its object. But the strength of this belief has been waning for some time, not least because we have become increasingly aware of its limitations for the practice of critique. "Criticism does not require us to step back from society as a whole but only to step away from certain sorts of power relationships within society. It is not connection but authority and domination from which we must distance ourselves."[18] Nonetheless, it remains counterintuitive to believe that intimacy and connection rather than distance and detachment can empower critique. For some, the phenomena of cultural pluralism and deep diversity only reinforce the received idea that in order for criticism to be successful, it has to rise above rather than enter into cultural differences and historical contexts.

Procedural conceptions of reason assume that the critical potential of reasons is greatest when (under highly idealized conditions) such reasons can meet with universal assent or agreement. Critique is thereby identified with universality, rendering weaker, if not parochial, any practice of critique that could not be fully identified with cognitive and moral universality. But the idea that critique needs such universality is, of course, just another way of saying that truth should be the goal of critique. Again, that supposes that transcendence lies upward, above the fray of conflicting values and goods, and the only self-decentering of cognitive and moral significance is self-decentering that arises from a process of abstraction (or detachment) from our cultural traditions, our social practices, our interests, and values. However, identifying critique strictly with universality weakens rather than strengthens the possibilities of critique. As I have already argued, abstraction from our form of life is not the only or most effective path to decentering our individual and collective self-understanding, cognitive and moral universality, not the only or most promising source of practical normativity. Indeed they are subject to the law of diminishing returns. We can only learn so much by the method of abstraction and decontextualization, a method incapacitated by the phenomena that calls for critical response: communication breakdowns, cultural disorientation, feelings of helplessness and lack of agency in the face of massive and baffling change, and the ongoing depletion of semantic and cultural resources. Learning in such cases is not equivalent to agreement or consensus, nor is initiated by it. We are talking about "how we can, and must, conceive of ourselves and our possibilities for acting." What learning amounts to here is facilitating a new beginning for ourselves that is made possible by the problem-solving and self-decentering activity of reflective disclosure.

Given the growing interdependencies and interconnections among nations and cultures, it is no longer possible to think of the "other" as separated from us geographically as well as culturally and historically. We live in a world of "strange multiplicity," to borrow James Tully's apposite phrase, a world in which disparate and diverse cultural lifeworlds encounter one another unforeseeably and unpredictably in a time horizon of contemporaneous noncontemporaneity. In this world formerly handy dualisms such as "distance and periphery," "us and them," no longer perform any useful function, no longer make sense. We are now equally distant from and equally near to each other in cultural space. "They" are our neighbor; "their" children go to school with ours. We have no choice but to get to know each other, to enter into each other's lives, into each other's differences, into each other's fears, into each other's pain, even, into each other's paranoia and hypocrisy. Our histories and cultures are fatefully intertwined. Detachment is no longer a real option; on the other hand, a great deal may be gained from taking a critical attitude that begins from rather than denies acknowledged connection and dependence.

Now I should make clear that the idea of *intimate critique* that I have been evoking does not depend, as does Michael Walzer's idea of internal social criticism, on the difference between identifying with our own traditions as opposed to standing outside them. It is not the difference between internal and external social criticism. While I agree with Walzer that identification with the object of critique is essential to its success, the kinds of identifications that are now necessary are identifications that go beyond "our" cultural traditions and social practices, especially since they have themselves become an issue for us, and since they have been challenged and infused by alternative cultural traditions and social practices to which they stand in uneasy tension. Intimate critique is called for by the conditions of deep diversity and global interconnectivity that are both enabling and disabling. Once we accept that culture plays an irreducible and constitutive role in social and political life, once we acknowledge the irreducibility of reasonable disagreement, we may find that the critique of others with whom we must nonetheless find a way to live requires an intimate mode of criticism; a mode of criticism based on reciprocal recognition, on re-knowing one another in terms different from those on which we previously relied. In such circumstances critique can no longer enjoy the privilege of distance and detachment, and can no longer justify the "pragmatic presupposition" or "regulative ideal" of a single correct answer, one right solution, to moral, cultural, and political conflict. Not only that, it may even be unwise to seek such an answer, and to deprive ourselves access to a richer field of possibilities. Moreover, because such a pragmatic presupposition privileges one kind of decentering (i.e., decontextualizing abstraction), it is an inappropriately narrow normative orientation for practical discourse in pluralistic, multicultural societies. The regulative ideal of practical discourse must be one that seeks to facilitate what truth-oriented normative procedures cannot: the broadest and most varied processes of self-decentering possible. There is no one practice of self-decentering which is fully adequate to our needs. We need different kinds of self-decentering, kinds not imaginable by proceduralists, kinds not possible within practical discourses aiming at convergence or consensus. The more one examines these issues, the more one comes to see that proceduralist models of reason have had a distorting effect on our conception of the scope and limits of practical reason, which effect can be corrected if we shift the focus imaginarius of such discourses from consensus or convergence to self-decentering learning that makes possible a new beginning for ourselves, a new way to "go on" together.

A recent paper of James Bohman's allows me to make this point a little more sharply. Bohman argues that social criticism is now divided between two contrary normative goals. One goal is to generate insights that allow agents to "see their circumstances correctly"; the other is to generate insights that allow them to see their circumstances "more reflectively and thus differently."[19] This is more or less the choice that faces contemporary critical theory, a choice that ultimately depends on whether "there is a fact of the matter about the human world, a single right answer independent of agents' needs, interests, and self-interpretations that would underwrite the pragmatic presupposition" of the single correct answer.[20] Of course, what impels us toward the goal of the single correct answer is the "craving for objectivity," to use Putnam's apt phrase, a craving for more than a merely human view, for a view from nowhere rather than from somewhere. But this goal gets in the way of facilitating a freely willed change in our self-understanding and social practices. And it is only this goal that answers the need of our times, the need that calls philosophy, and recalls critical theory to its unending task of facilitating just such change as enables human beings "to realize concrete possibilities for a better and less threatened life, on their own initiative and in accordance with their own needs and insights."

So what we have before us is the choice between a practice of critique oriented toward (the procedures for making) correct or true statements and one oriented toward the reflective disclosure of alternative possibilities and perspectives. To be properly oriented to the latter goal, the practice of critique would need to deepen its normative commitment to the position of the second speaker, the speaker who speaks second; for it is the normative standpoint of the second person that is crucial to intimate critique, and not just as the discursive analogue of the personal pronoun. As I argued in part IV, the philosopher or critic should not speak first; she should speak second. And this respondent's role is complemented and underwritten by the normative perspective of the second person. Drawing upon Gadamer's model of hermeneutic dialogue, the regulative ideal of which is a "fusion of horizons," James Bohman clearly specifies the normative function of the second person perspective in acts of social criticism.

The normative attitudes of the second person are neither true descriptions nor self-expressive claims. Rather, they are assessments that become explicit only in actual dialogue. By treating what others are saying as true or taking them to be correct or incorrect in their performance, the interpreter establishes nothing more than the possibility of more and perhaps better interpretations and thus the possibility of future dialogue or interpretive exchange. Gadamer puts this in a practical way: "Every interpretation establishes the possibility of a relationship with others." Such a relationship could only be established in the normative attitude. Gadamer goes on to say that these relationships institute obligations, since, "there can be no speaking that does not bind the speaker and the spoken to." It is to this binding power of interpretations and the implicit know-how of establishing normative relations that critics appeal, to the ability to open up or close off various practical possibilities with others with whom we are engaged in the process of mutual interpretation or of reaching understanding.[21]

Thus the practical consequence of dialogue regulated by the ideal of a "fusion of horizons" is not just an enlarged interpretive perspective but also a change in the normative self-understanding of the participants, a change in how they "go on" *together*. This is just how I would like to characterize the practice of intimate critique—as a practice of critical dialogue that aims to preserve and renew trust, and to facilitate commitment to ongoing processes of cooperative problem solving. It is a practice that is based on the recognition and performative acknowledgment of the fact that we are the facilitators and guarantors of one another's fragile freedom, not just the legal framework of rights and freedoms we enjoy as citizens of a democratic polity, but the freedom exemplified in our capacity to criticize and innovate, to bring about such change as can initiate better and more reflective ways of life. Intimate critique thereby escapes from the resentment-breeding limitations of winner/loser models of argument, making it more appropriate to the practices and institutions of deeply pluralistic societies, more capable of preserving and fostering the cooperative achievements and the mutual trust of their members.

3   Critical Theory's Time

Unlike models of critique based on the ideal of truth (including the ideal of total unmasking), a model of critique based on the disclosure of possibility is, for that very reason, in a position actually to respond to the problems of self-confidence (self-reassurance), skepticism, and the exhaustion of utopian energies. As a possibility-disclosing practice, critique neither requires nor must suppose a determinate utopia, for that would turn it into a possibility-foreclosing practice. To reiterate, the relation of critique to "utopia" is both indeterminate and necessary, enjoining it to prevent the foreclosure of possibility, to keep the possibility of a different future open, resisting resignation and accommodation to what is. Critique that has become skeptical about its own products ends up undermining its "normative foundations" not because it fails to preserve its orientation to truth, as Habermas claims (PDM 106–130), but because it fails to preserve its orientation to possibility. Unless critique can disclose "possibilities that contrast with actual conditions," the future cannot be the bearer of utopian hope; if the future cannot bear such hopes, if it appears unreceptive to our needs, the present will remain disoriented. Current interpretations of possibility, like the arteries of our aging hearts, harden every day. The point is not to let those interpretations dictate our future possibilities.

Once it loses touch with modernity's relation to time, the practice of critique, whatever its normative standpoint, becomes inanimate, dissolute. But for critique once again to draw its normativity from modernity's consciousness of time it must renew the very source from which it must draw. As Habermas has noted, modernity's consciousness of time has had to be "revitalized" time and again, by "radical historical thinking" (PDM 13). This is most definitely one of those times, and that kind of "thinking," as exemplified by "philosophers of the future"—the Young Hegelians, Emerson, Nietzsche, Heidegger, and Benjamin—is, by definition, the kind in which historical consciousness and utopian thought are fused.

The more we reflect on the distinctiveness of modernity, namely its "openness to the novelty of the future," the less inclined we are exclusively to regard it as a distinctive epoch, a caesura in historical time of evolutionary significance. We are instead prompted to regard modernity as defined by a distinctive experience of, and distinctive relation to, historical time. Employing the concepts "space of experience" and "horizon of expectation" as metahistorical categories, Reinhard Koselleck identifies modernity—*Neuzeit*—with the emergence of this new experience of, and new relation to, historical time.

[E]xperience is present past, whose events have been incorporated and can be remembered. Within experience a rational reworking is included, together with unconscious modes of conduct which do not have to be present in awareness. There is also an element of alien experience contained and preserved in experience conveyed by generations or institutions. . . . Similarly with expectation: at once person-specific and interpersonal, expectation also takes place in the today; it is the future made present; it directs itself to the not-yet, to the non-experienced, to that which is to be revealed. Hope and fear, wishes and desires, cares and rational analysis, receptive display and curiosity: all enter into expectation and constitute it.[22]

Neuzeit, however, "is first understood as a *neue Zeit* from the time that expectations have distanced themselves evermore from all previous experience."[23] If modernity's distinctiveness resides in an apparently unclosable gable between "experience" and "expectation," between past and future, then this accounts for why the significance of the present moment can appear both urgent and obscure, portentous and opaque—why, in other words, normative disorientation is an ever-present possibility. It also explains why modernity's relation to time will always stand in need of renewal. The picture of modernity that emerges here is one in which we see further evidence of the links between arising problems of intelligibility and arising needs for the disclosure of alternative possibility. Getting oriented, finding our way, requires disclosing the significance of the present moment, reconnecting it, if only tentatively and temporarily, to an inscrutable future and impermanent past.

Under different circumstances, circumstances in which the gulf between experience and expectation had not yet become unbridgeable, getting oriented was a matter of drawing upon inherited experience to open up the horizon of expectation, a matter of connecting what we've known to what may be. "Experiences release and direct prognoses." "The penetration of the horizon of expectation . . . is creative of new experience."[24] But experience must not only have an open relation to the future, it must be able to illuminate the future, to serve as a bridge to what is to come, to what might be. The relation to time distinctive of *Neuzeit*, however, is one in which "the previously existing space of experience," call it the logical space of possibility, "is not sufficient for the determination of the horizon of expectation."[25] It can no longer be derived or deduced from previous experience: that is the very condition of being modern, of living *Neuzeit*. When the past no longer casts its light upon the future, the experience of obscurity, opaqueness, is the default position from which we must begin to make sense of the predicaments we face.[26] In living *Neuzeit*, we become aware of just how much our sense-making practices, including our critical practices, depend on the disclosure of alternative possibilities, on our capacity to begin anew—on our ever-arising need "to call something into being which did not exist before, which was not given, not even as an object of cognition or imagination, and which therefore, strictly speaking, could not be known."

Contrary to some of Richard Rorty's suggestions about how we get from worn out concepts to possibility-disclosing ones, getting reoriented under the inherently disorienting conditions of *Neuzeit* is not a matter of simply replacing the old concepts with which we made sense of our predicament with new ones. The new concepts must be *called* into being. But calling something into being that did not exist before is neither a hit and miss affair nor a cognitive process that we can "master." It requires a much misunderstood and undervalued activity that consists in imagining this form of life differently by disclosing other possible ways of carrying it forward, other ways of "going on." This is not an ad hoc activity; it is a response to genuine problems and crises whose solution requires the disclosure of those alternative possibilities. It requires, among other things, attending to the way our sense-making concepts function either as concepts that "register" experience or as concepts that "generate" (possible) experience— or as conceptual switch points between one and the other. Koselleck draws a distinction between concepts (*Begriffe*) and "anticipations" (*Vorgriffe*). Let us retranslate the latter as *anticipatory concepts*. Under conditions of *Neuzeit* we have need of anticipatory concepts precisely because our expectations are radically underdetermined by our experience. Because they are "based on the experience of the loss of experience . . . [anticipatory concepts] . . . preserve or awaken new expectations."[27] Put a little differently, it is the capacity to be receptive to what has been lost or to what we are now losing that makes us capable of calling upon concepts that can generate, not just register, experience.[28]

In this connection it is worth noting that Koselleck's distinction between *Begriffe* and *Vorgriffe* is similar to Kant's distinction between empirical concepts of the understanding and regulative ideas of reason. Empirical concepts must conform to experience; by contrast, ideas of reason make demands on experience, demands that draw their normativity from possibility (the possibility of speaking, acting or thinking otherwise than we do)—from what ought to be, rather than from what is. An idea of reason can make demands on experience but cannot be derived from it. Similarly a *Vorgriff* can be constructed from a *Begriff*, but it cannot be logically deduced from it: a "pure concept of expectation [has] no correspondence with an empirical past."[29] *Vorgriffe* can "open up a new future" only to the extent that they can draw from and enlarge the space of experience by disclosing that "alien" moment of experience, the surplus of meaning and significance contained within its space. When successful, *Vorgriffe* can facilitate "the beginning of a beginning"—a possibility-disclosing break in time.[30]

Famously, Nietzsche claimed that "only that which has no history can be defined."[31] The claim can be taken as a historicized, proto-Wittgensteinian claim that concepts have a history of use, the multiple extensions of which are such that their meaning cannot be circumscribed by a single stable definition. That is certainly part of what he is claiming. However, it is not just the claim that concepts have a nonsubsumable history of use but, if one may put it this way, that history makes use of concepts. History inheres in the concepts with which we live our lives, and in responding to history, we alter and adjust the meaning and implications of our concepts. Now it is precisely because concepts have been permeated by historical experience, because they register it, that once they are transformed into anticipatory concepts, they can also generate possible experience. In this respect, then, they are a species of world-disclosing concepts, opening up the normative horizon of the future, preserving or awakening new expectations.

The activity of mind by which ordinary concepts are transformed into anticipatory concepts possessing both world-disclosing power and normative force is akin to what the early Marcuse called "phantasy." By this term he meant a reflective process of disclosure that, by critical reflection on the crises of the present, reopens the future. And it does so by disclosing a bridge between past and future, making it possible to regain orientation under conditions of disorientation.

The abyss between rational and present reality cannot be bridged by conceptual thought. In order to retain what is not yet present as a goal in the present, phantasy is required. The essential connection of phantasy with philosophy is evident from the function attributed to it by philosophers, especially Aristotle and Kant, under the title of "imagination." Owing to its unique capacity to "intuit" an object though the latter may not be present and to create something new out of given material of cognition, imagination denotes a considerable degree of independence from the given, of freedom amid a world of unfreedom. In surpassing what is present, it can *anticipate* the future. . . . Phantasy does not relate to the other cognitive faculties as illusion to truth (which in fact, when it plumes itself on being the only truth, can perceive the truth of the future only as illusion). Without phantasy, all philosophical knowledge remains in the grip of the present or the past and severed from the future, which is the only link between philosophy and the real history of humankind.[32]

Both anticipatory concepts and "phantasy" are instances of reflective disclosure, of a redisclosure of the world capable of reopening the future, and reconfiguring the normative relationship between past, present, and future. Now it is precisely through this activity that philosophy maintains its link to the "real history of humankind." If it failed to articulate possibilities that respond to the needs of humanity, philosophy would have failed to answer its own calling, a calling from the future. It is in this sense too that we can speak of the "philosopher of the future," for such a philosopher is responding to her time in the normative light of possibility, a future present that can normatively orient our own. Such a philosopher may or may not speak as a representative of "professional" philosophy. Anyone who can anticipate the future philosophically, who can provide concepts that can generate, not just register experience, will speak in the voice of philosophy, even if that voice is not today recognized as a genuinely "philosophical" voice. Whatever the case may be, it is very difficult for a "philosopher of the future" not to have a problematic, even adversarial relation to professional philosophy. That, as Nietzsche recognized, is simply the inescapable "untimeliness" by which such a philosopher is marked, a philosopher for whom it is not enough to overcome her time but also to overcome her own time in herself.

Although it may at first seem paradoxical, the "philosopher of the future" cannot be called by the future if she is not also called by the past, for it is a calling that recalls what may be lost to us forever, what needs to be preserved and passed on. It is this to which Marcuse refers when he writes: "Critical theory must concern itself to a hitherto unknown extent with the past—precisely insofar as it is concerned with the future."[33] As Marcuse, Benjamin, and Arendt, among others, came to see, if we wish to preserve the openness of the future, we must also preserve the *unclosedness* of the past.

In Arendt's preface to *Between Past and Future*, a remark from René Char's *résistance* writings serves as the focal point for a meditation that encompasses not only the relation between past and future but also the relation between inheritance and testament—that is, the problem of what to pass on to the future, how to will it across time. Char's remark that "our inheritance was left to us by no testament," refers to the loss of a certain cultural "treasure," lost because it was not preserved for the future, and not preserved because it was not recognized as such.

The testament, telling the heir what will rightfully be his, wills past possessions for a future. Without testament or, to resolve the metaphor, without tradition—which selects and names, which hands down and preserves, which indicates where the treasures are and what their worth is—there seems to be no willed continuity in time and hence, humanly speaking, neither past nor future, only sempiternal change of the world and the biological cycle of living creatures in it. Thus the treasure was lost not because of historical circumstances and the adversity of reality but because no tradition had foreseen its appearance or its reality, because no testament had willed it for the future.[34]

Just as it could not be named or called into being as a living possibility, the continuity in time across which it could be bequeathed could also not be willed. Thus the relation between past and future, testament and inheritance, provides a reminder that the disclosure of possibility also requires the *preservation* of possibility. The connection between the contracting space of possibility and the exhaustion of utopian energies cannot be fully understood if we ignore the degree to which our efforts to keep the future open, to prevent its foreclosure, requires keeping alive possibilities under threat of erasure, either from global systems of power or, as Benjamin reminds us, from our own lapses of memory, from our own collective failure to recognize them, to recognize their claim on us, and so to rescue them, not just for ourselves, but for the future.

It is on the basis of this connection between past and future that Benjamin was able to criticize the modern understanding of history, both for its inconstancy towards the past and its attempt to neutralize "the provocation of the new and the unexpected" (PDM 11)[35]. Thus what may seem paradoxical or strange, the simultaneous affirmation of the claims of the new (the future) and the claims of the old (the past), is entirely consistent with the normative relation to historical time abidingly central to critical theory. Benjamin was able to explicate and draw the normativity within this relation in a significantly new way, correcting modernity's one-sided orientation toward the novelty of the future, by acknowledging the normative claims of the past. "To all past epochs [Benjamin] ascribes a horizon of unfulfilled expectations, and to the future-oriented present he assigns the task of experiencing a corresponding past through remembering, in such a way that we can fulfill its expectations with our weak messianic power" (PDM 14). Benjamin's horizon-reversing corrective reveals the degree to which prior attempts to bring about equilibrium between continuity and discontinuity sacrificed or suppressed the unfulfilled expectations of the past.

In place of the previous asymmetry between past and future, Benjamin introduces an ideal of reciprocity into the normative relationship between past, present, and future. So it now becomes a matter of how to conjoin past, present, and future in such a way that whatever reopens the future by disclosing rather than foreclosing possibility is made possible and, in turn, makes possible, a remembering and a reawakening of the suppressed claims of the past.

Thus, the constellation of the present in relation to the past and future has undergone a specific change. On the one hand, under the pressure of urgent problems from the future, a present that is challenged to historically responsible activity gains ascendancy over a past that is to be appropriated for its own interests; on the other hand, a purely transitory present sees itself brought to account before the future for its interventions and omissions. Because Benjamin extends this future-oriented responsibility to past epochs, the constellation shifts once again: The tension-laden relationship to basically open alternatives in the future now touches directly the relationship to a past mobilised in turn by expectations. The pressure of the future is multiplied by that of the past (and unfulfilled) future. (PDM 15)

The goal of our relation to time is now no longer the typical modernist goal—to be liberated from the dead hand of the past. The goal is to be more deeply enjoined by the past—not to just any part of the past, but to that part that demands the recognition of needless suffering and cruel injustice, squandered possibilities, and unfulfilled expectations. In reply to Benjamin's unacceptably "theological" construal of remembrance and our obligation to the past, Horkheimer is certainly right to say that the "slaughtered are really slaughtered": "Past injustice can never be made up; the suffering of past generations receives no compensation."[36] But Benjamin was by no means as naïve as all that, nor must he be taken so literally. No, the dead cannot be brought to life, nor their suffering made good. However, what the present owes to the past is to prevent *its* foreclosure, and this it can do by recovering the speech of those who would otherwise have been silenced, reawakening hopes and expectations that might seem "unrealistic" or "utopian" to the past-erasing temperament of the times.

Habermas's treatment of the "theological" motifs of Benjamin's thought is, as always, hermeneutically sensitive and illuminating. But he too quickly assimilates Benjamin's normative enlargement and reorientation of modernity's relation to time to the framework of his communicatively reformulated universalism Thereby Habermas disperses the normative force of Benjamin's time-oriented and time-bound conception of "rescuing critique" (*rettende Kritik*). True, it does have the one normative implication that Habermas picks out: the idea of human solidarity across time (across generations) and not just across space (one's own time). But Benjamin's reflections are also intended to *unclose* the past in all its "provinciality" in relation to the present and the future, to normatively shield it against those who unreflectively treat it as just one more thing to be burst asunder or blotted out. His proposed reorientation of modernity's relation to time was meant to draw attention to the need for conserving cultural "treasures" not yet named, without which name they cannot be bequeathed to the future, to preserve possibilities not yet understood, let alone realized. To speak in more Heideggerian language, what is called for is a relation to the past that *uncloses* that which may be closed to us forever, not as something to be "preserved" for posterity in a museum of culture, but as that without which we may find ourselves hopelessly unintelligible to ourselves.

In an illuminating paper, Christian Lenhardt enlists the Benjaminian idea of "anamnestic solidarity" to provoke critical theorists into taking a more resolutely "conservative" attitude to the cultural traditions and "treasures" they inherit. The task of preserving the semantic contents of cultural traditions should not be left to today's political conservatives, who, in any case, have little genuine interest in conservation.[37] "Amnesia threatens to be the most capital of sins among emancipated posterity, unless properly conservative habits are implanted in the minds of the successors."[38] Otherwise, as Lenhardt shows, Habermas's worry that one day an emancipated humanity, robbed of the semantic light of tradition, might find itself unable to judge its own life as good, could easily (and more plausibly) turn into the worry than an emancipated humanity may find itself in "the absurd position of enjoying a life not of its own making"[39]—the lucky but not necessarily deserving beneficiary of sacrifices made by previous generations.

Since it emphasizes the interdependence of preservation and innovation, Benjamin's view of cultural preservation and conservation is quite unlike anything typical of cultural conservatism. He regards the process of cultural preservation as continuous with discontinuity, as dependent upon the occurrence of breaks in historical time. "To articulate the past historically . . . means to seize hold of a memory as it flashes up at a moment of danger. Historical materialism wishes to retain that image of the past which unexpectedly appears to humanity at a moment of danger. The danger affects both the content of the tradition and its receivers."[40] Of course, responsiveness to cultural dangers of this kind, and the capacity to retrieve an image of the past as it "unexpectedly appears in a moment of danger," can hardly be described as necessary to the practice of philosophy understood as an extension of the "normal business of science", but they are necessary to the practice of reflective disclosure and intimate critique. Its success does not depend on detaching itself from its time, seeking a critical standpoint beyond it—such as the standpoint of an ideal communication community. Rather, it connects itself to its time as intimately and critically as possible: intimacy and critique are not mutually exclusive; they are complementary. Since its success is also dependent on its contact with historical time, which time it is supposed to disclose anew, it is a practice of critique that cannot do "without the notion of a present which is not a transition, but in which time stands still and has come to a stop."[41] Without such a relation to historical time, critique would be sequestered in "homogeneous, empty time." If critique does not intervene in time, detaining it, allowing it to linger for a while, critique is unable either to experience or to facilitate the "beginning of a beginning," for a new beginning supposes connection, rich and complex, to what came before.[42]

Clearly, Benjamin's notion of "rescuing critique" is a form of possibility-disclosing critique. It draws its normativity from the thought that the failure to preserve the semantic contents of traditions, traditions that have become problematic for us but on which we nonetheless depend, is fatal to the human aspiration for a just world. Such an aspiration requires keeping open not only the future but also the past. In this respect critique plays the role of an incomplete (because incompletable) testament, willed across time to a future present prepared to inherit it in all of its incompleteness and potential ambiguity. Still, for all the posthumous attention upon Benjamin's life and thought, critical theory has yet to get over its modernist embarrassment about the idea of conserving culture, as though it were fearful of not being with it, of not being at the cutting edge of progress, of not being sufficiently *modern*. Of course, it is not easy to engage in such conservation. That it is a potentially risky enterprise almost goes without saying, least of all because one may end up looking like a Luddite or a fool. Adorno was fond of repeating Rimbaud's exhortation: "*il faut être absolument moderne.*" But to be "absolutely" modern requires alertness not only to modernity's achievements and possibilities but also to its destructiveness and to its *unreflective* modernism—which is to say, its unrelenting inconstancy, if not hostility towards the past, its intoxication with, indeed, its addiction to, the new for its own sake.

Reflecting on the very possibility of philosophy in the midst of a barbarous century, "Why Still Philosophy?", Adorno asked "whether philosophy, as a conceptual activity of the interpretive mind, is still the order of the day, whether it has fallen behind what it should conceptualize—the state of the world rushing toward catastrophe."[43] A melodramatic claim perhaps, but even if, like me, you think that there is a place for melodrama in philosophy (not only because it has always found its way into philosophy, and in places where you would least expect it), there is something about this claim that just sounds the wrong note—especially in dark times. That philosophy once enjoyed such a privileged access to the social totality as to be able confidently to conceptualize the state of the world rushing anywhere, is as untrue of its past as it is irrelevant to its future. Of course, it has long been a part of philosophy's metaphysical hubris that it believed itself to enjoy such a privilege, a privilege Adorno would not wish explicitly to reclaim. Nonetheless, what he seems to be mourning is less the state of the world rushing to catastrophe than the loss of philosophy's decidedly avant-garde position in relation to history. This impression is reinforced when Adorno stakes the future to philosophy in its capacity to regain its avant-garde foothold: "philosophy must prove itself the most advanced consciousness—permeated with the potential of what could be different—but also a match for the power of regression, which it can transcend only after having incorporated and comprehended it."[44]

According to Adorno, if philosophy is to preserve its critical diagnostic power, it must become (once again?) the "most advanced consciousness" of its time. This basically vanguardist self-understanding has blemished critical theory's history, but not only critical theory's; it is a self-understanding that has shaped "modernist" and "postmodernist" forms of social criticism ever since critique began to draw on the normativity of modernity's relation to time. The presumption that attunement with modernity's relation to time gives one an epistemically privileged relation to the present is an understandable temptation, but it is an unjustifiable, self-undermining presumption. It is absolutely essential to the success of possibility-disclosing critique that it lets itself be "permeated with the potential of what could be different." Letting oneself be permeated by "the potential of what could be different" is to let oneself suffer one's time, making oneself vulnerable to it by letting oneself be marked by it. As such it is an act of generosity, not the means by which one can gain an epistemic advantage over one's time. As it is, there is *nothing* in virtue of which the social critic enjoys any epistemic privilege in relation to her own times, not even "the potential of what could be different." There is no methodology, interpretative or nomological, that on its own can verify or confirm the insights of the social critic: for better and for worse their confirmation involves a cooperative relation between the social critic and her addressees, neither of whom enjoys an epistemic privilege vis-à-vis the other. However, the addressees enjoy a moral and political privilege: the right to decide for themselves whether to endorse or reject the value of critical insights by reflectively testing the possibilities they disclose. And as I argued earlier, since that test is going to be pragmatic, at once holistic and experimental, and since the test of possibility depends on future verification, the possibility in question is not tested against the world as it is, but as it might be, and, then, only when it might be other than it is. Thus we cannot say in advance whether those possibilities are rightly rejected or endorsed, rejected or endorsed for the right reasons. To repeat: Any disclosure of meaning and possibility is *underdetermined* by the "world."

Now it is worth noting that the idea that the success of critique or philosophy presupposes a historically "advanced consciousness" has no place in Benjamin's "theology." If each second is the "strait gate" through which the messiah may pass, no individual or group, no historical position, is any closer or any further from redemption in history—put less "theologically," the normativity of modernity's relation to time does not offer epistemic advantages to those that can get in touch with it. Thus to say, as Adorno does, that "[h]istory promises no salvation and offers the possibility of hope only to the concept whose movement follows history's path to the very extreme"[45] is to propose another kind of "theology" (an eschatology?) oriented one-sidedly to the future, and supposing that philosophy, by some special act of critical self-reflection, can divine the path of history. By all means, philosophy should be "permeated with the potential of what could be different," but it is in no position to know in advance its own "truth-potential." Nor is it in a position to know in advance whether it is a "match for the power of regression," let alone whether it can "transcend" the power of regression. With the further claim that philosophy can "transcend" the "power of regression" "only after having incorporated and comprehended it," Adorno seems to be recycling Nietzsche's claim, made in connection with the "Cagliostro of modernity," that once one has identified *the* pathological illness of modernity, one must voluntarily succumb to that illness if one is properly to immunize oneself against it.[46] This medical model of critique and corresponding image of the social critic as pathology-diagnosing superhero is one that we should resist, not revive. The putative immunization of the critic by the disease he is seeking to overcome, even at the risk of self-annihilation, is just one more variant of the vanguardist mentality from which critique must make a permanent break.[47] Just as it must eschew the goal of truth, critique must repudiate the very idea of an "advanced consciousness" in light of which it can acquire and justify its insights: critique does not have an epistemically privileged relation to its time, only an ethically shaped obligation to make sense of its time. If critical elucidation of our historical circumstances is to take place at all, circumstances in which, unlike those of Nietzsche and Adorno, are permeated by deep diversity and global interconnectivity, it will have to take the form of *reciprocal elucidation*, as James Tully conceives it. Similarly, if the renewal of utopian energies is at all possible, and if they are to have any practical effects on the world, they must be *democratically organized*—from the bottom and middle up.

Habermasian critical theory has never sought to occupy the position of the historical avant-garde, but it has sought, unsuccessfully, to circumvent the conditions of historicity and finitude by placing its normative standpoint both inside and outside time. Unbinding itself from its time, and binding itself ever more tightly to a foundationalist (or objectivistic) normative standpoint, deprives critical theory of the contact with historical time on which the practice of critique depends. By binding itself to time the right way, critical theory does not give up the possibility of transcending its time—only the possibility of transcending time as such. To invoke Emerson once again, around this circle another can be drawn. And so, the relevant contrast is not between the ideal and the real, or between facts and norms. Insofar as we are prepared to acknowledge our dependence on historically disclosed possibilities in light of which our normative orientations can and, perhaps, ought to change, the contrast in terms of which we should think is between the actual and the possible, between what is and what might be. The tension between the ideal and real, between facts and norms, as Habermas formulates it, is a persistent background tension, and, in a sense is "timeless." When we are facing crises and breakdowns of one kind or another, however, it is not enough to appeal to that difference to reorient ourselves and our practices: we have crossed a particular historical threshold, and have become aware that we no longer know our way around. The tension that arises between what is and what might be is not timeless; it is in time, and of its time. And it is for this reason that our sense of disorientation is relieved by the possibility of reorientation, by a possibility that we were previously unable to formulate or foresee—not by anything built into the tension between facts and norms or the ideal and the real.

4   Suppressed Romanticism (Inheritance without Testament)

What is critical theory for in times of need? This question, each half of which frames the first and last part of my book, obviously evokes the line from Hölderlin's poem "Brod und Wein," "what are poets for in times of need?" Just as obviously it evokes Heidegger's essay on Hölderlin, for which this line serves as its title. Above all, however, it is meant to evoke the romantic insight into the connection between the consciousness of crisis and the possibility of transformation—an insight articulated in what is arguably the first "romantic" text of the critical theory tradition, "The Oldest System-Program of German Idealism."[48] Whether Hölderlin had a hand in the writing of this text or not, another line from one of his poems reframes the connection between crisis and possible transformation: "where danger is, there also grows that which saves" (*Wo aber Gefahr ist, Wächst das Rettende auch*). As is well known Heidegger referred to this line often; less well known is Habermas's own appeal to this romantic figure of thought. Consider the concluding remarks of two of his most important books—*The Theory of Communicative Action* and *The Philosophical Discourse of Modernity*. At the end of the former he notes that it is only because the "symbolic structures of the lifeworld" were threatened by the "systemic imperatives of autonomous subsystems" that "they have become accessible to us"—which is to say, only when the resources of the lifeworld were sufficiently endangered did we become aware of them also *as* resources, resources upon which we could draw to respond to what threatens them. At the end of *The Philosophical Discourse of Modernity*, the same figure of thought reappears in the following form:

Modern Europe has created the spiritual presuppositions and the material foundations for a world in which this mentality ["social Darwinism"] has taken the place of reason. That is the real heart of the critique of reason since Nietzsche. Who else but Europe could draw from *its own* traditions the insight, the energy, the courage of vision—everything that would be necessary to strip from the (no longer metaphysical, but metabiological) premises of a blind compulsion to system maintenance and system expansion their power to shape our mentality. (PDM 367)[49]

It is not so easy to engage in a possibility-disclosing critique of the present if one is not prepared to think romantically. We simply cannot do as Benjamin reminded us without a break in time, a break that is crisisridden but that at the same time discloses possibilities we could not have foreseen, and that portend more than the mere reform of our practices and self-understanding. In my view, romanticism is not just some superseded period of cultural history, it is the frequently unacknowledged position from which we engage in a critical, time-sensitive interpretation of the present. To ask the question "What is critical theory for in times of need?" is to *romanticize* it; it is to ask the question of critique romantically. "Is there a way alternative to the romantic to ask the question? If you do not produce such an alternative; and if nevertheless you desire to keep hold of the question; then you will have not only to conclude that we are not beyond the demands of romanticism, but you will have to hope that the demands of romanticism are not beyond us."[50]

It is no accident that utopian energies have become exhausted. Modernity as we have known it is an exhausting form of life: to live it is to invite exhaustion. That modernity makes exhausting demands on all those who choose—or are forced to live—its form of life is an observation familiar to readers of Marx, Baudelaire, Freud, and Benjamin. As Benjamin put it, "it takes a heroic constitution to live modernity." By "heroic," however, he meant the amount of energy and faith required to live even the most ordinary, mundane existence in "a hostile atmosphere and place."[51] That the pursuit of our hopes and aspirations in such an atmosphere and place might have exhausted us, that our cultural and semantic energies may be used up, is the thought with which we are now haunted. That thought haunts us because we have come to realize that modernity is a possibility-exhausting form of life. Think of romanticism as the response to that haunting realization, and hope that "the demands of romanticism are not beyond us." In other words, hope that we are not too exhausted to proceed with the romantic transfiguration of modernity.

The relentlessly exhausting character of our modernity is why the famous quip from *The Communist Manifesto* that under conditions of modernity "all that is solid melts into air, all that is sacred is profaned," continues to find resonance in our time. John Berger has updated this experience in words appropriate to our time:

People everywhere, under very different conditions, are asking themselves: Where are we? The question is historical not geographical. What are we living through? Where are we being taken? What have we lost? How to continue without a plausible vision of the future? Why have we lost any view of what is beyond a lifetime? The well heeled-experts answer: Globalization. Postmodernism. Communications Revolution. Economic Liberalism. The terms are tautological and evasive. To the anguished question of Where are we? the experts murmur: Nowhere. Might it not be better to see and declare that we are living through most tyrannical—because the most pervasive—chaos that has ever existed?[52]

Said otherwise, we are much less confident than Marx and Engels once were, and, indeed, than all of the twentieth century avant-gardes (cultural and political), that the change that is "gonna come" is change we can welcome with open hearts. Having arrived after the meltdown, we do not begin with something solid that we watch helplessly or joyfully melt into air; we begin with fluidity, uncertainty, and chaos. Having lived fluidity, uncertainty, and chaos for some time now, we understand better than before that modernity is exhausting, not only because of the accelerating pace of change and the exponential compression of time, but also because living with fluidity, uncertainty, and chaos is just that much harder, that much more disorienting, that much more exhausting, than living through the change from a solid to a fluid form of life. There is far less exhilaration, and far more exhaustion. (The beginning of the twenty-first century is very different in this respect from the beginning of the twentieth—it is the difference between being terrified and being exhilarated by the change that is "gonna come.") Paradoxically the more rapidly change multiplies, overwhelming our already overtaxed capacity to make sense of, let alone, direct its course, the more deeply felt the contraction of our possibilities.

When all is fluid, in flux, be they identities, traditions, institutions, human relationships, then the difference between old and new, past and future, is all that much harder to experience, to identify, to articulate, sharply decreasing its capacity to serve as a source or point of orientation. Thus we are living under conditions that thwart our efforts to mark a difference in time, without which difference we are unable to initiate or facilitate the "beginning of a beginning." I have tried to show throughout the many pages of this book that critical theory's understanding of its calling is given to it by its time. Critical theory is not an inquiry that can define itself independently of its time, only in relation to it, and in responding to it. And I have tried to argue that the times in which we live, these taxing and exhausting times, require cultural practices that can reopen the future and unclose the past, cultural practices that can regenerate hope and confidence in the face of conditions that threaten to make even their regeneration meaningless. Philosophy, critical theory, critique, whatever name one wants to use, have been and can still be possibility-disclosing practices. To the extent that they can contribute to the "disclosure of possibilities that contrast with actual conditions," they are cultural practices that can facilitate the renewal of utopian energies, the regeneration of confidence and hope.

All this talk of disclosing possibility will sound rather romantic—much too romantic—to some ears. It most certainly is romantic, but I think it is an open question whether it is *too* romantic or whether critical theory has not been romantic enough of late. After all, the philosophical discourse of modernity is a *romantic* discourse initiated by the romantic critique of the Enlightenment. The Young Hegelians were romantics, self-critical romantics, to be sure, but romantics nonetheless. So were the various participants to this discourse whom Habermas acknowledges as the ones most responsible for revitalizing it: Nietzsche, Heidegger, Foucault, among others.

Indeed it is their shared romanticism, their dissatisfaction with the narrowness and destructive character of the Enlightenment project, and their utopian orientation, their passionate interest in how things might be otherwise, that connects all of the principal participants in this discourse.

Habermas's "recapitulation" of this discourse, for all of its various insights, is nonetheless an attempt to de-romanticize it, to curb it, to temper it, because he identifies its romanticism with its skepticism. Habermas overreacts to both, and fails to distinguish the value (indeed, necessity) of the former from the limitations of the latter. By claiming that the paradigm of the philosophy of the subject is exhausted, Habermas is implicitly claiming that the romantic impulses of the philosophical discourse of modernity are exhausted. But that claim, were it true, would mean that the philosophical discourse of modernity is also exhausted. (Is it any wonder that Habermas responds with alarm at the apparent exhaustion of utopian energies only a few years after announcing the exhaustion of the philosophy of the subject?) If that is the case, traditions of critical inquiry such as critical theory are just as exhausted, just as incapable of "going on," since their "going on" requires reappropriating, reclaiming their romanticism.

If critical theory no longer wishes to be romantic, if it is no longer capable of being romantic, if it finds that "the demands of romanticism" are beyond it, it effectively dissolves itself. Devoid of the critical impulses that can be drawn only from the "spirit of modernity," a "spirit" it came to have only because romanticism responded to the Enlightenment with *time-sensitive* critical energy, it most certainly must resign itself to the contraction of possibility. The readiness it has shown to discard its romantic inheritance is in some measure due to the hold that the right-Hegelian interpretation of modernity has on contemporary critical theory, an interpretation by which talk of social complexity and differentiation precludes any romantic talk about new beginnings and alternative possibilities. As it has identified itself almost exclusively with a procedural (i.e., discursive or deliberative) conception of law and democracy (to which the right-Hegelian interpretation of modernity neatly fits), critical theory has turned principally into a theory of the normative order of democratic societies. Such a theory, however, can only allow itself a "reformist" view of normative and cultural change, and can no longer be a critical theory in any approbatory sense of the term. Speaking in his romantic, rather than in his naturalistic voice, Richard Rorty rightly warns that insofar as critical theory "declines to be romantic, it is inevitably retrospective and inclined towards conservatism."[53] Again, the conservatism in question is not of a political kind. As I have said before, the problem is not that critical theory has become politically conservative; rather, the problem is that critical theory has become conservative about possibility—that is, it has become unromantic.

Another reason why critical theory has discarded its romantic past has to do with the rather common but erroneous assumption that critical theory cannot be romantic because democratic politics cannot be romantic, therefore critical theory cannot be romantic without being antidemocratic. But the question of whether democratic politics can be romantic will look very different if one thinks of democratic politics not as Habermas does—as grounded in normative procedures, but as Dewey, Arendt, and Castoriadis think of it—as grounded in the human capacity to begin anew. In any case, there is no way that I can see for critical theory to be critical without being romantic, no other way for it to respond to modernity's relation to time and its need for hope and confidence. Since the availability of confidence and hope depends on discourses and practices that facilitate the enlargement of meaning and possibility, then, to the extent that critical theory forsakes its romantic self-understanding, it becomes literally deaf to its calling.

Critical theory's conservatism about possibility and its reluctant romanticism reveal that it is as drained of utopian energies as the rest of the *fin de siècle* culture of modernity. "For academics, revolution is a notion of the nineteenth century."[54] Habermas pointed reply to a question about the possibilities of an "emancipatory" politics is noteworthy, not because its makes a controversial claim but because of what it implies, and what it leaves unaddressed. It implies that any kind of politics that isn't reformist is naïvely romantic ("I don't think that there can be any type of revolution in societies that have such a degree of complexity; we can't go back anyway, in spite of all the romanticist anti-movements").[55] Of course Habermas is right about the fact that the revolutions of the nineteenth- and twentieth-century type are not an option for us, but that has much less to do with the degree of social complexity that we have achieved than it does with their necessarily violent and undemocratic character. It is this to which we do not wish to go back, even if we could. More to the point, Habermas's reply leaves unaddressed the question with which all models of critique are faced today—the question of what accountable practice of social and cultural change, change we can attribute to our own agency, can take the place of revolution. This is an urgent question, not only because "reformist" politics are far less hopeful and far less appealing to those whose own circumstances are dire, to those in pain without promise of relief (and the latter greatly outnumber those whose circumstances are relatively comfortable and relatively painless). It is also urgent because our capacity to counteract the contraction of possibility requires something that can replace the concept and practice of revolution—something, in which, unlike revolution, social transformation depends on social cooperation, the extraordinary on the everyday, and discontinuity on continuity. That something is the practice of reflective disclosure, the practice of cooperatively disclosing the world anew.

A critical theory prepared fully to embrace its romantic self-understanding, would be a critical theory more capable of responding to its own time, and more attuned to the needs of its time. Is there anything more urgent today than to resist the sense that our possibilities are contracting or that they are exhausted? And is there anything more important for critical theory to do, any way for it to be more receptive to its calling, than to once again take on the task of disclosing alternative possibilities, possibilities through which we might recapture the promise of the future— through which we might recapture the future as a promise?

Notes

Part I

1. Stanley Cavell, *Conditions Handsome and Unhandsome: The Constitutions of Emersonian Perfectionism* (Chicago: University of Chicago Press, 1990), p. 21.

2. Immanuel Kant, *Critique of Pure Reason*, trans. Werner Pluhar (Indianapolis: Hackett, 1996), p. 8.

3. For the history of the connection between critique and crisis in the seventeenth and eighteenth centuries, see Reinhart Koselleck's rewarding study, *Critique and Crisis: Enlightenment and the Pathogenesis of Modern Society* (Cambridge: MIT Press, 1988). For an analysis and an attempt to resolve the current crisis of critique, see my "Reorienting Critique: From Ironist Theory to Transformative Practice," in *Philosophy and Social Criticism* 26, 4 (2000): 23–47.

4. G. W. F. Hegel, "The Preface to the *Phenomenology*," in Walter Kaufmann, ed., *Hegel: Texts and Commentary* (Notre Dame: University of Notre Dame Press, 1977), p. 20.

5. Karl Marx, *Early Writings* (New York: Vintage Books, 1975), p. 206. The same idea is played out even more dramatically in this famous passage from *The Eighteenth Brumaire of Louis Bonaparte*: "The social revolution of the nineteenth century cannot draw its poetry from the past but only from the future. It cannot make a start until it has stripped away all superstitions concerning the past. Earlier revolutions needed the recollections of world-history to render them insensible of their own significance. The nineteenth century revolution must let the dead bury the dead if it is to appreciate its own significance." (*The Portable Karl Marx*, New York: Penguin, 1983, p. 290).

6. Friedrich Nietzsche, *Beyond Good and Evil*, Section 212, in Walter Kaufmann ed., *The Basic Writings of Nietzsche* (New York: Modern Library, 1966), p. 327.

7. Of course, this conception of what a philosopher is, depending on how it is interpreted, is one far removed from the self-understanding of the majority of

professional philosophers. Nietzsche's conception is by no means naïve: he is less interested in what philosophers are or have been than in what they should be.

8. The "new beginning" has been made all the more difficult and complicated since the unification of Germany, which "unification" was wholly unforeseeable at the time Habermas wrote this essay.

9. Bernard Williams, *Ethics and the Limits of Philosophy* (Cambridge: Harvard University Press, 1985), p. 163.

10. This last remark is meant as an alternative to Habermas's Peircian/Kantian conception of transcendence as transcendence of cultural space and historical time—a "transcendence from within"—that is conceived as a movement upward rather than outward. See "To Seek to Salvage an Unconditional Meaning without God is a Futile Undertaking: Reflections on a Remark of Max Horkheimer," in *Justification and Application*, pp. 133–46.

11. Samuel Beckett, *The Unnamable* (New York: Grove Press, 1958), p. 3.

12. Hilary Putnam, *Words and Life,* (Cambridge: Harvard University Press, 1994), p. 194.

13. See Benjamin, *The Arcades Projects* (Cambridge: Harvard University Press, 1999); Adorno, *Minima Moralia* (London: Verso, 1974), and Horkheimer and Adorno, *Dialectic of Enlightenment* (New York: Continuum, 1972).

14. Samuel Beckett, *The Unnamable*, p. 3.

15. See my "The Idea of a New Beginning: A Romantic Source of Normativity and Freedom," in Nikolas Kompridis, ed., *Philosophical Romanticism* (London: Routledge, 2006), especially pp. 40–47, for critical discussion of the new both as a seductive piece of capitalist ideology and as a normative challenge to our current practices and normative resource for going beyond them.

16. Friedrich Nietzsche, "On the Uses and Disadvantages of History for Life," in *Untimely Meditations* (Cambridge: Cambridge University Press, 1983), p. 94.

17. Stanley Cavell, "The Future of Possibility," in Nikolas Kompridis, ed., *Philosophical Romanticism* (London: Routledge, 2004), my emphasis. To establish the affinities between Nietzsche and Emerson, Cavell cites first from Emerson's "Experience" and then from Nietzsche's *Beyond Good and Evil*. "In liberated moments we know that a new picture of life and duty is already possible. . . . The new statement will comprise the scepticisms as well as the faiths of society, and out of unbeliefs a creed shall be found. . . . The new philosophy must take [these scepticisms] in and make affirmations of them, just as much as it must include the oldest beliefs" (Emerson, "Experience"). "More and more it seems to me that the philosopher, being *of necessity* a man of tomorrow and the day after tomorrow, has always found himself, and *had* to find himself, in contradiction to today" (Nietzsche, *Beyond Good and Evil*).

18. I return to this question in part V, where I treat in far more detail its relation to Heidegger's emphasis on openness and receptivity.

19. Martin Heidegger, *Being and Time* (New York: Harper and Row, 1962), p. 63

20. I'm thinking of insights such as the following: "For every image of the past that is not recognized by the present as one of its own concerns threatens to disappear irretrievably." "To articulate the past historically does not mean to recognize it 'the way it really was' (Ranke). It means to seize hold of memory as it flashes up at a moment of danger. . . . The danger affects both the content of the tradition and its receivers." Walter Benjamin, "Theses on the Philosophy of History," in *Illuminations* (New York: Schocken, 1969).

21. It will become clearer in the course of my discussion that although I begin with the Frankfurt School tradition of critical theory, the normative model of critical theory I am working toward is fully pluralistic in its intentions. It is meant to work in partnership, not in competition, with other traditions of critical inquiry. However, it is a conception that remains normatively and historically attuned to the German philosophical tradition from Kant and Hegel to Habermas.

22. *Differenz des Fichteschen und Schellingschen Systems der Philosophie*, in Werkausgabe, vol. 2 (Suhrkamp: Frankfurt, 1970), p. 20. English translation in *The Difference between Fichte's and Schelling's System of Philosophy* (Albany: SUNY Press, 1977), p. 89. I have translated *Entzweiung* as diremption rather than as dichotomy.

23. *Differenz des Fichteschen und Schellingschen Systems der Philosophie* p. 22, (my translation). English translation in *The Difference between Fichte's and Schelling's System of Philosophy*, p. 91.

24. "Since the close of the eighteenth century, the discourse of modernity has had a single theme under ever new titles: the weakening of the forces of social bonding, privatization, and diremption—in short, the deformations of a one-sidedly rationalized everyday practice which evoke the need for something equivalent to the unifying power of religion" (PDM 139).

25. See Bernard Williams, *Ethics and the Limits of Philosophy* (Cambridge: Harvard University Press, 1985), pp. 169–73.

26. See Max Horkheimer, *Critical Theory: Selected Essays* (New York: Continuum, 1986), pp. 188–252.

27. John Dewey, *Art and Experience* (Carbondale: Southern Illinois University Press, 1989) p. 349.

28. "Epistemological Crises, Dramatic Narrative and the Philosophy of Science," in *The Monist* 60 (1977): 453–71.

29. Here I am reformulating for my own purposes a phrase of Emerson's from "Circles," in *Essays: First and Second Series* (New York: Vintage Books, 1983), p. 183.

30. Habermas tends to use "philosophy of consciousness" and "philosophy of the subject" interchangeably, without indicating that there is any noteworthy difference between them. Although I think that they are not as synonymous as this use implies, I will not press the point here. Later, at various points in my text, I challenge Habermas's unwarranted subsumption of the German tradition from Hegel to Heidegger under the category of the "philosophy of consciousness."

31. Immanuel Kant, *Critique of Pure Reason* (New York: St. Martin's Press, 1965), B708/A680.

32. Nikolas Kompridis, *Aesthetic Models of Critique* (in preparation).

33. Of course, I'm using the term "acknowledgment" in its particular Cavellian sense.

34. The way in which Habermas reconstructs the narrative of the problem of self-reassurance in *The Philosophical Discourse of Modernity* can leave one puzzled as to why such a central problem can be resolved so neatly.

35. For analysis of another set of problems not rendered objectless by the paradigm change to linguistic intersubjectivity, see Peter Dews, "Communicative Paradigms and the Question of Subjectivity: Habermas, Mead, and Lacan," in Peter Dews, ed., *Habermas: A Critical Reader* (Oxford: Blackwell, 1999), pp. 87–117.

36. Obviously I agree completely with David Hoy that the question of "how to 'inherit' the tradition of critical theory may be the most pressing controversy in the recent decade of European philosophy." See David Couzens Hoy and Thomas McCarthy, *Critical Theory* (Oxford: Basil Blackwell, 1994), p. 144.

37. Derrida, especially in such texts as *Glas* and *La Carte Postale*, is, to Rorty's mind, at least, the exemplary philosophical instance of such "self-creation."

38. In his recent exchange with John Rawls, Habermas described the differences between the conception of justice modeled by his discourse ethics and the conception modeled by Rawls's "justice as fairness," as differences bounded within a "familial dispute" ("Reconciliation through the Public Use of Reason: Remarks on John Rawls's *Political Liberalism*," in *Journal of Philosophy* 92, 3 (March 1995): 110. Surely there is as little need to regard these two traditions as adversarial as there is to regard them as members of the same family. They can stand in relation to each other as good neighbors do, neighbors who share some important goals and values but who also differ significantly on some others. Otherwise, we may be unable to answer Nancy Fraser's still pertinent question: "What's critical about critical theory?" For an instructive feminist critique of the "liberal" assumptions of Habermasian critical theory, see the essay that this question entitles in Fraser's *Unruly Practices* (Minneapolis: University of Minnesota Press, 1989).

39. While Thomas McCarthy is right to hold that Habermas has recombined Kant and Hegel, rather than simply abandoning Hegel, it remains obviously the case that the role of the Kantian conception has grown at the expense of the Hegelian.

40. Worries about critical theory's provinciality are not unique to Habermas. One finds them in Adorno as well, whereas Habermas reached out to the universalism of Kant's moral theory, Adorno reached out to avant-garde art and music. No doubt, the emergence of these worries within critical theory and the German tradition can be explained by the circumstances of a belated nation that seemed to have missed or evaded the best of the Enlightenment. But perhaps these circumstances also show that what is distinctive about critical theory's "calling" is not contingently related to its origins, that its provinciality may have something to do with its emancipatory orientation. Its provincial origins in a nation where emancipatory ideals lacked an empirical embodiment, where these ideals were most strongly resisted, may explain critical theory's responsiveness to the need that gave rise to its activity. At least, this was Adorno's view. But it may also have further implications concerning the relationship of "provinciality" to "universalism."

41. For Habermas, this required taking critical theory out of its defensive, peculiarly elitist, deliberately aporetic, and increasingly "aesthetic" stance. One might compare what Habermas did for critical theory to what Talcott Parsons did for sociological theory: he made it respectable and serious qua theory—and less "provincial."

42. Charles Taylor, *Sources of the Self* (Cambridge: Harvard University Press, 1989), pp. 509–10.

43. Thus it should not have come as any surprise when Habermas appealed to an "ethics of the species" in his timely intervention in the debate over the normative regulation of genetic technologies (*The Future of Human Nature*, MIT Press, 2003). Habermas correctly understood that these technologies possess the power to fundamentally alter what it means to be a human being, some generalizable understanding of which he articulated as the "normative self-understanding of the species." That this understanding is one which can be derived neither from a universalist conception of justice nor a culturally specific conception of the good is something which he takes to be an advantage normatively speaking. What he does not explicitly add is that his need to appeal to the normative content of what it means to be a human being exposes both the shortcomings and limitations of distinctions fundamental to his whole project—the sharp distinctions between the right and the good, the moral and the ethical. I return to some further implications of all this in part IV, chapter 2.

44. Habermas, "Reply to My Critics," in J. B. Thompson and D. Held, eds., *Habermas: Critical Debates* (Cambridge: MIT Press, 1982), p. 262.

45. In a recent paper, I argue against the view that critique needs universalistic criteria to be effective and "context-transcending," as though lacking in universality it lacked critical potential. And, conversely, I argue against the presumption that the putative universality of a critical norm promises an increase (rather than a decrease) in critical potential. See "From Reason to Self-realization? On the Ethical Turn in Critical Theory," *Critical Horizons* 5, 1 (summer 2004): 323–60. One of the most

eloquent recent statements of the view that I have in mind can be found in the closing pages of Clifford Geertz's most recent book:

The commitment of liberalism to state neutrality in matters of personal belief, its resolute individualism, its stress on liberty, on procedure, and on the universality of human rights, and, at least in the version to which I adhere, its concern with the equitable distribution of life chances is said to prevent it either from recognizing the force and durability of ties of religion, language, custom, locality, race, and descent in human affairs, or from regarding the entry of such considerations into civic life other than pathological—primitive, backward, regressive, and irrational. I do not think this is the case. The development of a liberalism with both the courage and the capacity to engage itself with a differenced world, one in which its principles are neither well understood nor widely held, in which indeed it is, in most places, a minority creed, alien and suspect, is not possible, it is necessary. . . . This fact, that the principles that animate liberalism are not so self-evident to others, even serious and reasonable others, as they are to liberals, is evident these days everywhere you look . . . [I]t is clear that Locke, Montesquieu, Jefferson, and Mill are particular voices of a particular history, not equally persuasive to all who hear them or their present-day champions. Those who would therefore, promote the cause for which these names, and others more nearly contemporary—Dewey, Camus, Berlin, Kuron, Taylor—in their various ways variably stand (for "liberalism," too, is neither compact nor homogeneous, and it is certainly unfinished), need to recognize its culturally specific origins and its culturally specific character. They need . . . we need . . . most especially, to recognize that in attempting to advance it more broadly in the world, we will find ourselves confronting not just blindness and irrationality, the passions of ignorance (those we know well enough at home), but competing conceptions of how matters should be arranged and people related to one another, actions judged and society governed, that have a weight and moment, a rationale, of their own; something to be said for them. The issue is not one of "relativism," as it is often put by those who wish to insulate their beliefs against the force of difference. It is a matter of understanding that talking to others implies listening to them, and that in listening to them what one has to say is very unlikely, not at the close of this century, not in the opening of the next, to remain unshaken. Clifford Geertz, "The world in pieces: Culture and politics at the end of the century," *Available Light: Anthropological Reflections on Philosophical Topics* (Princeton: Princeton University Press), pp. 258–59.

46. Similarly drawing upon the resources of pragmatism, James Bohman questions the limitations of the procedural mentality of Habermasian critical theory, and its misleading construal of neutrality: "On this reading, the democratic commitments of pragmatists leave them with no substantive political point of view, only the cooperative and second-order testing of a variety of alternative procedures, goals, and frameworks. However, the substantive commitments of such democratic and egalitarian practices are not politically neutral and inform the social scientist about what norms and consequences are relevant and important. Nor does a practice such as science remain neutral among competing claims, seeking some de facto consensus." James Bohman, "Participants, Observers, and Critics: Practical Knowledge, Social Perspectives, and Critical Pluralism," in William Rehg and James Bohman, eds., *Pluralism and the Pragmatic Turn: The Transformation of Critical Theory* (Cambridge: MIT Press, 2001), p. 110.

47. Axel Honneth, "The Social Dynamics of Disrespect," Peter Dews, ed., *Habermas: A Critical Reader* (Oxford: Basil Blackwell, 1999), p. 328.

48. John Dewey, "Construction and Criticism," *The Later Works*, Vol. 5 (Carbondale: Southern Illinois University Press, 1984), pp. 125–44.

49. The Sloterdijk affair, which inflamed German intellectuals through the summer and autumn of 1999, is one more sad and regrettable reminder of the volatility of Heidegger's (and Nietzsche's) thought when it can be associated, even in the most oblique, thoughtless, or unintentional way, with the language and aspirations of National Socialism.

50. Thomas McCarthy, *Ideals and Illusions: On Reconstruction and Deconstruction in Contemporary Critical Theory* (Cambridge: MIT Press, 1991), p. 96.

51. Michel Foucault's critical histories are probably the most successful attempt to bring about such a combination of approaches, but it is probably not quite what Marcuse had in mind.

52. For critical assessments of Heidegger's controversial and influential analyses, see the contributions of James Bohman, Martin Seel, Christina Lafont, and Nikolas Kompridis in *Thesis Eleven* 37 (1994): 29–45. (These contributions appeared originally in a special issue of the *Deutsche Zeitschrift für Philosophie*, 3/1993.)

53. Heidegger, p. 284. Translation amended.

54. Charles Taylor, *Philosophical Arguments* (Cambridge: Harvard University Press, 1995) p. 114.

55. Stephen Mulhall, *Heidegger and Being and Time* (London: Routledge, 1996), p. 96.

56. *The Basic Problems of Phenomenology*, pp. 169–70.

57. Heidegger, *Being and Time* , trans. John Macquarrie and Edward Robinson (New York: Harper and Row, 1962), p. 269. Original in *Sein und Zeit* (Tuebingen: Niemeyer, 1986), p. 226. Heidegger's depiction of the interdependent relationship between Dasein and truth is stated somewhat differently but to the same effect by Hilary Putnam: "without *values* we would not have a *world*." See "Beyond the Fact/Value Dichotomy," in *Realism with a Human Face* (Cambridge: Harvard University Press, 1990), p. 141. Whether he realizes it or not, Putnam's is using the term "world" in Heidegger's special sense. In *Reason, Truth, and History*, (Cambridge: Cambridge University Press, 1981), p. 201, Putnam made the same point in the following way: "A being with no values would have no facts either."

58. Hans-Georg Gadamer, *Truth and Method*, 2nd, rev. ed., trans. rev. Joel Weinsheimer and Donald Marshall (New York: Crossroad, 1989), p. 443, translation amended. Original in *Wahrheit und Methode* (Tübingen: J.C.B. Mohr, 1990) p. 446.

59. For clarification, see Frederick Olafson, "The Unity of Heidegger's Thought," in Charles Guignon, ed., *The Cambridge Companion to Heidegger* (Cambridge: Cambridge University Press, 1993). pp. 97–121.

60. See the following essays by Charles Taylor: "The Importance of Herder," in *Philosophical Arguments*, pp. 79–99, and "Theories of Meaning," in *Human Agency and Language* (Cambridge: Cambridge University Press, 1985), pp. 248–92.

61. "The [e]lucidation of the concept of world is one of the most central tasks of philosophy. The world-concept, or the phenomenon thus designated, is what has hitherto not yet been recognized in philosophy." Heidegger, *The Basic Problems of Phenomenology*, trans. Albert Hofstadter (Bloomington: Indiana University Press, 1988), p. 165.

62. Charles Taylor, *Philosophical Arguments*, pp. 12, 15.

63. Ibid., p. 77.

64. Ibid., p. 77–78.

Part II

1. "Life Forms, Morality, and the Task of the Philosopher," in Peter Dews, ed., *Habermas, Autonomy and Solidarity: Interviews with Jürgen Habermas* (London: Verso, 1986), p. 195.

2. Fritz Ringer, *The Decline of the German Mandarins: The German Academic Community, 1890–1933* (Wesleyan University Press, 1990).

3. All of these are relatively accurate renderings of *das Man*. Most of the time I use "one" or "anyone" in this book to render its meaning in English; occasionally I use the "they" where the context seems more appropriate.

4. For an illuminating comparison of Habermas's and Lacan's conceptions of subjectivity and intersubjectivity, I refer the reader once again to Peter Dews, "Communicative Paradigms and the Question of Subjectivity: Habermas, Mead and Lacan," in Peter Dews, ed., *Habermas: A Critical* Reader (Oxford: Basil Blackwell, 1999), pp. 87–117. For a contrast between Hegel's and Habermas's conceptions of intersubjectivity, see Robert Pippin's "Hegel, Modernity, and Habermas" in his *Idealism as Modernism* (Cambridge: Cambridge University Press, 1997), pp. 157–84.

5. *The Basic Problems of Phenomenology*, op. cit., p. 297, translation amended (my emphasis). I return to the implications of this difference in part III.

6. "The world comes not afterward, but beforehand, in the strict sense of the word. ... World is that which is already previously disclosed and from which we return to the beings with which we have to do and among which we dwell. We are able to come up against intraworldly beings solely because, as existing beings, we are always already in a world." *The Basic Problems of Phenomenology*, p. 165.

7. For an interesting variation of this dispute, removed from the charged atmosphere of Habermas's polemic against Heidegger and those influenced by the idea of

disclosure, see John McDowell's critical reply to Robert Brandom's Habermasian worry that "anyone who refuses to reduce the necessary sociality of language to interactions between individuals must make a super-person of a *we.*" John McDowell, "Gadamer and Davidson on understanding and relativism," Jeff Malpas, Ulrich Arnswald, and Jens Kertscher, eds., *Gadamer's Century: Essays in Honor of Hans-Georg Gadamer* (Cambridge: MIT Press, 2002), pp. 188–90.

8. Here I am in disagreement with Hubert Dreyfus's view that Heidegger is not offering a theory of intersubjectivity. What Heidegger is offering—regardless of whether this is clear to Heidegger himself—is an account of intersubjectivity, an admittedly incomplete and one-sided account, placed within a larger framework whose focal concern is, as Dreyfus rightly argues, the conditions of social intelligibility. But those conditions, though they are logically prior to intersubjectivity as such, are conditions that stand in a feedback relation to structures of intersubjectivity. Thus Dreyfus underestimates the resources that *Being and Time* can offer for a richer theory of intersubjectivity than we currently possess. By developing its potential, we can strengthen the models of intersubjectivity offered by Hegel and Habermas as well as defend certain of its features against both Hegelian and Habermasian criticisms. For an example of the former, see Robert Pippin, "On Being Anti-Cartesian: Hegel, Heidegger, Subjectivity, and Sociality," in *Idealism as Modernism: Hegelian Variations* (Chicago: University of Chicago Press, 1997) pp. 375–94. Unfortunately, Pippin accepts Dreyfus's claim that Heidegger's account of social intelligibility is not a theory of intersubjectivity, from which he then draws the wrong conclusions.

9. For obvious and (perhaps) not so obvious reasons, I have taken the liberty of changing the personal pronoun from he/him to she/her.

10. Another one of those rare occasions can be found in the discussion of "Mutual Understanding and Calculation" in volume one of Heidegger's lectures on Nietzsche, whose discussion is cited by Habermas in *PDM*, p. 137.

11. I believe the translation of *Entschlossenheit* as "resoluteness" is deeply flawed and very misleading, but I will stick with it until I thematize its shortcomings and propose an alternative in chapter 3 below.

12. "Der Ruf kommt *aus* mir und doch *über* mich." The connection between Heidegger's use of "*über* mich" here and Freud's *Über-Ich* is worth exploring.

13. Here we have an instance of a general problem with Heidegger's transcendental-hermeneutic mode of inquiry in *Being and Time*. Just as Kant left unresolved the problem of mediating between the transcendental and empirical "I," Heidegger left unresolved the problem of mediating between ontological and ontic, existential and existentiell, levels of analysis.

14. In this passage, Heidegger sounds more like an exponent of a 1960s Californian "ethics of fulfillment" than a German mandarin of the 1920s—or so it first

sounded to my ears. It took some repeated listening before I found another way to hear it, making it sound both more appealing and more internally consistent with the analyses of *Being and Time*. I come to that in the next chapter.

15. Stanley Cavell, *Conditions Handsome and Unhandsome* (Chicago: University of Chicago Press, 1990), pp. xxxi–xxxii.

16. Richard Rorty, *Contingency, Irony, and Solidarity* (Cambridge: Cambridge University Press, 1989), p. 27.

17. Hegel, *Phenomenology of Spirit*, trans. A. V. Miller (Oxford: Oxford University Press, 1977) p. 110, translation amended.

18. Of course, in practice it is not so easy to distinguish when we are getting in the way of others from when we are clearing the way for them. That will always be something that must be negotiated and codetermined *with* others.

19. *Enzyklopädie der philosophicschen Wissenschaften*, vol. 8, in G. Hegel, *Werke*, E. Moldenhauer and K. Michelet, eds. (Frankfurt: Suhrkamp, 1970), p. 84, my translation.

20. For a detailed and compelling elaboration of this view, see Robert Pippin, "What is the question for which Hegel's Theory of Recognition is the Answer?" *European Journal of Philosophy* 8, 2 (2000): 155–72. Also illuminating is Pippin's "You Can't Get There from Here: Transition Problems in Hegel's *Phenomenology*," in Frederick C. Beiser, ed., *The Cambridge Companion to Hegel* (Cambridge: Cambridge University Press, 1993), pp. 52–85.

21. G. W. F. Hegel, *Elements of the Philosophy of Right*, trans. H. B. Nisbet (Cambridge: Cambridge University Press, 1991), p. 42.

22. G. W. F. Hegel, *Enzyklopädie der philosophischen Wissenschaften*, p. 84, my translation and my emphasis.

23. Stanley Cavell, *Conditions Handsome and Unhandsome*, p. xxxii.

24. For the elaboration of this point, I'm indebted to Robert Pippin's "What is the Question for which Hegel's Theory of Recognition is the Answer?" *European Journal of Philosophy* 8, 2 (2000): 155–72. For further development of my own view of recognition see Nikolas Kompridis, "Struggling over the Meaning of Recognition: A Matter of Identity, Justice, or Freedom?" *European Journal of Political Theory* 6, 2 (2007), and "Recognition, Agency, and Voice," in Danielle Petheridge, ed., *The Critical Theory of Axel Honneth* (Leiden: Brill, 2007).

25. Heidegger can be charged with an unduly obstinate commitment to (ontological) formalism, but not with decisionism. The formalism of his categories rendered them sufficiently plastic to suit the purposes of his political misadventure. In any case, the entire attempt to correlate purported decisionism with his commitment to Nazi ideology has been pressed beyond the point of credibility. As Hans Sluga has

shown, it was more typical to defend the truth of National Socialism by appealing to a theory of "objective values." See his "Metadiscourse: German Philosophy and National Socialism," in *Social Research* 56, 4 (1989): 795–818.

26. In an interview with Richard Wolin, Habermas describes the influence of Sartre on his understanding of *Being and Time*. See "Jürgen Habermas on the Legacy of Jean-Paul Sartre," *Political Theory* 20, 4 (1992): 496–501.

27. Unfortunately, even sympathetic Heidegger commentators continue to misconstrue the meaning of *Entschlossenheit* and, thereby, reproduce the "decisionistic" interpretation of it. See, for example, Taylor Carman's, Randall Havas's, and John Haugeland's contributions to the recent *Festschrift* for Hubert Dreyfus. For example, Haugeland completely ignores the meaning of *Enthsclossenheit* and its connections to *Erschlossenheit*, imposing upon it the English meaning of "resoluteness." "The word 'resolute' means firmly or unwaveringly determined or decisive." John Haugeland, "Truth and Finitude: Heidegger's Transcendental Existentialism," Mark Wrathall and Jeff Malpas, eds., *Heidegger, Authenticity, and Modernity: Essays in Honor of Hubert L. Dreyfus*, vol. 1, (Cambridge: MIT Press, 2000), p. 68.

28. I offer a more detailed account and defense of receptivity in part V, chapter 2.

29. Even if one wanted to insist on treating the "call" intrasubjectively, making sense of its call/response structure requires acknowledging that its intelligibility as a call is derived from an intersubjective understanding of what it is to call and be called. Any intrasubjective understanding of the call would be derivative, parasitic upon its intersubjective structure.

30. "Resoluteness does not first take account of a situation and then places that situation before itself; it has placed itself in that situation already" (BT 347/SZ300).

31. Contrary to the views of some of Heidegger's critics, there is an inherently reflexive dimension to resoluteness. Such reflexivity is not alien to but an essential part of any mode of reflective disclosure. In *Self-Consciousness and Self-Determination*, Ernst Tugendhat skillfully demonstrates the deliberative structure of *Entschlossenheit*, but his otherwise instructive analysis is undermined by his very disappointing (and very wrong) interpretation of disclosure as "awareness."

32. Soren Kierkegaard, *Either/Or*, trans. Alastair Hannay (London: Penguin, 1992), p. 517.

33. On this point, see Charles Taylor, *Ethics of Authenticity* (Cambridge: Harvard University Press, 1991), pp. 38–39.

34. It is not a "Thus, I willed it" so much it as a "Thus, I let it."

35. For a critique of such models of self-creation, see Susan Bordo's *Unbearable Weight: Feminism, Western Culture, and the Body* (Berkeley: University of California Press, 1993).

36. They are: language (*Rede*), affectedness (*Befindlichkeit*), understanding (*Verstehen*), and falling (*Verfallen*).

37. Charles Taylor, "Heidegger, Language, and Ecology," in *Heidegger: A Critical Reader*, p. 259.

38. Hubert Dreyfus, *Being in the World* (Cambridge: MIT Press, 1991), p. 177.

39. Alasdair MacIntyre, "Epistemological Crises, Dramatic Narrative, and the Philosophy of Science," pp. 56–57.

40. Heidegger here anticipates the role of the friend, which is so crucial to Cavell's conception of moral perfectionism.

41. Although, Habermas is right to claim that there is a connection between *Being and Time* and Heidegger's political writings of the 1930s, the connection is primarily external, not internal. Heidegger could not have put to use the categories of *Being and Time* toward the goal of National-Socialist revolution without violating their normative integrity—without instrumentalizing their meaning. The normative language of *Being and Time* does not lend itself so easily to the simplistic, overwrought language of national revolution as Habermas claims it does, as though its ethical content can be transposed into the political content of National Socialism as easily, or, as mechanically, as a piece of music can be transposed from one key to another. (Of course, this will appear to be the case if, like Habermas, one thinks that the ethical content of *Being and Time* is reducible to the subjectivistic framework of Sartrean existentialism.) Habermas is well aware of the trouble to which Heidegger would go to bring his thought manipulatively and coercively into conformity with his self-image. But Habermas does not seem to see this very same tendency at work in Heidegger's attempt to bring his thought into conformity with his political goals: Heidegger the Nazi instrumentalized Heidegger the philosopher. That the latter was all too willing to allow genuine philosophical insights to be instrumentalized, distorted, and exploited in the name of something totally incompatible with them raises a number of psychological as well as moral questions about Heidegger. Whether anything of philosophical value can be gained by taking up these questions is not clear; what is certainly clear is that there is something to be gained by examining Heidegger's inconstant and opportunistic relationship to the ethics of *Being and Time*. Otherwise, the degree to which *Being and Time* resists both its author's manipulations and the goals of National Socialism will be drastically underestimated, if not missed completely.

42. For a discussion of the role moral perfectionism can play in democratic life, see Stanley Cavell, "The Conversation of Justice," *Conditions Handsome and Unhandsome*, (Chicago: University of Chicago Press, 1990), pp. 101–26. For commentary on and elaboration of Cavell's argument, see Stephen Mulhall, "Promising, Consent and Citizenship: Rawls and Cavell on the Social Contract," *Political Theory* 25, 2 (1997): 171–92, and "Politics, Perfectionism and the Social Contract," *Journal of Political*

Philosophy 2, 3 (1994): 222–39. See also David Owen, "Cultural Diversity and the Conversation of Justice", *Political Theory* 27, 5 (1999): 579–96.

43. For an instructive analysis of the continuities of Heidegger's thought, see Frederick Olafson's "The Unity of Heidegger's Thought," *The Cambridge Companion to Heidegger*, pp. 97–121.

44. It is in connection to this failure that Habermas should have made the point that Heidegger's analysis of the *Mitsein* chapter should have "illuminated the very processes of mutual understanding (*Verständigung*) and not merely understanding (*Verstehen*)" (PDM 149), and not as evidence that Heidegger's philosophy never shook free of the presuppositions of the philosophy of consciousness.

45. Anyone familiar with Stanley Cavell's recent writings will be aware of the important affinities between Emerson and Heidegger (and Nietzsche). The deepest disagreement among them arises from their different estimations of democracy. Still I think Emerson would agree with Heidegger's *das Manish* critique of the "average everydayness" of currently existing democracy. But unlike Heidegger, Emerson would hold onto the hope, the possibility, that democratic forms of life could engender more open, less totalizing forms of everyday practice.

46. Ralph Waldo Emerson, *Essays: First and Second Series* (New York: Vitange Books, 1990), p. 40.

47. J. S. Mill, *On Liberty and Other Essays* (Oxford: Oxford University Press, 1991), p. 73.

48. Emerson, *Essays*, p. 48.

49. Mill, *On Liberty*, pp. 74–75.

50. Emerson, *Essays*, p. 38.

51. Mill, *On Liberty*, p. 77.

52. Hubert Dreyfus, *Being in the World*, pp. 141–62. For detailed comparisons of Wittgenstein and Heidegger, see Charles Taylor's "Lichtung and Lebensform," in *Philosophical Arguments* (Cambridge: Harvard University Press, 1995), and Karl-Otto Apel's "Kritische Wiederholung und Ergänzung eines Vergleichs," in the symposium on Wittgenstein, *Der Löwe spricht . . . und wir können ihn nicht verstehen* (Frankfurt: Suhrkamp, 1991), pp. 27–68.

53. See the opening pages of "Individualization through Socialization: On Mead's Theory of Subjectivity," in *Postmetaphysical Thinking* (Cambridge: MIT Press, 1992), pp. 149–204.

54. Ibid., p. 190. My emphasis.

55. "[L]anguage is an inheritance. Words are before I am; they are common . . . [T]he question whether I am saying them or quoting them—saying them firsthand or

secondhand, as it were—which means whether I am thinking or imitating, is the same as the question whether I do or do not exist as a human being and is a matter demanding proof." Stanley Cavell, *In Quest of the Ordinary. Lines of Skepticism and Romanticism* (Chicago: University of Chicago, 1988), p. 113.

56. This group of philosophers and poets to which I refer constitutes a distinct tradition of modern thought, one I call philosophical romanticism. See the essays in Nikolas Kompridis, ed., *Philosophical Romanticism* (London: Routledge, 2006) for a reassessment and rearticulation of this tradition of thought.

57. The work of James Bohman is one exception. See his *Public Deliberation* (Cambridge: MIT Press, 1996), pp. 197–236. The work of Jay Bernstein is another. See Bernstein's, *The Recovery of Public Life: Jürgen Habermas and the Future of Critical Theory* (London: Routledge, 1995), pp. 197–234.

58. See especially the last section of his essay "Walter Benjamin: Consciousness Raising or Rescuing Critique," in Gary Smith, ed., *On Walter Benjamin: Critical Essay and Recollections* (Cambridge: MIT Press, 1988), pp. 120–24, and the chapter on the "colonization of the lifeworld" in volume 2 of *The Theory of Communicative Action*).

59. Charles Taylor, *Sources of the Self* (Cambridge: Harvard University Press, 1989), p. 510.

60. With his recent intervention in the debate over genetic engineering (*The Future of Human Nature* (Cambridge: MIT Press, 2002), Habermas had to abandon the normative asceticism which previously restricted both the role and scope of philosophical reflection. Returning to his roots in philosophical anthropology, he offers a view of what it is to be a human being that he derives from the "ethical self-understanding of the species." I return to the implications of this move in part IV.

61. Heidegger, *The Question Concerning Technology*, p. 11.

62. See Nikolas Kompridis "On World Disclosure: Heidegger, Habermas, and Dewey," *Thesis Eleven* 37 (1994): 29–45.

Part III

1. Once again, I remind the reader that Habermas treats the philosophy of the subject as synonymous with the philosophy of consciousness, but this treatment is disputable, since Habermas takes the philosophy of consciousness to be the basic conceptual framework of the philosophy of the subject. As I argued in part II, the lines that Habermas would like to draw between philosophies of the subject and philosophies of intersubjectivity are not nearly as firm as Habermas claims. There is more to the philosophy of the subject than the philosophy of consciousness, and Habermas is simply wrong to ignore the differences between them: the exhaustion of the philosophy of consciousness is not the exhaustion of the philosophy of the subject.

2. Robert Pippin, "You Can't Get There from Here: Transition Problems in Hegel's *Phenomenology of Spirit*," in Frederick C. Beiser, ed., *Cambridge Companion to Hegel* (Cambridge: Cambridge University Press, 1993), pp. 52–85.

3. Of course, the epistemological construal of reason expresses its own ideal of freedom and self-determination. But this ideal of freedom and self-determination depends on what Charles Taylor has called an "ontology of disengagement," giving the epistemological construal of reason its apparently irresistible inevitability. See Taylor's "Overcoming Epistemology," in his *Philosophical Arguments* (Cambridge: Harvard University Press, 1995).

4. See Peter Dews's introduction to *Habermas: A Critical Reader* (Oxford: Basil Blackwell, 1999), pp. 1–28.

5. It is worth noting that despite the bulk of the book being concerned with the challenge of world disclosure, there is not a single index entry for this idea in either the English or German versions of the text. Very few commentators recognized that the challenge posed by the renewed application of this idea in poststructuralist France, in the work of Taylor, Rorty, and Dreyfus, was the central preoccupation of *The Philosophical Discourse of Modernity*, providing evidence of the most significant theoretical reconsiderations (not necessarily changes) in Habermas's work since *Knowledge and Human Interests*. It could have been a turning point for Habermas and critical theory, but that was not to be the case for reasons that are the preoccupation of much of my book.

6. The fiercely polemical nature of the book often undermines Habermas's stated claim to take the position of a "participant" in this two-centuries long discourse, and his concerns about the skeptical implications of world disclosure outrun his commitment to dialogue, giving his lectures the character of an admonition, and making his contemporaries sound as though they needed a good philosophical scolding.

7. That is not to say that Habermas is of the rather naïve view that the use of communicative reason will exclude the possibility of violence altogether, only that he is of the questionable view that violence does not inhere in communicative reason as it inheres in subject-centered reason.

8. This way of talking about reason seems illegitimately to anthropomorphize reason, to give it subject-like properties. I think this is to some degree unavoidable, given that *we* are the reason that we use.

9. For an alternative treatment of the concept of mimesis in Adorno, see Nikolas Kompridis, "Amidst the Plurality of Voices: Philosophy of Music after Adorno," *Angelaki, Journal of the Theoretical Humanities* 8, 3 (2003): 167–180.

10. This act of taking the role of the object was recognized by George Herbert Mead as a generalization and expansion of subject-subject relationships through which

young children acquire an understanding of the difference between self and other, and through which they acquire essential communicative abilities. On this neglected aspect of Mead's theory of intersubjectivity, see Hans Joas, *George Herbert Mead: A Contemporary Re-examination of His Thought*, (Cambridge: MIT Press, 1985), pp. 153–159.

11. "Since the turn to autonomy, art has striven mightily to mirror one basic aesthetic experience, the increasing decentration of subjectivity. It occurs as the subject leaves the spatiotemporal structures of everyday life behind, freeing itself from the conventions of everyday perception, of purposive behaviour, and of imperatives of work and utility" (MCCA 17).

12. "Truth, Semblance, and Reconciliation," in Albrecht Wellmer, *The Persistence of Modernity* (Cambridge: MIT Press, 1991)

13. It is worth noting that Habermas employs the Weberian terminology of "cultural action systems" (*Handlungsysteme*) to describe science and morality, and the much weaker term "enterprise" (*Betrieb*) to describe art. It seems that in order to be given a new place in the theory of modernity, art can no longer be conceived as autonomous cultural action systems—which is more or less to make it "placeless."

14. Although I was first trained as an instrumentalist and composer, through no fault of my teachers at the University of Toronto and at Yale University, not once were such capacities "administered" to me, nor to any one of my fellow music students. I can't think of any occasion when even the expectation that "this is the sort of thing we *should* be learning" was expressed—that failure to acquire the requisite world-disclosing capacities before graduation would warrant blaming one's teachers or oneself. It would be hard to imagine a professor of music, art, or literature running a practical course like, "Techniques of World Disclosure" or "World Disclosure for Composers." Musicians, artists, architects, as with most everyone else in professional schools, learn problem-solving skills—like how to get a certain kind of sound out of one's instrument, how to get from here to there in the piece one is composing, how to get better at correcting one's own mistakes. If at this point one needs to acquire world-disclosing capacities, it is already too late. It should be noted that for Heidegger to be an agent at all is to be in possession of the capacity for disclosure; there cannot be agents who have such a capacity in virtue of the practices (or cafés) they favor, and agents who do not. The idea that a value sphere could *specialize* in disclosure shows only the degree to which Habermas is himself under the sway of the "expert culture" thinking he is critical of.

15. I can't help but cringe at Habermas's vocabulary in this context, conceiving the "products" of culture as though produced on reason's assembly lines, each of which "specializes" in producing the three main products of modern culture: science, morality, and art.

16. See Nikolas Kompridis, *Models of Aesthetic Critique* (in preparation).

17. Charles Taylor, *Sources of the Self*, p. 214.

18. Habermas's ongoing political worry is that this "wholly other" might speak with the voice of charismatic or sacred authority, a world disclosing *Fuehrer*.

19. John Dewey, "Construction and Criticism," *The Late Works, 1929–1930*, vol. 5 (Carbondale: Southern Illinois University Press, 1984), p. 141.

20. Obviously this is the history that is told when one takes pragmatism, Heidegger, later Wittgenstein, and Cavell as the point of reference.

21. Stanley Cavell, *This New Yet Unapproachable America*, p. 66.

22. Ibid., p. 90.

23. Ludwig Wittgenstein, *Philosophical Investigations*, trans. Elizabeth Anscombe (Oxford: Basil Blackwell, 1999), see. 108.

24. Habermas dismisses such suggestions for "becloud[ing] the sober insights of pragmatism" (*PDM*, 206); he fails to see just how *selective* is his own appropriation of the insights of pragmatism. He ignores Dewey in favor of Peirce, and takes from Mead only what is conducive to the intentions of his discourse ethics.

25. As the example of Sweden shows, it is not just a matter of the state providing generous paternity as well as generous maternity leave. In Sweden men generally do not take advantage of their right to a rather generous paternity leave. They prefer the familiar world of their workplace to the disruption of what is genuinely new in their home.

26. A world that makes so little of birth makes just as little of death. In either case we have the suppression, if not the erasure, of the extraordinary in everyday life.

It has been observable for a number of centuries how in the general consciousness the thought of death has declined in omnipresence and vividness. In its last stages this process is accelerated. And in the course of the nineteenth century bourgeois society has, by means of hygienic and social, private and public institutions, realized a secondary effect which have been its subconscious main purpose: to make it possible for people to avoid the sight of the dying. . . . In the course of modern times dying has been pushed further and further out of the perceptual world of the living. There used to be no house, hardly a room, in which someone had not once died. . . . Today people live in rooms that have never been touched by death, dry dwellers of eternity, and when their end approaches they are stowed away in sanatoria or hospitals by their heirs. Walter Benjamin, "The Storyteller," *Illuminations*, trans. Harry Zohn (New York: Schocken, 1969), pp. 93–94.

27. Hannah Arendt, *The Human Condition* (Chicago: University of Chicago, 1958), p. 246.

28. John Dewey, "Construction and Criticism," *Later Works*, vol. 5 (Carbondale: Southern Illinois University Press, 1988) p. 127.

29. Notice how the meaning of *Vernunft* is collapsed into the meaning of *Verstand*.

30. "Questions and Counter-Questions," in Richard Bernstein, ed., *Habermas and Modernity* (Cambridge: MIT Press, 1985), p. 202.

31. Habermas's view that world-disclosing argument is not philosophical argument, not argument as such, is shared by Richard Rorty (who, unlike Habermas, enthusiastically endorses the practice). For Rorty's view of this issue see, "Is Derrida a Transcendental Philosopher," in *Essays on Heidegger and Others: Philosophical Papers*, vol. 2 (Cambridge: Cambridge University Press, 1991), pp 119–28, and, "Habermas, Derrida, and the Functions of Philosophy," in *Truth and Progress: Philosophical Papers*, vol. 3 (Cambridge: Cambridge University Press, 1998), pp. 307–26. For criticism of Rorty's view of what counts as argument and what reason can mean, see my "So We Need Something Else for Reason to Mean," *International Journal of Philosophical Studies* 8, 3 (2000): 271–95.

32. I am not by any means endorsing Apel's conception of philosophy as *Letzbegründung*, a conception that tries to make philosophical reflection the ultimate, unsurpassable meta-discourse of modernity. The claim that philosophy is the "*Reflexionsform* aller denkbaren Sprachspiele und Lebensformen und insofern der geschichtlich-kontingent Lebenswelt" is just wishful thinking, more naïve than metaphysical. See Karl-Otto Apel, "Wittgenstein und Heidegger: Kritische Wiederholung and Ergänzung eines Vergleichs." in Brian McGuiness, Jürgen Habermas, et al., eds., *Der Löwe spricht . . . und wir können ihn nicht verstehen* (FraukFurt: Suhrkamp, 1991), p. 44.

33. I owe this point to Charles Taylor's highly instructive essay, "The Validity of Transcendental Arguments," in *Philosophical Arguments* (Cambridge: Harvard University Press, 1995), pp. 20–33, especially pp. 31–33.

34. For an example of this rhetoric-based approach, see James Bohman, "World Disclosure and Radical Criticism," *Thesis Eleven* 37 (1994): 82–97.

35. For a critique of attempts to give the conclusions of transcendental arguments the character of an inviolable rule (in order to crush the moral skeptic once and for all), see Ernst Tugendhat's analysis of the use to which Habermas and Apel put the so-called performative contradiction argument in their respective discourse ethics in his *Vorlesungen über Ethik* (Frankfurt: Suhrkamp, 1994), pp. 161–76.

36. Charles Taylor, *Philosophical Arguments*, p. 63.

37. "Both Wittgenstein and Heidegger had to struggle to recover an understanding of the agent as engaged, as embedded in a culture, a form of life, a world of involvements, ultimately to understand the agent as embodied." Ibid., p. 61–62.

38. Ludwig Wittgenstein, *Philosophical Investigations*, trans. G. E. M. Anscombe, (Oxford: Basil Blackwell), sec. 123.

39. Wittgenstein, *Philosophical Investigations*, sec. 255.

40. Stanley Cavell, *This New Yet Unapproachable America*, p. 73.

41. Friedrich Nietzsche, *The Gay Science*, trans. Walter Kaufmann (New York: Vintage, 1974), sec. 355.

42. If we are going to speak, in the manner of Sellars and McDowell, of a "normative space of reasons," we have to remember that the logical space is made possible, and is nestled within, a historically shaped culture of reasons. I take this to be the point of Robert Pippin's criticism of Henry Allison for trying to describe Kant's conception of reason as a "historically conditioned faculty," and of Pippin's qualified endorsement of John McDowell's quasi-Hegelian, quasi-Gadamerian, account of the historically conditioned character of the logical space of reason. See Pippin, "Naturalism and Mindedness: Hegel's Compatibilism," *European Journal of Philosophy* 7, 2 (August 1999): 210.

43. Hilary Putnam, *Realism with a Human Face* (Cambridge: Harvard University Press, 1990) pp. 163–78.

44. Hubert Dreyfus, "Being and Power: Heidegger and Foucault," in *International Journal of Philosophical Studies* 4, 1 (March 1996): 4.

45. For an elaboration of this point see, Hubert Dreyfus, "Heidegger on the connection between nihilism, art, technology and politics," in Charles Guignon, ed., *The Cambridge Companion to Heidegger*, pp. 289–316. See also Hubert Dreyfus and Charles Spinosa, "Further Reflections on Heidegger, Technology, and the Everyday," in Nikolas Kompridis, ed., *Philosophical Romanticism* (London: Routledge, 2004).

46. Heidegger, *Basic Writings*, trans. David Farrell Krell (New York: Harper and Row, 1977), p. 217. Heidegger goes on to describe the interpretive disagreements that inevitably arise among those who engage in critical histories of ontologies as like a "lover's quarrel"—a not unfamiliar genre of discourse.

47. That suggestion, developed in two early essays in the 1920s is very carefully reconstructed by Thomas McCarthy, "Heidegger and Critical Theory: The First Encounter," in *Ideals and Illusions. On Reconstruction and Deconstruction in Contemporary Critical Theory* (Cambridge: MIT Press, 1991), pp. 83–96. It's too bad that critical theorists remain skeptical, treating it as of merely historical interest at best.

48. Horizons of meaning, understandings of being, and the like, must not be confused with logically closed systems of meaning. See Donald Davidson, "On the Very Idea of a Conceptual Scheme," in *Inquiries into Truth and Interpretation*, (Oxford: Oxford University Press), pp. 183–96. See also Hans-Georg Gadamer, *Truth and Method* (New York: Seabury Press, 1989), p. 304.

49. The ontological difference offers two standpoints from which we can understand cultural change. We can move dialectically back and forth between these two standpoints, as though between observer and participant standpoints, but we

cannot dissolve the difference between them. These standpoints—the ontological and the ontic—are analogous to (and modeled on) the intelligible and empirical standpoints from which, according to Kant, we can understand human freedom. But they have a different function. Just as we must presuppose the intelligible standpoint to make sense of our selves as agents, we must presuppose the ontological standpoint to understand our prior dependence, as knowers, doers, and speakers on a linguistically mediated and holistically structured understanding of the world. Both standpoints must be disclosed by world-disclosing argument since they are not immediately "obvious," and not directly accessible.

50. Albrecht Wellmer, *The Persistence of Modernity* (Cambridge: MIT Press, 1991), pp. 36–94.

51. See Jay Bernstein, *Recovering Ethical Life* (London: Routledge, 1996), pp. 212–13.

52. For a helpful discussion of the difficulties facing Habermas's pragmatic theory of meaning, see Albrecht Wellmer, "What Is a Pragmatic Theory of Meaning? Variations on the Proposition 'We Understand a Speech Act When We Know What Makes It Acceptable,'" in Axel Honneth, Thomas McCarthy, Claus Offe, and Albrecht Wellmer, eds., *Philosophical Interventions in the Unfinished Project of Enlightenment* (Cambridge: MIT Press, 1992) pp. 171–219.

53. Ibid., p. 213

54. James Bohman, "Two Versions of the Linguistic Turn."

55. Jay Bernstein, *Recovering Ethical Life*, p. 216.

56. John Dewey, *The Public and its Problems*, in *The Later Works of John Dewey, 1925–1953*, vol. 2 (Carbondale: Southern Illinois University Press, 1984), p. 255. For an application of this point to the theory of deliberative democracy, see James Bohman, *Public Deliberation. Pluralism, Complexity, and Democracy* (Cambridge: MIT Press, 1996), pp. 197–236.

57. Rorty makes this point in *Philosophy and the Mirror of Nature* (Princeton: Princeton University Press), p. 271, after which he goes on caustically to comment on the pretensions of philosophers who think they are in a position to tell the rest of us when we "could start meaning something different" (p. 272).

58. Dewey, "Philosophy and Civilisation," *The Later Works*, vol. 3, p. 4.

59. Dewey, Ibid., pp. 4–5.

60. They are, as Ian Hacking points out, "self-authenticating," which is, to be sure, unsettling for a number of reasons. See "Style for Historians and Philosophers," in Ian Hacking, *Historical Ontology* (Cambridge: Harvard University Press, 2002), pp. 191–92.

61. Taylor, "Heidegger, Language, and Ecology," p. 252.

62. Ibid., p. 253.

63. Dewey, *Experience and Nature* (La Salle: Open Court, 1929), p. 156, my emphasis.

64. Dewey's pragmatic test differs fundamentally from the kind of "pragmatic" test for new meaning Rorty has in mind: "One can only savour it or spit it out." Neither savoring it nor spitting it out tells us very much. We may be inclined to savor something now that we will want to spit out later, or spit out now what we might one day wish to savor. In either case our reaction to the "taste" of something new is not very informative. What's missing in Rorty is precisely what is so crucial to Dewey: the moments of experiment and reflection. See Rorty, *Contingency, Irony, and Solidarity* (Cambridge: Cambridge University Press, 1989), p. 18.

65. Habermas, "Hermeneutic and Analytic Philosophy: Two Complementary Versions of the Linguistic Turn," in Anthony O'Hear, ed., *German Philosophy Since Kant* (Cambridge: Cambridge University Press, 1999), p. 429.

66. Ludwig Wittgenstein, *On Certainty*, trans. G. E. M. Anscombe and G. H. von Wright (Oxford: Oxford University Press, 1974), p. 16.

67. Needless to say, there is a standard interpretation of Wittgenstein that is open to Habermas's criticisms, but as in the case of the standard interpretation of Heidegger (standard among critical theorists, anyway), this is not the only, or most plausible interpretation. For the alternative to the Kripke, Baker and Hacker, and Rorty line of Wittgenstein interpretation, see Stanley Cavell's *The Claim of Reason* and *Conditions Handsome and Unhandsome*, the illuminating collection of essays in Alice Crary and Rupert Read, eds., *The New Wittgenstein* (London: Routledge, 2000), and Richard Eldridge, *Living a Human Life: Wittgenstein, Intentionality, and Romanticism* (Chicago: University of Chicago, 1997). See also Robert J. Fogelin, "Wittgenstein's Critique of Philosophy," in Hans Sluga and David G. Stern, eds., *The Cambridge Companion to Wittgenstein* (Cambridge: Cambridge University Press, 1996), pp. 34–58.

68. Ibid., p. 439.

69. Lev Vygotsky, *Mind in Society* (Cambridge: Harvard University Press, 1978), p. 86.

70. Ibid., p. 89.

71. Jerome Bruner, *Actual Minds, Possible Worlds* (Cambridge: Harvard University Press, 1986), p. 141, my emphasis.

72. We can say that the pre-reflective and reflective disclosure of meaning is a condition of possible learning, but further learning (which is not the same as the acquisition of more "knowledge") is also a condition of successful disclosure.

Part IV

1. If we accept the premises of the procedural conception of philosophical argument, we end up with some unacceptable conclusions. For example: Derrida is not a philosopher who likes to argue (PDM 193), ergo, Derrida must not be a real philosopher. If Derrida *is* a philosopher, a procedural conception has no way of explaining how that can be. Conversely, if Derrida does not count as a philosopher, a procedural conception has a lot of explaining to do.

2. Of course, this is just how Richard Rorty thinks that we should balance those two ways of doing philosophy. Neither "edifying" or "systematic philosophy," neither "world-disclosing" or "argumentative" philosophy should dominate the practice of philosophy. See *Philosophy and the Mirror of Nature* (Princeton: Princeton University Press, 1979), pp. 357–89, and "Habermas, Derrida, and the Functions of Philosophy," in *Truth and Progress*, Philosophical Papers, vol. 3 (Cambridge: Cambridge University Press, 1998), pp. 307–26.

3. Karl-Otto Apel, *Diskurs und Verantwortung* (Frankfurt: Suhrkamp, 1988), p. 347.

4. Richard Rorty, *Philosophy and the Mirror of Nature*, p. 392.

5. Immanuel Kant, "Architectonic of Pure Reason," *Critique of Pure Reason*, trans. and ed. Paul Guyer and Allen W. Wood (Cambridge: Cambridge University Press), pp. 694–95.

6. Although I cannot I argue this here in detail, I would suggest that the lifeworld is a much less settled sphere than that selectively highlighted aspect of it which functions as a "conservative counterweight" to massive dissensus. The lifeworld is not only the holistically structure background of myriad presuppositions and everyday knowledge, it is also the everyday form of life in which these presuppositions and knowledge are anchored, the place where they are variously lived. Under conditions of cultural pluralism characterised by deep diversity, far less of the lifeworld's background understanding can function as the sphere of what can be taken for granted. The background "certainty" of the lifeworld, has been shaken and overtaken by the "strange multiplicity," as James Tully calls it, of disparate and diverse cultural lifeworlds encountering one another in new and unpredictable ways. Such daily encounters amongst lifeworlds in a time horizon of contemporaneous non-contemporaneity cannot leave their respective background assumptions intact, or in a state of stable equilibrium. In any case there is a tendency to treat the holistic structure of lifeworld knowledge in a way that makes it sounds as though the threads of the lifeworld are woven uniformly tight throughout, as though each strand of the web is composed of many thickly woven threads. But I would think that such a characterization of the lifeworld (as resource) makes the lifeworld (as product) much more impervious to change and discontinuity, to reflective redisclosure and to unforeseeable breakdowns—which obviously it is not. And that is, I presume, because the various threads are not tightly woven throughout because they tear,

unravel, and wear out, and because there are places where they need to be woven anew.

7. Habermas treats the relation between philosophy as stand-in and interpreter as though devoid of possible tension, but that cannot be the case, given Habermas's own account of the roles they are supposed to play.

8. As a highly active public intellectual, Habermas is something of an exception, but even so, his appearances in the public sphere in some rather important and highly charged debates carried on in Germany's finest newspapers are nonetheless appearances in the comfortable discursive medium with which he carries on his professional activities. His voice, presumably raised as that of an ordinary citizen with no special expertise, is nonetheless heard as the voice of an "expert," and presented as such by the editors, and understood as such by the readers.

9. Hilary Putnam, "Why Is a Philosopher," *Realism with a Human Face* (Cambridge: Harvard University Press, 1990), p. 118.

10. It is worth noting that in its orientation to the world, Thoreau's sauntering kind of walk is markedly different from the walk of Baudelaire's *flâneur*, the walk of the disengaged, self-alienated observer/consumer of *la vie moderne*.

11. Henry David Thoreau, "Walking," in *Walden and Other Writings* (New York: Modern Library, 2000), p. 627.

12. Martin Seel, "The Two Meanings of 'Communicative' Rationality: Remarks on Habermas' Critique of a Plural Concept of Reason," Axel Honneth and Hans Joas, *Communicative Action* (Cambridge: MIT Press, 1991), p. 38.

13. The more there is at stake, the less clear, the more bewildering the phenomena that confront us, whether it concerns the reality of global warming, the risks to humans of a genetically manipulated food chain, not to mention, the genetic manipulation of the human race itself, or the emergence of previously unheard of strains of infectious diseases.

14. And even if it did, even if there were a common lingua franca, the problem of translation would nevertheless remain as a "domestic" problem. As the novelist, Russell Hoban, puts it: "After all, when you come right down to it, how many people speak the same language even when they speak the same language?" Cited in *The Globe and Mail*, Tuesday, May 6, 2003.

15. About this set of difficulties, Habermas has very little to say. Describing philosophy and literary criticism as performing analogous mediating roles on behalf of the lifeworld, he acknowledges that they

are both faced with tasks that are paradoxical in similar ways. They are supposed to feed the contents of expert cultures, in which knowledge is accumulated under one aspect of validity at a time, into an everyday practice in which all linguistic functions and aspects of validity are intermeshed to form one syndrome. And yet literary criticism and philosophy are supposed to accomplish this task of mediation with means of expression taken from languages specialised in questions of taste or of truth. They can only resolve this paradox by rhetorically expanding and enriching their special languages to the extent that is required to link up indirect communications with the manifest contents of statements, and to do so in a deliberate way. (PDM 209)

I hope that I have made clear that much more than linking indirect communications (rhetoric) with the manifest content of statements (fallible knowledge) is going to be required to resolve the paradox he describes. The fact that this problem appears in the form of a paradox is itself not fully appreciated, since Habermas proceeds as though it is a problem of straightforward translation and of employing the appropriate rhetorical means to serve the relevant semantic ends.

16. Drawing on the work of A. C. Crombie and Michel Foucault, Ian Hacking describes a "style of reason" or argumentation as one that opens up a whole field of possibility whose very intelligibility radically depends on that style of reasoning. Ian Hacking, "Styles of Scientific Reasoning," John Rajchman and Cornel West, eds., *Post-analytic Philosophy* (New York: Columbia University Press, 1985), pp. 145–65.

17. Like me, Peter Dews is very worried about the sectarian and restrictive nature of Habermas's conception of philosophy. He raises similar and complementary concerns about Habermas's conception of philosophy as performing the role of interpreter and stand in, but I find that Dews's laudable desire to make critical theory's vision of philosophy more inclusive by making room for genealogy, hermeneutics, deconstruction, and phenomenology actually gets in the way of seeing the problem clearly: these critical approaches are not engaged in mediation in the relevant sense—not yet, anyway. They are just as much as critical theory part of the problem that needs to be solved.

18. Each type of incursion names three types of possible alienation. The extreme self-alienation of the lifeworld can be the consequence of objectivistic self-descriptions of individuality, culture, and society when naturalistic strategies of social-scientific explanation functions as persuasive justifications to reorder the lifeworld under economic and bureaucratic imperatives. It can also be the consequence of moralizing incursions that either trespass upon the private intimate sphere of the individual or the family, or rob agents of the opportunity to collectively and co-operatively address their own moral dilemmas and conflicts. There is considerable empirical evidence to support the need to defend the lifeworld against the first two of these types of incursions. However, is it really the case that it needs defending against aestheticizing incursions? I suppose that a certain modernist conception of architecture (e.g., the International Style) can alienate the lifeworld from its own public spaces, and a certain aestheticized ideal of unencumbered, unconstrained self-creation pervades the lifeworld, visibly valorized and encouraged by popular culture. Still it is hard to see just how expert aesthetic "knowledge" (for Habermas, as for many other philosophers, a contradiction in terms) is being misapplied here. In the case of architecture, it is not so much an aesthetic perspective as much as economic and administrative imperatives that drive urban planning. In the case of the ideal

of self-creation, it is most certainly not an ideal that has illegally migrated from the sphere of art into the domain of the lifeworld but, rather, an interpretation of individual freedom that owes as much to our inherited conceptions of negative freedom as to more "romantic" conceptions of freedom as self-determination.

19. Perhaps it is unwise to speak of the "unity of reason," for that may be nothing more than a philosophical construction, a piece of Enlightenment mythology. If we are to be defenders of the lifeworld, we should not misconstrue the nature of its integrated rationality, whose nature is pluralistic, not monistic, a motley reason more truly reflecting the pluralistic nature of modern lifeworlds, and just as unsurveyable from any one perspective, just as resistant to subsumption under one category.

20. Habermas, *The Future of Human Nature*, trans. Wiliam Rehg, Max Pensky, and Hella Beister (Cambridge: MIT Press, 2002), p. 15.

21. Habermas, *The Future of Human Nature*, p. 39.

22. Habermas, *The Future of Human Nature*, p. 40.

23. Stanley Cavell, *This New Yet Unapproachable America*, p. 74.

24. I owe thanks to Stanley Cavell for taking the time to discuss this passage with me.

25. James Tully, "Political Theory as a Critical Activity," *Political Theory* 30 (August 2002): 551.

26. Putnam, *Realism with a Human Face*, p. 119.

27. I'm actually of the view that there is no such thing as "continental" philosophy, not if by "continental" philosophy we mean to refer to a distinct branch of philosophy, the way we refer to epistemology, logic, philosophy of language, or aesthetics. I think it is obvious to open-minded reflection that there is nothing intrinsically philosophical about the designation "continental" philosophy. It is not a field defined by a canonical set of problems and questions, and the "field" it does cover is so broad and diverse that consistent application of the term to all of its supposed instances leads to incoherence. Today the distinction between "analytic" and "continental" names a political or institutional difference, not a philosophical one. See Nikolas Kompridis, *Philosophical Romanticism*, pp. 1–18.

28. Bernard Williams, *Philosophy as a Humanistic Discipline* (Princeton: Princeton University Press, 2006), pp. 180–99.

29. John Dewey, *Human Nature and Conduct* (Carbondale: Southern Illinois University Press, 1988), p. 123.

30. George Herbert Mead, "Definition of the Psychical," James Reck, ed., *Selected Writings: George Herbert Mead* (Chicago: University of Chicago Press, 1964), pp. 42–43, 52–53, 58.

31. Ian Hacking, "Language, Truth and Reason," Martin Hollis and Steven Lukes, eds., *Rationality and Relativism* (Cambridge: MIT Press, 1982), p. 60. Of course, the possibilities in question are not just possibilities for truth-or-falsehood but for rightness-or-wrongness, not just potential truth candidates but also potential action and speech candidates.

32. As is well known, Mead's distinguishes between the "I" and the "me." The "I" stands for the novel, spontaneous, and creative dimension of human freedom and agency; the "me" is used to refer to the social self that is the product of the internalization of normed behavior and normative expectations.

33. Ludwig Wittgenstein, "Philosophy: Sections 86–93 of the 'Big Typescript' (Catalog Number 213)," in, *Philosophical Occasions 1912–1951* and Alfred Nordmann, eds., James Klagges (Indianapolis: Hackett, 1993), pp. 161–163.

34. Michel Foucault, *Politics, Philosophy, Culture* (London: Routledge, 1988), p. 14.

35. Hilary Putnam, *Realism with a Human Face*, pp. lxi–lxii.

36. Stanley Cavell, *The Claim of Reason* (Oxford: Oxford University Press, 1979), p. 125.

37. Hilary Putnam, *Realism with a Human Face*, p. 118.

38. Albrecht Wellmer, "Intersubjectivity and Reason," in L. Hertzberg and J. Pietarinen eds., *Perspectives in Human Conduct* (Leiden: E.J. Brill, 1988), p. 154.

39. Peter Dews, "Introduction," *Habermas: A Critical Reader*, p. 16.

40. It was Hegel, after all, who came up with this phrase to describe the new mundane concerns of "romantic" art, whose definition he produced, in part, through his encounter with seventeenth-century Dutch painting, where the focus was everyday subjectivity. Compare this body of work, the work of Rembrandt and Vermeer, for example, with what Descartes was up to at the same time in his *Meditations*. And then compare the protagonist of the *Meditations* to the protagonist of Cervantes's *Don Quixote*. Which one of them is most intimately conversant with the prose of the world?

41. Emerson, "Circles," in *Essays*, p. 171.

42. John Dewey, *Reconstruction in Philosophy and Essays: Middle Works*, vol. 12 (Carbondale: Southern Illinois University Press, 1988), p. 201.

43. I owe thanks to David Levin who helped me to see this point much more clearly than before.

Part V

1. Martin Heidegger, *On Time and Being* (New York: Harper and Row, 1972), p. 70, translation amended. The original in *Zur Sache des Denkens* (Tübingen: Max

Niemayer, 1969), p. 76. Other than Karl-Otto Apel, "Wittgenstein und Heidegger: Kritische Wiederholung and Ergänzung eines Vergleichs" in Brian McGuiness, Jürgen Habermas et al., eds., *Der Löure spricht . . . und wir können ihn nicht verstehen* (Frankfurt: Suhrkamp, 1991), pp. 27–68, I know of no other critical theorist who has acknowledged this very important amendment to late Heidegger's view of the relation between truth and disclosure.

2. James Bohman, "Two Versions of the Linguistic Turn: Habermas and Poststructuralism," in Maurizio Passerin d'Entrèves and Seyla Benhabib, eds., *Habermas and the Unfinished Project of Modernity: Critical Essays on The Philosophical Discourse of Modernity* (Cambridge: MIT Press, 1997), p. 201.

3. Heidegger, *On Time and Being*, p. 69, translation amended.

4. See Hubert Dreyfus and Charles Spinosa, "Further Reflections on Heidegger, Technology, and the Everyday," in Nikolas Kompridis, ed., *Philosophical Romanticism* (London: Routledge, 2004), and Charles Taylor, "Heidegger, Language, and Ecology," in Hubert Dreyfus and Harrison Hall, eds., *Heidegger: A Critical Reader* (Oxford: Blackwell, 1992), pp. 247–69.

5. Nietzsche, *The Gay Science*, p. 79.

6. Emerson, *Circles*, in *Essays*, p. 175.

7. Susan Bordo, *Unbearable Weight: Feminism, Western Culture, and the Body* (Berkeley: University of California Press, 1992), p. 246.

8. For example, by driving at ecstasy-generating speed on a road "liberated" from any obligations to others, others who have simply been "erased" from this image of ecstatic self-realization.

9. Nikolas Kompridis, "The Idea of a New Beginning: A Romantic Source of Normativity and Freedom," in Nikolas Kompridis, ed., *Philosophical Romanticism* (London: Routledge, 2006), pp. 32–60.

10. Hannah Arendt, "What Is Freedom?" in *Between Past and Future* (London: Penguin, 1993), p. 151.

11. Hannah Arendt, *On Revolution* (London: Penguin, 1990), p. 211.

12. Hannah Arendt, "Freedom and Politics," in A. Hunold, ed., *Freedom and Serfdom* (Dordrecht: Riedel, 1961), p. 215.

13. Hannah Arendt, *On Revolution*, p. 234.

14. Ibid., p. 232.

15. Albrecht Wellmer, "Arendt on Revolution," *Revue Internationale de Philosophie* 53, 208 (1999): 218–19.

16. Habermas's revealing remark brings his position remarkably close to Gehlen's "crystallization" thesis, a thesis that Habermas is quick to criticize in the opening

pages of *The Philosophical Discourse of Modernity*. But the talk of a "contracting space of possibility" to which we must resign ourselves does not appear essentially different—as different as it should—from Gehlen's claim that the possibilities of modernity "have all been developed in their basic elements. Even the counter-possibilities and antitheses have been uncovered and assimilated, so that henceforth changes in the premises have become increasingly unlikely" (PDM 3).

17. Heidegger, *The Question Concerning Technology*, p. 25.

18. I note now, and concede, that anyone employing the terminology of "fate" and "destiny," even with a fallibilistic orientation, is also going to employ a little hyperbole. That can't be avoided: it comes with the territory. Just as their ancient predecessors, the Old Testament prophets, modern social critics can hardly be expected to eschew hyperbole, though the best are aware that the more excessively it is used, the less effective it will be.

19. Emerson, *Essays*, pp. 254–55, my emphasis.

20. Ibid, p. 261.

21. Cavell, *This New Yet Unapproachable America*, p. 104.

22. See Henry Allison, *Kant's Theory of Freedom* (Cambridge: Cambridge University Press, 1990), pp. 36–37, for the discussion of epistemic spontaneity and practical spontaneity as an activity of "taking as."

23. A few years ago I was dumbfounded by an article in *The Guardian*, in which a journalist reported with considerable pride how she practically jumped out bed just moments after giving birth in order to interview, of all people, General Augusto Pinochet (he was being forcibly detained in Britain at the time pending ministerial review of possible judicial proceedings on charges of human rights violations). I take this to be a pretty clear case of *not* "letting it happen," of refusing to let oneself be "marked" or "struck" by any discontinuity between one's past and present self, refusing, denying, the opportunity of beginning anew, of answering anew to the claims of the new—in this case, the claims of a newly born child.

24. For a complementary treatment of this view of agency, see Martin Seel, "Letting Oneself be Determined: A Revised Concept of Self-determination," in Nikolas Kompridis, ed., *Philosophical Romanticism* (London: Routledge, 2006).

25. Cavell, *Conditions Handsome and Unhandsome: The Constitution of Emersonian Perfectionism*, pp. 101–26.

26. An example from recent history: After the results of a poll taken a few months after the end of the second Gulf war were released, various pollsters and political analysts were canvased to make sense of the astounding fact that despite all evidence to the contrary, a third of Americans believed that US forces found weapons of mass destruction in Iraq, and 22 percent believed that Iraq had used chemical or

biological during the war. Half of those polled before the war, in an earlier survey in January 2003, believed that Iraqis were among the 9/11 hijackers. Only 17 percent (!) of Americans stated correctly that no Iraqis were involved. All the analysts conceded that these Americans were actively resisting the experience of cognitive dissonance—the gap between their beliefs and the facts. But that resistance could not be sufficiently explained by how their beliefs came to be so distorted in the first place. One can take into account such factors as the short attention of the American public when it concerns "foreign news," the superficial and opportunistic treatment of such news by American media, and the Bush administration's deliberate policy of misinformation that a conformist media is only too ready to support. Although relevant, such factors do not fully explain resistance to readily available knowledge. Cognitive dissonance is a failure of rationality, indicative of an unreceptiveness to reason. Propaganda cannot succeed without our complicity. One analyst identified the problem as "a lack of understanding about other countries— that maybe many Americans don't know one Arab from another." That is more or less to say that a very large number of Americans actively resist re-cognizing the "other" and, thereby, themselves. Once again, we have a case of not listening, of rendering the "other" voiceless by subsuming a highly diverse and disparate group of "others" under a handy concept: "terrorist." As another analyst put it: "Saddam, Osama, they all sound the same, they're all ragheads, so who cares? I don't think a lot of Americans have taken the time or considerable trouble to find the difference between Shiite and Sunni or Saddam and Osama." See Frank Davies, "False War Beliefs Striking" (http/www.twincities.com/mld/pioneerpress/6136245.htm), and Michelle Goldberg, "Why don't we care about WMD?" (http://www.salon.com/news/feature/2003/06/19/deluded/print.html).

27. Hans-Georg Gadamer, *Truth and Method*, trans. Joel Weinsheimer and Donald B. Marshall (New York: Continuum, 1989), p. 356.

28. Anyone who "argues" with their fellow citizen, their neighbor, their spouse, their sibling, or their child the way that philosophers argue with one another in professional contexts will rightly be looked upon as someone who cannot let down their guard, as someone so alienated from their fellow human beings as to be from another planet.

29. Cavell, *Conditions Handsome and Unhandsome*, p. 20.

30. Heidegger, *The Question Concerning Technology*, p. 27, translation amended (my emphasis).

31. Ibid., p. 27. Translation amended (my emphasis).

32. Dreyfus and Spinosa, "Further Reflections on Heidegger, Technology, and the Everyday," p. 248.

33. Ibid., p. 271.

34. Naomi Klein, "Memories of Consumer Choice" (http://www.nologo.org/detailed.phip?ID=33). In this article Klein refers to a *New York Times* report in which the president of a well-known Canadian organic food company confessed that its crops had been contaminated by GM material. "We have found traces in corn that has been grown organically for 10–15 years. There's no wall high enough to keep that stuff contained."

35. Walter Kirn, "Signals from Nowhere," *New York Times Magazine* (June 22, 2003): 11–12 (my emphasis).

36. Heidegger, *On Time and Being*, p. 37.

37. In "On World Disclosure: Habermas, Heidegger, and Dewey," I draw a distinction between small-size, medium-size, and large-size disclosures of the world. I think that only small-size disclosures qualify as forms of reflective disclosure that we can attribute to our own agency, and that are compatible with an acknowledgement of human plurality.

38. For example, Maeve Cooke, "Argumentation and Transformation", in the journal, *Argumentation* 16, 1 (2002): 81–110.

39. For this reason I cannot endorse James Bohman's attempt to rescue Habermas from his highly inconsistent attempts to accommodate disclosure in his pragmatic theory of language. (See his "Two Versions of the Linguistic Turn: Habermas and Poststructuralism"). Bohman acknowledges that the aestheticizing strategy has been a complete failure, but he does not see that the debunking strategy is just as misguided as the aestheticizing strategy, which is why he does not give sufficient consideration to Heidegger's own view, as distinct from the one Habermas ascribes to Heidegger, a view that cannot be understood unless the place of receptivity within it is appreciated. Bohman's proposal for rescuing Habermas's account of disclosure rightly begins by rejecting the attempt to turn disclosure into some fundamental type of language use. Rather than making room for disclosure by creating a special linguistic category for it, Bohman assimilates disclosure to rhetoric in order to retrieve what he takes to be its most important attribute—its capacity to release us from rigid interpretive frameworks and, thereby, initiate innovative cultural change. However, by assimilating disclosure to rhetoric, Bohman makes it all the more difficult to distinguish it from propaganda. And it brings his view of disclosive social criticism in very close proximity to the views of rhetoric as an instrument of social change espoused by Richard Rorty and Stanley Fish. Both Rorty and Fish divorce innovative uses of language from "problem-solving," since they reject the view that such uses of language help us see things more clearly, help us "escape from something that had deceived us and held us captive." Thus Bohman ends up supporting a view of innovative uses of language as normatively neutral: they can equally disclose "just as and unjust worlds," as Bohman puts it. Or as Rorty likes to put it, *anything* can be made to look good or bad by being "redescribed." For a critique of Rorty's view that *anything* can be made to look good or bad by being "redescribed,"

see Nikolas Kompridis, "Reorienting Critique: From Ironist Theory to Transforma-tive Practice," *Philosophy and Social Criticism* 26, 4 (2000): 23–47.

40. Ian Hacking, "Style for Historians and Philosophers," p. 190.

41. Readers of *Knowledge and Human Interests* will recognize in this passage the traces of the Hegelian construal of reason favored by the early Habermas—before his turn to a stronger, far less historical conception of reason.

42. Seyla Benhabib, *Critique, Norm, and Utopia* (New York: Columbia University Press, 1986), p. 277.

43. C. S. Peirce, *Collected Papers*, vol. 5, ed. C. Hartshorene and P. Weiss (Cambridge: Harvard University Press, 1931–1935), p. 311. Cited in Habermas, *Between Facts and Norms*, trans. William Rehg (Cambridge: MIT Press, 1996), pp. 14–15.

44. In comparison Montaigne's vision of human intersubjectivity, which anticipates both Dewey's and the later Wittgenstein's view of it, is a vision that accepts all that makes it fragile and finite but no less worthy of our allegiance and endorsement than its divinized counterpart: "Since mutual understanding is brought about solely by way of words, he who breaks his word betrays human society. It is the only instru-ment by means of which our wills and thought communicate, it is the interpreter of our soul. If it fails us, we have no more hold on each other, no more knowledge of each other. If it deceives us, it breaks up all our relations and dissolves all the bonds of our society." Michel de Montaigne, *The Complete Essays of Montaigne*, trans. Donald Frame (Stanford: Stanford University Press, 1957), p. 505.

45. Albrecht Wellmer, "Truth, Contingency, and Modernity," in *Endgames* (Cambridge: MIT Press, 1998), p. 141.

46. Hegel draws an instructive contrast between the "independent, reserved, unre-ceptive" classical gods of classical antiquity and the incarnated divinity of Christ—"because here God himself descends into finite temporal existence." G. W. F. Hegel, *Aesthetics. Lectures on Fine Art*, vol. 1, trans. T. M. Knox (Oxford: Oxford University Press, 1975), p. 532.

47. Kant, *Critique of Pure Reason*, B584, p. 545.

48. Richard Rorty, "Universality and Truth," in Robert Brandom, ed., *Rorty and His Critics* (Oxford: Basil Blackwell, 2000), p. 10.

49. For lucid and compelling criticisms of the idea (shared by Habermas and others) that a distinct set of justificatory practices can and must ground all other social prac-tices, see James Tully, "Wittgenstein and Political Philosophy: Understanding Prac-tices of Critical Reflection," in Cressida Hayes, ed., *The Grammar of Politics* (Ithaca: Cornell University Press, 2003), pp. 17–43. See also Charles Taylor, "To Follow a Rule," in his *Philosophical Arguments* (Cambridge: Harvard University Press, 1995), pp. 165–80.

50. "In trying to do justice to the theoretical character of theory (rational reconstructions as 'pure' knowledge) and the practical character of practice (critique as bound to the system of action and experience), he seems to have reintroduced the gap between theory and practice, between reason and emancipation that *Knowledge and Human Interests* tried to close. More specifically, if it is only reflection in the sense of critique that pursues a direct interest in liberation from the self-deception embedded in systematically distorted communication; and if the identification of reason (in its purest form) with reflection makes sense only if reflection is understood as the reconstruction of the universal presuppositions of speech and action, then it seems to follow that *the interest in emancipation is not proper to reason as such,* but only to a particular employment of reason: critical self-reflection." Thomas McCarthy, *The Critical Theory of Jürgen Habermas* (Cambridge: MIT Press, 1978), pp. 101–102, my emphasis.

51. As is well-known, Kant distinguishes between two kinds of rationality: the "understanding" (*Verstand*) through whose concepts we make *sense* of experience, and reason (*Vernunft*) through whose ends-proposing and possibility-disclosing activity we make *demands* on experience.

52. See Kant, *The Critique of Pure Reason*, B582/B576; original in *Kritik der Reinen Vernunft*, R. Schmidt, ed. (Hamburg: Felix Meiner, 1954).

53. As though trying to appease Kant (and Habermas), Albrecht Wellmer has tried to grace the normativity of possibility with the normativity of universality in defending Arendt's conception of public freedom. But the "universal possibility" that Wellmer points out is actually a historically particular possibility: "the possibility of creating, in the midst of contingent historical circumstances, a space of public freedom; a space in which no law of progress and no eschatology holds sway; a space which no extrapolitical normative foundation secures or justifies." The possibility that Wellmer identifies is appealing enough without any false attributions of universality. See Albrecht Wellmer, "Arendt on Revolution," in Dana Villa, *The Cambridge Companion to Hannah Arendt* (Cambridge: Cambridge University Press, 2000), p. 229. However, note that this version of Wellmer's paper is somewhat different from the version cited above and published in *Revue Internationale de Philosophie*.

54. For my own attempt to develop the implications of this "romantic" idea of reason for democratic politics, see Nikolas Kompridis, *Kant and the Idea of a New Beginning: Rethinking Public Reason and Democratic Politics* (Lanham: Rowman and Littlefield, 2009).

55. Kant, *Foundations of the Metaphysics of Morals*, trans. L. W. Beck (New York: Bobbs-Merrill, 1969), p. 80. I am citing from Robert Pippin's highly informative essay, "Kant on the Spontaneity of Mind," in his *Idealism and Modernism. Hegelian Variations* (Cambridge: Cambridge University Press, 1997), p. 36.

56. Michel Foucault, *Politics, Philosophy, Culture* (London: Routledge, 1988), p. 27.

57. As Albrecht Wellmer points out, it is this assumption that more than anything else constitutes the "third dogma" of empiricism. See Wellmer, "Reason and Inter-subjectivity," L. Hertzberg and J. Pietarinen, eds., *Perspectives on Human Conduct* (Leiden: E. J. Brill, 1988), p. 154.

58. Charles Taylor, "Overcoming Epistemology," in *Philosophical Arguments*, p. 12.

59. Herbert Marcuse, *Negations: Essays in Critical Theory*, trans. Jeremy J. Shapiro (Boston: Beacon Press, 1968), p. 135.

60. Ibid., p. 135.

Part VI

1. Whether it is observed in the reactions to "political correctness," identity politics, feminism, affirmative action policies, or protests against globalization, and now, to self-critical explanations of the West's role in creating the conditions under which "terrorism" can flourish, what we find is widespread cultural fatigue with social criticism, a fatigue manifesting itself spontaneously in the form of impatience, dismissiveness, and outright hostility, as well as in the form of a highly organized backlash. More recently the events of 9/11 harnessed this resentful energy in a particularly intolerant manner, making the United States the democracy most unreceptive to self-criticism, making self-criticism nearly equivalent to treason.

2. One could trace the philosophical history of this form of skepticism by reading Hegel on the unhappy consciousness, Kierkegaard on despair, Nietzsche on the historical sense, romanticism, and nihilism, Heidegger on Nietzsche and nihilism, and, more recently, Charles Taylor on naturalism and Stanley Cavell on skepticism. I provide a synopsis of this philosophical history in "Reorienting Critique: From Ironist Theory to Transformative Practice," in *Philosophy and Social Criticism* 26, 4 (2000): 23–47. For illuminating analysis of how this skepticism is expressed in popular culture and in everyday discourse, see Susan Bordo's discussion of "plastic discourse" in *Unbearable Weight. Feminism, Western Culture and the Body* (Berkeley: University of California Press, 1993), pp. 246–65.

3. Hilary Putnam, *Renewing Philosophy* (Cambridge: Harvard University Press, 1992) p. 178, my emphasis.

4. Only the much too knowing ideologues of modernization and globalization continue to recommend as the cure to all that ails the modern world large-scale processes of change whose scope and unintended consequences they can neither comprehend nor foresee. In the same breath, however, they proclaim that these processes are as irresistible as they are necessary, that they represent "progress." With this exhortation to accept and adapt to what is inevitable, they unintentionally attest to and intensify our doubts.

5. Similarly Nancy Fraser in her discussion of the "post-socialist condition" also refers to the exhaustion of utopian energies, but she too fails to develop its implications for the practice of critique. Moreover I believe she errs in amending Habermas's diagnosis as referring not to an exhaustion of utopian energies *tout court*, but to the exhaustion "left-wing" utopian energies in particular. This error is a consequence of conflating political with utopian energies. Although right-wing *political* energies are far from exhausted, they can hardly be described as *utopian*. Indeed, they are anti-utopian. They are motivated by *ressentiment*, by the urge to destroy the "welfare-state" rather than by the urge to create something genuinely new. See Fraser's *Justice Interruptus* (London: Routledge, 1997), pp. 1–6.

6. This talk of dried up utopian oases is of course a reference to Nietzsche's characterization of modern nihilism as a spreading desert (*die Wueste wächst*). Perhaps, what we have now is not any new form of obscurity or opaqueness (*Unübersichtlichkeit*), but the belated recognition of the ever-increasing momentum with which *die Wueste* is spreading—and therefore the growing alarm that we are not creating any new utopian oases, and so unintentionally accelerating the loss of sense-making possibilities.

7. Hilary Putnam, *Renewing Philosophy*, p. 177.

8. Habermas, "Consciousness-Raising or Rescuing Critique," in Gary Smith, ed., *On Walter Benjamin: Critical Essays and Recollections* (Cambridge: MIT Press, 1988), p. 123.

9. Although the endorsement of its addressees is a necessary condition of the validity of any critical insight, it is not a sufficient condition of validity. For various independent reasons and social circumstances, the collective addressees of social critique may not be ready or inclined to accept it. Conversely, mere acceptance is also not a sufficient condition of validity. Once again, independent reasons and social circumstances may play a role in the acceptance of social criticism that turns out to be incorrect. Nevertheless, diagnostic social critique can never become an effective instrument of democratically achieved social change unless those to whom it is addressed reflectively endorse it.

10. Immanuel Kant, *Critique of Pure Reason*, trans. and ed. Paul Guyer and Allen Wood (Cambridge: Cambridge University Press, 1997), pp. 100–101. Translation slightly amended.

11. Friedrich Nietzsche, *The Gay Science*, p. 38.

12. On these issues, see Reinhard Koselleck, *Critique and Crisis* (Cambridge: MIT Press, 1988), especially ch. 8, pp. 98–126.

13. For a fuller account of the exhaustion of unmasking critique, see Nikolas Kompridis, "Reorienting Critique: From Ironist Theory to Transformative Practice," *Philosophy and Social Criticism* 26, 4 (2000): 23–47. See also Nikolas Kompridis "So

We Need Something Else for Reason to Mean," *International Journal of Philosophical Studies* 8, 3 (2000): 271–95.

14. Hannah Arendt, *The Human Condition* (Chicago: University of Chicago Press, 1958), p. 246.

15. John Dewey, *Art as Experience* (Carbondale: Southern Illinois University Press, 1989), p. 38.

16. Max Horkheimer and T. W. Adorno, *Dialectic of Enlightenment*, trans. Edmund Jephcott (Stanford: Stanford University Press, 2002), p. 18.

17. Nietzsche, *The Gay Science*, p. 38.

18. Michael Walzer, *Interpretation and Social Criticism* (Cambridge: Harvard University Press, 1987), p. 60.

19. James Bohman, "Participants, Observers, and Critics: Practical Knowledge, Social Perspectives, and Critical Pluralism," in William Rehg and James Bohman, eds., *Pluralism and the Pragmatic Turn: The Transformation of Critical Theory* (Cambridge: MIT Press, 2001), p. 100. Unlike inquiries that aim at the "rational reconstruction" of implicit rule-knowledge, critique is a form of self-reflection that can have practical consequences for how we live, and how we determine the proportion of continuity and discontinuity in the form of life we inherit and pass on. However, rational reconstructions, even *if* they were to able to produce uncontroversial, unchallengeable results, can only identify the "rules" governing a very limited range of human speech and action, outside of which fall the spontaneous and unforeseeable ways in which human beings change themselves and the world: such change is not rule-governed change, and does not refer back to any rule-governed competence for initiating change. While rational reconstructions may generate knowledge about their object domain, they have no necessary relation to the practice of critique. And this much Habermas himself acknowledged some time ago: "Self-reflection leads to insight due to the fact that what has previously been unconscious is made conscious in a manner rich in practical consequences: analytic insights intervene in life, if I may borrow this dramatic phrase from Wittgenstein. A successful reconstruction also raises an 'unconsciously' functioning rule system to consciousness in a certain manner; it renders explicit the intuitive knowledge that is given with competence with respect to the rules in form of 'know how'. But this theoretical knowledge has no practical consequences" (Habermas, *Theory and Practice*, trans. John Viertel (Boston: Beacon Press, 1974), pp. 22–23).

20. Ibid., p. 100.

21. Ibid., p. 107.

22. Reinhard Koselleck, *Futures Past. On the Semantics of Historical Time*, p. 272.

23. Ibid., p. 276.

24. Ibid., p. 275.

25. Ibid., p. 275.

26. Here I am paraphrasing an observation of de Tocqueville's in the closing pages of *Democracy in America*. Anticipating the condition Habermas would diagnose almost a century and a half later, he writes: "Since the past has ceased to throw light upon its future, the mind of man wanders in obscurity." Cited by Hannah Arendt in *Between Past a Future* (New York: Penguin, 1977), p. 7.

27. Koselleck, *Futures Past*, p. 263.

28. Ibid., p. 285.

29. Koselleck, *Futures Past*, p. 286. As examples of *Begriffe* turned into *Vorgriffe*, into future-directed "concepts of movement," Koselleck points to Kant's concept of *Völkerbund*, "league of nations," and to now exhausted or still highly contested concepts such as democracy, liberalism, socialism, communism, fascism, progress, and revolution.

30. Arendt, *Between Past and Future*, p. 11.

31. Friedrich Nietzsche, *Genealogy of Morals*, Second essay, Section 13, in *Basic Writings of Nietzsche*, ed. trans. Walter Kaufmann (New York: Random House, 1966), p. 516.

32. Herbert Marcuse, *Negations*, pp. 154–55, my emphasis

33. Ibid., p. 158.

34. Arendt, *Between Past and Future*, pp. 5–6.

35. Of course, as I pointed out in part V, chapter 4, Habermas's image of reason as an impregnable hull effectively does the same.

36. Max Horkheimer, "Materialism and Metaphysics," in *Critical Theory: Selected Essays* (New York: Continuum, 1986), p. 26.

37. For an instance of this "conservative" attitude in connection with questions concerning the political claims of culture, see Nikolas Kompridis, "Normativizing Hybridity/Neutralizing Culture," *Political Theory* 133, 3 (June 2005): 318–43.

38. Ibid., p. 154.

39. Christian Lenhardt, "Anamnestic Solidarity: The Proletariat and Its *Manes*," *Telos* 25 (Fall 1975): 154.

40. Walter Benjamin, *Illuminations*, p. 255.

41. Ibid., p. 262.

42. Regrettably, most normative theorizing continues to think within the idea of homogeneous, empty time, time that proceeds unbroken toward an ever-receding

point in the future. And although we have developed a deeply skeptical attitude toward the notion of progress, in our theorizing we nonetheless retain the conception of time on which it depends. We seem to be theorizing in a prison house of time, a prison house of our own making, hurtling forward toward a "future" from which we seem unable to escape—a "future" without a future.

43. T. W. Adorno, *Critical Models*, trans. Henry Pickford (New York: Columbia University Press, 1998) p. 13.

44. Ibid., p. 16.

45. Ibid., p. 17. Incidentally, if one were to substitute the Heideggerian term "being" for the Hegelian "concept," this statement would be open to the same dismissive criticisms critical theorists, including Adorno, have been aiming at Heidegger for decades. In this respect both fundamental ontology and historical materialism have been guilty of intellectual hubris.

46. "What does a philosopher demand of himself first and last? To overcome his time in himself, to become 'timeless.' With what must he therefore engage in the hardest combat? With whatever marks him as the child of his time. . . . Well, then! I am, no less than Wagner, a child of his time; that is, a decadent. . . . Others may be able to get along without Wagner; but the philosopher is not free to do without Wagner. He has to be the bad conscience of his time: for that he needs to understand it best. . . . 'Wagner sums up modernity. There is no way out, one must first become a Wagnerian.'" Nietzsche, "The Case of Wagner," in Walter Kaufmann, ed., *The Basic Writings of Nietzsche* (New York: Modern Library, 1992), pp. 611–12. On certain shortcomings of Nietzsche's critique of Wagner, see Nikolas Kompridis, "What Would an Ideal Have to Be Like to Be Dionysian?" *International Studies in Philosophy* 30, 3 (fall 1999): 123–31.

47. On the use and disadvantages of medicalised models of critique, see Nikolas Kompridis, "From Reason to Self-Realisation? On the Ethical Turn in Recent Critical Theory," *Critical Horizons* 5, 1 (Summer 2004): 323–60.

48. Written in Frankfurt in 1796, authorship of this two-page fragment has been attributed individually and collectively to Hölderlin, Hegel, and Schelling.

49. The surprise that greeted Habermas's call for "the rebirth of Europe" in response to the willful chaos unleashed by the Bush regime would have been unwarranted had sufficient attention been given to this passage. See Habermas's "Unsere Erneurung. Nach Dem Krieg: Die Wiedergeburt Europas," "co-authored" with Jacques Derrida, in *Frankfurter Allgemeine Zeitung*, May 31, 2003, p. 33. See also Rorty's contribution to this idea of Europe published contemporaneously in *Suddeutsche Zeitung*, and reprinted in English in *Dissent* (fall 2003).

50. Cavell, *This New Yet Unapproachable America*, p. 114. Cavell's reply to a different, but related question serves me here better than any I could come up with on my own.

51. Walter Benjamin, *Charles Baudelaire: A Lyric Poet in the Era of High Capitalism*, trans. Harry Zohn (London: Verson, 1976), p. 74. By "heroic constitution," Benjamin had something rather different in mind than what is commonly evoked by the word "heroic." The relevant notion of heroism is inspired, first, by Baudelaire's description of the working classes: "No matter what party one may belong to . . . it is impossible not to be gripped by the spectacle of this sickly population which swallows the dust of the factories, breathes in particles of cotton, and lets its tissues be permeated by white lead, mercury and all the poisons needed for the production of masterpieces . . . ; of this languishing and pining population to whom *the earth owes its wonders*; who feel a purple and impetuous blood coursing through their veins, and who cast a long, sorrow-laden look at the sunlight and shadows of the great parks" (Benjamin, *Charles Baudelaire*, p. 74). Second, by Baudelaire's description of the perseverance of those who strive to "go on" with cultural practices at once glorified and undermined: "When I hear how a Raphael or a Veronese is glorified with the veiled intention of depreciating what came after them, . . . I ask myself whether an achievement which must be rated *at least* equal to theirs . . . is not infinitely *more meritorious*, because it triumphed in a hostile atmosphere and place" (Benjamin, *Baudelaire*, p. 75).

52. John Berger, "Where are We?" *Harper's*, March 2003, p. 13.

53. *Essays on Heidegger and Others, Philosophical Papers*, vol. 1 (Cambridge: Cambridge University Press, 1991), p. 188.

54. This question was posed by Nancy Fraser during an exchange with Habermas at the conference celebrating the English language publication of Habermas's *The Structural Transformation of the Public Sphere*. Evidently Habermas had to "get over the shock to answer such a question." See Craig Calhoun, ed., *Habermas and the Public Sphere* (Cambridge: MIT Press, 1992), pp. 468–69.

55. Ibid., p. 469.

Index